10/20/80

Basic Technical and Business Writing

Basic Technical and Business Writing

JOANNA M. FREEMAN

THE IOWA STATE UNIVERSITY PRESS / Ames, Iowa

To TOM, MAE, and JOE

JOANNA M. FREEMAN, associate professor of English at Pittsburg State University, holds the B.S. in Education degree from Southwest Missouri State University, the M.A. degree in English from the University of Colorado, and the Ph.D. degree in English from the University of Kansas. She has taught in the English department of Pittsburg State University since 1958. As Coordinator of the Technical Writing Program, Dr. Freeman has developed both beginning and advanced technical writing courses, supervised the technical writing internships, and has presented technical writing workshops throughout the Midwest. She is a member of the Society for Technical Communication, the National Council of Teachers of English, the Modern Language Association, and the Kansas Association of Teachers of English.

© 1979 The Iowa State University Press
All rights reserved

Composed and printed by
The Iowa State University Press
Ames, Iowa 50010

First edition, 1979

Library of Congress Cataloging in Publication Data

Freeman, Joanna M   1929–
   Basic technical and business writing.

   Includes bibliographical references and index.
   1. Technical writing. I. Title.
T11.F68   808′.066′6   78-25818
ISBN 0-8138-1965-2

Contents

Preface

Basic Technical and Business Writing has been written to prepare college and university students as well as business, industrial, and government employees to handle successfully the paperwork with which they will be confronted in the first years on the job. This text will give them instruction and practice in organizing ideas and communicating them to a specific audience.

Summaries, sample papers, and writing topics suitable for students from every school on campus and for workers in all areas of the job market are given at the end of each chapter. Most of the sample papers were written for actual use in government and private enterprise and show a cross section of material produced by professional workers in the fields the students themselves will enter. In most of the writing assignments in this text, students and workers are encouraged to use material from first-hand experience and observation rather than from printed sources. They can select topics they are already familiar with, but they assume the responsibility of communicating their technical information to the instructor, to other students in the class, or to a supervisor. This approach is valid since rarely do those in industry, government, health, or education ask for reports telling them what they already know or complain that reports explain things too clearly, in language too simple.

A section on grammar is not included in this text since students and workers on the job can consult any of the reputable handbooks listed in the Introduction. However, basic rules for the use of numbers, abbreviations, and punctuation are included in Chapter 1; and appropriate systems of documentation are presented in Chapter 5.

Effective writing done on the job is a must for all employees who wish to advance in their chosen fields because skill in writing calls attention to other aspects of their work. This text presents the basic rules for technical writing, specimen writing produced in many different career areas, and writing topics appropriate both for students in technology, arts and sciences, and education and business and for workers in government and industry.

So many people have offered assistance and advice during the writing of this book that listing them all would be impractical. However, the following people, agencies, corporations, and businesses were extremely cooperative and contributed specimen writing and illustrations for use in this text: faculty and students of Pittsburg State University, Pittsburg, Kansas; Desoto, Inc.; *Mid-America Commerce & Industry;* Data-Pro Research Corporation; American Dental Association; Zoological Society of London; Ford Motor Company; Petersen Publishing Company for *Motor Trend; Worklife;* Kavanagh & Son's Insulation; McGraw-Hill Book Company for *Electrical World, Modern Plastics, Automotive Engines,* and *Construction Methods & Equipment;* American Marketing Association; Kansas Gas & Electric Company; Boeing, Wichita Division; Beech Aircraft Corporation; Racine Industrial Plant, Inc.; Farmland Industries, Inc.; Macmillan Publishing Company for *Introduction to the Bible;* W. B. Saunders for *A Textbook of Histology;* Hallmark Cards, Inc.; Music Educators National Conference; American Home Economics Association; *Wood & Wood Products;* St. Luke's Hospital, Kansas City, Missouri; *Kansas City Star;* Unified School District 250, Pittsburg, Kansas; KOAM-TV; Northwestern Mutual Life Insurance Company; Family Service Association of America for *Social Casework;* Modern Language Association of America; American Society for Public Administration; American Institute of Physics; G. P. Putnam's Sons for Art Buchwald; Black and Decker Manufacturing Company; *Annals of Botany; RN; Environmental Science & Technology;* National Council of Teachers of English; W. R. C. Smith Publishing Company for *Southern Automotive Journal;* Society of Plastics Engineers; *Wage-Price Law & Economics Review;* National Broadcasting Company; Specialty Projects Corporation; Kim-Tam Designs; York College; Alexanders Material Handling Company, Inc.; Pittsburg Bi Centennial, Inc.; Puritan-Bennett Aero Systems; True Temper Corporation; American Express Company; Thomas D. Williams; Engineering, Inc.; Comotara Business Park; Ellman Dental Manufacturing Company, Inc.; McNally Pittsburg Manufacturing Corporation; Society for Technical Communication; Ace Forms, Inc.; Kansas Power and Light Company; Massachusetts Mutual; Seidler & Associates; *Chemical & Engineering News;* and Whirlpool Corporation.

Introduction

SCOPE OF TECHNICAL WRITING

Technical writing is an important skill for students who wish to finish their degree programs successfully and for workers who must write for the advancement of their careers. Both students and professional workers must often communicate highly specialized information in simple, clear, concise language. It has long been recognized that technologists, engineers, scientists, and students training for such fields must master technical writing, but it is now apparent that home economists, nurses, teachers, business executives, artists, mathematicians, military personnel, sociologists, politicians, lawyers, psychologists, and all types of government workers must effectively communicate technical ideas. They must write letters, advertising copy, progress reports, feasibility studies, proposals, lab reports, formal reports, and articles for publication as routine duties of their jobs. Students training to enter these areas must become skilled in using explanations of processes, instructions, technical definitions and descriptions, and analyses. It is a fact of student and professional life that writing ability calls attention to technical skills.

TYPES OF TECHNICAL WRITING

Technical writing is important to students and to employees and employers at every stage of a project. Before the actual work begins, the project must be planned and its possibilities of success evaluated—all in writing. When the work does begin, problems will arise and memos and letters must sometimes be exchanged. Progress reports must describe every part of the work. When the job or the student project is completed, the final report must be written and the total undertaking publicized.

GENERAL CHARACTERISTICS OF TECHNICAL WRITING

It is unfortunate that the term *technical writing* suggests writing that uses as much technical language as possible. Nothing could be further from the truth.

This type of writing deals with facts; it appeals to the mind. It must have clarity, economy, and restraint. You, as technical writers both before and after graduation, must consider several possible word choices and choose the clearest and simplest. You must use as few words as possible to communicate your ideas. You must be objective and unbiased in your presentation of the facts.

Three characteristics of technical writing distinguish it from all other types of writing: headings, figures and tables, and various spatial devices. Headings are labels that identify each section and help the reader grasp the organization of the report. Technical writing is rarely read from beginning to end; the headings help the reader find the most relevant parts. Figures—drawings, charts, graphs, photographs—illustrate and clarify complex ideas. Tables convert statistical data to a readable form. Other spatial and visual devices such as numbers, indentations, and variations in size of print and in colors of ink all contribute to clarity.

Certain characteristics of effective writing are always desirable in every type of technical writing: correct grammar, punctuation, and spelling; clear organization; and a direct style. Effective technical writing is based on skill in writing in general. It will help you to complete your other university assignments; it will prepare you to handle the paperwork connected with your first professional position after graduation.

The sample business writings in this text can make you aware of the standards your future employers will expect you to meet because most have been written by trained employees already working in the various fields. Some student papers have also been included. Writing topics range from the general to the specific and are appropriate for students and workers from different interest areas. As a rule you will write short reports for the nonspecialized reader; you will write formal reports and proposals for experts in the field. For these more complex assignments you can depend on library research or company files as well as your own investigations.

NEED FOR TECHNICAL WRITING SKILLS

Technical materials in the various fields must be constantly updated, but the basic technical writing skills will remain useful during the rest of your educational program and throughout your career. If you are a student, technical writing will help you to handle successfully the term papers, reports, and essay examinations in your other classes; if you are enrolled in cooperative education, it will help you to deal with the paperwork associated with off-campus job experiences. If you have finished school and are employed, skill in technical writing will help you to advance easily and rapidly in your chosen work.

GRAMMAR HANDBOOKS

Any of the reputable grammar handbooks listed below will answer your questions about sentence and paragraph structure and word usage:

Corbett, Edward P. J. *The Little English Handbook: Choices and Conventions,* 2nd ed. New York: John Wiley & Sons, 1977.

Gorrell, Robert M., and Charlton Laird. *Modern English Handbook,* 6th ed. Englewood Cliffs, NJ: Prentice-Hall, 1976.

Hodges, John C., and Mary E. Whitten. *Harbrace College Handbook,* 8th ed. New York: Harcourt Brace Jovanovich, 1977.

Kierzels, John M., Walker Gibson, and Robert F. Willson, Jr. *The Macmillan Handbook of English,* 6th ed. New York: Macmillan Publishing Co., 1977.

McQueen, William A. *A Short Guide to English Composition,* 3rd ed. Belmont, CA: Wadsworth Publishing Co., 1977.

Basic Technical and Business Writing

C H A P T E R   1

Style

STYLE—along with the use of headings, figures, and tables—distinguishes technical writing from all other types of writing. It can be defined as "how writers arrange words to say what they want to say." Since deciding "how" to say something involves mechanics, as well as word choice, a special section is included in this chapter to explain the principles of abbreviation, capitalization, and use of numbers that apply specifically to technical writing. In literary work it is desirable to develop a very distinctive style; however, in technical writing the style should never call attention to itself. Writers must strive for clarity, economy, and restraint and present the facts so the readers can concentrate on the subject matter.

WORD CHOICE

Clarity

The first concern in writing the rough draft of any report is to get the main ideas down on paper. Then, while polishing those main ideas, the writer should pay special attention to word choice.

Stiff, pompous language must first of all be avoided. Too many inexperienced writers try to use a complicated, supposedly impressive word choice. This artificiality obscures important ideas. They use empty, elegant words and phrases such as those listed in the left-hand column below:

POMPOUS EXPRESSION:	REVISION:
it was noted by this writer	I saw
in the proximity of	near
prior to	before
afford an opportunity to	permit, allow
inasmuch as	since
red in color	red
twelve in number	twelve
washers of a small size	small washers

ORIGINAL: The senator used the overhead projector to present details of his investigation of the Kennedy assassination; the congressman further utilized this visual aid to compare his findings with those of the Warren Commission.
REVISION: The senator used the overhead projector to present his findings in the Kennedy case and to compare them with those of the Warren Commission.

Vagueness is closely connected to pomposity. The technical writer must be constantly on guard for expressions that refer to *the above, the latter,* or *the last mentioned.* The instruction sheet for a popular brand of vertical broiler warns the reader, in heavy print, that "Failure to follow the above procedure may support combustion." This warning is vague because the reader may not know what "the above procedure" is and may not immediately understand the meaning of "support combustion." A clearer statement would be, "Always unplug the cord before you remove the rack from the vertical broiler; otherwise, the food on the rack may catch fire."

Observe the vague language used in the paragraph below.

In such cases, all who are subjected to considerable noise must be tested. The new standard also requires that employees showing an increase in their hearing threshold must wear some type of hearing protection. A test should be taken soon after employment begins. This first test will give you a foundation upon which you can base the employees' later examinations.

When specific expressions are substituted for the original vague word choices, the paragraph is easier to read because the clearer language communicates additional information.

Under the new standards, employees who are subjected to a daily noise dose of 0.5 or more must have their hearing measured and recorded. Employees showing an increase in their hearing threshold must wear some type of protective earmuff or ear plug. An audiogram should be taken within the first 90 days of employment. This first test is known as the base line audiogram and gives a basis for comparison of later audiograms.

Passive voice, when it is overused or misused, also contributes to poor technical writing. A verb is passive voice when the subject is acted upon; it is *active voice* when the subject is the actor.

ACTIVE VOICE: The President signed the bill.
The chairman noted the report.
PASSIVE VOICE: The bill was signed by the President.
The report was noted by the chairman.

Use active voice when possible because most readers consider active voice more forceful.

Passive voice should be used to stress *what* was done rather than *who* did it. In a report written to explain increased construction costs, the following passive voice statement is effective since the damaged material is of prime importance.

PASSIVE VOICE: Three sections of Wallite paneling were damaged by the carpenters.

Active voice would stress how the paneling was damaged, not the extent, and might thus be inappropriate.

ACTIVE VOICE: The carpenters damaged three sections of Wallite paneling.

Passive voice can also be useful for developing an impersonal tone because it eliminates overuse of personal pronouns such as *he, she, they,* and *we.*

As a writer, you should not move pointlessly from one voice to another within a sentence or paragraph or report, needlessly shifting the attention of the reader from the chief focus of the sentence. When you find yourself switching between active and passive voice, decide which voice will make your writing stronger and then use it consistently.

Technical language, although it must be mastered by the technical writer, should not be overused. The limited use of technical language leads to clarity; too much technical language creates confusion. In this age of specialization persons in the individual sciences, professions, businesses, and their subdivisions tend to create words that have exact meaning only to members of that particular group. This kind of writing is known as jargon. When jargon is used in writing by professionals for professionals, it can be effectively used for clarity. But excessive use of jargon in writing intended for a wider audience and needlessly technical language seem to be overlapping areas. An example of this type of writing is found in an educational psychology text: "In the experimental study of learning it has been found that the contingencies of reinforcement which are most efficient in controlling the organism cannot be arranged through the personal mediation of the experimenter." Translated, these lines simply mean that "Learning studies show that it is impossible for the teacher to foresee all the possible responses of the student to a problem."

Words with double meanings often create much con-
fusion. Sometimes double meanings can be clever and can attract attention, but in technical writing they should be avoided. A sign often seen in pharmacy windows is "We dispense with accuracy." Here the reader is not quite sure whether the pharmacist makes up his prescriptions with great care or in a very haphazard manner. A mattress factory that advertises "We contribute to the growth of the community" adds a little humor but does not contribute to clarity.

Vague pronouns also are confusing in technical writing. Pronouns are vague when they do not modify a specific noun. The word *this* is the greatest offender.

ORIGINAL: The bigger car will be more expensive to operate. Not only will its repairs cost more but its gasoline consumption will be greater. The buyer should take this into account.
REVISION: The bigger car will be expensive to operate. Not only will its repairs cost more but its gasoline consumption will be greater. The buyer should take these added costs into account.

In the original, the pronoun *this* refers to two different costs and has no specific antecedent that is singular in form. The pronoun *which* can also contribute to lack of clarity.

ORIGINAL: The meatpacking company has agreed to curb the pollution of Indian River which pleases the community.
REVISION: The meatpacking plant has agreed to curb the pollution of Indian River, a decision which pleases the community.

In the original sentence *which* has no specific word to refer to but instead refers to the whole idea of curbing the pollution of Indian River.

Accurate mechanics increases the clarity of word choice. The same basic rules learned in other composition classes and in other job experiences can guide you in problems of mechanics. However, some principles of abbreviation, capitalization, and use of numbers apply specifically to technical writing.

Abbreviations are used more frequently in technical writing than in any other type of writing; writing out a technical term when it appears often in a short report will lessen the effectiveness of other details. Such terms should be abbreviated when they appear many times within a paragraph. But standard abbreviations should be used, as illustrated in the list below, and should be used consistently.

alkaline	alk
European melting point	EMP
gauss	G
gravity	gr
decigram	dg
hectometer	hm
infrared	IR
insoluble	insol
milliroentgen	mr
pounds per square inch gage	psig
relative humidity	RH

standard temperature and pressure	STP
ultraviolet	UV
viscosity index	VI
effective horespower	ehp

Also, there are some abbreviations that are even better known and more easily recognized than the terms written out.

revolutions per minute	rpm
manuscript	ms
Fahrenheit	F
Celsius	C
American Federation of Labor	AFL
International Brotherhood of Electrical Workers	IBEW

For additional authoritative information on abbreviations, see the *American Standards Association Abbreviations for Scientific and Engineering Terms* (ASA Z10.1–1941) or see a style manual published by a journal in your field.

When a technical term is used frequently enough to justify abbreviation, there are a few standard rules to follow:

1. The first time a technical term is used in a report, it should be written out in full; the abbreviation should be included in parentheses. Then throughout the rest of the report, the abbreviation alone can be used.
2. An abbreviation for a unit of measure is always shown in the singular: 50 lb and 100 gal.
3. Abbreviations are not ordinarily capitalized unless the words they stand for are capitalized.
4. Unless a term denoting a unit of measure is extremely short, such as *day, mile,* and *acre,* such a term is abbreviated when it follows a number: 3 lb, 4 oz, 2 gal, 4 yd, and 2 in. *Inch* should be abbreviated in., not quotation marks above the line; *feet* should be abbreviated ft, not an apostrophe. *By* should be written out instead of using an X. Thus you should write 12 ft by 12 ft, not 12′ X 12′.
5. As to whether or not a period should be placed after an abbreviation, the practice of books and journals in your professional field should be followed. However, a period should always be used after abbreviations that are used in writing in general: a.m., p.m., c.o.d., B.C., and abbreviations that are used in footnotes and bibliographies, such as vol. and p. A period should be used after an abbreviation that spells a word: in., a., and no.
6. If there is any doubt, technical terms should not be abbreviated.

Capitalization should be used sparingly in technical writing. However, capitalization is necessary in the following situations:

1. The names of organizations and business and government bodies should always be capitalized: The Federal Communications Commission, Veterans of Foreign Wars.
2. The title of a person should be capitalized if that title precedes the name: Judge John Smith. If the title follows the name in memo or letter addresses, that title also is capitalized. However, if the title follows the name in the context of a sentence, it should not be capitalized: John Smith, a judge of the district court.
3. Such words as *chemistry, history,* and *psychology* should be capitalized when they appear as part of the name of a course. They should not be capitalized when they refer to a general subject.

Numbers, in technical style, are more likely to be written with numerals instead of being spelled out. The main differences between ordinary and technical style are:

1. In technical writing, usually 10 and all numbers above should be expressed as numerals. All numbers below 10 should be written out, except when those numbers below 10 precede a unit of measurement: 5 in., 2 hr, but three windows and two doors. When the sentence begins with a number, that number should always be written out.
2. In a sentence or in a paragraph where numbers are used with great frequency, all these numbers should be expressed as numerals, even when they are below 10, rather than writing them out.
3. When one number appears immediately after another as part of the same phrase, one of the numbers should be spelled out: 6 one-inch blocks, three 2-girl teams.
4. Numerals usually are presented as decimals rather than ordinary fractions because decimals indicate a greater degree of precision: 0.25 rather than ¼. Decimal fractions should be preceded by a zero.

Accurate spelling is especially important to the technical writer because it, too, improves clarity. Often one misspelled word in a report gives the reader a general impression of inaccuracy, and sometimes the reader or supervisor either refuses to read the report or refuses to take action on that particular report believing that it may also include inaccurate facts. A good rule is always to look up a word in the dictionary when you are unsure of the spelling, paying special attention to any word used several times in a report. Making a list of problem spelling words and learning those words will also improve spelling.

Economy

Wordiness is the inevitable result of simply getting the main ideas down on paper. As the rough draft of a report is revised, often one word can be substituted for a whole phrase, clause, or even for a complete sentence. In the following samples, the *Revision* reflects greater economy and clarity than does the *Original.*

ORIGINAL: Several employees are requested to report to the dispensary. They are:
REVISION: Several employees are requested to report to the dispensary: (Then list the names)

ORIGINAL: This is to advise all branch managers that the telephone number of the institute was changed from Extension 001 to 002 effective February 20, 1979. This information is called to your attention that you may be so advised.
REVISION: The telephone number of the Institute has been changed from Ex. 001 to Ex. 002, effective February 20, 1979.

ORIGINAL: A portion of our latest order from your company, in specific (order #24781 U) item #82059, astro poster of the Pleiades starcoaster (1-2.75), was received in damaged condition. Knowing that this parcel was not insured it was my decision to bring this to your attention. The poster in question is damaged beyond applicable use by this department. We would like to have this order replaced, if possible, and we will gladly send you the damaged poster at your request. I would certainly appreciate your cooperation in this matter and hope that you answer this request soon as we do need this item for practical use before the end of March.
REVISION: Thank you for your prompt attention to our recent order (24781 U). Unfortunately one item, Pleiades starcoaster poster #82059, was badly damaged in shipment and had not been insured. Please send us another one immediately.

ORIGINAL: It is my personal hope that you will join Alpha Kappa Phi now and get in on some of its benefits.
REVISION: Join Alpha Kappa Phi and benefit from the programs.

ORIGINAL:	REVISION:
due to the fact that	because
in the event that	if
the number two	two
take into consideration	consider
give an indication	indicate
make use of	use
climb up	climb
connect together	connect
enter into	enter
inside of	inside
100% complete	complete
full capacity	capacity
component parts	components
It is stifling in this room.	The air in this room is stifling.
There are 16 people on the invitation list.	Sixteen people have been invited.

Objectivity

Enthusiasm or bias has no place in technical writing. Words such as *very, most,* and *unique* should be avoided and certainly eliminated during the revision process because effective technical writing is restrained. The sentence below is improved when *very, unique,* and *tremendously* are omitted.

ORIGINAL: The J. T. Bennett Company was the very first to develop unique water-based industrial coatings that tremendously reduce air pollution throughout the application process.
REVISION: The J. T. Bennett Company was one of the first to develop water-based industrial coatings that substantially reduce air pollution during the application process.

Qualifying statements are a necessary part of the restraint so desirable for technical writing. Careless judgments and sweeping statements should not be made. Certainties, possibilities, and probabilities should not be confused. The expert economist may, because of the detailed facts at his disposal, write "Rising food prices are not necessarily the result of grain sales to Russia." The Affirmative Action Officer, aware of the complexities of self-evaluation and the subsequent procedural changes, will cautiously say, "The Title IX program for the Department of Athletics may be implemented at the university a few months before the July 21 deadline." Only the uninitiated would dare to announce categorically, "The Title IX program for the Department of Athletics will be implemented by April 21."

Humor and sarcasm have no place in technical writing because some reports are kept on file for years. The humor that seems appropriate in 1979 may no longer be appropriate or in good taste in 1990. Often humor is difficult to interpret. Consider a memo sent out by the district insurance representative to all his local agents: "Reports have been sporadic lately. If you are still working for me, please let me know what you're doing." This is a clever memo, certainly, but it leaves so many questions unanswered that another exchange of letters or phone calls will be necessary. How often does the district manager want reports? What information does he want included in these reports?

SENTENCES

Not only must attention be given to word choice in the drive for a style that reflects clarity, economy, and restraint, but also close attention must be paid to sentence structure. Here, again, extremes must be avoided.

Length

Primer sentences—very short, choppy sentences in which there is a poor relationship of ideas—may be the result of the drive for economy. Brief, monotonous sentences make the paragraph below difficult to read.

The Rector Company offers 1,200 wall covering patterns. Some are the roll-type conventional wallpaper. Some are fabric vinyl. Many of these patterns are prepasted. Some are pretrimmed. Some are strippable and scrubbable. Many wall covering patterns have flocked designs. Most are sold under the Rector name. There are a few rolls, in specialty patterns, sold through mass merchandiser catalogs, however.

Excessively long sentences can be equally offensive; note the confusion in the following paragraph.

The Rector Company offers 1,200 wall covering patterns in roll-type conventional wallpaper and in fabric-backed vinyl, prepasted, pretrimmed, strippable and scrubbable, flocked designs which are sold under the Rector name, although a few specialty patterns are sold through the mass merchandiser catalogs.

Varying the length of sentences can make such paragraphs more readable and interesting. When you have been using long, smooth-flowing sentences and you come to an idea that you especially want to stress, you can put that idea in a short, simple sentence to call attention to it. Such variety in sentence length helps avoid monotony. The following two paragraphs illustrate the effectiveness of varied sentence lengths; examine them closely and then rewrite the above paragraph about the Rector Company for greater effectiveness.

There are still a few open issues concerning emissions. Although the tests performed by Brownlow give some assurance that the Stirling burner can produce low emission levels, we do not know what compromises will be required as a result of vehicle development. Also, we do not know the problems associated with achieving 50,000 miles of low emissions durability or the extent of engine maintenance and manufacturing tolerances required to produce engines with low emissions, although major problems are not envisioned. Facilities costs and manufacturing costs are also open issues.

There is no drug that specifically helps parenchymal necrosis. Corticosteroids are not usually indicated in cirrhosis, but in a few clinical situations they are apparently helpful: postnecrotic cirrhosis with cholestasis will often show a rapid serum bilirubin decrease after administration of prednisone for four to six weeks in gradually decreasing dosages; and the jaundice, SGOT, and serum gamma globulin levels decrease while appetite and serum albumin level increase in postnecrotic cirrhosis with chronic active hepatitis after prednisone administration. The corticosteroids may occasionally facilitate diuresis and reduce pruritis. If the patient is receiving over 10 mg of prednisone per day, antacids should be administered between meals and at bedtime.

Complexity

Rearranging the elements of a sentence can add variety. The basic pattern for the English sentence is subject, verb, and object: "The operator carefully checked the computer." In this sentence the subject *operator* is the actor; the object *computer* receives the action of the verb *checked*. These basic elements can be rearranged so the object *computer* becomes the subject of the sentence, followed by the passive voice verb *was checked*: "The computer was checked carefully by the operator."

Adverbial elements can be moved from one position to another in the sentence or can be expanded upon:

Working carefully, the operators checked the computer.

If the operators will carefully check the computer, they can probably discover the malfunction.

The operators will probably discover the malfunction when they check the computer.

After a conference with the manufacturer's representative, the computer operators discovered the malfunction.

The loose and the periodic sentences relieve monotony. In the loose sentence the main idea is put first and then the other elements are added: "The Thomas B. Jones Company has developed an adhesive that can be used to bind the layers of plastic and foil in plastic food pouches that are used in home freezing." The periodic sentence begins with modifiers and other elements, and the main idea comes last: "Wishing to improve the plastic food pouches that are used in home canning by binding the layers of plastic and foil, the Thomas B. Jones Company has developed a new adhesive."

The balanced sentence makes thoughts easier to understand. It contains two or more parts of equal importance; the second part states an idea parallel to that of the first or exactly opposite to the first: "Design has become the selling point of Jason Furniture; fine craftsmanship has become the hallmark of the Joseph Furniture Company."

Punctuation

Adequate punctuation determines the effectiveness of most sentences. The clearest word choices and the most effectively written sentences are confusing if they are not punctuated correctly.

The easiest way to solve punctuation problems is to find the subject and verb of the main clause, then punctuate the elements that make up the rest of the sentence. Listed below are the six elements that can be added to the subject and predicate of the main clause to complete the sentence. The clue to their arrangement is the punctuation—the commas, semicolons, and the dashes.

1. *Introductory Element:* A number 1 comma signals the end of an introductory element, an element placed before the main part of the sentence.
   a. First of all,[1] consider the function of your report.
   b. After listing all the details that you can think of,[1] arrange those details into groups according to subject.
2. *Interrupting Element:* A number 2 comma [or dash] signals an interrupting element, an element placed within the sentence rather than at the beginning or end.
   a. There is no reason,[2] however,[2] to be unduly concerned if you are asked to write a report.
   b. Public speaking can—[2]if you prepare carefully—[2]be a relaxed, enjoyable experience.
3. *Afterthought:* A number 3 comma [or dash] signals an afterthought, an element placed at the end of the sentence.
   a. There are many varieties of reports that fit into no special classification,[3] reports that perform multiple functions.
   b. The supervisor interviewed the candidates—[3]all of whom seemed well qualified.

4. *Coordinate Clauses:* A number 4 comma [semicolon or dash] signals a compound sentence composed of two coordinate clauses.

    a. An appendix is sometimes omitted in a report,[4] but it permits the writer to make material available without placing it in the main text.

    b. Some subjects deal in proven facts;[4] other subjects are idea-oriented.

5. *Series:* A number 5 comma signals that three or more sentence elements—nouns, verbs, phrases, or clauses—are used in a series.

    a. There are some reports that are not classified as letters,[5] memoranda,[5] or laboratory reports.

    b. Plan,[5] write,[5] and proofread each report that you write.

When commas are used within the elements in a series, semicolons should be used to mark the end of each element in the series; too many commas create confusion.

    a. Mrs. Loretta Smith, president of the PTA;[5] Mrs. Roy Jones, school counselor;[5] and Mrs. S. C. Long, third grade teacher, attended the planning session.

6. *Two or More Modifiers of the Same Word:* A number 6 comma signals that two adjectives or adverbs modify the same noun, verb, or adjective and are not connected with *and.*

    a. A clear,[6] concise report performs a variety of functions smoothly and efficiently.

    b. Read the report carefully,[6] completely.

(Courtesy Jean McColley and Thomas Hemmens [1])

As you read for instruction or entertainment, you should try to number punctuation marks. If you can decide why an editor used a certain mark of punctuation, then you can also read your own rough draft and decide what punctuation marks are needed and why.

In summary, there are five rules for writing sentences:

1. Write concrete sentences that avoid vague language.
2. Write easily understood sentences that are free from unnecessarily technical language.
3. Write emphatic sentences by displaying the main ideas prominently.
4. Write uniform sentences in which all the parts of the sentence support the main idea.
5. Write effective sentences by punctuating them clearly.

PARAGRAPHS

Paragraphs provide relief for the eye and indicate the orderly arrangement of the main ideas. Using at least one paragraph per page will help the reader. Do not, however, use so many paragraphs on one page that the smooth flow of ideas is interrupted.

Organization

The topic sentence expresses the main idea of the paragraph and can appear anywhere in the paragraph. Often it comes first and is supported by explanatory sentences. This pattern is called deductive and is illustrated in the following paragraph; the topic sentence is italicized.

DeSoto is many things to many people. To some, the company is a paint manufacturer, one of the largest and most innovative in the business. To others, it's a supplier of protective coating to the interiors and exteriors of airplanes and appliances. To the homeowner, DeSoto is known for its fine furniture and wall coverings. To still others, DeSoto is recognized as a quality manufacturer of detergents and cleaning compounds, many of them marketed under the Sears, Roebuck and Co. label.

(Courtesy DeSoto, Inc. [2])

Sometimes the supporting sentences come first in a paragraph and the topic sentence is last as an effective summary. These supporting sentences can be arranged chronologically, spatially, or in the order of importance. But the important thing to remember is not to stray from the topic sentence even though it comes last. The following paragraph is a good example of this type of inductive reasoning; the topic sentence is italicized.

If the college freshman enjoys shopping for groceries and trying new recipes in her leisure hours, she should consider home economics as a major. If she is fascinated by the new fabrics or is interested in fitting patterns, then she will be successful in home economics. If she takes up home economics, she will probably get dreamy-eyed and absentminded, but she'll be joining an enthusiastic cult. She and her fellow majors will have a good time because *home economics is fun.*

Coherence

Coherence simply means that the sentences in a paragraph are woven together so the reader moves easily from one sentence to the next without feeling that there are gaps in thought, puzzling jumps, or points not made. A consistent grammatical pattern running through the whole paragraph can give it coherence. In the earlier paragraph about DeSoto, similar sentence patterns—*To* and then the name of a specific group of people—cause the sentences to flow into each other. In the paragraph about home economics, repetition of *If* at the beginning of the sentences contributes to the continuity of thought.

Coherence is also achieved by using pronouns that will allow you to repeat the subject throughout the paragraph without any obviously monotonous repetition. *One* and *it* can be used to refer to DeSoto; *she* and *her* can refer to the home economics major; *he* or *she* can be used for *manager.*

Transitional words and expressions contribute to the coherence of a paragraph by clearly relating one idea to another. They can link together sentences and improve the unity and coherence of the whole paragraph: *a second characteristic, to sum up, despite this fact, finally, to illustrate, another, next, in addition to,* and *consequently.* Transitional sentences can smoothly connect paragraphs: "After the spin cycle has been completed, the clothes must be placed in the dryer." "In spite of these apparent disadvantages, there is one overriding advantage: the total weight of the component."

But each transitional expression has its own precise application; these words cannot be loosely interchanged. The following list of words illustrates these precise meanings; one or two possible interpretations of each word are also included.

however	in spite of that, all the same
thus	in the way just stated, in the following manner
therefore	as a result of this, for that reason
moreover	in addition to what has been said, besides
consequently	by logical inference
similarly	in like manner, likewise

In the sample paragraph below, the sentences are not connected, so the reader is forced to consider each one separately and loses the continuity of idea.

I was hired as managerial trainee and started work at the restaurant. My experience had been derived chiefly from books. I was not prepared to clean deep fat fryers, scrub down the kitchen, and settle petty squabbles among the waitresses. I soon became so discouraged with the long hours and the frustrations that I considered quitting. The manager must have sensed this. He called me into his office and praised my ability to get along with others and pointed out the rewards of being assigned an assistant managership. I realized that I had been doing a better job than I had thought, and I decided to remain.

The following version of the above paragraph is much more effective because it is coherent; transitions have been added to connect the ideas. Sometimes the italicized transitions supply a needed thought, and sometimes they simply add words and phrases that tie the sentences together.

I was hired as managerial trainee and started work at the restaurant. *Until then,* my experience had been derived chiefly from books, *and unfortunately* the books had not prepared me to actually do kitchen work and deal with other employees—*problems that every managerial trainee must face.* *Thus* I soon became so discouraged with the long hours and the frustrations that I considered quitting. *I think* the manager must have sensed this *because* he called me into his office and talked to me *both* about my ability to get along with others and the rewards of being assigned an assistant managership. *That talk encouraged me. From that time on,* I realized that I had been doing a better job than I had thought *and that experience would solve most of my problems,* and I decided to remain.

Rewriting the following paragraph improves the flow of sentences and eliminates short, choppy sentences and repetitious word choices.

Original   The SCS system uses a solenoid-operated valve in the vacuum advance line near the distributor. The solenoid valve is energized at road speeds below approximately 35 miles per hour. It is de-energized by a centrifugal switch. This switch is located in the speedometer cable assembly. It can be mounted to the transmission or frame side member and interconnected with the speedometer drive. This allows normal spark advance. A thermal switch is also incorporated into the SCS system. It prevents engine overheating during periods of prolonged engine idle.

Revision   The SCS system uses a solenoid-operated valve that is energized at road speeds below 35 miles per hour. This solenoid valve in the vacuum advance line near the distributor prevents normal spark advance. At speeds in excess of 35 miles per hour a centrifugal switch, located in the speedometer cable assembly or mounted to the transmission or frame side member and interconnected with the speedometer drive, de-energizes the solenoid valve and allows normal spark advance. A thermal switch is also incorporated into the SCS system to prevent engine overheating during periods of prolonged engine idle.

Introductory and Concluding Paragraphs

Introductory and concluding paragraphs deserve special attention. The introductory paragraph in a report must attract the reader's attention and give background on the subject. The concluding paragraphs must reach a logical conclusion, summarize the main points, and/or present the writer's final emphasis.

In a report on solid lubricants, the following introductory paragraph gives background information and explains the approaches:

Background of the problem   The trend in recent years to subject sliding surfaces to an ever-increasing range of thermal, mechanical, and environmental stresses has inevitably posed new problems in friction and wear. Conventional mineral oils are unable to lubricate effectively at temperatures much in excess of 150°C, and even the newer synthetic hydrodynamic lubricants are limited to temperatures below 350°C. At lower temperatures also there are many applications in which hydrocarbon lubricants are ineffective because of solidification or inadmissible because of contamination.

Two approaches   There are two main approaches to the solution of these problems. The first, and most immediately attractive, is to use thin films of solid lubricants, such as graphite and molybdenum disulfide, interposed between sliding surfaces of conventional materials. The ultimate solution, however, lies in the development of new composite materials that will exhibit low friction and wear.

The concluding paragraph summarizes the advantages and disadvantages of solid lubricants:

Advantages   Solid lubricants have a wide range of applicability. They can be used at temperatures beyond the useful range of conventional oils and greases. The low volatility of many of these materials provides them with the capability of functioning effectively in vacuum. Their high load-carrying ability makes them useful with heavily loaded components. Solids, however, do

Disadvantages   lack some of the desirable properties of mobile lubricants: life and the ability to carry away frictional heat.

AUDIENCE

As you work to perfect your word choice, sentence structure, and paragraphing—whether in the classroom or at a full-time job in an office or plant—you must consider the audience for which the report is intended. An awareness of the audience will guide your word choice, selection of details, and the arrangement of those details.

Type

Rarely does the audience include just one type of reader. Even in the classroom situation, you must write for all the students as well as for the teacher. A few of the students will probably be from your major area, but most of them will be from other departments on campus. The nursing student explaining the latest treatment for cirrhosis of the liver will be writing perhaps for two other nursing students, five auto technologists, two mathematicians, three chemists, four home economists, three English majors, and four history majors. When you write a longer formal report, you may be writing not only for your technical writing instructor who will have only a general knowledge of the subject but perhaps for your major advisor who, as an expert in the field, may be evaluating the technical content of the report. Awareness of such a mixed audience will help you to make decisions not only about the style you will use but also about the material you will include.

In an on-the-job situation, the audience will be just as diverse. You should write the report so the members of the board can understand it, even though they will probably have only a generalized knowledge of your technical area. Yet you must include enough technical information to satisfy the supervisor of your unit. All these facts should be communicated so clearly that your subordinates, who may be familiar with only one part of the process, can still be made aware of the whole procedure.

Primary Reader

The primary reader, who is the person to whom the report is addressed, may be a supervisor or executive who needs background information and basic facts and definitions for a general picture of the problem. In such a case, you should use as little technical language as possible. You may wish to compare the unfamiliar to something you believe is familiar to this segment of your audience; if necessary, to explain a highly technical point, you should use a more common word that this audience can better understand. Major concepts can be illustrated with bar graphs and pie charts that are less accurate than the more exact tables but easier to read, and conclusions can be drawn for the executive that will facilitate an administrative decision on your report.

The primary reader, on the other hand, may be a technical specialist who will need only the highly specialized information and complex, detailed tables. For this reader, you may suggest several possible conclusions and let the specialist reach the final conclusion while evaluating the technical information of the report.

Secondary Reader

Regardless of which type of primary reader you anticipate, you should remember that the report will often have several other readers so you must plan for their needs too. For the specialist who is called in to assist, advise, and evaluate the technical details of the report, some detailed figures, mathematical tables, and accurate technical facts to support those general statements should be included; for the secondary reader with a general background, illustrations and comparisons should be included.

Effect of the Audience on the Report

To be a competent technical writer you must anticipate the needs of both types of readers. You must visualize both the reader who has a general knowledge and the one who has specific technical information. To put your readers in a receptive mood, tell them at the beginning of the report what it is about and why it was prepared. The report should be organized clearly with a summary placed first, then general background information in the introduction, and specific conclusions to help the reader who has only general information. Detailed technical information and statistical tables should be included in the body and in the appendix at the end of the report for the technical expert. The paper should be divided into parts and clearly labeled so each type of reader can find the relevant sections. Most technical reports are not meant to be read straight through; busy supervisors and technical experts each read only those parts of the report that seem most valuable to them.

In the introduction printed below, the writer has given background information for the reader who has general information and has included a statistical table for the specialist.

Despite the recession, the unions are now busy organizing employees in one particular area. That sector covers the white collar employees of companies *where unions already have contracts for the production employees.* As evidence of that trend, the National Labor Relations Board held a record total of 1,281 white collar elections in 1974. Most were in offices where the unions held contracts for the production workers. The accompanying table tells the story.

WHITE COLLAR ELECTIONS				
Yr.	Elec-tions	Won By Unions	% Won By Unions	No. Em-ployees In Units
1961	395	177	44.8	4,660
1962	462	273	59.0	5,880
1963	443	255	57.5	6,495
1964	471	268	56.9	6,730
1965	514	318	61.8	7,600
1966	579	352	60.7	9,085
1967	868	567	65.3	15,090
1968	808	422	52.2	11,175
1969	752	422	56.1	10,695
1970	809	428	52.9	11,110
1971	825	437	52.9	12,085
1972	1,010	574	56.8	21,780
1973	1,031	548	53.1	15,965
1974	1,281	725	56.6	22,790

During the last four years, I have analyzed 212 union victories in white collar elections in a whole variety of industries. Of the 212 companies, 17 were in insurance and banking; the remainder were the offices of manufacturing companies. I found that timely precautions could have prevented most of these union victories.

In the conclusion to this same article, the writer keeps the reader who has only general information in mind and lists specific conclusions.

As a result of our comprehensive study, several conclusions became evident.
1. Most white collar elections in which wages and hours were alleged to be the main issue (about 60%) were won by the unions because of employee ignorance of the competitive situation of the company. Employer speeches in the election period had no effect. They were too late.
2. Most complaints about white collar working conditions (a basic cause of nearly 30% of the elections) were well founded and reflected real issues. Election speeches had no effect here either.
3. About 50% of the elections named arbitrary, tyrannical, and abusive supervisors as an issue. This is truly the result of poor supervisory methods. The elections could have been avoided with proper supervisory training.

Even with disputes over money, almost all labor unrest could have been quelled before unions took control of the office force. How? By setting up a two-way communications system and training supervisors in modern management methods.

(Courtesy *Mid-America Commerce & Industry* [3])

SUMMARY

You should strive for clarity, economy, and restraint as you present the facts so your reader can concentrate on the subject matter. Clear word choice will be the result of avoiding pompous language, vague pronouns, overuse of the passive voice, too much technical language, and words with double meanings. Accurate mechanics increases clarity, so mastering the principles of abbreviation, capitalization, and use of numbers that apply specifically to technical writing is advantageous. As a general rule, three words should not be used when one word would communicate the idea just as effectively. A biased report of the facts should not be given; excessive enthusiasm and humorous statements should be omitted.

Varying the length of sentences contributes to effective technical writing. Rearranging the subject-verb-object pattern of the English sentence and using transitional expressions to weave sentences into a coherent pattern make reports easier to read. Loose, periodic, and balanced sentences help the writer avoid monotony.

The main ideas of the report should be paragraphed, and each paragraph should contain its own topic sentence that clearly states that main idea. The topic sentence can be placed anywhere in the paragraph, but all the details in the paragraph should clearly support, explain, and illustrate it.

An awareness of the audience that will read the report will help you make decisions about style and about the material you will include. There are basically two types of readers in any audience: the reader who has a general knowledge of the subject and the one who has specific technical information. The parts of the paper should be labeled so both types of readers can find the sections intended for them. As you strive to develop a clear, readable style in report writing, you must be guided by a concern for your readers' interests. If you communicate facts and ideas that prove to be useful, you have written a good report; if you communicate those facts in such a way that they can be quickly and easily understood, you have written an excellent report.

EXERCISES

Rewrite the sentences in the following exercises. These sentences are similar to those you may encounter as you proofread your own rough draft. Remember that problems in word choice are solved during the revision of the rough draft—after you get the main ideas down on paper.

A. Correct the stiff, pompous language of the following sentences.

1. It was apparent that the conflagration resulted from the excessively arid conditions.
2. The newest employee was cognizant of the necessity to ameliorate interoffice relationships.

3. You will doubtless be gratified to ascertain that our various group supervisors have communicated to our nonoffice personnel the fact that it is the chief executive officer himself who has laid down the directive that said employees are not to delay their return of the monthly report beyond the first day of each period.

B. Rewrite the following sentences substituting specific words for vague expressions.

1. In the evening I took care of the unfinished projects.
2. Before preparing your proposal, get suggestions from at least three different people.
3. For greater safety, the bolt should be fixed.
4. If specific problems arise and can be brought out, it may be necessary to treat these problems realistically.

C. Correct the needlessly technical language and jargon of the following sentences.

1. In terms of the underachiever, meaningful activities along the lines of the overall objectives provide little stimulation.
2. When the absorption of the Chapius bank of ozone in the visible spectrum was added to the Rayleigh theory, the calculated sky brightness came into agreement with observation of solar depression angles below the horizon from about 0 to 6.
3. Television daytime dramas are psychologically complex, dwelling on parallel themes of disjuncture and ambiguity.
4. The decortication of the tree progressed at a rate parallel to the debilitation of the tubular system.

D. Make each of the following sentences more concise and direct.

1. At this point in time it is the understanding of those who work in the bookkeeping department that she will continue to work part-time for the city in the role of inspector.
2. What we have involved here is a situation where it appears that we have one transportation company and a taxi company providing all public transportation in the city.
3. It has been reported by the street commissioner that improvement of Prospect and Adams Streets will be accomplished by a new surface being applied.

E. Combine some of the short *primer* sentences below into longer, smoother-flowing sentences. The order of ideas may be changed so that closely related ideas may be together and less closely related ideas may be put in separate sentences.

1. You will meet foreign educators who are developing cooperative education programs. Opportunities to discuss foreign exchange programs will be available. Educators will come from France. Some will come from England. They will come from Africa. Other representatives will be from the Near East. They will have fresh insights into existing problems.
2. Buying a small building does not mean you sacrifice quality. The roof and wall panels are the same ones used on the preengineered buildings. They have an exclusive, full-sidelap corrugation. It provides extra strength. It is a better fit for weather tightness.
3. The selection of a material best suited for a particular product application is important. It is often determined by two important factors. The first is cost. The second is overall performance. Appearance is important. Toughness and durability concern the designer. Ease and speed of processing influence the final decision of the manufacturer.

F. Break each of the following long sentences into shorter sentences. You may change the order of the ideas if necessary.

1. In fairness to all registrants, it is necessary for us to make an assessment of $25 when a registrant cancels attendance less than seven days prior to the workshop because late cancellations in our limited attendance meetings not only deprive other registrants of the chance to attend but can force cancellation of a meeting so we hope you will recognize the need for this policy and will cooperate fully.
2. In 1925, when airplanes were still a rare sight, such developments as the faired-in-engine cowling, negative-stagger wing, controlled-pitch propeller, retractable landing gear, the safety harness, and the "V" tail were innovations but today, the sky is no longer the limit as cryogenic systems circle the moon in Apollo spacecraft and supersonic missile targets test our nation's defenses.
3. Normally, the hourly kill at Farmcrop beef plant is 115 animals, but it had been reduced to 50 as of April 4 when John Coewene, president of Farmcrop Foods, said the real test of the boycott was yet to come on Thursday, Friday, and Saturday when shoppers did their weekend buying and customarily purchased meat for Sunday dinner.
4. Although typewriter housings were made exclusively of metal a few years ago, not only the housings but many carrying cases, keys, space bars, and carriage ends for standard machines, portables, and the electric models are now made of plastic without sacrificing protection of delicate parts because toughness, light weight, and portability combine with new beauty in both color and design, plus a surface that is mar, chip, and stain resistant and easy to clean.

G. Rewrite the following paragraphs, adding transitional expressions to link the sentences together and to supply needed thoughts.

When the fishing vessel finished the rescue operation, the crew radioed that they were changing course and proceeding at full speed to New York. The decks were full of survivors. Some were dressed in borrowed clothes; some were only partially dressed. They were stupefied by shock and exhaustion. Some survivors were hysterical with relief, and some were very angry over lost suitcases. Some were grieving over missing family members. Some were rejoicing over finding relatives at first thought to be lost.

Business executives pay large sums of money to lure political conventions to their city. A cab company can clear an extra $20,000 a day on convention business. One manufacturing company may do a half million dollars worth of business in campaign buttons. The delegates and their friends spend millions on chartered flights into the city, on food, hotel rooms, recreation, and novelty items such as ball-point pens, auto stickers, bumper strips, campaign wrappers, and other souvenirs. The delegates increase newspaper circulation 15% to 20% during the convention, and major candidates must establish headquarters in the city and staff them.

H. Clearly state the topic sentence in the paragraph below and rearrange the sentences so they effectively develop it.

Supervisors can gain the faith of employees by showing they are devoted to the workers and to the company, by making employees' problems their problems, by being knowledgeable enough to try to answer all the worker's questions, and by listening to complaints and personal problems. To be an effective leader a person must gain respect from employees and have enough enthusiasm to drive and inspire workers. Good supervisors must be able to show subordinates that they are good and fair leaders. Bittle says, "Leadership is the knack of getting other people to follow you and to do willingly the things you want them to do."

I. Edit the following paragraph for repetitious and vague word choices.

When a product reaches the decline stage, the company should determine if its product is contributing to the company. This usually determines the product's future. There is usually someone in the organization who will defend the product on the basis that "The product is our company—without it, our company image will not be the same." Another argument may be that "The product may not be profitable in itself, but it gives us a full product line to offer to consumers." The different arguments concerning the product may or may not be valid but all of them should be investigated thoroughly before any decisions about the product are made.

WRITING ASSIGNMENTS

Use the memo form shown below. In the first paragraph discuss the problem; in the second paragraph explain the solution you propose. As you plan each memo, carefully consider the needs of the designated reader. Give special attention to clarity, economy, and restraint in word choice; to variety in sentence structure; and to logical paragraph development.

To: DATE:

FROM:

SUBJECT:

1. Assume that you are the president of an organization. Inform the members of your group of a change in meeting time.
2. Assume that you are the president of an organization. Inform the members of your group that they must spend all day Saturday working on the house in which the organization is quartered.
3. Assume that you are the president of an organization. Inform the members of your group that they must come to a two-hour study session each week.
4. Assume that you are a graduate assistant. Suggest to an instructor that some piece of equipment be purchased to be used in a course that you are teaching.
5. Suggest to the newest part-time employee of the place where you are now working that some action be taken to improve efficiency.
6. Suggest to your next-door neighbor that some action be taken to improve your relationship.
7. Suggest to the city commission that some improvement be made in a certain street.
8. Suggest to your landlords that they make a specific improvement in their rental property.
9. Suggest to the paper carrier that a certain improvement be made in deliveries.
10. Suggest to your roommates that they take some action calculated to improve your relationship during the coming semester.
11. Assume that you are president of an organization. Inform the members of your group of an increase in dues.
12. Write a memo to a librarian explaining a problem related to checking out books and magazines and suggest a solution.
13. Write a memo to the Campus or Company Beautification Committee requesting that they take some action to improve a certain area of the grounds.
14. Assume that you are the president of an organization. Write a memo to the members informing them that they are required to attend the annual picnic.
15. Write a memo to your employer requesting that a specific action be taken to solve a personnel problem.

REFERENCES
1. Jean McColley and Thomas Hemmens. *Preface to Composition.* Englewood Cliffs, NJ: Prentice-Hall, Inc., 1968.
2. *DeSoto . . . People and Products.* Des Plaines, IL: DeSoto, Inc.
3. A. A. Imberman, "Unions Aim at a New Target," *Mid-America Commerce & Industry,* Sept. 1975, p. 8.

CHAPTER 2

Organization and Outlining

ORGANIZATION is the first step in communicating facts so a reader can quickly understand them. Organization involves an awareness of all the necessary points to be made and a deliberate attempt to arrange them effectively; it is usually the result of planning before the writing actually begins. The well-organized report helps the reader grasp the main points immediately and see important relationships among them.

PURPOSE

Effective technical writing begins with a clear and definite purpose. The ideas conveyed, the audience selected, and the effect desired all contribute to the purpose of the report. Even before a serious investigation of the subject has been made, the following questions must be answered:

1. What do I want to say?
2. To whom do I want to say it?
3. What effect do I want to have on my audience?

These three considerations are so closely related that they are really three ways of looking at one purpose—not three separate parts of the purpose. Each is influenced by the other.

Subject

The general subject of the report will usually be determined by the circumstances of the job itself. The problem will already exist; the effect will have been recognized. Perhaps a student has investigated an assigned topic and must report the findings to a professor. Or a chemist, a sociologist, a historian, or a lawyer has done some research and wants to tell other members of the profession about it. An engineer in a pipeline company must write a report to the supervisor explaining the leaks in the sewer lines in a certain sector. A corporation executive must explain to the board members the implications of the year-end report. A government biolo-

gist must report the results of a field trip to collect water samples from drainage ditches. A doctor wants some colleagues to know about a new technique to drain off fluids from patients who have had thoracic surgery.

There are times, of course, when you must choose your own subject; perhaps you have been asked to speak on "A Health Topic of General Interest" or you have been asked to contribute an article to a professional journal. In such cases, there are four requirements for a suitable subject:

1. One that you know a great deal about
2. One important enough to merit the time and space devoted to it
3. One that is interesting to the audience that you wish to reach
4. One that is appropriate to the occasion

As early as possible in the planning process, you must begin narrowing down your general topic:

GENERAL TOPIC	LIMITED SUBJECT
A Health Topic of General Interest	Swine Flu Vaccine for Local Hospital Employees
A Recent Trend in Drafting	Computerized Drafting at Central Aviation
Improvement of the Cardiac Pacemaker	Substitution of a Radio Isotope–Powered Electrical Generator for the Batteries in the Cardiac Pacemaker

Audience

In technical writing the audience determines what is to be said and how it is to be said. For example, when publicizing a cooperative education program to potential employers, the coordinator will prepare a brochure that stresses (1) the high-caliber worker hired for a minimum wage set by the employer, (2) the inexpensiveness of this type of recruitment program for potential permanent employees, (3) the inexpensiveness of training the student in contrast to employees trained through the established training programs, (4) the employer's personal satisfaction at influencing educational programs, and (5) the desire for public service in the local community. When writing an article to be published in the college newspaper, the coordinator will stress the advantages for the student who enters the co-op program: (1) practical experience related to academic studies, (2) the testing of career goals, (3) confirmation of the student's choice of a major, (4) understanding of human relations, and (5) financial assistance. To appeal to both audiences the coordinator will have to keep each audience clearly in mind.

In deciding on the purpose of the report, in planning the best way to develop it, in writing sentences, and even in choosing words, you must remind yourself of the nature and size of your audience. If the circumstances have not chosen your audience for you, you must decide for yourself exactly what type of audience you hope to reach.

Effect

You must also decide what effect you want to have on your audience; this specific effect will influence your subject matter, your plan, tone, and style. The cooperative education coordinator will stress career investigation when persuading students to sign up for the co-op program but will stress the financial savings afforded by hiring co-op students when persuading employers to give them jobs. The corporation executive may stress net profits when instilling confidence in board members but may stress lost work-hours when directing a vice-president to reorganize a certain department.

PRELIMINARY PLANNING

A good plan is the structure through which the purpose is achieved. The plan is that pattern or a combination of patterns by which you can best communicate your purpose to the audience; it must show the relationships of ideas. Technical reports are often developed by one or by a combination of the patterns listed below:

General to Particular	(General statements are followed by explanatory details.)
Cause and Effect	(Causes are discussed first and the effect is reached as the next logical step, or the effect or effects are classified into the causes.)
Problem and Solution	(A problem is explained and then a solution is proposed.)
Comparison-Contrast	(Two or more subjects are measured one against the other.)
Elimination	(A subject is clarified by telling what it is not. This pattern is usually followed by another telling what the subject is.)
Narration	(Processes, investigations, and experiments are described in the order of their occurrence.)
Description	(Objects are described by components and order in space.)
Definition	(Objects or principles are identified and distinguished.)
Division and Classification	(Wholes are divided into parts; then each part is developed by whatever pattern best suits it.)

Because of the type of subject, you sometimes cannot decide on an overall plan immediately after determining the purpose. You should write down labels identifying the key ideas in the block of information you have gained from reading, investigation, and experiment; then you should study the list and group similar ideas together. After you have grouped the ideas in categories, the relationships of the various groups should be determined. Usually, you can now decide on the idea you wish to emphasize. Some of the details may be discarded as irrelevant. Then you can choose an overall plan of development and write down a one-sentence statement (your thesis) that will guide you in making decisions about the specific details you will include.

Thesis

A thesis is a short, simple sentence that states the central idea of the report. The thesis reflects your awareness of the audience and the effect you wish to have on that audience. Notice that the emphasis in the thesis below changes, depending on the group addressed:

(CONSTRUCTION COMPANY)	The concrete floor of the new community center was damaged by a 2-inch rainfall on September 2.
(LOCAL NEWS MEDIA)	A 2-inch rainfall damaged the concrete floor of the community center now under construction.
(CHAMBER OF COMMERCE)	The new community center, specifically the concrete floor, was damaged by a 2-inch rainfall.
(INSURANCE COMPANY)	Damage to the concrete floor of the community center now under construction was extensive.

The thesis can announce the plan of the report:

Oil wells are drilled in three phases: setting up the derrick, boring the hole, and completing the well.

It can state the solution to a problem, as in each of the following sentences:

The only cure for overweight is selective eating.

Expansion of Parking Lot B is the least expensive solution to the employee parking problem at Ajax Chemical Company.

The thesis must reflect your decisions about the choice and limitation of subject, type of audience, and the effect that you wish the report to have on that audience.

Types of Introductions

After the body of the report itself has been planned, the introduction must be considered. The introduction can give background, state the thesis, and indicate the main divisions of the paper—as in the following introductory paragraphs:

Background Since 1927, automobile designers have made a concerted effort to improve cars both aesthetically and mechanically. Contoured and upholstered seats, key start, powerful engines, and several other improvements have helped make the car more appealing to the public. One of the major *Thesis* mechanical improvements in the automobile has been the development of the automatic transmission. The automatic transmission has eliminated *Main* the need for a clutch and shifter; its basic parts *divisions* are the torque converter, hydraulic system, planetary gear set, and the clutch and band.

Background Disclosure of the Nixon tapes has created a new awareness of electronic surveillance. A shocked American public in 1974 learned that every word spoken in the sanctity of the Oval Office had been recorded and those tapes stored in the basement of the White House, thanks to the efforts of Rose Mary Woods, H. R. Haldeman, Stephen Bull, assorted secret service men, and President Richard Nixon himself. Even though it was subsequently learned that Eisenhower, Kennedy, and Johnson had also taped conversations in their offices, the Nixon tapes generated a deep fear of too much secrecy and power behind the shield of executive privilege. Americans began to recollect the words of the eighteenth-century French political writer, de Maistre, who said, "Every nation has the government it deserves," and began to change the system. In a flurry of purging, a reexamination of the privacy statutes began and continues to the present time. Any *Thesis* reassessment of the electronic surveillance that threatens the privacy rights of the United States *Main* citizen must include (1) the legal history of *divisions* wiretapping and electronic surveillance, (2) the present laws governing wiretapping and electronic surveillance, and (3) the audio devices that will affect such laws in the future.

The introduction also can explain equipment, conditions, and skills necessary in implementing the ideas in the report, as illustrated in the paragraph below.

Thesis Tree skiing gives the average skier an opportunity to develop reflexes and to think ahead while enjoying powdery snow longer because the snow among the trees is more protected during warm, sunny weather. There are, howev-

Equipment er, two necessary pieces of equipment: grips that don't require straps and goggles that will protect *Conditions* the eyes from branches. Skiing in forest areas should not be scheduled too early in the season because a fresh snowfall can conceal obstacles beneath the surface. The only skill necessary for the *Skill* intermediate skier is that of keeping speed under control.

A more formal type of introduction can describe the way in which the report project was initiated, and the structure of the report itself, instead of the subject of the report. This kind of introduction may include subheadings such as Purpose or Objective, Scope or Limitations, Sources of Information, and Authorization. Notice that the following introduction includes Purpose, Sources of Information, and Authorization and that headings are used to identify each part.

INTRODUCTION

PURPOSE

The John Kenneth dealership has announced that Mazda automobiles will be introduced in its showrooms and on the lots in September. Because the service department has previously serviced only American-made cars with piston engines, a detailed inventory has been taken of the tools and equipment currently used that can be adapted to servicing the Wankel engines in the Mazdas. The purpose of this report is to present the results of the tests and experiments made to adapt our present service equipment to the Wankel engine.

SOURCES OF INFORMATION

Information on servicing the Wankel engine has been received from the Toyo Kogyo Company in Japan, which produces several hundred thousand Wankel engines for its Mazda cars each year. General Motors, now developing a small car powered by a Wankel engine, has acquainted us with the necessary service operations and metric wrenches and sockets. Most of the facts presented, however, were obtained by the direct testing and experimentation done in our service department.

AUTHORIZATION

This report and the investigation on which it is based were authorized by John L. Kenneth, owner of John Kenneth's, on March 10, 19—.

Types of Conclusions

One type of conclusion often effective in explanations of processes, instruction sheets, and in other brief reports is the kind that ends with one more detail or step—as in the concluding paragraph below.

Reason The final reason for advocating the merger of the Jones Tool Company and Atlas Supply is a financial one. Competitive lease buying has cost *Explanation* both companies together about 60 million dollars annually. For instance, last year Jones Tool Company spent 30 million dollars buying such leases and Atlas Supply spent 45 million dollars. Unfortunately, all these leases were worth no more than 15 million dollars.

If the report is lengthy, ending with a restatement of the

thesis and a summary of the key points is most helpful. See the following paragraphs of conclusion.

Legal history Wiretapping, which first became popular after
(first the invention of the telegraph in 1836, is a
division) technological improvement on simple eavesdropping by the unaided ear. Federal law regulating wiretapping has ranged from the first statute written only for the duration of World War I to the expectation of privacy doctrine expressed in the *Katy* v. *United States* decision of 1967 and based on the Fourth Amendment, a doctrine that has become the basis for most of the laws now governing wiretapping and bugging.

Present laws Title III of the Omnibus Crime Control and
(second Safe Street Act of 1965 governs electronic sur-
division) veillance. It prohibits (1) wiretapping without the consent of one of the persons involved, (2) the production, distribution, possession, and advertising of communication interception devices, and (3) court-ordered electronic surveillance unless authorized by the state legislature and only after certain requirements have been met pertaining to the type of crime and identification of the specific conversation, offenders, time limits, and continuing surveillance plans. The primary exception to this statute is based on national security.

Audio Audio surveillance equipment can be divided
devices into telephone surveillance, microphones, radio
(third and optical transmitters, and recording devices.
division) Although there is no guaranteed method of protection against these devices, a limited defense can be had through approved locks, burglar alarms, periodic security sweeps of the premises, an electronic analysis of the telephone system, and a physical search.

Restatement Wiretapping and electronic surveillance may
of thesis become an accepted reality in the next decade. Because of technological advances, people can never again be assured of absolute privacy.

Ending with a projection into the future is an effective device when the thesis suggests some warning or question about the future. The conclusion below follows this plan.

Thesis Management goals of productivity at Kelly, Inc., can be reached in the future through improved relationships with employees. Five basic
Summary rules for effective human relations must be introduced and implemented in this corporation:

    1. The employee should be given an honest and respectful appraisal of work.
    2. The employee should be informed of the reasons things are done as they are.
    3. The employee should be acquainted with his present status and prospects for the future.
    4. The employee should be told of changes before they occur.
    5. The employee should be asked for opinions and suggestions.

Future If these practices are followed by all levels of management at Kelly, Inc., approximately 95% of management goals for productivity can be reached by 1982.

ORGANIZING BRIEF REPORTS

Organizing a short report usually involves only (1) listing the key ideas to be included and (2) arranging those ideas in the form easiest to understand. The plan may be merely a short list. For the brief explanation of a process in Chapter 4, "Special Rigs Push Trans-Alaska Pipeline through Wilderness," the plan might have consisted of only five items:

1. Need for special rigs
2. Purpose of ACCO Model 2535 insulator unfolder
3. Lifting
4. Unfolding
5. Guiding

When preparing a short report of a standardized type, you must work within a rigidly prescribed pattern that permits few choices. Check, for example, the specimen blank form below. The specific information asked for in each blank allows the supervisor very little choice in the organization of facts. Thus arrangement of information is no problem here. However, word choice is often a serious problem in filling out blank forms because of the limited space available and because of the obligation to give only the information requested. The most serious error made in using blank forms usually involves failure to limit yourself to the information asked for.

Supervisor's Accident Report

Name _____ Plant location _____
Date of the accident _____ Time _____
Place of occurrence _____ Dept._____
Description of how the accident occurred_____
_____
_____
_____
Description of the injury_____
_____
_____
_____
What unsafe act on the part of the employee caused this accident? _____
_____
_____
What unsafe condition was responsible for this accident? _____
_____
_____
What corrective action has been or will be taken? _____
_____
_____
The injured employee reported to Dr. _____
    Hospital_____
Date of this report_____ Signed _____
    (Supervisor)

ORGANIZING LONGER REPORTS

There are two types of outlines for detailed reports: (1) the working plan, which is the first step in preparing a complex formal report or proposal, and (2) the independent document, which can be submitted to superiors instead of the finished report. Each type of outline will force you to make decisions early in the writing process about major divisions and the coordination and subordination of the supporting points.

In preparing the working plan outline, you should try to divide the mass of information connected with your general subject into five or six parts because most readers have difficulty dealing with a large block of information. This type of outline is the primary organizational device of most technical writers. It can create order out of the facts at your disposal, and it is valuable because it helps you to visualize the completed report before you begin to write. If the relationship of the major points is obvious, they can be grasped immediately and can be remembered more effectively. Roman numerals, capital letters, and indentation clearly spell out these relationships in the outline; headings and transitional words such as *first, then, thus, however, for example,* and *next* can be used in the text to assist the reader.

An outline can sometimes be considered an independent, finished product to be submitted as is to a superior or used as an aid to speechmaking. Such an outline can be filed with the permanent records of the organization; or, if the information in the outline is judged to be of permanent value, a written report based on it can be requested.

But regardless of which type of outline you prepare, the advantages of outlining are not solely for the reader. Outlining is advantageous for the writer, too, because it clarifies thinking and forces decisions about subject matter, style, and form. The outline helps (1) to determine the function of any paper and the limits of the subject, (2) to reflect an awareness of the needs of the audience, and (3) to present a well-thought-out pattern that gives a sense of continuity.

Steps in Outlining

After you have surveyed all the information at your disposal, write down the main idea or thesis of the report you intend to write.

Arrange all your information in five or six basic groups. These will be the main divisions of the outline. Usually the introduction and conclusion of the report are not included in the outline. You have several alternatives in the arrangement of the main divisions, so let the needs of your audience dictate your final arrangement of points. Pause to check the logic of these main divisions. Are they of equal importance? Do they all make a similar contribution to the thesis?

After formulating the general plan, work out the details. Examine all the facts under one roman numeral division, and arrange those facts in not more than six subdivisions. Then, if the subject is extremely complex, subdivide each subdivision, but no more than five or six times. On the other hand, if you can think of only one point in a subdivision, do not divide it because the word *division* implies at least two parts. If you have enough information to subdivide an entry, you should have enough information for at least two subdivisions. If there are facts for only one subdivision, allowing an entry representing so little information would be misleading in the overall plan. Theoretically, if there is an A, there should be at least a B; if there is a 1, there should be a 2. Fill in the necessary minor subdivisions, but do not waste time devising subdivisions that may disappear or at least alter in the course of writing.

The outline should clearly indicate the importance of each entry through subdivision. The space devoted to the development of a main division in the outline should indicate the amount of space devoted to that division in the paper itself. For instance, the most detailed roman numeral entry in the outline should also become the longest and most detailed section of the report. Examine the following outline for the major points, the relationship of those main points to the thesis, and the subdivisions that indicate the amount of space to be devoted to each roman numeral division in the report itself. This outline shows the typical pattern of a complex formal report.

THESIS: *The patient suffering from cirrhosis of the liver has a chance of recovery because of modern treatment and skilled nursing.*

CARE OF THE PATIENT WITH CIRRHOSIS
I. Etiology
II. Symptoms
   A. Pathophysiology
   B. Progression
III. Treatment of cirrhosis
   A. Nutrition
   B. Drugs
   C. Surgery
IV. Nursing care
   A. General
      1. Hygiene
      2. Nutrition
      3. Emotions
      4. Education
   B. Care during complications
      1. Portal hypertension
         a. Causes
         b. Treatment
         c. Nursing considerations
      2. Edema and ascites
         a. Causes
         b. Treatment
         c. Nursing considerations
      3. Esophageal varices
         a. Causes
         b. Treatment
         c. Nursing considerations
      4. Hepatic coma
         a. Causes
         b. Treatment
         c. Nursing considerations
V. Prognosis

Suitable Rank for Each Point

Unless you are forced to follow a preexisting pattern, create a plan that gives each point a rank appropriate to its actual importance. In your plan avoid faulty coordination and subordination.

Excessive coordination sometimes is the result of overusing the classification plan. Classification is the grouping of like with like, the arrangement of things according to certain common qualities or characteristics. Classification, or establishing set divisions, is an easy type of outline to prepare but sometimes you finish with subpoints in the lower levels of the outline about which you have little to say; it is often quite impossible to develop each entry into at least one paragraph in the paper itself. The subpoints always bear the same relationship to their main points and appear very logical and orderly. But classification does not take into account the variations in thought development. Levels have been created that are logical but quite hollow.

Similar points can be organized in a similar manner only as far as subject matter permits, and then overlaps occur. Overusing the classification plan can result in creating so many subdivisions that they are no longer separate and distinct, and so they overlap. If a point is shown as equal to another when it is logically subordinate, excessive coordination is the result. Identify the overlapping entries in the parts of outlines below, and then rewrite them.

A. Uses of geodesic domes
   1. In industry
   2. In the armed forces
   3. As living quarters
   4. As vacation homes

. . . .

1. Computer control of power plants
   A. Computer applications in steam plants
   B. Computer applications in nuclear plants
   C. Computer applications in privately owned plants
   D. Computer applications in hydroelectric plants

Illogical subordination occurs when you place a subpoint under the wrong main point: the so-called subpoint may be equal in rank to the main point or it may belong under another main point. Correct the faulty subordination in the parts of outlines below:

   I. Functions of motor oil
      A. Friction
      B. Coolant for engine parts
      C. Cost
  II. Classification of oil
      A. Viscosity
         1. Importance
         2. Test
         3. Index
      B. Rating
         1. SAE
         2. ASTM
         3. API
         4. CRC
      C. Additives

. . . .

  II. Video display terminal
      A. General description
      B. Function
      C. Advantages
      D. Disadvantages
         1. Cathode ray tube
         2. Keyboard
         3. Low cost

The part of an outline below is an example of the classification plan used effectively:

 III. Exhaust emission control systems
      A. Engine modification types
         1. Controlled combustion
         2. Improved combustion
         3. Cleaner air system
         4. Chrysler Lean Burn
      B. Air injection types
         1. Thermactor
         2. Air Injection Reaction
         3. Air Guard
      C. Catalytic converters
         1. Pellet type
         2. Monolithic type
  IV. Fuel evaporation emission control systems
      A. Vapor transfer
      B. Charcoal canister
      C. Crankcase storage
      D. Carburetor vapor
      E. Fuel tank

Arrangement of Topics

The set of topics internal to each section or subsection should always be given some logical order: they probably will not appear in the order in which you thought of them. Usually you will not use the same system or sequence to arrange the topics in all sections or subsections of the outline. The roman numeral divisions may be arranged in order of importance, the capital letter divisions may be arranged chronologically, and further subdivisions may be arranged in yet another pattern.

The topics in an outline should always be arranged with the audience in mind—their background, willingness to accept your ideas, and the questions they will want answered. In technical writing the needs of the audience should override the dictates of some logical pattern of arrangement. According to logic, evidence is presented before the conclusions; but out of consideration for the audience, this order is often reversed in report writing.

Parallel Treatment of Similar Points

Just as classification helps the readers grasp the main points, so parallel structure helps them to comprehend the main points and also their relationships. Parallel structure puts ideas of equal importance in the same grammar form. Main points should be phrased alike as far as possible—perhaps nouns, nouns and modifiers, or verbs with *ing* endings. Subdivisions under a certain roman numeral should be phrased alike, perhaps all expressed as nouns and prepositional phrases. Parallel structure makes the part of an outline below easy to understand.

THESIS: *The community recreation program must provide for the mentally retarded and for the physically handicapped.*

COMMUNITY RECREATION FOR THE HANDICAPPED

I. Program for the mentally retarded
  A. Definition of the retardate
    1. Learning
    2. Remembering
    3. Functioning
  B. Needs of the retardate
    1. Leisure time
    2. Class time
      a. Development of physical fitness
      b. Development of coordination
  C. Teachers of the retardate
    1. Training
      a. College classes
      b. Internship programs
    2. Personality
II. Program for the physically handicapped . . .

Sentence and Topic Outlines

There are actually three types of outlines: the topic, the sentence, and a combination of the two. The most useful type is the topic outline because entries in this type of outline can be transferred directly into the report as headings and also into the table of contents. A topic is usually a noun, a modifier, or a noun and modifier combination—no clauses should appear in this type of outline, also no complete sentences or questions. The first word of each entry should be capitalized. All the outlines used as examples thus far in this chapter have been topic outlines.

Unlike the topic outline, the sentence outline expresses each topic entry with a complete, declarative sentence rather than with a word or phrase. The sentence outline will not provide a ready-made set of headings for the report, but it will supply all the necessary information when the outline is submitted instead of the final written report; and it will, of course, force the writer to make decisions about the report early in the writing process. Observe the detail of the specimen sentence outline below and the arrangement of ideas.

THESIS: *The conversion to metrics in the United States is advantageous to industry.*

METRIC CONVERSION IN INDUSTRY

I. There are two significant advantages to industry in adopting the metric system.
  A. A universal measuring system is advantageous.
    1. Increased world trade is a result.
    2. Increased productivity is another result.
  B. Forecasting in business and industry is simplified.
    1. Accuracy is increased.
    2. Calculations are easier.
II. There are two significant disadvantages to industry in converting to the metric system.
  A. The creation of training programs is expensive.
    1. Employee education is the responsibility of the employer.
    2. Nonconformists hamper the success of training programs.
  B. Temporary reduced productivity is expensive.
    1. Employees must be taught the theory of metrics on company time.
    2. Employees must be taught the operation of new equipment on company time.
III. There are several methods by which industry is converting to the metric system.
  A. Congress subsidizes the conversion.
    1. The conversion cost for industry amounts to 30% of the $100 billion total cost.
    2. The federal conversion will take 10 years.
  B. Dual dimensioning eases the difficulties of conversion.
    1. Tools currently in use have been designed for easy conversion.
    2. New tools will bear both metric and English markings.

Sometimes the two types can be combined by using complete sentences for the roman numeral divisions and topics for the subdivisions. This kind is valuable because it avoids the repetition of the sentence outline. Just remember to use parallel structure for the sentences and also for the subpoints, as in the sample outline below.

THESIS: *The high school instructor who teaches standard English to nonstandard-speaking students needs special training.*

TEACHER PREPARATION FOR APPLIED SOCIAL AND REGIONAL DIALECT STUDY ON THE SECONDARY LEVEL

I. The teacher must be prepared scholastically and culturally.
  A. Scholastic qualifications
    1. Theoretical subject matter
      a. Linguistics
      b. Phonetics and phonemics
      c. Morphology and syntax
    2. Practical subject matter
      a. American English structure
      b. Language testing
  B. Cultural qualifications
    1. Attitude toward the students
      a. Avoidance of prejudiced feelings
      b. Avoidance of preconceived, stereotyped ideas
    2. Attitude toward the dialect
      a. History of the dialect
      b. Sociocultural environment of the dialect
II. The teacher must be made aware of the necessary student adjustment.
  A. Background and environment
    1. Family history
    2. Living conditions

B. Attitude toward the teachers
  1. Previous experiences
  2. Previous educational opportunities
III. The teacher must plan the curriculum for the nonstand-
ard-speaking students.
  A. Relevant literature
    1. Anthropological study
    2. Representative authors
  B. Self-expression in speaking and writing
  C. Evaluation of the grading system
  D. Stimulating atmosphere
    1. Learning to listen
    2. Learning to reason

Two Forms for the Outline

Regardless of the type of outline, there are two forms it may take: (1) the number-letter sequence that has been used in examples thus far in this chapter and (2) the decimal sequence. The relative importance of each entry in the number-letter sequence is indicated both by the number or letter and by the indentation. The number-letter type of outline, theoretically, can be developed only through the 26th level while the decimal system is unlimited. In actual practice, though, the number-letter or alphabetic sequence is often developed in greater detail than the decimal sequence, which is usually carried no further than the fourth level (what would be the lower-case letters in the number-letter sequence). The decimal sequence does permit the reader to comprehend at a glance the relative importance of one item to another. A number-letter sequence for one major item and its subdivisions is shown below:

I.
  A.
    1.
    2.
      a.
      b.
      c.
    3.
      a.
      b.
        (1)
        (2)
          (a)
          (b)
          (c)
  B.
    1.
      a.
      b.
    2.
      a.
      b.
      c.
        (1)
        (2)
    3.

The decimal sequence for the same principal item and its subdivisions is shown in the next column:

1.0
  1.1
    1.1.1
    1.1.2
      1.1.2.1
      1.1.2.2
      1.1.2.3
    1.1.3
      1.1.3.1
      1.1.3.2
        (To prevent confusion, subordination is sel-
        dom carried beyond the fourth figure in the
        decimal sequence.)
  1.2
    1.2.1
      1.2.1.1
      1.2.1.2
    1.2.2
      1.2.2.1
      1.2.2.2
      1.2.2.3
    1.2.3

An example of the decimal sequence is found below:

THESIS: *The airbrush is useful to the layout and design department in a printing company.*

THE AIRBRUSH

1.0 Construction of an airbrush
  1.1 Control of the air spray
  1.2 Control of the flow of paint
    1.2.1 The needle valve
    1.2.2 The needle
2.0 Types of airbrushes
  2.1 Conventional design
    2.1.1 Paasche Model V
    2.1.2 Thayer and Chandler Model AA
  2.2 Special design
    2.2.1 Paasche Model AB
    2.2.2 Wold Model BB
3.0 Air supply
  3.1 The liquid carbonic unit
  3.2 The electric compressor-reserve tank
  3.3 The hand- or foot-operated pump
4.0 Operating the airbrush
  4.1 Holding procedure
  4.2 Correct movement
  4.3 Methods of working
    4.3.1 Vertical
    4.3.2 Horizontal
5.0 Applications
  5.1 Airbrush rendering
    5.1.1 Posters and illustrations
    5.1.2 Mechanical renderings
    5.1.3 Design
    5.1.4 Product rendering
    5.1.5 Technical figures
  5.2 Airbrush photo retouching
    5.2.1 Editorial retouching
    5.2.2 Mechanical retouching
    5.2.3 General advertising

Items in either form of outline can be arranged in

order of importance, chronologically, spatially, familiar to unfamiliar, simple to complex, or sequentially as in the steps in a process. The type of development best suited to the purpose, subject, and audience should be chosen. Chronological arrangement of details is appropriate for instructions, progress reports, investigations, and experiments. Order of importance or spatial order is effective for technical descriptions; familiar to unfamiliar and simple to complex arrangements are helpful in technical definitions. Sequential development best suits explanations of processes performed by machines. Spatial and sequential ordering is often grasped most quickly by professionals; moving from the simple and familiar to the complex and unfamiliar is helpful to audiences with less specialized training.

Regardless of the form you use, the outline is a safeguard against repetition of ideas and omission of vital information because it keeps you moving in a logical direction. It helps you to visualize the finished report with all the interrelations of ideas because the outline breaks a complex subject into parts. The carefully written outline helps you to spend less time later on rewriting the report.

CHECKLIST FOR A FINISHED OUTLINE

Checking the finished outline is a must. Checking the mechanical aspects is fairly simple, but problems in content are more difficult to identify.

Form

1. There should be at least two and no more than five or six main divisions and subdivisions under each main division, and no more than five or six subpoints under each subdivision.
2. At the other extreme, if there is an A, there should be a B; if there is a 1, there should at least be a 2. If there is not enough information for at least two divisions, the entry should not be subdivided at all.
3. Each main division should be expressed in the same grammatical form; each group of subdivisions should be expressed in the same grammatical form; and each group of subpoints under a subdivision should all be in the same form.
4. Each subseries should be indented.
5. A period should be placed after each roman numeral, each capital letter, each Arabic number, and each small letter. Such punctuation should be used consistently throughout the report.

Content

1. Each main division should contribute equally to the thesis statement.
2. The whole main division, including the subdivisions and subpoints, should be examined thoroughly before the next main division is considered.
3. The subdivisions should be clear and should accurately reflect the development of the ideas in the paper.

4. Classification should accurately reflect the relationship of ideas. Sometimes classification can appear to be logical but does not accurately reflect the content of the proposed idea; often it lists several ideas that appear of equal importance but that carry a different weight in the paper itself.
5. The introduction and conclusion should not be included in an outline.

When you finish checking the outline, remember it is subject to constant revision because of the additional information you will discover as you continue reading and writing.

EXERCISES

A. Examine the parts of outlines printed below. Identify the weakness or weaknesses you find in each.

(1)

I. Weather problems
   A. Subzero temperatures
   B. Ice storms
   C. Heavy snowfall
   D. Severe winters

(2)

I. Sheet-fed offset
   A. Size
      1. Single color
      2. Multiple color units
   B. Speed
      1. Past
      2. Present
      3. Future
   C. How much the runs cost
      1. Short runs
      2. Long runs
   D. Quality of work
      1. Line work

(3)

I. Fortran
   A. Advantages
      1. Processing time
      2. Initial cost
   B. Disadvantages
      1. Cost of cards
      2. Complexity of the operation
II. Basic
   A. Brief processing time
   B. Low cost of cards
   C. Poor terminal access
   D. Complexity of the total operation

(4)

I. Top management
   A. General manager
      1. Basic principles
         a. Charts
         b. Supervisors
         c. Information
         d. Pride
         e. Production
         f. Records
         g. Files
II. Middle management

(5)

V. The spray gun
    A. What is a spray gun?
    B. How does it work?
    C. What are the principal parts of a spray gun?
    D. Adjusting the spray gun
        1. Check pressure at the gun
        2. Testing the pattern
    E. Using the spray gun
        1. Type of coats
        2. Banding
    F. What happens when you handle the gun improperly?
        1. Runs
        2. Starved or thin film
        3. Orange peel
        4. Tilting the gun
        5. Arcing the gun

(6)

II. The teacher's role in the open classroom
    A. The teacher as an initiator, encourager, and guide
        1. Student-oriented class
    B. The teacher as a lesson planner
        1. Open-ended lesson plans
        2. Individualized and group lesson plans
        3. Activity-centered lesson plans

B. Using the facts listed below, outline a report analyzing the feasibility of a furniture manufacturer switching from wood frame chairs to molded plastic frame chairs. Write a suitable thesis; then develop a topic outline using either the number-letter sequence or the decimal sequence.

1. Wood is a renewable natural resource.
2. The plastic frame allows the company to produce more units at lower cost.
3. This last fiscal year of producing wood frames has been the company's peak year.
4. Dry kilns can be shut down entirely if a full conversion is made to plastic frames.
5. The petroleum supplies necessary to plastic are getting more controversial.
6. Plastic molded frames eliminate most of the basic woodworking operations.
7. The plastic frames will require a "cutting" to be run in minimum quantities of 500.
8. There are no structural variations in the plastic frame chairs.
9. Fifty-six percent of the forces currently employed on woodworking will be available for transfer into upholstering if the plastic frames are used.
10. If a particular wood frame type does not hold up in the market, it can be dropped or modified.
11. Each molded plastic arm section replaces wood component assemblies of at least eight to ten parts per side.
12. Twenty percent of the entire force of the plant will be uprooted and shifted into new functions that will require retraining if plastic frames are introduced.
13. Several wood frame chair styles have certain standardized parts.
14. The plastic frame chair has a one-shot molded back that replaces a wood assembly of 14 different parts, each of which has to be dimensioned, machined, and assembled.
15. Retention of the wood frames maintains the corporate image and protects the workers' job functions.
16. Plastic frame chairs will increase the output capacity by 30% to 35%.
17. A covering can be applied to the plastic frame chair exactly as sewn from the cutting room.
18. There is no absolute commitment to a given volume figure for the wood frame chairs.
19. With the molded plastic frames, there are no problems with seam alignment or adjustments to accommodate dimensional or contour variations.
20. Retention of wood construction involves no new costs for existing styles.
21. Standard guns and staples can be used to apply upholstery to the molded plastic forms.
22. The trend in furniture markets is swinging back to natural wood for all exposed parts.
23. Some machines used in the woodworking process will be shut down.
24. Plastic molded frames eliminate the need for the most expensive equipment investments.
25. Twenty percent of the total woodworking force will have to be laid off if the plastic frames are adopted.

TOPICS FOR OUTLINES

Choose one of the subjects listed below and write a topic outline containing 25 to 45 entries. Use either the number-letter sequence or the decimal sequence. Give the outline a title.

1. Criteria to consider when selecting a microscope
2. Reasons for the popularity of your major department's honorary society
3. Steps in tuning an engine
4. Steps in patching breaks in an asphalt road
5. Steps in solving a transit problem used in surveying courses
6. Criteria to consider when planning refreshments for a party
7. Steps in performing the slump test on concrete
8. Steps in changing a bandage
9. Steps in pruning a tree
10. Steps in giving an injection
11. Steps in using a computer
12. Criteria for selecting an elective
13. Criteria to consider when renting a place to live for the summer session

14. Criteria to consider when selecting a college for graduate study
15. Criteria to consider when purchasing a certain piece of sports equipment
16. Reasons for the popularity (or unpopularity) of a certain course
17. Criteria to consider when buying a new car
18. Criteria to consider when selecting a pet
19. Reasons for the popularity of a certain organization in your hometown
20. Criteria to consider when taking a part-time job
21. Criteria to consider when buying some article of clothing
22. Criteria to consider when joining a campus organization

Headings, Tables, and Figures

THE use of headings, tables, and figures sets technical writing apart from all other types of writing. Technical writing is the communication of highly specialized information in the simplest terms possible, and headings and illustrations contribute to that simplicity and clarity.

USE OF HEADINGS

Headings are labels that identify the various parts of a report. They are used in the body of the report and in a very formal introduction, but seldom in the conclusion. Headings (1) clarify the organization of the report and help the reader to understand the relationships among its various parts, (2) make it possible for the reader to read only the relevant sections, and (3) catch the reader's attention and arouse interest. Headings also help the writer: they force the writer to arrange material logically.

Transitional sentences should be used to link the headings together. Between the title of the report and the first heading there should be a transitional sentence, a paragraph, or perhaps several paragraphs. Between the first main heading and the following subheading there should be a sentence of transition, if at all possible, because this transitional sentence prepares the reader for the heading to follow. Observe the use of headings and transitional sentences in part of a report on noise reproduced below.

EFFECTS OF NOISE EXPOSURE

The known effects of noise exposure are of two types: auditory effects, which consist of temporary hearing loss and permanent hearing loss; and nonauditory effects, which cause interference with communication by speech or which otherwise influence behavior. First we will examine the auditory effects.

Auditory Effects

Loss of hearing is any reduction in the ability to hear from that of a normal person. Such a loss may be classified into two general categories.

Temporary hearing loss results from the exposure to loud noises for a few hours, with hearing returning after a brief rest period. Sometimes the recovery period may take minutes, hours, days, or even longer, depending on the individual and the severity and length of exposure. The major portion of the temporary loss occurs during the first one or two hours of exposure. This temporary loss is roughly constant for the same person from day to day, but it varies from person to person according to a normal statistical distribution.

Permanent hearing loss may occur as a result of the aging process, disease, injury, or exposure to loud noises over an extended period of time. Hearing loss associated with noise exposure is referred to as "acoustic trauma." This type of hearing loss is not reversible, as it is a result of nerve or hair cell destruction in the hearing organ. Usually hearing losses of this type are only partial.

Also observe in the above example that the sentence following a heading does not use a pronoun to refer to the heading because it is *outside* the text. Avoid using *this, these,* and *it* in the sentence following a heading. For example, if the heading is "The Radio Frequency Amplifier," the first sentence should be "The Radio Frequency (RF) amplifier strengthens the weak signal picked up by the antenna." It should not read "It strengthens the weak signal picked up by the antenna."

Headings of Different Rank

Headings must be used systematically; they must not be casually inserted into the text. If you are writing from an outline, the roman numeral, capital letter, and arabic number entries (but not necessarily the numerals or letters themselves) are transferred into the report as headings. Try to use at least one heading on each page, but do not use so many that they are distracting and seem to cut up the text into too many sections. Use enough headings to keep the reader constantly aware of what is being discussed but not so many as to reduce continuity. If you have very limited information on each entry in the outline, you might choose to transfer only the roman numeral and capital letter entries into the report as headings.

The Most Important Headings. The roman numeral entries in an outline are transferred into the paper as headings that are centered in the middle of the page and are placed in capital letters and underlined. These are often called *center heads*. Center heads should not be placed close to the bottom of the page.

The Headings Second in Importance. Capital letter entries in the outline are placed on the left-hand margin and are underlined. Important words in the heading are capitalized. These are called *side heads.* They are placed above the paragraph that they identify and introduce.

The Headings Third in Importance. The arabic number entries from the outline are incorporated as the first words or phrases of the paragraph. They are called *paragraph heads.* They are underlined and end with a period or with a colon. Two spaces separate the paragraph head from the first sentence in the paragraph. Only the first letter of the first word of this heading may be capitalized, or the initial letter of each important word may be capitalized. Whichever system is used, the capitalization of paragraph heads in a report should be consistent. If the paragraph head is identical with the first few words of a paragraph, you may avoid repetition by omitting the spacing and incorporating the heading into the first sentence. Again, any series of paragraph heads should be handled consistently—all separated from the first sentences by periods or colons and spacing or all used as parts of the first sentences.

Notice the accurate use of the center head, side head, and paragraph heads in a section of a paper below.

TYPES OF AIRBRUSHES

There are many types of brushes on the market, although the differences are mainly in the design of the body of the brush. Internally, the working parts are essentially the same. Better workmanship may account for a slightly higher price of one make of brush while quantity production and adequate tooling may reduce the cost of another make. Another difference in the types of airbrushes is the quality of line that is possible to draw with them. Some will draw a line as fine as a hair, when properly adjusted, but will not throw a wide spray, while others will deliver a broad spray for covering large areas quickly but will not draw as fine a line. Some makes combine both of these desirable features in the same brush.

Conventional Design

The conventional design airbrush works on the syphon, gravity, or pressure feed fluid tank system. The tank is mounted to the side of the airbrush and is adjustable to different positions. The conventional design airbrush has two types of control valves. The two way or double action valve system has a valve which, when pushed down with the index finger, emits only air. The amount of air emitted is controlled by the pressure applied to the valve; the more the pressure, the more air emitted. The control of paint comes from pulling back on the valve—the further pulled back, the more paint emitted. The second type of valve is a single action valve. The amount of air and paint emitted is controlled by the downward pressure applied to the valve—the more pressure applied, the more air and paint emitted.

The Passche Model V is designed for artists, illustrators, designers, and photographers who require a generous flow of color for blending, shading, and covering larger areas. The Model V type airbrush has a double action finger lever which controls the air and amount of color desired from a fine line to a gradually widening finely atomized color for backgrounds or realistic cloud effects.

The Thayer and Chandler Model AA also has a double action finger lever control. It can spray a fine line to a gradual wide pattern. The Model AA is designed for general color blending, shading, and covering large areas.

Headings of the Professional Printer

The typist uses capital letters, underlining, and placement on the page to indicate the importance of the headings that label the various sections of a report. The professional printer uses different positions and sizes and types of print to distinguish the various ranks of headings.

Headings for the Brief Memo or the One-Page Report

Headings all of the same rank make memos and brief reports easier to read. Headings of second importance or of third importance may be used. For instance, each paragraph in the body of the memo may be labeled with a side head separated from the paragraph itself. Or the beginning of each paragraph in the body of the same memo can be underlined; just make sure that each of these paragraphs begins with the same grammatical form. Regardless of how simple your plan for headings is, make sure that they stand out on the page and indicate the organization of the body of the report or memo. Headings are seldom used in the introduction and conclusion of a short report because these sections are often only one or two sentences in length. See the following progress report in memo form with paragraph heads.

To: President Johnson   Date: March 1, 19—
From: Affirmative Action Committee
Subject: Activities of the Affirmative Action Committee

This progress report is submitted by the Affirmative Action Committee to acquaint you with its activities and concerns thus far in the school year of 19— to 19—.

Past actions. The Affirmative Action Committee, meeting on the first and third Thursdays of each month at 3:30 p.m. in the Student Union, has concerned itself primarily with two problems: (1) monitoring the hiring practices of the college and (2) revising the Guidelines.

In October we acted as a screening committee for the 64 applicants for the position of Personnel Officer. After evaluating them according to the education and experience required in the job description, we recommended 7 top candidates for interview.

The revision of the Guidelines must be submitted to HEW by July 1, 19—. In November, December, and January the committee revised the Guidelines to correct three deficiencies listed in the HEW evaluation of 19—. The Director of Employee Relations appeared before the committee to furnish information and availability data needed for the revision.

Present concerns. The committee is studying the Guidelines of another university which have been approved by HEW. We are comparing their specific goals and timetables with similar statements in our Guidelines to get a better idea of how ours should be revised.

<u>Future concerns</u>. The Affirmative Action Committee has set up several possible areas of future concern: (1) the outlining of a detailed grievance procedure to be written as a document separate from the Guidelines, (2) the development of a formal policy for monitoring the part-time, temporary faculty, and (3) the publication of a newsletter designed to disseminate useful information to classified and unclassified personnel.

We are an advisory body and are here to help the administration, faculty, and classified personnel. Our primary, overall goal is to keep our school in full compliance with federal regulations. Perodic reports will be sent to acquaint you with our various activities designed to accomplish this goal.

Economy and Clarity of Headings

Effective headings are the result of following rather specific rules. Some of the basic principles are reviewed below.

Pattern. All headings, regardless of their rank, should be topics—usually nouns and modifiers. If you doubt your ability to phrase headings as nouns, consider the heading as the title for the section. Verbals are often helpful; gerunds clearly label the steps in an explanation of a process, for instance.

Parallelism. Parallel structure means using the same grammatical form for headings that are logically equal, and such structure makes the headings of equal rank easier to read and remember. The grammatical form may vary, however, from one series of headings to another: the headings of first rank may be expressed as nouns and the headings of second rank may be gerunds. In spite of which grammatical form is used, the first heading of a certain rank sets the pattern for all other headings of that rank.

Empty Headings. Such headings as "Discussion" and "Comments" tell little about the content of the section and usually should be avoided. Headings should be informative.

Length. Headings should be neither too long nor too short. As in other areas of technical writing, moderation is desirable. The heading "Codes" is too brief to be very informative; "Building Codes for Multiple Family Dwellings in Zone Six of Brooklyn" is cumbersome and distracting. "Applicable Building Codes" would be more effective.

Capitalization and Punctuation. Center heads should be capitalized throughout. The first letter in each important word in side heads should also be capitalized. The initial letter in each important word of the paragraph head may also be capitalized or only the first letter of the first word, depending on the writer's choice. Periods or colons should be placed after paragraph heads. All ranks of headings should be underlined in typed copy.

Numbers and Letters. Occasionally the decimal or number-letter sequence is used with headings, but the danger here is that the page will appear cluttered and will be difficult to read. This system does, however, facilitate reference in complicated analyses or in lengthy formal reports and proposals. The decimal sequence is used in the following brief excerpt from a lengthy formal report that included many headings.

1.0   SINGLE WIDTH SECTIONALS

Single width sectionals are made by placing two 10 ft, 12 ft, and 14 ft wide sections side by side. Sections can be two piece single story, three piece, two story stack on, or two story sectional boxes. The principle that sets the sectionals apart from mobile homes is their construction specifications.

1.1   The Strengths

The erection and completion of a single width sectional for living purposes take place in two or three days. Such speedy completion is due in part to building codes and zoning and to the seasonal demand.

1.1.1   <u>Building codes and zoning</u>. Sectionals are in every aspect conventional houses; there are no problems concerning local or state building codes. Sectional units are designed and assembled to meet basic building code requirements. Since they meet conventional building codes, they are affixed to permanent foundation systems.

1.1.2   <u>Seasonal demand</u>. The smaller builders keep a relatively constant flow in ordering the sectionals. It is easy to program the drop in demand during the winter months to their response.

1.2   The Weaknesses

Housing competition in urban areas and distance from the point of supply are the most obvious problems for the modular industry. These problems will have a lasting effect on the future of the modular industry.

1.2.1   <u>Competition</u>. A good conventional operation can beat the sectional operation even with the extra site and labor costs for the conventional home. A great percentage of sectional growth will be limited to the rural market where demands are rapidly growing and to vacation homes in small towns and in low value subdivision markets where sales are too slow to permit an efficient, on-the-site operation.

1.2.2   <u>Transportation</u>. For better delivery service and minimum trucking cost, the job site should be fairly close. The maximum distance a sectional can be transported is usually 250 miles.

USE OF ILLUSTRATIONS

Illustrations clarify technical information in proposals and reports. They are ordinarily not used in memos and letters; therefore, those reports in the memo and letter forms should not be dependent on illustration. In some reports, though, it is impossible to communicate technical information in words alone; for these, the article-report form should be used, and tables and figures should be added. The main conventions for the use of tables and figures will be given here, but you must also observe the ways in which nonverbal forms are used in the publications of your major area. Systematic observation of the various uses for tables and figures will increase your resourcefulness.

As you decide when to use illustrations in your report, keep your audience in mind. Is your audience *eye minded* or *word minded?* If the illustration is self-explanatory, resist the impulse to explain it. Do not give a complicated explanation and then refer the reader to the figure that simplifies the information. Refer to the table or the figure first, and then offer additional explanations if necessary. Observe the sample table below and the context in which it is used:

Most of the recently installed minicomputers are being used in industrial control and laboratory instrumentation. Among the biggest markets for minicomputers are industrial control, research, data communications, and education. As a follow-up to the article in *Datapro Research Corporation,* a Minicomputer Reader Survey Form was sent out and 1,268 readers responded. Table 1 shows how the users of minicomputers rated their minicomputers.

TABLE 1. User Experience with Minicomputers

	Excellent	Good	Fair	Poor
Overall performance	42%	46%	10%	2%
Ease of programming	19%	58%	17%	6%
Ease of operation	34%	57%	7%	2%
Hardware reliability	40%	44%	12%	4%
Maintenance service	24%	46%	23%	7%
Technical support	13%	38%	30%	19%
Manufacturer's software	16%	44%	25%	15%

From Table 1 a few conclusions can be drawn. It is clear that minicomputer users are generally pleased with the reliability and effectiveness of their minicomputers. Also the users are partly satisfied with the quality of the maintenance service they are receiving. But it also shows that many of the users are much less pleased with the technical support and manufacturer's software.

(Courtesy Datapro Research Corporation [1])

Tables

Tables have column headings across the top row and headings from the left side (the stub); they usually present statistical information. A table is often the result of hours of work in compilation and analysis, but the time spent on a table is well worth it in terms of the reader's understanding. It is possible to grasp information in tabular form that would be impossible to understand in ordinary prose because tables usually present extensive data obtained under varying conditions.

The following general rules will guide you in the preparation of tables:

1. The table should be referred to in the text of the report so the reader will know when to consult it. The table should be placed in the text as close as possible to but following the first reference to it.
2. The column headings should have parallel grammatical form. They should be arranged in some logical order: alphabetical, geographical, quantitative, etc.
3. The identification of the table (arabic number and title) is placed at the top. Tables are usually numbered consecutively throughout a short report. However, when tables are used in a textbook, they are numbered consecutively by chapter—the first number indicating the chapter

and the second number the placement of the table in the chapter (3.1, 3.2, 3.3, etc). The title should be expressed as a topic and be as concise as possible. A sentence or two of explanation (the legend) may follow the title or may be included in an unnumbered footnote placed at the bottom of the table and introduced by the word *Note* followed by a colon.

4. Spacing should be used to separate columns, or dotted lines should be used. Too many solid lines should be avoided.
5. Numbers should be arranged in the columns by the right-hand digit or by the decimal point.
6. Decimals should be used instead of fractions unless decimals are not customary for the subject area involved.
7. Large numbers should be labeled in the column heading in terms of thousands, millions, etc.
8. Large numbers should be rounded off when reading ease is more important than accuracy.
9. Standard abbreviations should be used to save space.
10. When a note is needed to explain some part of a table, a lower-case letter, a number, or a symbol should be placed above the line at the point where the note is needed and the note placed at the bottom of the table. Do not confuse a table footnote with a footnote in the text that always goes at the bottom of a page and is designated by a number rather than a lower-case letter.
11. A table should not extend over the normal margins of the page. If it does, the table should be placed lengthwise on the page with the top at the left side of the page.
12. A table should usually not be continued from one page to another, but if this must be done, *continued* should be written at the bottom of the first page and the top of the second. If appropriate, subtotals should be placed at the bottom of the first page and at the top of the second page.
13. When a table has been copied, credit should be given to the source in an unnumbered footnote placed at the bottom of the table and introduced by the word *Source* followed by a colon—the practice followed in this text. Credit can also be given with a raised footnote marker after the title referring the reader to notes at the end of the report or with a reference number in parentheses after the title or the title and legend referring the reader to the numbered list of references at the end of the report. Occasionally, the author's name, publication, and date are placed in parentheses after the title of the table.
14. The long table should be divided into two parts. If, however, a long table must be used, the long list of numbers should be divided into shorter sections by spacing or by dotted horizontal lines.

Although statistical information is most often presented in tabular form, the table can also be used to compare other kinds of information. It may consist of words arranged in column form. Just remember, though, that a table is more than two or three lists placed side by side.

Tables 3.1 to 3.5 illustrate some of the principles and rules that have been discussed in this chapter.

TABLE 3.1. Combined visual-tactile and radiographic findings for IU examiner, on the baseline examination and after each year of study for teeth present at the baseline examination in children present at all examinations, Santa Clara County

n	Control (N = 116)	Treatment (N = 123)	% difference	t value
Baseline prevalence				
DMFT	4.16 (0.267)*	4.56 (0.326)		0.92
DMFS	6.85 (0.504)	7.59 (0.597)		0.95
Proximal surfaces	2.27 (0.263)	2.87 (0.333)		1.42
No. erupted permanent teeth	20.93	21.02		
One-year increment				
DMFT	1.20 (0.151)	0.87 (0.159)	−27.4	1.50
DMFS	2.35 (0.293)	1.83 (0.286)	−22.0	1.26
Proximal surfaces	1.29 (0.216)	0.90 (0.187)	−30.2	1.37
Two-year increment				
DMFT	2.22 (0.215)	1.56 (0.205)	−29.8	2.23†
DMFS	4.56 (0.528)	3.31 (0.397)	−27.4	1.89†
Proximal surfaces	2.41 (0.349)	1.77 (0.277)	−26.6	1.44
Three-year increment				
DMFT	2.70 (0.241)	2.15 (0.241)	−20.2	1.64†
DMFS	5.97 (0.622)	4.62 (0.489)	−22.7	1.71†
Proximal surfaces	2.99 (0.414)	2.50 (0.335)	−16.3	0.92

Source: The American Dental Association in *Journal of the American Dental Association* [2].

* Standard error of the mean
† Significant at P = 0.05; one-tailed Student's *t* test

TABLE 3.2. Distribution of stalls by type of work

Planning Volume	Customer Service Stalls	New Car Preparation Stalls	Used Car Conditioning Stalls	Subtotal Stalls
100	5	1	1	7
200	8	1	1	10
300	11	1	1	13
400	13	1	2	16
500	15	1	2	18
600	17	1	2	20
700	19	1	2	22
800	21	1	2	24
900	22	2	3	27
1000	24	2	3	29
1100	27	2	3	32
1200	29	2	3	34
1300	31	2	3	36
1400	33	2	3	38
1500	34	3	4	41
1600	36	3	4	43
2000	43	4	5	52

Source: The Ford Motor Company [4].

TABLE 3.3. A comparison of three major labor relations laws

Contract Item	Wagner Act	Taft-Hartley	Landrum-Griffin
Individual bargaining and individual rights	Union certified by NIRB is exclusive agent in respect to wages, hours, and conditions of employment. Also individual employee can present grievances.	Individual employee can present grievances to have them settled without the "interference of the bargaining representative."	Union democracy and protection of individual rights guaranteed by union members "Bill of Rights."
Free speech	No set provision.	Employer views that do not threaten reprisal, force, or promise of benefit are permissible.	No provision.
Secret ballot	Used only to determine the collective bargaining unit.	Used to determine collective bargaining unit, to accept or reject employer's final offer, and to determine whether group desires union shop.	No provision.

TABLE 3.4. BIRD CENSUS

	E. Java	Bali	Lombok	Sumbawa
Total bird count	2412	1587	674	1421
No. recording sites	25	15	12	26
No. birds per site	96.5	106.5	56.1	54.6

Source: The Zoological Society of London for *Journal of Zoology* [3].
Note: The study was made by four observers in 78 ten-minute recording periods during a journey through East Java, Bali, Lombok, and Sumbawa, September 1973.

TABLE 3.5. Comparison of new part prices and used part prices

Item	New Price:$	Used Price:$
Late model V8 engine		
Short block	600	300 Exchange
Complete	1200	400 Outright
Automatic transmission with convertor	500	200
Starter motor		
New	100	
Rebuilt	50	15 Exchange
Wiper motor	50	15 Exchange
Brake caliper	75	10 Exchange
Front fender	85	65

Source: Petersen Publishing Company for *Motor Trend* [5].

Figures

Figures are all types of visuals that are not classified as tables and include graphs and curves, bar charts, pie diagrams, flow sheets, photographs, diagrams, and drawings. Figures must serve some useful purpose and not just decorate the page; they can summarize the technical information in the text and can illustrate details passed over in the general text. Figures effectively present numbers, structures, and pictures by vividly stressing general trends or comparisons. They should be simple, accurate, properly labeled, and smoothly integrated with the text so the figures and text reinforce each other.

As you decide on the placement and function of figures in the report, always keep your readers in mind. If they may not be able to understand a certain figure, give them that information in another type of figure that will be easier to grasp.

The following general rules will guide you in the preparation of figures:

1. The figure should be referred to in the text of the report so the reader will know when to consult it. Place the figure in the text as close as possible to but following the first reference to it; if the first reference is near the bottom of the page, place the figure at the top of the next page.
2. The identification of the figure (arabic number and title) is placed a double space beneath the figure; this identification should be closer to the figure than to the text so it will not be confused with the text. If space is limited, the identification can be placed to the left of a small figure. A sentence or two of explanation (the legend) may follow the title, which is expressed as a topic. Figures are usually numbered consecutively through a report. In a book, figures are numbered by chapter (3.1, 5.1, etc.).
3. Each figure should be surrounded by plenty of space to separate it from the text or should be enclosed in a line border. Examine the periodicals in your field to discover the practices of others in your major area. Just remember to be consistent in the handling of figures throughout the report.
4. Standard abbreviations may be used to save space.
5. A figure should not extend over the normal margins of the page. If it does, place the figure lengthwise on the page with the top at the left side of the page.
6. Each figure should be neatly drawn in India ink and should be no larger than necessary for clarity.
7. The figure should contain all the information that the reader needs so he will not have to refer to the text. Label the parts of the figure.
8. Lettering must not be placed slantwise. Place the lettering so that it can be read with the bottom of the figure down.
9. A complicated figure should be divided into two simpler ones.

10. If you have copied the figure, give credit to the source under the illustration or at the end of the legend, with the author's name, publication, and date in parentheses or with the number of the reference in parentheses. The copyright holder may require a certain form of credit line.

Graphs and Curves. A brief examination of technical books and periodicals will indicate that the types of figures often used are graphs and curves. They present the same data that might also be included in a table. In fact, the first step in drawing a graph is to compile a table. Graphs are especially effective when showing past and present trends and forecasting future trends when the data used are continuous. They show a continuous relationship between two or more quantities. The rise and fall of the line visually suggest the changes. The line may be a jagged one that goes from point to point, or it may form a smooth curve. See Figures 3.1 and 3.2. Although the smooth curve is less accurate, it does indicate a general trend.

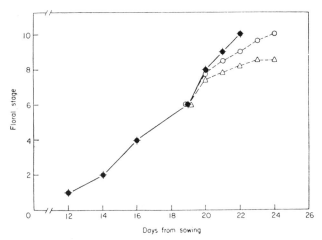

Fig. 3.1. A graph showing the rate of development of the first initiated flower bud of plants of variety P47 in different photoperiods. o——o, 11 h; +——+, 12 h; o---o, 13 h; Δ---Δ, 14 h. Each point represents the mean of five plants. (Courtesy *Annals of Botany* [6])

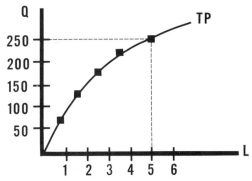

Fig. 3.2. A curve showing the levels of output obtained from different amounts of labor input. (Courtesy Pittsburg State University [7])

There are several rules for the drawing of a graph. Include no more than three or four lines on one graph and label each line either on the graph or curve itself or explain the meanings of the lines in the sentence of explanation after the title. When you use different symbols for each line on the graph, remember that a solid line looks more important than a line of dashes; a line of dashes looks more important than a line of dots. Do not let the symbols used change the meaning of the graph. If possible, keep the labels horizontal so they will be easy to read; do not print along the curve of the graph. Place the independent variable across the bottom of the graph and the dependent variable along the left side. The dependent variable is affected by changes in the independent variable. Each usually begins at zero (Fig. 3.3). But when large numbers such as thousands or millions are used, as in Figure 3.4, the zeroes are suppressed in the interests of clarity.

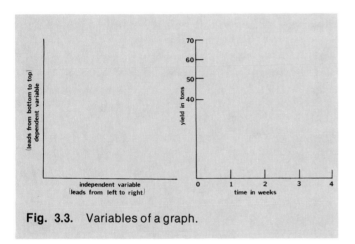

Fig. 3.3. Variables of a graph.

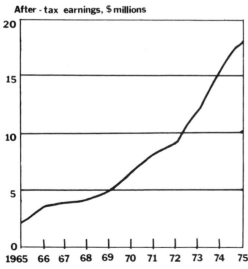

Fig. 3.4. Accurate presentation of earnings gains. (Courtesy *Chemical & Engineering News* [8])

The graph can be misleading when charting business statistics and must be planned carefully. The more the vertical values are "stretched" or the more the horizontal values are compressed, the greater will be the significance or change the graph depicts. Since a sharp rise or fall suggests an important change, compression of the horizontal values can be misleading. In Figure 3.4, the information is presented accurately; in Figure 3.5, compression of the horizontal values gives a false impression.

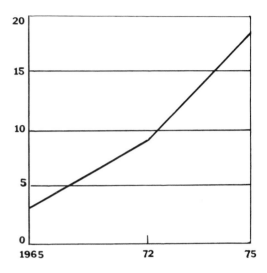

Fig. 3.5. Inaccurate presentation of earnings gains due to compression of the horizontal values.

Bar Chart. The bar chart is a series of bars that picture comparisons among a number of items. It is the figure most closely connected to tables. It converts the statistical information found in tables to bars that can be understood at first glance; however, these bars are not as accurate as the table. The bars can be either vertical or horizontal depending on the type of subject; vertical bars would be appropriate for altitude studies or increase in sales and the horizontal bars for time or distance studies. They can be shaded with varying degrees of intensity but are seldom solid colors.

The bar chart or graph is quite useful because it permits immediate comparison of amounts. It can show different amounts at different times, amounts of several different things at one or more times, and the amounts of different parts that make up a whole. Observe the types of bar charts in Figures 3.6 to 3.9.

The bar can be presented pictorially in a pictogram or picture chart; for instance, a string of oranges can represent the increase in orange production in Florida for a certain period. Such a pictorial treatment can popularize the material, but it is not often used in technical reports because it is difficult to maintain accuracy in such pictures. Occasionally, a different size object is used to represent different amounts; in the example cited above, a different size orange would be used to show the growth in orange production in Florida for a number of successive years. However, it is better to use ordinary bars that vary only in length rather than to

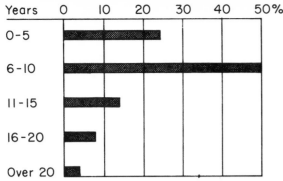

Fig. 3.6. Horizontal bar chart measuring the length of the changeover to the metric system in the United States.

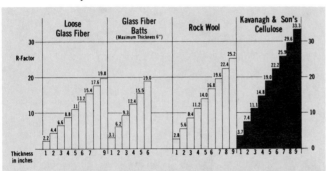

Fig. 3.7. Vertical bar chart. "R" stands for resistance; the greater the "R" value, the better the insulation. (Courtesy Kavanagh & Son's Cellulose Insulation Co. [9])

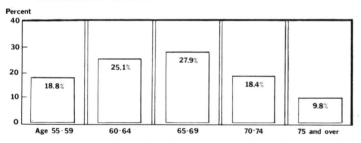

Fig. 3.8. Vertical bar chart showing the ages of workers in the senior community service employment program. (Courtesy *Worklife*[10])

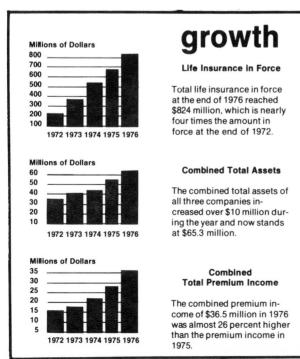

depend on varying dimensions that make it difficult to decide which objects are larger than others.

Two picture charts are presented in Figures 3.10 and 3.11. Figure 3.10 is more suitable for technical reports because accompanying statistics interpret the string of pictures. Figure 3.11 does not give the specific information required in technical writing.

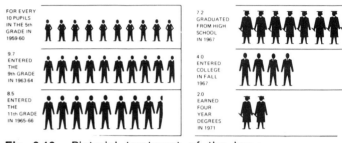

Fig. 3.10. Pictorial treatment of the bar chart showing school retention rates.

Fig. 3.11. Pictorial treatment of the bar chart showing the ranking of issues in an election year.

The steps in compiling a bar graph are few. Select a scale—perhaps one inch on the bar to represent 300 graduates or 500 new Fords. Or if you want to fit the bar graph in a small space, you may decide to let ¼ inch represent the 300 graduates or the 500 new Fords. Try different possibilities until you are satisfied with the heights of your highest and lowest bars. Draw in the others accordingly. Shade the bars to make them stand out. Add appropriate headings and a border if you so desire. To include more information in the bar graph, you may wish to segment each bar. Give each segment a different shading or cross-hatching so it can be easily identified. See Figure 3.12.

Fig. 3.9. Bar charts showing the growth of the Farmland Insurance Program. (Courtesy Farmland Industries, Inc. [11])

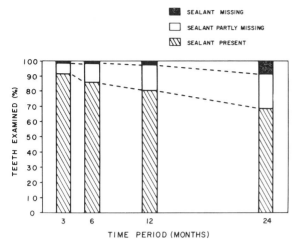

Fig. 3.12. Bar graph with vertical segmented bars showing sealant retention on paired permanent teeth at 3, 6, 12, and 24 months. (Courtesy American Dental Association for the *Journal of the American Dental Association* [12])

Pie or Circle Diagram. More than any other visual aid, the pie offers comparison of parts to each other and to the whole at the same time; it shows the fractions or percentages that make up a whole. The pie diagram or chart is invaluable for giving an easily understood picture of proportions, but for maximum effectiveness there should be obvious differences in each segment. The pie cannot be interpreted quantitively as quickly as a bar graph, which is more effective than the pie when there is little difference between each segment. The pie diagram is most often used to picture expenditures or sources of income.

There are several rules for drawing a pie diagram: (1) The values compared must be expressed as whole numbers that add up to 100%. (2) Pie diagrams should not be divided into more than eight segments. (3) One-dimensional diagrams are easier to read than three-dimensional ones. For instance, in Figure 3.13 the pie diagram on the left is clearer than the one on the right.

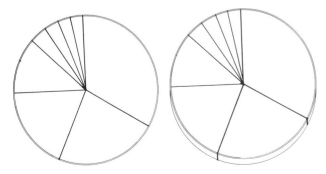

Fig. 3.13. One-dimensional and three-dimensional pie diagrams.

(4) The largest segment should be placed at twelve o'clock with the other segments arranged clockwise in decreasing order. (5) If one segment is less than 2%, it should not be shown; several small segments can be lumped together as "miscellaneous." (6) All segments should be labeled horizontally, not slantwise. The labels may be placed outside the segments or within them. Also these two methods of labeling may be combined: The labels for large segments may be placed within and the labels for small segments may be placed outside the pie. See Figure 3.14.

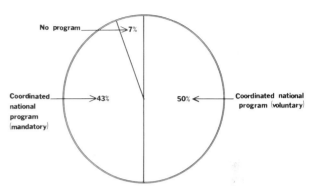

Fig. 3.14. Pie diagram showing the results of a local opinion poll on the best course of action for United States conversion to the metric system.

Flow Chart. The flow chart is not concerned with statistics. It traces pictorially the movement of material through the manufacturing process and shows the process from raw to finished product. Machines and processes are shown as circles or rectangles; these are connected by arrows indicating the direction in which the product moves.

Similar to the flow chart is the organizational chart. The organizational chart shows fixed positions in the structure of the business rather than movement. It can reveal the different levels of responsibility in the company or institution and their relationships—the persons responsible to a certain official and the superiors of that official. The chart that shows the chain of command by listing the positions rather than those who fill the positions does not become outdated quickly because there are fewer changes in the structure of the organization than there are in the job holders. Circles or rectangles, properly labeled, are drawn to represent the positions that make up a business staff.

There are several steps you must take to draw an effective flow chart or organizational chart: (1) List each phase or position that you want to include. (2) Arrange them and put them in boxes. (3) Label the boxes, keeping the lettering horizontal. (4) Connect the boxes with arrows. (5) Label the point where the reader should begin with *start* if such labeling seems appropriate.

Notice in Figures 3.15 and 3.16 that labels are printed in the boxes if the boxes are large enough. If the boxes are too small, the labels are placed outside. Arrows clearly connect the boxes.

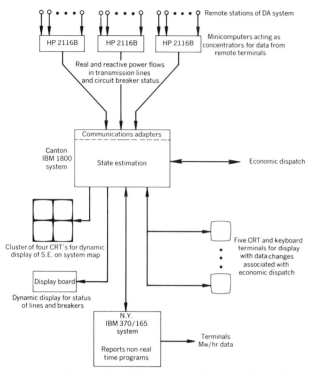

Fig. 3.15. Flow chart of the state-estimation package. (Reprinted from Feb. 15, 1976, issue of *Electrical World* [13], copyright, Mc-Graw-Hill)

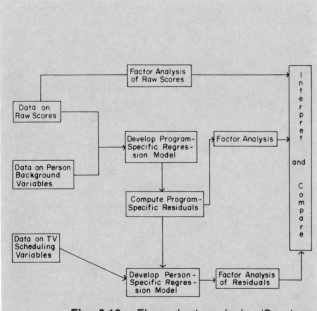

Fig. 3.16. Flow chart analysis. (Courtesy American Marketing Association for *Journal of Marketing Research* [14])

Tree Diagram. Similar to the flow chart is the tree diagram. It is appropriate for clarifying the organization of technical reports as well as for depicting the structure of various projects and chains of command because it clearly shows the relationship of one idea or part to another. The formal outline of a technical report can be compared to a tree structure: the purpose statement or thesis is the apex of the tree; the main arguments used to support the thesis (roman numeral divisions) are the middle level of the tree; the subdivisions of the main divisions (capital letter divisions) are comparable to the next lower level of the tree; and the lowest level of the tree is representative of the arabic numeral divisions. Figure 3.17 illustrates this concept.

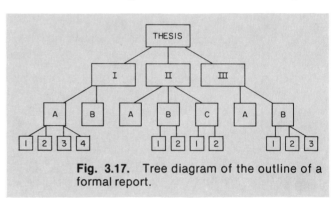

Fig. 3.17. Tree diagram of the outline of a formal report.

Photographs. External appearances are most effectively shown in photographs. The best photos are those taken at close range; when appropriate, they should also suggest action. They contribute vividness to a report because they can substantiate statements in the text as well as assist the verbal description. Photographs can present precise details of what to look for during an inspection and of how to assemble and disassemble equipment.

To use photographs skillfully, strive for sharp contrast in the photos, and retouch those that have a cluttered or unattractive background. Label the important parts if such labeling would add clarity, using white ink on black areas and black ink on white areas. Then explain the labels in a sentence of explanation in the legend or in the text. Artists' renditions can be used in the same way as photographs. See Figures 3.18, 3.19, and 3.20.

Diagrams and Drawings. Sometimes diagrams and drawings are more valuable than photographs because they can show not only the outward appearance of the object but also the intricate parts and internal workings. In a drawing, only those parts discussed in the text are included; in a photo all the camera sees is included. A simple drawing is often better than the realistic clutter of a photograph. The drawing that emphasizes what will be most helpful to the audience should be selected and further simplified.

There are several types of diagrams and drawings: (1) The process drawing emphasizes a step-by-step sequence of sketches that illustrate the steps in a process. It helps the reader's performance. The installation diagram shows the relationship of the various parts, and the schematic helps the reader visualize the whole process or system. (2) An exploded view blows apart the object but maintains the arrangement of its parts. (3) The cutaway drawing removes the outer casing to show the inside of the mechanism. (4) Cross-sectional views cut the object in half, showing its size and all the relationships of the parts. But regardless of the type of diagram, the reader should proceed from left to right. These diagrams and drawings can show how equipment operates, and also the shape and location of objects. See Figures 3.21 to 3.27.

Fig. 3.18. Photograph of the Xerox 1824 microfilm printer. (Courtesy Kansas Gas and Electric Company [16])

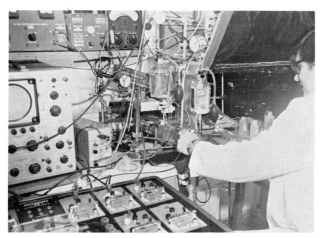

Fig. 3.19. Photograph showing a graduate student using a chart recording device, oscilloscope, a pressure recording system, and a light beam device to study the effect of intraocular pressure upon retinal impulse activity. (Courtesy Pittsburg State University [17])

Fig. 3.20. Artist's rendition. (Courtesy Rudi/Lee/Dreyer, Ames, Iowa)

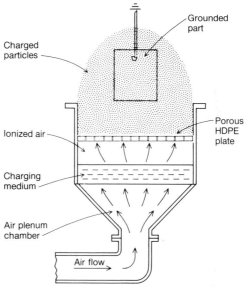

Fig. 3.21. Process drawing of the porous HDPE shield. (Courtesy McGraw-Hill Book Company for *Modern Plastics* [19])

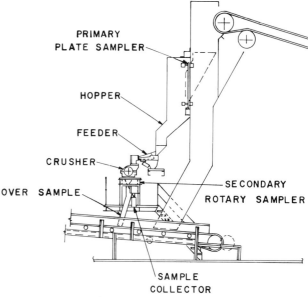

Fig. 3.22. Typical installation diagram of a plate and rotary sampler. (Courtesy McNally Pittsburgh Manufacturing Corporation [15])

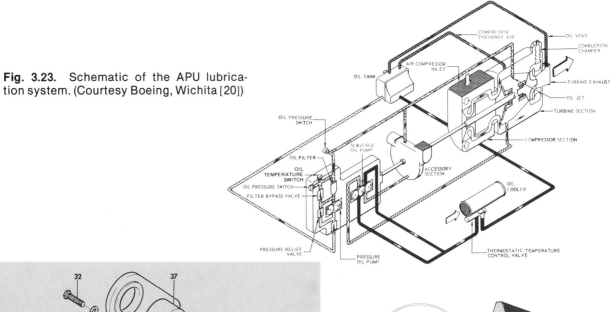

Fig. 3.23. Schematic of the APU lubrication system. (Courtesy Boeing, Wichita [20])

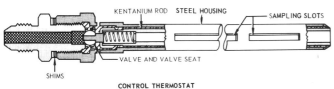

Fig. 3.24. Exploded drawing of an aircraft nose steering disconnect linkage. (Courtesy Beech Aircraft Corporation [22])

KENTANIUM ROD STEEL HOUSING SAMPLING SLOTS

VALVE AND VALVE SEAT

SHIMS

CONTROL THERMOSTAT

Fig. 3.25. Cutaway drawing of a control thermostat. (Courtesy Boeing, Wichita [20])

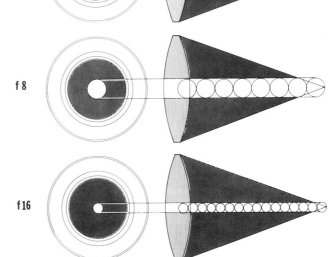

f 4

f 8

f16

Fig. 3.26. Cutaway drawing of the f-stop in a camera. (Courtesy Pittsburg State University [21])

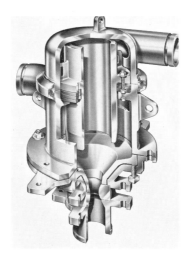

Fig. 3.27. Cross-sectional view of the McNally Visman Tricone. (Courtesy McNally Pittsburg Manufacturing Corporation [15])

Maps. Statistical information can be presented clearly and dramatically with a map. A map can be simplified considerably before publication by deleting all the unnecessary names and lines. Such deletions will focus the reader's attention on the important aspects of the map (Fig. 3.28).

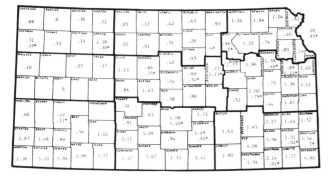

Fig. 3.28. A map showing precipitation for the week ending May 29. The asterisk indicates precipitation for May 30–31, omission of an entry indicates the report was not received, and T means trace.

Placement of Tables and Figures

Placement of the table or of the figure in the text is determined by (1) the size and (2) the reference to it in the text. The visual must be placed right after the first mention of it in the text; tell the reader when to refer to it. If it is small, place it on the right side of the page; place the text on the left. If the visual is larger, interrupt the text and extend it across the page; then continue the text below the visual. When visuals are not essential to understanding the technical information, refer to them in the text and place them in the appendix section at the end of the report.

If there is not enough space left on the page to include the figure right after the first mention of it in the text, put it at the top of the next page. A table can be continued from the bottom of one page to the top of the next if necessary. Remember to leave enough white space around a figure or table to adequately separate it from the text, even if the figure is already enclosed in a border.

The table or figure that must be viewed over several pages presents a special problem. There are three solutions: (1) put the table or figure on a double fold-out page at the end of the report with a tab identifying it (Fig. 3.29); (2) put it on the bottom or top half of the last page on which you refer to it and use horizontally split pages for the text leading up to that point (Fig. 3.30); or (3) if the table or figure is long and narrow, put it on the right side of the page on which you make the last reference to it and vertically split the pages coming before that page so the reader can view the table or figure while reading the text (Fig. 3.31).

Fig. 3.29. The double fold-out page.

Fig. 3.30. Horizontally split pages.

Fig. 3.31. Vertically split pages.

SUMMARY

Headings and visuals distinguish technical writing from all other kinds of writing. Headings label the parts of a report, and there are usually three different ranks: (1) headings of first importance that are centered, put in capital letters, and underlined; (2) headings of second importance that are placed on the left-hand margin, underlined, and the important words capitalized; and (3) headings of third importance that are placed at the beginning of the paragraph, underlined, the first letter of the first word or of all important words capitalized, and a period or colon at the end. Paragraph heads can also be incorporated into the paragraph as the first word or phrase of the first sentence. All headings, regardless of their rank, should be phrased as topics, and the headings must be informative. "Discussion" and "Comments" are not very helpful. In some types of complicated analyses or lengthy reports, numbers and/or letters from the outline may also be used with the headings.

Statistics and technical information bombard both students and employees each day. Visuals clearly communicate such information. Visuals are like summaries and lists in that they are the focal points of the report. They do not replace words, but they do make economy of word choice possible. They should be placed in the text immediately after the first reference to them.

Tables give specific, detailed information when accuracy is more important than attracting attention. In a highly technical report prepared for fellow workers and superiors, more tables than figures should be used. Identification should be placed above the table and too many solid lines should be avoided.

In a report prepared for the less specialized audience, figures should be used to dramatize the facts. Figures may or may not be enclosed in borders, but they should be handled consistently throughout the report. Identification should be placed below the figure. Graphs and curves are the figures most often used in technical writing; bar charts present the statistics that can be found in tables; the pie diagram shows percentages of the whole; the flow sheet traces the manufacturing process from raw material to the finished product; photographs show outward appearances; and drawings and diagrams reveal the internal workings.

Headings, tables, and figures are all used to present information in such a clear, concise manner that the reader can immediately understand it.

EXERCISES

1. Construct a table that clearly presents the age, sex, class rank, and majors of five other students in your class.
2. Construct a table showing the high and the low temperatures in a 24-hour period for five cities. Record the temperatures for today and for one year ago today.
3. Construct some type of bar chart showing the total annual contributions to the alumni association for five consecutive years.
4. Determine the amount of money you spend each month. Construct a pie (circle) diagram or some type of bar chart showing how you spend this money.
5. Draw a line graph showing the number of majors in the history, English, biology, and mathematics departments for five consecutive years. Or draw a line graph showing the number of employees in the drafting, accounting, and personnel offices of several local industries.
6. Develop an organizational chart showing the structure of a campus organization or of a local civic club.
7. Construct a visual for the registrar showing specific percentages of students who received grades of A, B, C, D, F, or W in two imaginary classes. Then construct another type of visual that will communicate the same information more quickly to a high school student. Select the illustration most appropriate for each reader.
8. Write a paragraph introducing one of the figures or tables described in the above exercises. If additional explanations are necessary after the reader has looked at the illustration, write another paragraph offering this information, one which can be placed in the text after the figure or table.

REFERENCES

1. *All About Minicomputers.* Datapro Research Corp., 1973.
2. Herschel S. Horowitz and David Bixler, "The Effect of Self-applied SnF_2ZrSiO_4 Prophylactic Paste on Dental Caries: Santa Clara County, California," *Journal of the American Dental Association,* Feb. 1976, p. 370.
3. G. A. Lincoln, "Bird Counts on Either Side of Wallace's Line," *Journal of Zoology* (London), Nov. 1975, p. 352.
4. Ford Facility Guide. Dearborn, MI: The Ford Motor Co.
5. Herb Adams, "Save Money with Used Auto Parts," *Motor Trend,* Nov. 1975, p. 74.
6. M. S. Zehni and D. G. Morgan, "A Comparative Study of the Effects of Photoperiod on Flower Bud Development and Stem Elongation in Three Varieties of *Phaseolus vulgaris, L.,*" *Annals of Botany,* Jan. 1976, p. 19.
7. Gladys A. Kelce School of Business and Economics. Pittsburg State University. Pittsburg, KS.
8. "Mallinckrodt Plans More Records in 1976," *Chemical & Engineering News,* Mar. 1, 1976, p. 9.
9. Kavanagh & Son's Cellulose Insulation Co. 114 W. 20th Street, Pittsburg, KS.
10. "Works and Figures: Older Americans," *Worklife,* Feb. 1976, p. 27.
11. Farmland Industries, Inc. P.O. Box 7305, Kansas City, MO.
12. Helen Guthrie and Susan Shank, "Nutritional Counseling for Prevention of Dental Caries in Adolescents," *Journal of the American Dental Association,* Feb. 1976, p. 382.
13. Jorge F. Dopazo, "State Estimator Screens Incoming Data," *Electrical World,* Feb. 15, 1976, p. 56.
14. Vithala R. Rao, "Taxonomy of Television Programs Based on Viewing Behavior," *Journal of Marketing Research,* Aug. 1975, p. 356.
15. McNally Pittsburg Manufacturing Corp. Pittsburg, KS.
16. Kansas Gas and Electric Co. 201 N. Market, Wichita, KS.
17. Department of Biology. Pittsburg State University. Pittsburg, KS.
18. "Idea Exchange," *Modern Plastics,* Jan. 1976, p. 28.
19. The Boeing Co. Wichita Division. Wichita, KS.
20. Instructional Media Center. Pittsburg State University. Pittsburg, KS.
21. Beech Aircraft Corp. Wichita, KS.

C H A P T E R 4

Short Reports

IN the first years of college or career, the student or employee is often required to write different kinds of short reports while under pressure on the job: feasibility reports, progress reports, lab reports, and biographical and organization sketches. Various methods of expository development—such as technical definitions, technical descriptions, sets of instructions, explanations of processes, and analyses—can be used for these reports. It is necessary to master each of the methods of exposition and types of reports separately because they often are written as complete, independent reports. At other times, these short reports become parts of longer, more formal papers.

DEFINITION

A report can generally be defined as technical data that have been collected, analyzed, and presented in an organized form to the person or organization requesting that information. Such a report acquaints those in authority with the normal operations of the business, with special problems, or with the progress made on new projects. Even when this information is presented orally, it must usually be converted to written form for permanent records. In large organizations the distance between executives and employees is often great; effectively written reports bridge the distance.

The short report usually has several distinguishing features. It does not exceed three or four pages and is presented in one of the three formats discussed in this chapter: memo, blank form, or article-report form. The letter format is discussed in detail in Chapters 9 and 10. The short report does not include any additional elements such as a title page, table of contents, summary, or bibliography. In the text of the report, all the headings are usually of only one rank.

DESIRABLE QUALITIES
Interest

The one who reads the short report is seldom as interested in it as the writer. The reader's attention must

be attracted at the beginning by stressing the practical benefits to be gained from reading it or by clearly stating its significance. In technology, business, education, and the professions, *time* and *money* are the magic words. Instead of telling the reader that the report will be "interesting and important," you should stress the time and/or money that will be saved by reading it. Since one-third of the readers are often lost by the time they reach the third page, the conclusions and recommendations may be placed at the beginning to stimulate reader interest. The following excerpt from a report from the president of Farmland Industries, Inc., illustrates the principle of stressing financial achievements to gain the reader's attention. Notice that the president first states the thesis, offers statistics to prove the thesis, and briefly mentions problems and interprets them.

Thesis   Farmland Industries' performance during the difficult 19— to 19— fiscal year is evidence of Farmland's strength and stability.

Supporting evidence   Volume rose by $66.9 million to a record total of more than three-quarters of a billion dollars. And savings, although down some $1.3 million from the previous year, topped $21 million.

Problems   The year's problems included abnormal weather that interrupted some planting and harvesting patterns. Naturally, those interruptions affected farm supply volume.

The problems that affected savings most, however, were decreasing meat processing margins and increasing crude oil costs and unstable petroleum product prices.

Interpretation   Although it reduced savings of Farmland Foods, the problem of lower meat processing margins was not without its bright side. The lower processing margins were caused by higher market prices for hogs and cattle. They boosted incomes to livestock producers, Farmland's owners. . . .

(Courtesy Farmland Industries, Inc.[1])

Self-Sufficiency

At the beginning of a report, you should clearly state the reason for writing it. Include all the background information necessary so the reader will not have to refer to previous reports, memos, or letters. Remember that your report may be passed around to others who do not have the background of the one to whom you are writing. Use enough specific technical information to add an authoritative note so the reader will feel you have not overlooked anything—but not so much that it detracts from the key points you wish to make. Notice in the following specimen memo that the purpose and background information are clearly stated in the first paragraph, past actions and work in progress and future accomplishments are discussed in turn, and the date of the next memo is given in the last paragraph.

To: Tom Armstrong
From: Cathie Daster
Subject: Transferral of insurance policies to the computer
Date: October 1, 19—

Purpose and background On September 1 you asked for a report of my progress in transferring the insurance policies to the computer in C Department by October 1. I began this job on August 28 and it should be finished by October 8.

Past actions The claims for the entire past year and the present year up to September have been transferred to the computer—with the exception of three claims. These claims could not be found on Alpha file: the names are Robert Brown, Dale McGrew, and Dallas Euring.

Work in progress The automobile policies are being transferred to the computer at the present time. There have been no conflicts with the policies thus far; however, I have two hundred more policies to transfer.

Future accomplishments The homeowner policies which were included in this job have not been delivered to my desk from the fifth floor. When I receive these policies, I will give them prompt attention.

Next reporting date I will send a final memo dated October 29 to inform you of the completion of this job and of the final results.

Omission of Unnecessary Detail

There is a significant difference between papers written in college classes and reports written on the job; failure to recognize this difference can lead to embarrassment. In the college paper, you must include much background information and details on the process of research and on the theory behind the process—just to let the instructor know that you are familiar with all these facts. The library is usually the main source of information. But after graduation, you must visualize the person who will see your report and ask yourself what facts will be needed. The employer assumes you have used the correct procedure and have mastered the theory and is interested only in the results of the investigation. Most of the facts come from the company files and from your own experiments and investigations.

Objectivity

As you write to further your career, you must report only the facts. Report them fairly, even to the point that you carefully examine arguments opposing your proposal; otherwise the readers may think you are unaware of opposition to your ideas. As you counter opposing

ideas, be as diplomatic as possible so others in the organization will not be unnecessarily offended.

Be careful not to be carried away by enthusiasm. A report will be more persuasive if the facts speak for themselves. Emotionally loaded words, such as *desperately* and *heartrending,* and negatively charged words, such as *claim* and *fail,* detract from the facts. Avoid the excessively enthusiastic *tremendously.*

Personal and Impersonal Tones

The tone of a report is usually the result of word choice. Often a personal tone can be the result of avoiding pompous words, excessive technical detail, Latin expressions, or even long sentences, but ordinarily it comes from using *I, you,* and the contractions of verbs. The sentences below illustrate the personal and impersonal tones.

Personal: I heard the slap of the loose belt fifty feet from the machine.

I conducted the experiment on October 18.

You should always check your equipment.

The operator shouldn't leave the machine unattended.

Impersonal: The slap of the loose belt was audible from a distance of fifty feet.

The experiment was conducted on October 18.

One should always check the equipment.

The operator should not leave the machine unattended.

A personal tone suggesting informality is often effective in letters, memos, and for most of the writing intended for subordinates. *I* creates a personal tone. *You* is definitely personal and gives the impression that the reader is being directly addressed and personally involved in what is being said. This textbook, striving for reader involvement, makes frequent use of *you;* the tone is often personal.

Much of the time, however, impersonality is preferable in technical writing because it stresses what is being done instead of who took the action. The language used in any formal style of writing is very impersonal. Contractions of verbs and first and second person pronouns such as *I, we,* and *you* are not used. Technical jargon should be used very sparingly. *The writer* is often substituted for *I,* and *one* can be substituted for *I* and *you.* There is some danger, though, that the formal, impersonal tone will be too stiff, aloof, and vague. *It is believed that* might better be *I believe.*

Informal and formal styles can both be used effectively. The personal tone involves the reader. Such informality is appropriate when there is a personal relationship with the reader, when that person is likely to be the only reader, when the subject is one of only temporary concern, or when you especially want to involve the reader in what is being said. On the other hand, the impersonal tone gives some dignity to the sentences. It is desirable when the report will probably be given to other readers as well as the one addressed or when the report will be a matter of permanent record.

FORM

The short report, regardless of whether it is a memo, a blank form, or an article-report, consists of general background information in the beginning section; specific details in the paper itself; and, usually, an overall evaluation, summary, or list of conclusions in the final section. The introductory and concluding sections ordinarily are stated in simplified terms, especially for the supervisor with a general knowledge of the subject or for the supervisor who may not choose to read the detailed information in the body of the report. The report should move from the general to the particular, from the overall picture to the statistical information needed by the technical specialist. A short report can vary both in length and cost: it can be a one-page, ditto master copy giving instructions to a crew of workers or a four-page, full-color brochure for stockholders.

Memo

The memo is an informal communication between employees and between departments within the same company; increasingly, it is also being used for communication outside the company. It is brief, seldom more than one page since it usually deals with a single problem, does not include tables or figures, and is usually directed to just one person or one group of persons. Even though the memo is brief, it is easier to read if the main ideas are paragraphed; often the first and last paragraphs are single sentences. Most companies print their own memo forms; but if no form is provided, use one such as shown in the following examples.

NOTICE

To: All employees
From: Jacqueline Harlinger, Assistant Controller
Subject: Telephone service
Date: September 16, 19—

Purpose   The following telephone reminders are being given to assure that we are receiving the best possible service at the best possible cost.

Explanation of the procedure   Directory assistance is now being charged to Clark Corporation for information requests for our area code cities. Any city with an area code of 316 will be billed at the rate of 10¢ per request. To keep our telephone service at reasonable cost, your cooperation is needed. A frequently called

number file maintained in each office and used when placing calls might be advantageous.

Costs   Although the charges for in-state calls and directory assistance are not charged directly to your department at this time, the charges per minute on completed in-state calls and directory assistance requests are paid from the general operating budget. If these services are abused, there is a possibility these charges will be distributed to the departments.

Limitations   Please limit your calls to five minutes. Do not hold the line while the other person leaves the line but arrange to call back later.

Collect calls accepted at any time must be reported to the central switchboard operator. Occasionally, circumstances may require you to charge a call made from your home to Clark Corporation. If this occurs, you should report it to the central operator on the next business day.

Future   For further information or for questions on billing, you may contact me in the Business Office, extension 592.

To: Coffeyville Council of the Camp Fire Girls Board
From: Lue Barndollar, President
Subject: Council House cleaning
Date: August 27, 19—

Problem   When the Council House at 602 Beech was vandalized on Friday night, August 20, everything was removed from cupboards, shelves, and drawers and thrown on the kitchen floor. The dining room walls and windows were also sprayed with paint.

Solution   To put the Council House in order, the board members will have a workday on Saturday, August 28, 19—, from 9:00 a.m. until 4:00 p.m. Please come in your work clothes, bringing sponges, a bucket, dustcloths, and a paintbrush. Brooms, dustpans, and ammonia for cleaning will be available at the Council House. Sherwin-Williams will furnish two gallons of antique white oil-based paint, and Coffeyville Mill Supply will donate two quarts of turpentine and four drop cloths. The Pepsi-Cola Company will supply drinks for the group, but each worker should bring her own sack lunch.

To: Ed Gorman   Date: September 8, 19—
From: Paul Stevens
Subject: The removal and replacement of the front motor seal on No. 9 combine

Background and purpose   On August 27, 19—, you assigned the motor work on No. 9 combine to me and asked that I report my progress by September 8.

Past work   Preparatory Work. Since late August I have been working on No. 9 combine on Saturdays and Sundays only. During these weekends I have removed the radiator assembly and the harmonic balancer.

Present work   Removal. At the present time I am ready to remove the front seal. This job should take about five minutes. I now have the parts to fix the motor: a front crankcase seal and a sleeve assembly for the harmonic balancer. I charged $15 worth of parts to you at Fort Scott Truck and Tractor.

Future work   Replacement. By September 12 I should have the front seal replaced and the combine back into operation in time for the fall harvest.

Blank Form

The blank form is used extensively by most companies and businesses because the information is organized in the same way, it demands the same information from each person, and it discourages wordiness. A report made by filling in a blank form is easy to read and easy to file. But one disadvantage of the blank form is that some workers feel frustrated because they want to include additional information not asked for in the various blanks. More and more companies are now adding a section labeled *Additional Information*. See the following examples of the blank form.

SUPPLEMENTARY EDUCATION REQUEST
(Please type)

NAME _____ TITLE_____
      (Last)   (First)   (Initial)
DEPARTMENT _____ DIVISION_____

COURSE INFORMATION

COURSE TITLE _____ COURSE SPONSOR_____
WHERE HELD_____ LENGTH OF COURSE_____
COSTS_____ PROJECT CHARGE_____
     Tuition   Travel   Accommodations

COURSE CONTENT AND DESCRIPTION   (Briefly state how this course will benefit you in relation to your job and the overall objectives of the company.)

APPROVALS

SECTION SUPERVISOR_____ DATE_____
DIVISION DIRECTOR_____ DATE_____
DEPARTMENT DIRECTOR_____ DATE_____
(When approved please send to the Personnel Division.)

EMPLOYEE GRIEVANCE

                                    Date_____
Name of Union_____
Employee _____
Nature of the grievance in detail (be specific) _____
_____
_____
_____
_____
_____

Section of the contract violated _____ Paragraph _____
Action requested _____
_____
_____
_____

Signature of the employee's committee chairperson _____
_____

Signature of the employee _____
Supervisor's answer_____
_____
_____

Supervisor's signature _____ Date_____
Disposition of the grievance _____
_____
_____

Manager's signature _____ Date_____

RECORD OF PHONE CORRESPONDENCE

Talked with: _____He/She called:__ Date:_____
                        I called:__ Time:_____
He/She represents: Self____ Company_____
His/Her location:_____
Subject or model:_____
Discussion or message:_____
_____
_____
_____
_____
_____
_____
_____
_____
_____
_____
_____
_____

CC: _____   _____
Project File No._____
Signed: _____

Article-Report

The article-report form is patterned after articles in newspapers and periodicals. It includes a title in the center of the top line and then the introduction, body, and conclusion. Tables and figures can be used to illustrate and reinforce specific details; headings can identify the various sections. This narrative form is usually longer than the memo and allows the writer considerably more freedom than the blank form.

THE AUTOMOTIVE GAS TURBINE

Thesis   Gas turbine power plants in automobiles will be advantageous to the American consumer. The maintenance schedule is more lenient on the turbine than on the piston engine automobile. The
Supporting evidence   overall fuel mileage will be superior on the gas turbine; the longevity of the turbine is also superior, comparatively. Cars powered by gas turbines will be decidedly different in styling, with shorter hoods and more glass area, due to compactness of the turbine, and also different in comfort since the smoothness of the turbine is not as annoying as the vibration of the reciprocating engine.
Disadvantage   The main disadvantage is the expense. The turbine car will be at least $600 higher than the piston engine automobile. When the tooling procedures become standardized, the cost will begin to stabilize and will drop about 10%.
Restatement of the thesis   All facts considered, the gas turbine engine will be more practical for the automobile than the present piston reciprocating engine.

METHODS OF EXPOSITORY DEVELOPMENT

There are five basic types of exposition for the short report: the technical definition, technical description, instruction, explanation of a process, and analysis.

Technical Definition

The purpose of a technical definition is to explain clearly the meaning of a term. Such a definition often is just one brief sentence that is part of a longer paper. It includes, in addition to the term itself, two parts: the genus and the differentia. The genus is the general group, class, or category to which the term belongs and should be limited as much as possible. The differentia include the characteristics that distinguish this item from all others in its general class.

Seldom do readers complain that a definition is too easy, so the simplest, clearest words should be used. Derivations of the word being defined should be avoided. The following definition is not very helpful: "Landing weight is the weight of the airplane when it lands." For greater clarity, the genus should be expressed as a noun right after the term to be defined: "A tachometer is an *instrument* (genus) which registers the rpm of the gas generator with 100% representing a gas generator speed of 37,500 rpm" (differentia).

The audience determines the language and information included in a technical definition. You should always ask yourself, Who is the reader? Why does he need this definition? What, if anything, does he already know about this term? Your audience may never have heard the term before and need only a general understanding of it, or your audience may already be familiar with the term but need more specialized in-

formation about it. When the audience requires more than a very brief definition, it must be expanded to include more information: "A clearway is an area beyond the airport runway (genus) not less than 300 feet on either side of the extended center line of the runway, at an elevation no higher than the elevation at the end of the runway, clear of all fixed obstacles, and under the control of the airport authorities" (differentia).

Four basic methods of expanding a definition—illustration, elimination, comparison-contrast, and a listing of the parts—can be used when a whole paragraph is needed to define a term satisfactorily. The expanded definition developed through illustration is most valuable when the readers understand and are familiar with the examples used.

In the following definition the term is defined in the first sentence, two illustrations are given, and an interpretation of the illustrations is included in the final sentence.

Definition   Antinepotism policies are those practices that prohibit the simultaneous employment of two
Illustrations   members of the same family. A wife cannot be hired in the public relations office because her husband is already working for the company as a supervisor in the assembly division. A college student is not eligible for employment in a corporation's summer employment program because her mother works there as a bookkeeper in the ac-
Interpretation   counting department. Such regulations are discriminatory if they limit the opportunities available to women more than to men.

In some cases, an audience can better understand an expanded definition when first told what something is not. You should be careful, however, to always clearly define the term or object before ending the definition. In the definition below, the writer first gives several definitions of what literature is not, then defines *literature,* and ends with a positive example.

Elimination   Literature is not the writing found in a compilation of facts. It is not a list of instructions on how to hold a baseball bat, how to catch a fly ball, or how to run for home base. It is not a
Definition   recipe in a cookbook. Literature should be conceived as a written expression on such a level that it becomes one of the fine arts, perhaps a
Example   story about a boy who struggles to overcome a physical handicap so that he can earn a place on the school team.

A definition can also be developed through comparison or contrast to assist the reader's understanding. In the excerpt below, the definition of *flood accounts* is given, one paragraph is devoted to the Mesopotamian account, and one paragraph to the Hebrew story.

Definition   The Mesopotamian and Hebrew flood accounts are stories that illustrate the truly unique features of the Hebrew God, Yahweh.

First point   In the Mesopotamian polytheism the gods dis-
of the pute among themselves the wisdom of the deluge,
comparison and the motive for it is not in every case apparent. They display their human foibles, cringing in fear before forces which they cannot control and crowding like flies about the sacrifice upon which their lives depend. There is no one omnipotent will directing events toward purposeful and moral ends. The immortality granted the flood hero is incidental, since, as Gilgamesh discovers, it is not made available for the common lot of mankind.

Second point   Yahweh, by contrast, is undivided in his
of the decision to use the flood as a punishment for
comparison wickedness and to provide a fresh beginning with a faithful remnant. It is human corruption and not divine caprice that brings on the flood in the Hebrew account. God's purpose, furthermore, is a universally significant one, a binding covenant with the newly purged race for all ages to come.

(Courtesy Macmillan Publishing Co. for
Introduction to the Bible [2])

Another method of expanding a definition involves a listing of the parts or components. The following paragraph of definition first tells what a high worker is not, then defines *high worker* and lists the various types.

Elimination   A high worker is not a worker that has been boozing it up or is on drugs, but is anyone who
Definition reaches an off the ground working position by means other than protected stairways and stand-
List of ard elevators. This includes construction work-
types ers, iron workers, tower and chimney mainte-
included nance workers, oil and chemical tower operators, ship fitters, bridge painters, building and window washers, and overhead traveling crane operators.

(Courtesy *Mid-America Commerce & Industry* [3])

The basic parts of a technical definition, in summary, are the term itself, the genus, and differentia. The definition may be a single short sentence or several paragraphs, depending on the purpose and audience. The differentia may be expanded through illustration, elimination, comparison-contrast, or a listing of the parts. Usually, more than one of these methods of expansion can be used in developing a single definition.

Following are seven tips for writing effective definitions.

1. Avoid using derivations of the word to be defined: "Myopic is of or having myopia."
2. Always state the genus in the form of a noun immediately after the term to be defined: "History is the *essence* of innumerable biographies," not "History is when" or "History is if" or "History is where."
3. Be sure the genus is as narrow as possible: "Matting is a woven fabric," not "Matting is a material."

4. Avoid language with which the readers are unfamiliar. If they have no familiarity with the term, the simplest language is desirable. If they are specialists in the field, then precise, technical language would be appropriate.
5. Explain the root or roots from which the term is derived. "Omnipotent" might be fixed in the reader's mind by explaining that *omni* means *all* and *potent* means *powerful.*
6. Mention the point of view when a definition is written from a special one: "The pinna, in anatomy, is the external ear, the auricle."
7. Use figures to increase the clarity of technical definitions when the standard report form is used. Avoid the use of headings in expanded definitions because of their relatively short length.

The specimen technical definition describes *torque* and explains it through brief examples. Then torque is contrasted with power and work. In the last paragraph there is a technical discussion of torque.

TORQUE

Definition   Torque is a turning or twisting effort. When
Examples you reel in a fish, you are applying torque to the reel crank. You apply torque to the steering wheel of an automobile to guide it around a curve. You apply torque to the top of a screw-top jar when you loosen the top. See the figure.

Torque or twisting effort.

Other   Torque should not be
definitions confused with power or with work. In an automobile, torque is the rotary or twisting force that the engine applies, through shafts and gears, to the car wheels. Power is something else—it is the rate at which the engine works. Work is the energy expended, or the product of force and distance. Both work and power imply motion. Torque does not; it is merely a turning effort and may or may not result in motion.

Explanation   Torque is measured in pound-feet (do not confuse this with foot-pounds of work). For instance, if you apply a 20-pound push to a windlass crank that is 1½ feet long (from center to handle), you would be applying a torque of 30 pound-feet. In the metric system, torque is measured in kilogram-meters. Thus, our example would be: If you apply a 9.972-kilogram push to a windlass crank that is 0.457 meter long (from center to handle), you would be applying a torque of 4.146 kilogram-meters.

(Courtesy McGraw-Hill Book Company
for *Automotive Engines* [4])

Technical Description

The purpose of a technical description is to present facts objectively so a specific decision can be reached. It is a word picture of an apparatus, mechanism, structure, layout, place, or condition. Technical description will be a part of just about every report you will be asked to write: manuals, instruction sheets, proposals, feasibility reports, and explanations of processes.

Keep in mind that the technical description is quite different from the literary one. In a literary description of a wrecked car, the writer will stir the emotions as the accident is described: the bone-wrenching jar at the moment of impact, the sound of shattering glass, the cloud of dust, the moment of stillness after impact, and the chill of fear as the twisted wreckage is seen. In a technical description you will not elicit an emotional response from the reader. You will report the damage to the engine and the frame, the glass areas that will need to be replaced, and the body work that will be required so an estimate of the cost of repairing the car can be made and a decision can be reached as to whether or not it should be repaired or replaced.

Technical description, usually, is part of a longer paper. It can, however, be a separate piece of writing, ranging from the relatively simple classified ad or catalog entry to the detailed description of a multimillion dollar piece of coal-washing equipment.

The audience determines the type of information included in a technical description. If the readers are familiar with the object, it is not necessary to define it before describing it. If they are totally unfamiliar with the object, it may be necessary to define it and even to describe its function in general terms. Words such as *large* and *small* can be misleading; what is large to a watchmaker would not be large to a foundry worker. Words denoting position can be helpful to readers: *above, below, beside, under, over,* and *behind.* If an unfamiliar part can be compared to something with which the audience is familiar, the description will be easier to understand: *an S-shaped rod, a bowl-shaped cavity,* or *nerve fibers in small treelike figures.*

The basic parts of the technical description move from the whole to the parts to the whole again. The introduction gives a general picture of the object to be described, the body includes a detailed analysis of each part of the object, and the conclusion presents an overall view so the reader will not be left with details of the last part described.

Several techniques may be used in the introduction to give an overall picture of the object. If the reader is totally unfamiliar with it, a definition will be helpful and also a general description of the object that would include overall dimensions, material, and color. A brief description of how the object is used or how it works can also be valuable. Regardless of whether you decide to use one of the above suggestions for developing the introduction of a technical description, or even all three of them, you will want to list the parts of the object that you intend to describe in detail in the body of the paper.

You will discuss each part in the same order in which you list it in the introduction.

The following two-paragraph introduction to a technical description of the heart includes a definition, general description of the heart, function of the heart, and a list of the three main layers of the heart that will be discussed in detail in the body of the article.

THE HEART

Definition
General
description   The heart is a thick, muscular, rhythmically contracting portion of the vascular system. It lies in the pericardial cavity within the mediastinum. It is about 12 cm long, 9 cm wide, and 6 cm in its anteroposterior diameter, and consists of four chambers: a right and left *atrium* and a right and

General
function   left *ventricle.* The superior and inferior venae cavae bring the venous blood from the body to the right atrium, from which it passes to the right ventricle. From here the blood is forced through the lungs, where it is aerated, and it is then brought to the left atrium. From there it passes to the left ventricle and is distributed throughout the body by the aorta and its branches. The orifices between the atria and the ventricles are closed by the *tricuspid valve* on the right and the *mitral valve* on the left side. The openings to the pulmonary artery and the aorta, from the right and left ventricles, respectively, are closed by the aortic and pulmonary *semilunar valves.*

Listing of
the three
layers and
definition
of each   The wall of the heart, in both the atria and the ventricles, consists of three main layers: an internal, the *endocardium;* an intermediate, the *myocardium;* and an external, the *epicardium.* The internal layer is directly exposed to the blood; the myocardium is the contractile layer; and the epicardium is the visceral layer of the *pericardium,* a serous membrane that forms the pericardial sac, the serous cavity in which the heart lies.

(Courtesy W. B. Saunders Company for *A Textbook of Histology* [5])

The discussion of the parts in a technical description is developed in greatest detail. As you describe each part, you can use a pattern similar to that used in the introduction: a definition of the part, a general description of that part, the function of that part, and perhaps its relationship to the other parts. One paragraph or several paragraphs can be devoted to the description of each part.

In actual practice, the technical description can be much briefer than the introductory paragraphs of the "Heart" section indicate. The introduction can be a single sentence. The parts are not listed in the one-sentence introduction because such a list would be repetitious with the parts listed in the body of the report. Sometimes a single sentence is adequate to describe each part—as in the example below. Each sentence can be paragraphed separately or all sentences can be incorporated in a single long paragraph.

SEALING WAX

Overall   Hallmark Sealing Wax continues to enjoy
evaluation tremendous retail success and consumer acceptance. Features in-
clude:

Superior color clar-
ity—Hallmark Seal-
ing Wax colors are
brighter and more
fade-resistant.

Interchangeable han-
dles and seals—These
are a better value for
the consumer and en-
courage multiple pur-
chases of seals.

Hallmark Sealing Wax.

Discussion   Large wax sticks—Hallmark sealing sticks are
of each part larger than major competitors. They give more
seals per wax stick.

Dramatic merchandiser—It attractively presents wax, seals, handles, and gift boxes. This
merchandiser measures 25 in. by 25 in. by 12 in.

Convenient reorder system—A complete re-
serve stock file and ticket organizer is shipped
with each selection and merchandiser.

General   Selection SWX66 @ $242.00 includes 24 each
description of the 16 colors of wax sticks; 72 walnut handles;
and cost a balanced selection of 104 general design seals; a
balanced selection of 176 initial seals (multiple
quantities of most popular letters); and 8 gift
ensembles. All items may also be ordered open
stock.

(Courtesy Hallmark Cards, Inc.[6])

To leave the reader with a picture of the object as a
whole and not with a lapful of parts, the conclusion may
stress the cost of the object, the time it will save the user,
or the overall dimensions and weight if this information
was not included in the introductory paragraph.

Use of spatial and visual devices for clarity can add
much to the technical description. Figures are especially
important and should be included in the body of the
paper, seldom at the beginning or end. It is your responsibility to decide which parts can be best explained to
your audience through use of figures, and then you
must decide what type of illustration will be most effective. You may wish to reinforce only certain parts with
figures, or you may choose to place an overall view of
the object with each part identified right after you list
the parts in the introduction—between the introduction
and the body of the paper.

Headings should be used in the body of the report to
identify each part—whether you devote a whole
paragraph to describing that part or only a single
sentence. Remember that business and technical reports
are rarely read from beginning to end. Label each part
of the object as you describe it so the reader interested in
only one part will not have to read the whole description.

The specimen technical description that follows illustrates the whole-parts-whole format and the use of

headings and figures. The writer first gives background
on the use of the building, a general description of it,
and a listing of the five main areas in the introduction.
Then the function of each area in the body of the report
is described, and the conclusion gives an explanation of
the communication system that links all five areas
together.

GIBBS-COOK BUILDS FOR EFFICIENCY

Background   When executives of Gibbs-Cook Equipment
Function of Company, the Des Moines-based Caterpillar dis-
the building tributor, decided to build a new facility, the primary concern was increasing customer service
capabilities without loss of efficiency or an un-
manageable increase in operating costs. Both executives and employees of the company agreed
that a new building should be designed around
job functions as opposed to the usual practice of
shaping operations around building layout.

General   The new facility consists of two buildings
description totaling 92,000 square feet located at 104th and
Hickman. The two buildings are further sepa-
Listing of rated into five separate areas: the main office, the
five areas warehouse, the loading and unloading ramps, the
washroom, and the repair areas.

General   The main office comprises 14,100 square feet,
description which allows ample room for expansion. This
and function area accommodates four employees working in
of the the credit department, five working in the ac-
five areas counting department, and an undesignated number working in the data processing section.

The warehouse area of 14,500 square feet
features high-density storage and planned traffic
patterns. Parts inventories normally consist of
some 22,000 items with a value of more than $1
million. Parts numbers are listed with microfilm
and viewers, and the requisition is passed on to
the computerized locator system. The size of the
parts bins in the warehouse was determined by
computer for maximum storage density. Locations of bins also were determined by parts turn-
over so that fastest moving items would be
located close to customer service desks.

The loading and unloading ramps are adjacent
to the main en-
trance on the south
side. Two ramps ac-
commodate both
pickup and flatbed
trucks (figure 1).
The receiving desk
and unloading
ramps for incoming
parts are located on

Fig. 1. Ramps accommodating
either lowboy trailers or flatbed
trucks.

the opposite side of the storage area. Three ramps
here have adjustable dock boards to enable lift-
truck handling of all shipments regardless of the
vehicle in which they were shipped. Heavy components are placed on 15-foot high racks on the
perimeter of the receiving area to hold lift-truck
traffic in the warehouse to a minimum.

The washroom can clean three large earth-
movers simultaneously with high pressure
washers and a steam cleaner. The floor slopes to

a four-stage settling basin. After sediment settles, the water runs into storm sewers. Sediment is periodically removed with a wheel type loader. All trade-in machines plus those received from customers for repair are routed first to the washroom for complete cleanup.

The repair areas consist of two 30-by-60-foot bays that accommodate up to four machines each. Floors are eight-inch reinforced concrete with ¾-inch driving track laying equipment into the repair bay without damage to the floors. When repair of a major component such as the engine or transmission is required, the machine is taken to the component repair shop. There the component is removed and the machine pulled or lifted from the building and into an outside storage area. This permits maximum utilization of shop space as well as a better quality repair. All rebuilt engines are tested four hours on a 1,500 hp dynamometer (figure 2) while transmissions are checked three hours on the transmission test bench.

Fig. 2. The 1,500 hp dynamometer for testing diesel engines.

General description of system that links all five areas A primary concern in the overall planning of this new facility was time lost in internal communication. An internal pneumatic tube system which permits routing of memos, work orders, parts requisitions, etc., to the proper station in the five separate areas without loss of production time was installed. In a service industry where high labor input traditionally pares profit margins, Gibbs-Cook has taken positive action to eliminate wasted work hours while improving quality standards of repair.

(Courtesy *Mid-America Commerce & Industry* [7])

Instructions

The purpose of a set of instructions is to tell the readers how to do something, perhaps how to operate a certain machine. Enough detail must be included so they will not only understand the process but also be able to perform it properly. This is the type of technical writing most often read by employees and most often written by supervisory and management personnel.

It is impossible to describe the many different types of instruction sheets written each year. Instructions are written to improve the efficiency of workers; they are put out for new automobiles and heavy equipment, for appliances, construction (do-it-yourself) kits, and all types of products requiring care. They vary from the businesslike instructions from manufacturers to dealers who sell and service their products, to the diplomatic, public-relations–minded instructions manufacturers write for the adult consumer, to information manuals in comic book form for school children. The length of these instructions can range from a 214-page maintenance manual for the Beechcraft Super King Aircraft to the very brief caption, "Mix well before using."

But regardless of type, tone, and length, instructions must be clearly written in simple language or there will be countless complaints from employees; there may be a loss of customer goodwill and perhaps a drop in sales. You must know your subject; you must organize your ideas and then double-check the organization of your thoughts before you begin to write.

The audience determines what information will be included in the instructions. Such information should be limited to those facts the audience needs, should be arranged so they can immediately grasp the facts, and should be communicated in words that can be easily understood.

Psychologists say that if workers understand why they are performing a process, they will follow the steps more intelligently. Such explanatory material should be placed near the beginning of the instructions.

The basic parts of a set of instructions are the definition of the process, the steps, and the advantages of following the steps. The introduction and conclusion stress the process as a whole and the body lists specific steps that must be taken to perform the process correctly.

The introduction, depending on the type of audience, could include a definition of the process if the reader might be unfamiliar with it, a list of tools necessary to perform the process, the special skills needed by the worker, conditions necessary for success, or an explanation of any preparations that should be made before the actual process is begun. For lengthy sets of instructions explaining a complex process, a separate paragraph giving the underlying theory behind the process—in a nontechnical way if possible—and a list of the steps to be performed are added after the introductory paragraph. For briefer instructions, this paragraph can be omitted.

In the body, the most important part of the instructions, the five or six steps necessary to perform the process should be listed. If the process is quite involved, it may be necessary to further subdivide each step as in the following set of instructions.

1. Hoist the aircraft.
    a. Obtain two broad band support straps of flexible material for encircling the nose and midsection of the fuselage.
    b. Locate one band at station 107.0 in the nose area and station 266.5 of the midsection area.
    c. Attach the bands to each end of a heavy timber 15 feet long. Attach the cable or chain from the hoisting crane to the beam at a position corresponding to station 180.0.
    d. Station a person at each wing tip to offset any unbalanced weight in the wings.
    e. Remove all loose equipment from the aircraft. Take up the slack in the hoist and begin the lift gently, watching carefully for any unbalance.
2. Check the landing gear.

Special instructions that apply in unusual circumstances can be given after the instructions for normal conditions are completed. These special instructions could be introduced with a sentence similar to the following: "It may be necessary when the humidity is above 80% to modify steps three and four."

Readers should always read completely through the instructions before they begin the process, but in actual practice they rarely do. Therefore, warnings at the end of the instructions are often worthless. A warning should be placed before the step involved. It may be placed in heavy print, in a different color of ink, or enclosed in a box. If the step is repeated, repeat the warning; do not depend on the reader's memory:

4. **CAUTION:** DO NOT IMMERSE THE TEMPERATURE CONTROL IN THE WATER. Wipe the Temperature Control and cord with a damp cloth or sponge and dry thoroughly.

The conclusion should be written in general terms that will help the reader see the process as a whole again. Perhaps time and money saved can be emphasized, or a carefree future can be envisioned because of the excellent service to be received from the product.

Spatial and visual devices are more important to instruction sheets than to other types of technical writing. These devices should especially be used in the body of the instructions. Steps should be indented and numbered. Headings should label each step. Underlining can highlight important words, definitions, and procedures. Variation in style of lettering and in colors of ink can add to clarity, especially when used to warn the reader of dangerous practices or unsafe procedures and to add explanatory notes.

Figures are a must for instructions. Small drawings and diagrams should be used when the space is limited, and drawings should be simplified to show only the essential details. If you try to show every part of a device, the illustration may become cluttered with nonessentials. Photographs, line drawings, and charts are helpful.

But remember that spatial and visual devices, as with all other aspects of technical writing, must not be overdone. The too-cluttered look that detracts from the steps themselves should be avoided.

The tone at the beginning and end of a set of instructions should be pleasant. Instructions to subordinates get better results if given courteously. A few companies still inject *sell* or public relations in the introduction and conclusion of instructions calculated to impress the buyer with the wisdom of his purchase:

Your new central vacuum cleaning system will make it so easy for you to keep your home clean. There's no heavy machine to drag around, no recirculation of fine dust, no messy bag to change. And because the power unit is located away from the living area, you'll clean without being disturbed by noise. Read this booklet over before you use your Hidden Vac and you'll find many suggestions to make cleaning easier still.

More companies, though, separate the instructions from the *sell* information by preparing a separate descriptive brochure to accompany the instruction sheet.

The tone in the steps themselves can be personal. Do not be afraid to give commands; include *you* in the commands or let it be understood as in the following sentences: "Prove analytically that the diagonals of a rhombus are perpendicular." "Draw a sketch of the graph of the equation on this page."

The style for instruction sheets is distinctive. Since clarity is all-important, use short, simple sentences, especially in the steps themselves. Avoid all words and phrases that are not immediately clear; be brief, concise, and to the point. Transitional expressions linking the steps can be merely *first, second, then, next,* and *last.* The continuity provided by longer, smoother transitions is generally not as important in instruction sheets as in other types of technical and business writing, although such expressions are sometimes valuable in the introductions and conclusions of instructions.

A consistent verbal point of view will add to clarity. Use the same tense of verbs throughout the paragraph or section if logically possible. Avoid aimlessly shifting from active to passive voice and changing the focus of the paragraph. Retaining the same voice often makes the writing stronger.

Also be consistent in the use of pronouns. Avoid shifting from one person to another, from *I* to *you* to *he* or *she* within a paragraph or section, and from singular pronouns to plural. Shifting from *they* to *she* or *he* to *they* again lessens the effectiveness of sentences and paragraphs.

When you use headings to label each step, you should use the same grammar form for each heading. These headings may be separate from the sentences explaining the steps and may take the form of nouns and modifiers or gerunds. Or you may wish to begin the first sentence that explains each step with a verb that stresses the action to be taken, and underline that verb as a heading. In the safety tips below, each sentence begins with a verb and direct object, which are underlined and used as headings.

4. <u>Keep children and pets</u> at least 15 feet away from the power mower when it is in operation.
5. <u>Disengage all blade and drive clutches</u> before starting the engine.
6. <u>Start the engine</u> carefully with your feet well away from the blades.

In the drive for clarity and simplicity, remember to use sentences. They are preferable to phrases for giving instructions because they are clearer, more complete. Always include the articles *a, an,* and *the.* You do not save enough space by leaving them out to justify the resulting confusion:

<u>Push down</u> until handle is securely in place. Insert bolt through small holes of handle pieces and secure with nut. Tighten nut with screwdriver.

These instructions are easier to read when *a, an,* and *the* are added:

<u>Push down</u> until the handle is securely in place. Insert the bolt through the small holes of the handle pieces and secure it with the nut. Tighten the nut with a screwdriver.

The specimen instructions below show the writer giving a general description of the cleaner and the necessary preparations in the introductory paragraph, explaining each of the three steps, and ending by pointing out the advantages of this method of cleaning carpets.

THE RACINE METHOD
FOR CLEANING CARPETS

Description of the cleaner itself   Racine Carpet Cleaner is vacuum-packed for better quality and may seem hard or solid when you first cut open the plastic bag. If so, loosen the top layer with a sharp object. The remainder will crumble easily. Reseal the bag and store the box on its side when not in use.

Preparation   Remove the carpet cleaning machine from the tray by stepping on the edge of the tray and, with a firm pull, lifting the machine out by the lower handle. Plug in the cord. Now you are ready to give your carpet a Racine beauty treatment. Follow these simple directions:

Directions for each step   1. SPRINKLE THE CLEANER ONTO THE CARPET.

Racine is ready to apply—nothing to mix. Use about two handfuls per square yard (3 ft by 3 ft). Cover one 9 ft by 12 ft area or less at one time. See Figure 1.

Use as much Cleaner as you need for a good job. There is no danger of soaking the carpet.

NOTE: Ventilating the room during cleaning helps to speed the evaporation of the cleaner.

Fig. 1. Sprinkling the cleaner by hand.

2. GLIDE THE MACHINE OVER THE CLEANER IMMEDIATELY.

Unlock the handle and turn on the machine. Glide it slowly back and forth over the Cleaner in one direction; then crosswise; then in the first direction. See Figure 2. Sprinkle fresh Cleaner on the traffic paths and brush some more.

The more you brush, the better the results. Keep the Cleaner under the brushes.

Fig. 2. Operating the carpet cleaning machine.

3. VACUUM.

Vacuum slowly one way, then crosswise. See Figure 3. The longer the Cleaner is left on the carpet, the easier it is to pick up. Beater-type vacuums work best.

NOTE: Always wrap the soil from the vacuum bags in paper for disposal.

Fig. 3. Vacuuming.

Advantages of using this method   Replace the furniture and use the room immediately. The Cleaner left in the carpet will help remove the new soil during later vacuumings.

(From *The Racine Method for Cleaning Carpets* [8]. Copyright 1975 by Racine Industrial Plant, Inc. Reprinted by permission.)

Explanation of a Process

The purpose of an explanation of a process is to help the reader understand the process in order to judge its results, its efficiency, and its practicality. This type of writing differs in one important way from instructions: the reader of an explanation of a process does not want to perform the process.

Most of the explanations of processes considered here will deal with processes performed by human action. A new method of collecting lunch money may be explained in a memo to parents by an elementary teacher so the parents can judge whether or not it will be more efficient than the present system; the sales manager may want to explain to the sales staff a new, less expensive way of processing contracts; or the lab technician may explain how certain tests are performed so the validity of the results may be judged. Since the reader of the explanation does not actually want to perform the process but just to understand it, there are no commands given.

The audience determines the details included in an explanation of a process. This audience may consist of supervisors or executives who wish to understand the process but not to do it; it may include fellow employees who want to understand a process used in other departments. The explanation is likely to appear in a report, article, or proposal.

The basic parts are similar to the parts of a set of instructions. There is a fairly standardized pattern to follow when writing an explanation of a process that leads to an easy-to-understand memo or report. This pattern includes an overall description of the process with a list of the main steps that make up the process, an explanation of each step in the order in which the steps have been listed, and a summary or evaluation of the process if one would contribute to the clarity of the report.

The introduction should be limited to information the reader will really need. If the process is an unfamiliar one, a definition would be in order. Maybe the reader will need to know what special tools or physical plant will be needed to perform the process, what special skills the worker will need, or what specific conditions will contribute to the desired results. Sometimes the reader needs to be told about what other preparations should be made before the process is performed.

The introduction should be followed by a general picture of the whole process, perhaps by explaining the theory on which it is based. Then the steps that make up the process should be listed, in chronological order if possible. Limit the steps to five or six; if the process is more complex, as in instructions, subdivide each of the five or six steps so the reader can still easily retain the overall picture. Discuss each step in order.

In the explanation of each step, follow basically the same pattern as that used in instructions: a definition of the step if necessary; useful information about tools, skills, conditions, or preparations required for this step; further subdivision if needed; and a detailed report of what is done when this step of the process is performed. Always stress the results of the step instead of the step itself. This emphasis can be illustrated by comparing the following two examples. In the first, the steps are emphasized; in the second, the results of the steps are emphasized.

First, apricot jam must be boiled and brushed over the cake. Then sufficient undercoat should be rolled out to cover the cake. This should be rolled on to an ordinary rolling pin, and then lifted up and spread out over the cake. Any folds should be carefully smoothed out by rubbing with fingers and palms in a circular fashion from the center of the cake. Next the surplus undercoat at the base of the cake is trimmed off, the result being that the cake is now ready for icing and decorating.

.   .   .   .   .   .

To prepare a cake for icing and decorating, first boil some apricot jam and brush it over the cake. Then sufficient undercoat must be rolled out to cover the entire cake. This should be rolled on to an ordinary rolling pin, then lifted up and spread out over the cake. Any folds should be carefully smoothed out. . . .

The second example is easier to understand because the result of the steps is stated first. The reader does not get lost in a maze of steps before being told what the steps are intended to accomplish.

Transitional expressions—such as *first, second, third, next, then, last,* etc.—are especially important when the steps do not follow a chronological order. When several workers perform steps at the same time, it is absolutely necessary to keep the reader aware of the process as a whole and of the stage reached in the process at any given moment.

Remember that you do not have to give equal time to the explanation of each step. One step may be a standardized procedure and familiar to your audience; the next may be an unusual procedure that will require a detailed explanation.

Whether or not to use a conclusion to end the expla-

nation of the process is your choice. If it is a part of a longer paper, no conclusion is necessary. Often the explanation that is written as a short, separate report ends with the discussion of the last step or action taken. But in the involved explanation of a rather complex process, a conclusion would be desirable and would probably restate the steps that make up the process or evaluate the effectiveness of the whole process.

Two other types of explanations of processes include the processes performed by machines and natural processes. The process performed by machinery begins with an introduction similar to that performed by human action. But in the steps themselves, the function of the machinery should be stressed. Confusion sometimes results when the explanation begins to sound like technical description. This happens when the steps emphasize the facts about the machine and deemphasize the actual operation of the machine. The explanation of a process performed by a machine should stress what the machine does as it operates; the description of the machine should be secondary. As in instructions, headings often include verbs that emphasize the steps to be taken in the process instead of the usual noun-modifier headings.

In the following explanation, the two-paragraph introduction gives background, explains the general function of the insulation unfolder, and lists the steps performed by the machine. Each step in the process is discussed, and *then* and *finally* are used as transitions to link the steps together.

SPECIAL RIGS PUSH

TRANS-ALASKA PIPELINE THROUGH WILDERNESS

Background Working under rigorous Arctic field conditions, unique machines designed expressly for the Trans-Alaska pipeline project are proving to be highly capable performers. With over half the 798-mile line completed, they've been well-tested in service, and most of the special equipment, costing millions of dollars, is working as planned.

Function One special machine performs almost ideally as it handles kerfed fibrous glass and steel insulation panels on over 400 miles of elevated pipe. The

Steps performed by the machine ACCO Model 2535 insulation unfolder (1) lifts the insulation panels, (2) unfolds them, and (3) guides the insulation manipulator.

Explanation of each step in the process The insulation unfolder lifts the panel on a hydraulic scissors-lift table. This table raises each 15-by-24-ft panel (folded 8 ft wide for shipping) to the top of the machine.

"Then" and "Finally" as transitions Then the machine unfolds the panel by hydraulically driven steel forks and channels that rotate vertically around the machine's long axis and grip halves of the 700-lb panel. This enables a half to be flipped slowly up and outward. See the figure.

The unfolder machine on a flatbed hitched to a crane spreading a 700-lb panel of insulation into the open position.

Finally the insulation unfolder guides by its vertical channels the insulation manipulator so that it can snug the kerfed insulation around the pipe.

(Courtesy McGraw-Hill for
Construction Methods & Equipment [9])

Use of active voice is appropriate in describing the action of a mechanism. *Voice* refers to the relationship between subject and verb. In active voice, the subject does something. In passive voice, the subject is acted upon by the verb.

ACTIVE: The oscilloscope draws a picture of the ignition-system voltages on the face of the tube.
PASSIVE: A picture of the ignition-system voltages is drawn on the face of the tube by the oscilloscope.
ACTIVE: The crankcase ventilating system removes the water vapor.
PASSIVE: The water vapor is removed by the crankcase ventilating system.

In an explanation of a natural process, the introduction could include one or more of the following: a definition, a general explanation of the exact nature of the process, a discussion of the theory behind the process, or a description of the conditions under which the process occurs. This introduction could best be followed by a paragraph giving an overall picture of the process and a list of the not more than five or six stages it includes. Then each stage should be explained chronologically. This explanation should include telling what happens in the stage and, if possible, why it happens. The same decisions about the conclusion must be made in this type of explanation as in an explanation of a process performed by a person. The following is an explanation of a natural process:

CELL DIVISION

Definition   The cell, in biology, is the morphological and physiological unit of the organism. It is essentially the same in plants and animals and is usually of microscopic size.

Overall picture of the process   Cell multiplication takes place from the division of a cell into two equal parts, all parts of the cell (cytoplasm, nucleus, and centrosome) being involved. The process of cell division varies in different cases; however, mitotic division seems the more usual type. Four series of phases may be recognized in the mitotic division of cells: (1) the prophase, or preparatory changes; (2) the metaphase, or acme of the division process; (3) the anaphase, or aggregation of nuclear material at the centers; and (4) the telophase, or that in which the cytoplasm divides and the two new nuclei are established. See the figure.

Listing of steps

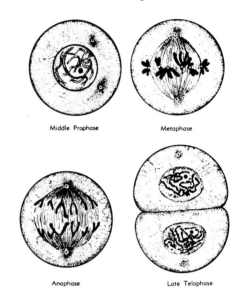

Middle Prophase   Metaphase

Anaphase   Late Telophase

Mitotic cell division.

Prophase

Explanation of what happens in each phase of the process   The centrosome becomes double, if not so already, and the two centers move apart. A set of radiations (the asters) now make their appearance, having the centrosomes at their centers. Between the centrosomes the asters pass over into each other, making a spindle-shaped figure composed of lines (the karyokinetic spindle). At the same time changes are occurring in the nucleus. The chromatin becomes condensed into a deeply staining thread, coiled within the nuclear membrane (skein or spireme stage). Eventually this thick thread breaks into a number of deeply staining rods (chromosomes). The number of chromosomes is constant in each species throughout the whole series of cell divisions in the individual and is always even. In the threadworm *(Ascaris)* there are 2 or 4 chromosomes; in certain liverworts, 8; in the frog, 24; in humans, 48.

Metaphase

The spindle has come to lie in the equator of the nucleus, and the nuclear membrane has disappeared. Each chromosome splits lengthwise in equivalent parts, one half of each going toward each pole. Consequently, each of the daughter nuclei receives exactly equivalent portions of the chromatic substance of the mother nucleus.

Anaphase

The separated parts of the chromosomes move to the two poles of the spindle, and these group themselves closely together. For a time the spindle fibers still persist as fine threads connecting the chromosomes, and in the middle of their course a plate of fine granules often appears lying across the fibers. The asters fade away, and the process of nuclear division is accomplished.

Telophase

In the last stage, the whole cell now divides, the division plane passing through the plate of granules, which plate helps form the new cell wall. The chromatophores expand, pressing against each other, and form spherical nuclei. Alongside each nucleus is found the centrosome of the new cell.

Spatial and visual devices are important to the explanation. Each step or stage should be numbered in the introduction (especially if there are three or more). In the body of the report each step should be labeled with a heading; remember that since the headings are of equal importance, they should be in the same grammar form. Indentations and underlining all help the reader to see how each step contributes to the final result—how each stage contributes to the overall major development. Figures and tables are also helpful in reinforcing and further illustrating the more complex steps.

The tone of an explanation of a process is one of calm, reasoned reporting of the facts. It is diplomatic. It does not give commands; it avoids *you*.

The style of an explanation of a process is smooth-flowing. The sentences are longer and more involved than those found in a set of instructions. Transitional words and expressions contribute to the flow.

In the following *explanation of a process,* the thesis is clearly stated and explained, karaya sheets are described, and the steps are listed. Each step is explained with suitable transitions. Finally, precautions are mentioned and the advantages stressed.

APPLICATION OF KARAYA SHEETS

Thesis   Application of karaya sheets is most beneficial to postoperative patients with large draining *General* wounds. Traditional dressings, saturated with *explanation* drainage fluids, often dry out on the edges and become stiff and scratchy, causing the patient added discomfort. And the odor may be embarrassing for the patient and nauseating for the visitor. Using karaya sheets as a "second skin" can speed wound healing and prevent skin excoriation.

General   Karaya sheets, *description* available from a number of surgical supply companies, range in size from 4 by 8 to 8 by 8 inches.

Listing Application consists *of steps* of four steps: (1) cutting an opening in the karaya sheet, (2) cleansing the skin around the wound,
Using two sheets of karaya. (3) applying the karaya sheet, and (4) positioning the dressings.

Explanation of each step in the process   First, an opening should be cut in the karaya sheet the same size as the wound opening. If the wound is large, two sheets should be used. See the figure.

Second, the skin around the wound should be gently but thoroughly cleansed with saline solution. The nurse must be sure to remove all secretions. Cleansing will stimulate circulation and help prevent tissue breakdown.

Third, the karaya sheet must be applied to the wound area, the opening in the sheet aligned with the wound opening. The sheet should be pressed into place, allowing the warmth of the body to soften the karaya and form a bond between the skin and karaya. All the surrounding skin exposed to drainage should be covered with the karaya sheet. The karaya thus acts as a second skin.

Fourth, the dressings should be placed over the wound and karaya sheet. Montgomery straps will hold the dressings in place and eliminate the need to apply new adhesive strips each time the dressing is changed, reducing skin irritation from the tape. A wide piece of stockinette placed around the patient's waist (similar to a binder) and fastened with pins or tape is also useful to hold dressings in place.

Precautions for the whole process   The karaya sheet and dressings should be checked every two to four hours to make sure that drainage isn't seeping under the sheet onto the patient's skin. They should be changed at least every 24 hours, since the karaya will become *Restatement* soft and melt, thus losing its effect. With this *of advantages* technique, the skin will be protected from injury, healing will be facilitated, and the patient will be more comfortable.

Analysis

An analysis is the systematic division of a subject so it can be better understood. It is necessary to analyze conditions, trends, causes, results, processes, ideas, and problems of every kind. Analysis, then, shows all the parts into which an apparently simple suggestion or situation can be broken down.

Perhaps a high school English teacher proposes to her principal that technical writing be taught to second-semester juniors who are not planning to attend college. To analyze this suggestion, the proposal could be divided into available teachers, suitable textbooks, existing classroom space, student demand, and the types of classes from which these students would be diverted.

In government, industry, business, and some institutions, a set pattern for analysis may already have been established and this pattern can be followed. But if no set pattern has been established, there are several ways to list and arrange significant facts.

The audience determines the facts to be included. Do not report all the facts you have at hand; use only those that your audience will need. Ask yourself why they need this analysis. Will they have to decide on whether or not they can afford to implement the proposal or on its practicality or appropriateness? Can the readers better understand the analysis if you consider the main points separately? The writer in the first specimen analysis at the end of this section ("Would You Enjoy One of Your Rehearsals?") believes his readers can better understand the subject if he divides it into parts. He breaks rehearsal language into four categories and examines each in detail. Or should the main points be interwoven as subheadings under general criteria? The writers of the second specimen analysis ("Are Community Nutrition Programs Meeting the Needs of the Elderly?") use the general criteria of the Kalamazoo programs, the survey, the results, and the conclusion. Under each of these divisions they use the subheadings of Meals-on-Wheels and the Golden Diners Club so their readers will not have to retain large blocks of information about Meals-on-Wheels as they read about the Golden Diners Club. As you decide what information to include in an analysis and how to arrange it, always keep the audience and the function of the analysis firmly in mind.

Types of analyses vary. Every kind of technical writing depends on analysis to some degree. The technical description divides an object into parts and then describes each part. It describes the arrangement of parts in a physical or conceptual subject: a cell, mathematical equation, political theory, animal, tool, or machine. This is a type of structural analysis that tells how something is put together. The explanation of a process divides the procedure into steps and describes each step to help the reader understand the process. The reader is not expected to perform the process. Each step is explained in detail and continuity is important. This is a type of descriptive analysis that tells how something is done. The set of instructions divides a task into steps and describes each so the reader can actually do it. The steps are listed in sequential order, each step is explained, and visuals are used to illustrate key steps in this instructional analysis that tells how to do something.

The analysis is usually a part of a longer technical report, but sometimes it can be presented separately. There are two basic kinds of analyses, depending on the type of units into which the subject is divided: (1) classification, which logically divides a plural subject into related groups, and (2) partition, which divides a singular subject into its parts.

CLASSIFICATION. Classification is a type of analysis that sorts items connected with the subject under discussion into related groups. Its subject is always a plural one. That subject is divided into clearly defined coordinate and equal groups that have one characteristic in common. Chairs, for example, can be divided into lounge, dining, and rocking, but the members of each group are still chairs. The one characteristic all groups have in common is that all are chairs.

Suppose you are going to interview for a part-time job. Before you report for an interview, you may wish to jot down your qualifications:

1. You kept books successfully for The Jones Company during the summer of 19—.
2. You have completed 20 hours of accounting courses.
3. You worked as a bookkeeper in the County Clerk's office during the summer of 19—.
4. You still have two more years of college and you need this job to help pay your expenses.
5. You have recently married.
6. The County Clerk of Allan County recommends your work highly.
7. You worked part time at a local theater during your senior year of high school and successfully kept the financial records.
8. You are working for a Bachelor of Science degree in accounting.
9. You can type 60 words a minute.
10. You are personally acquainted with the supervisor of Plant No. 1.

The process of organizing these random notes about yourself into groups or categories is analysis through classification. The above facts seem to fall into the following groups: experience, education, personal information, and references. If you had included a category called "high school bookkeeping classes," the categories would no longer be equal because high school classes would be a part of *education*. Experience, education, personal information, and references are mutually exclusive: each is a clearly defined group that would still exist without the other three groups. Education would still be a valid category even if the other three were unnecessary. Also these four groups do not overlap; any item of the list can be placed in only one category.

Any plural subject can be classified: the subject may be objects, concepts, or processes; it may be classified into a variety of categories or groups. Objects such as chairs can be classified by size, style, fabric, or color. Concepts can be classified according to significance or origin. Processes can be classified according to type.

But whatever the subject, the categories must be

1. Coordinate—The subject is divided into equal groups that are related by a common characteristic.
2. Mutually exclusive—Each category must be separate from the others, a clearly defined group even if the other groups were not considered. It cannot depend on any of the other categories.
3. Nonoverlapping—If any item on the list can be placed in more than one category, those categories should be limited or perhaps renamed.
4. Complete—The categories must identify all the groups into which the subject may be divided; nothing can be left out. For example, college students cannot be divided into only two categories: blondes and redheads. A number of students would have no category into which they could fit.

These categories, which must be parallel in content as well as in grammatical form, should be presented in the most effective order: most familiar to least familiar in classifying breeds of dogs, order of importance in classifying the effects of the metric system on a draftsperson or in classifying the qualifications of a potential employee, and simple to complex in classifying sleeve patterns. If it seems that the order of the categories is of no special importance, the best order for the reader's convenience can be used.

The usefulness of the classification system is dependent on its purpose; the categories considered and their form will be determined by the reader's needs. Depending on those needs, classification can be the method of organizing an entire paper, a section of a paper, a paragraph, or even a part of a paragraph.

The facts communicated by classification may be presented in outline form, in written reports, in visuals, or by a combination of these forms. The four categories in the following illustrative outline are coordinate, mutually exclusive, nonoverlapping, and complete and are arranged chronologically.

CHRONOLOGICAL CLASSIFICATION OF THE PRODUCT LIFE CYCLES

I. Product introduction
   A. Idea creation
      1. Existing need
      2. Brainstorming
   B. Development
      1. Prototype
      2. Test market
II. Product growth
   A. Information check
      1. Sales
      2. Consumer attitude
   B. Future growth
III. Product maturity
   A. Market
   B. Image
      1. Packaging
      2. Promotional theme
      3. Adaptations of the original product
IV. Product decline
   A. Indicators
      1. Competition
      2. Costs
   B. Phaseout

Although the outline can be used alone, it is more often accompanied by a written explanation similar to the one below.

The Cycles

All products and ideas that are produced go through various life cycles. The cycles may contain many possible stages, but basically they start with the product introduction, go through a growth period, reach some kind of peak, and—sooner or later—pass from the scene. Products may make an indefinite pattern with these stages and not all product cycles involve all the basic stages.

Implications

The design firm can look at products presently on the market to better understand the life of them. A product passing the maturity stage does not always have to go through the decline stage. A creative designer, understanding these stages, can revive an older product by new approaches in promotion or modification of the product itself. The more information a designer has when developing and promoting a product, the greater chance a product will live a longer life.

Written explanations can be accompanied by a graphic illustration as well as an outline. Figure 4.1 visually reinforces the outline and explanation by tracing the various cycles through which the product may go.

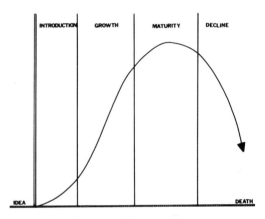

Fig. 4.1. Product life cycles.

PARTITION. The partition type of analysis is a specific analysis. Its subject is singular and that subject is divided into parts, steps, or aspects. This type is generally a part of a larger whole, a dependent part of a formal report or proposal. If the partition system is going to be useful, it—like the classification system—must have divisions that are parallel, mutually exclusive, nonoverlapping, and complete.

The parts in a partition analysis do not necessarily have anything in common except for being parts of the same item. A chair can be divided into the back, seat, legs, and arms, but any one part—such as the back—is not a chair. The base, dial, and receiver of a telephone have no particular relationship other than that they are all parts of a telephone. This division contrasts with the classification system in which all members of a category have the same characteristic in common. Partition parts can be arranged in any effective order: chronological in classifying the steps in a process or spatial in describing the parts of a device.

CAUSAL ANALYSIS. Closely related to the partition and classification analyses is the causal analysis, which investigates possible causes or effects and determines which cause or effect is most probable. The causal analysis frequently includes other forms of writing such as definition, description, explanation of a process, classification, and partition. Exactly which other forms of writing are to be included is determined by the writer's conception of the reader's needs. But most causal analyses include a statement of the existing problem, a detailed explanation of the possible causes, and then a decision as to the most probable cause.

In a problem-solving situation, the cause may be known and several effects observed. In this case, the parts of the analysis would be (1) statement of the problem or cause, (2) consideration of each observed effect, and (3) a decision as to the most important or key effect.

There are two major pitfalls in writing a causal analysis: (1) assuming that an earlier event necessarily causes a later one and (2) concluding that an effect can be created only by one cause when there may be several causes.

The specimen partition analysis below shows that each category is a part of the whole; no one category, by itself, is a rehearsal. The writer begins with a surprising observation to attract attention to his singular subject. He explains his observation and states his thesis. Then he analyzes in detail the four parts of a rehearsal, arranging them chronologically, and concludes with an evaluation of the whole rehearsal. He uses headings to guide the reader and a figure to reemphasize the complete cycle.

WOULD YOU ENJOY
ONE OF YOUR REHEARSALS?

Singular subject

Attention-getter

A close observation of music rehearsals reveals one overriding fact: Most conductors and directors talk too much! Some of this verbalization is extraneous and redundant. Some of it is nonproductive and ambiguous. However, verbalization by the conductor is important and at times vital to a successful rehearsal. The numerous and varied comments made by a director usually fall into four categories.

Explanation

Thesis

Four categories that are
1. coordinate
2. mutually exclusive
3. nonoverlapping
4. complete

The Appraisive Phase

In essence, appraisive language measures distance between an actual performance and perfection. A skilled conductor has acquired the ability to "hear" a perfect or near-perfect rendition of a work of music, and with this image or model in mind, he or she can determine how close a performing group comes to reaching a preconceived level of excellence.

It is often difficult to know when to praise and to what extent, but if in doubt, the director should err on the side of hyperbole rather than its opposite, litotes. Hyperbolic language tends to upgrade everything a notch, so a "good" performance is called "excellent," and an "excellent" performance becomes "fantastic." Litotesic language downgrades achievement slightly, so that an "excellent" performance is termed "not bad," and a "good" performance is evaluated as "nothing to be ashamed of."

Appraisive language, then, is positive, reasonable in its level of expectation, and honest, and it occasionally strays a little toward hyperbole. Appraisive discourse reveals both the quantity and the quality of achievement in music. It prepares the way for apprisive, or informative, language functions.

The Apprisive Phase

Verbalized instruction is necessary at every rehearsal, but verbalized thought is not always a precise way of communicating. Words can be given differing connotations, and these differences are the hazard of apprisive language.

Categories arranged in chronological order

Instructive discourse makes up a goodly portion of most music rehearsals. "Let's take it from measure 30, page 4"; "Ready on the count of three"; "Turn to the 'Hymn for All Ages' in your folder." It is easy to fall into verbal ruts. The use of the word "OK" is a common fault, as is repetition of the phrase "OK, ready now." A good way to become aware of the way you use apprisive language is to tape your rehearsals and then listen to these tapes in private. Try to place yourself in the role of a performer. Would you enjoy one of these rehearsals? Are the instructions clear, precise, direct? Are there ways to vary your instructions in order to avoid monotony?

Each category expressed in the same grammar form

The Prescriptive Phase

The third type of rehearsal language is prescriptive, which means that the conductor uses verbalized methodology to evoke specific psychomotor responses. These pedagogical devices, called "action patterns," are related to the performance elements of music. They are intended to improve intonation, blend, tempo, rhythm, articulation, diction, timbre, and so on.

For instance, the choral director might tell a certain tenor to press his tongue firmly against the ridge of his lower gum when he sings an "oo" vowel. The orchestral conductor might advise a violinist to use more "wrist" in a down-bow attack. Master teachers have acquired a whole repertory of "action patterns." However, these action patterns involve more than mere verbalization by the director. Straight verbalization is usually in the apprisive realm, whereas language that is truly prescriptive calls for a psychomotor response from the performer—a response that is very specific and that requires repetition for mastery.

The Consummative Phase

After the director has appraised weaknesses, informed the musicians of needed improvements, and outlined a course of remediation, a fourth function for language in a rehearsal still remains. There is a perfective stage toward which we all strive, the consummative urge to better all previous attempts. This arena is the domain of true leadership and, I might add, the test of true leadership.

In this phase, the conductor uses all the powers of inspiration at his or her command. This might involve merely admonishing the musicians, or it might call for insisting that certain standards and traditions be maintained. It involves reiteration, guidance, repetition, review, and finally, a transmutation that culminates in a vitalized expression of the composer's intentions. This in turn leads to individual and collective achievement.

Repetitive The Continuing Cycle
cycle   The cycle of rehearsal language functions goes on and on: appraise, apprise, prescribe, and consummate: evaluate, inform, remediate, and perfect (see the figure). In each phase of the cycle, there may be initial, medial, and terminal steps that move from passivity to activity, abstraction to concretion, obscurity to lucidity, and discovery to fulfillment.

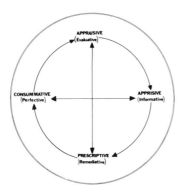

The cycle of rehearsal verbalization.

Evaluation   Verbalized language can impel or impede
of the whole progress with music. It can inspire or discourage,
rehearsal enlighten or confuse, humanize or degrade. If our use of language at each rehearsal causes us to surpass ourselves, we are on our way toward realizing both our own potential and the potential that lies within the performers and the music we serve.

(Courtesy *Music Educators Journal* [10])

The specimen classification-partition analysis illustrates the practice of combining these two types of analyses in the same report: classification to identify the categories and partition to divide each category into separate parts. The authors first give background information on their plural subject of Kalamazoo Programs, classifying their subject into two separate groups. They explain their survey and report the results, partitioning each group into two parts: satisfaction with food and the socialization need.

ARE COMMUNITY NUTRITION PROGRAMS
MEETING THE NEEDS OF THE ELDERLY?

Background   Nutritionists everywhere agree that proper diet is essential to good health. There is increasing evidence that good nutrition even changes the rate at which we age, while "over" or "under" nutrition can alter for the worse the age at which we die.

Plural The Kalamazoo Programs
subject   Community nutrition programs are provided for the elderly in the Kalamazoo, Mich., area

List of through the Meals-on-Wheels program for the
categories homebound and the Golden Diners Club for those who need low-cost, nutritionally adequate meals in a social setting.

Two cate-   Meals-on-Wheels serves approximately 100
gories that persons in and around Kalamazoo. Meals are de-
are livered 6 days a week, with an extra frozen meal
1. coordinate sent along for the seventh day. Program partici-
2. mutually pants may have a hot meal delivered for as many
exclusive days a week as they request and they may also
3. nonover- receive breakfast and a cold lunch. The packaged
lapping meals are delivered around midday by volunteer
4. complete drivers and helpers. Hot food is kept hot in insulated cabinets placed in the volunteers' cars.
   The Golden Diners Clubs were started in the Kalamazoo area in 1974 under the new Title VII of the Older Americans Act of 1965. This program offers group meals in a community setting as well as social and health-related services.
   More than 150 persons a day are fed at group meals provided at five sites in Kalamazoo that have a high density of older residents. On at least 5 days a week, a hot meal is served that provides one-third or more of the current daily recommended allowances as established by the Food and Nutrition Board of the National Research Council/National Academy of Sciences.

The Survey
   Just how satisfied are the participants with the meals provided by both programs? Because this question had not been answered on any large scale in the Kalamazoo area, we decided to survey the participants to measure their satisfaction.

Procedure   We adapted an attitude questionnaire that had been designed and used for evaluating the Pittsburgh area's Meals-on-Wheels program. We surveyed three groups: participants in the Meals-on-Wheels, the Golden Diners Clubs, and a small sampling of nursing home patients (to see how elderly people react to meals provided through institutionalized and public services).

Results of the Survey
   The participants surveyed were pleased with the meals and service in all three programs (see Table). The findings support the hypothesis that meals served in a socialized setting provide participants with more than the basic nutritional requirements and actually improve their interest in good food.

KALAMAZOO GERIATRIC NUTRITION SURVEY

Program	Participants			
	Number Surveyed	Age Range	Mean Age	Average Median Score*
Meals-on-Wheels	26	56–98†	75	2.40
Golden Diners Club	31	53–98	73	1.99
Nursing Home	11	34–90	73	3.58

*The possible median range is from 0.9 to 10.2, with a low score indicating a high degree of satisfaction with the program. The median score in the evaluation of the Pittsburgh area Meals-on-Wheels program was 2.19.

†One respondent did not indicate age.

Partition of In the nursing home group, 7 out of the 11
each category surveyed reported that they did not eat some of
1. satisfac- the food provided; 7 said that meals at home were
tion with better; and 4 said the nursing home's hot foods
food were not served hot. On the other hand, the
2. socializa- survey showed that the home delivery service for
tion need meals is working well. Recipients reported that
the hot foods were hot and the cold foods cold,
and that the quantity of food was adequate. The
Golden Diners Club participants in either program thought the meals prepared at home were
better.

All Meals-on-Wheels recipients in the sample
reported that the people delivering their food
were friendly; the same was reported of the meal
site managers for the Golden Diners Clubs. Of
the 26 persons responding to the Meals-on-
Wheels questionnaire, 21 indicated a desire for a
visitor from the program to come, but only 18 of
the 31 surveyed in the Golden Diners Club expressed the need for a visitor.

Conclusion

Summary Study results show that there is a definite need
for socialization by the elderly, and that the socialization factor affects their response to their
meals. As people become older, their satisfaction
with their food decreases. Meals-on-Wheels recipients—who are isolated in their homes—appear to have a greater need for visitors from the
program and socialization than the participants
in the Golden Diners Clubs, which appear to meet
socialization needs.

Evaluation Data obtained in this informal survey clearly
show that the elderly participants in the
Kalamazoo nutrition programs have a high
degree of satisfaction with the meals provided.
The programs are effectively meeting a community need and have brought a continuous stream of
positive, enthusiastic responses from their participants.

(Courtesy American Home Economics Association [11])

TYPES

Many different types of short reports can be written
either as complete, independent reports or as parts of
longer, more formal presentations. Four easily iden-
tifiable types are feasibility reports, progress reports,
laboratory reports, and biographical and organization
sketches.

Feasibility Reports

The purpose of the feasibility report is to present
evidence that a certain proposal or recommendation will
succeed. This type of report proves the potential success
of one proposal over others submitted. Feasibility
report writing is stimulated by a desire for change,
which may involve the creation of new products or the
modification of old ones or development of more
economical methods. Some of the proposals for change
will be valid and some will not. Supervisors and executives must judge them, and the feasibility report
helps them to decide for or against a proposal. If the

report is accurate, it helps management reach important
decisions quickly. Inaccurate feasibility reports may
cause wrong decisions leading to loss of profit, prestige,
and customer goodwill.

Some feasibility reports are the result of months of
work and are more than a hundred pages long. These
complex, detailed studies are formal presentations and
include title pages, tables of contents, lists of figures
and tables, and the appendixes—in addition to the
report proper. Often though, feasibility reports are
shorter, less formal, and are prepared in weeks or even
days.

Criteria, the standards by which the proposals and
recommendations are judged, are established in a
feasibility report after a careful consideration of the
needs of the readers. These standards often determine
the success or failure of the proposal and, if possible,
should be grouped under two headings: cost and
capability. Such limitation of the major criteria clarifies
the issues for the readers and helps the writer by limiting
the investigation and speeding the writing.

In the cost section, costs are usually divided into initial costs and into operational and maintenance costs. If
this section is lengthy, a summary might be helpful to
the audience; if this section is short, such a summary
would be repetitive.

The capability section is often a catchall section for
the other considerations. It includes items that would be
difficult to translate into accurate cost data; these are
items for which precise data are usually not available.

Problem: A small town needs more hospital beds
Alternatives: 1. Expand the present hospital
              2. Build a new hospital at site A
              3. Build a new hospital at site B
              · · · · · · · · · · ·

Criteria: 1. Cost
             A. Initial
             B. Operational and maintenance
          2. Capability
             A. Land available
             B. Adjacent thoroughfares
             · · · · · · · · · · ·

Presentation of the data under each criterion:
          1. Cost
             A. Initial
                (1) Expansion of the present hospital
                (2) Building at site A
                (3) Building at site B
             B. Operational and maintenance
                (1) Expansion of the present hospital
                (2) Building at site A
                (3) Building at site B
          2. Capability
             A. Land available
                (1) Expansion of the present hospital
                (2) Building at site A
                (3) Building at site B
             B. Adjacent thoroughfares
                (1) Expansion of the present hospital
                (2) Building at site A
                (3) Building at site B

When all the cost and capability criteria data for a proposed project can be expressed, the readers sometimes find the feasibility report easier to understand. These readers can evaluate the alternatives according to just one criterion, "years to recover," when all the data can be converted into cost figures. Their final decision will be based on the time necessary for the firm to recover the money invested in the equipment. The readers will consider the proposal feasible and recommend the suggested change when estimates of the potential market and of the firm's share in that market are included.

The basic parts of the short feasibility study include the summary, introduction, a discussion of each criterion, conclusions, and the recommendation.

The summary is an explanation of the main points of the study. It can be up to one-tenth the length of the entire report.

The introduction first includes a statement of the purpose and the definition of the problem. Then comes the scope, which explains the possible alternatives and lists the criteria that will be examined to determine the probable success of each alternative proposal.

The body of the feasibility report may include additional background and introductory information on the various alternatives. Each criterion must be defined; then the data for all the alternatives must be judged according to that particular criterion. This process should be repeated until each criterion has been dealt with.

Conclusions include the evaluations of the success of the various proposals. The recommendation points out the one proposal that seems assured of success.

Visual and spatial devices should be included in the feasibility report. Figures and tables are used primarily in the cost section because the data here can be presented better with these aids than the data in the capability section. However, the data in the capability section should also be presented visually when possible. Headings, indentations, and numbers are also helpful in calling attention to the basic parts of the feasibility report.

The specimen feasibility report below includes the purpose statement and a general explanation and evaluation of the two alternatives in the summary. The introduction gives the purpose of the report, the existing problem, and the scope of the report. The cost section analyzes Plan A and Plan B in detail, and the conclusion and the recommendation follow.

SUMMARY

Purpose   The purpose of this report is to examine the feasibility of two different methods of unloading materials in the receiving department of the warehouse of Miller Manufacturing Company.

Explanation of Plan A   Plan A is the present plan by which all the unloading is done by hand. Annual disbursements for this labor and for certain closely related expenses are $9,200.

Explanation of Plan B   Plan B, the alternative proposal, is to build an unloader and conveyor belt that will reduce labor

costs. The initial cost of the unloader and conveyor belt will be $15,000. It is estimated that this equipment will reduce annual disbursements for labor and "labor extras" to $3,300. Extra annual disbursements for income taxes over those required with Plan A are estimated to be $1,300. Annual payments for power, maintenance, and property taxes must also be considered. The equivalent uniform annual cost of capital recovery is $2,235.

Evaluation   The total annual cost for Plan A is $9,200, and the total annual cost for Plan B is $8,635. Therefore, Plan B is more economical.

INTRODUCTION

Purpose

The purpose of this report is to determine which of two plans for unloading materials in the receiving department of the warehouse of Miller Manufacturing Company is most economical.

Problem

Miller Manufacturing Company has been in operation at its present location since October 10, 1954. Since that date, materials have been unloaded in the receiving department of the warehouse by hand labor. The problem is whether or not to continue in the same way or to mechanize the operation.

Scope

The two plans will be evaluated according to one criterion: cost. In the present operation, the cost of labor and labor extras will be considered. In the proposed plan, the annual cost of capital recovery, labor and labor extras, power, maintenance, property taxes and insurance, and extra income taxes will be considered.

COST

Plan A

Annual disbursements for labor and labor extras such as social security taxes, industrial accident insurance, paid vacations, and various employees' fringe benefits amount to $9,200. Plan A refers to the present method of unloading materials by hand in the receiving department of the warehouse.

Plan B

This alternative proposal to build an unloader and conveyor belt will reduce the labor cost to $3,300. The initial cost of mechanization will be $15,000 but the equivalent annual cost of capital recovery will be only $2,235. Annual payments for power will be $400, for maintenance $1,100, and for property taxes and insurance $300. Extra annual disbursements for income taxes over those required for Plan A are estimated at $1,300.

It is expected that the need for this particular operation will continue for 10 years and that, because the equipment in Plan B is specially designed for the particular purpose, it will have no salvage value at the end of that time. It is assumed that the various annual disbursements will be uniform throughout the 10 years. The minimum attractive rate of return after income taxes is 8%.

Everything but the initial $15,000 is already assumed to be a uniform annual disbursement. The only compound interest calculation needed is a conversion of this $15,000 to its equivalent uniform annual cost of capital recovery. The equivalent uniform annual disbursements may then be tabulated for each plan and their totals may be compared.

EQUIVALENT UNIFORM ANNUAL DISBURSEMENTS

Plan A		*Plan B*	
Labor and labor extras	$9,200	CR = $15,000 (A/P, 8%, 10)	
		= $15,000 (0.14903) = $2,235	
		Labor and labor extras	3,300
		Power	400
		Maintenance	1,100
		Property taxes, insurance	300
		Extra income taxes	1,300
Comparative equivalent uniform annual disbursements	$9,200	Comparative equivalent uniform annual disbursements	$8,635

CONCLUSION

Plan B, costing $8,635 per year, will save $565 annually over Plan A.

RECOMMENDATION

Plan B should be adopted immediately and continued for the expected 10 years of operation.

Progress Reports

There are many forms for progress reports. Some companies supply printed forms so thay can get the same information from each employee. If blank forms are not furnished, brief routine progress reports can be put in memo form or letter form (if no figures or tables are included). Lengthy annual progress reports or final progress reports on complex projects use the more formal article-report form.

The purpose of a progress report is to describe the advancement made on a continuing project. It gives an account of the work completed up to the present time, of work now under way, and of work planned for the future. It tells about changes that are being made to reach a desired end—the completion of a particular job or project.

The progress report may be used for adjustment of schedules, work assignments, and budget allocations. State and federal projects as well as other types require regular monthly and quarterly progress reports.

The audience for progress reports often includes readers with much technical training who will need only the necessary details about complex technical aspects and not details about the familiar, commonplace operations. These readers will probably find the same type of organization in each progress report helpful. They may find the past-present-future format clearest for brief reports. If the report deals with a complicated project, they may prefer that the job be divided into the various aspects and past, present, and future applied to each aspect.

The basic format of a progress report includes background information in the introduction, the chronological report on the progress of the project, and the future of the project.

The introduction should be self-sufficient so previous reports will not have to be consulted. The job, the date of completion, your function, and the assignment that you have received should all be included. Any chronological background that seems necessary should also be given.

The body of the progress report should consist of several paragraphs that give a chronological report on the project or job: work already completed in earlier report periods as well as in the current one and work under way now. This account may also report past and present difficulties with workers and evaluate the methods used in both past and current situations.

The conclusion should use a tone of cautious optimism. It should include a summary of the work still to be done and of what can reasonably be expected in the way of problems. The agreed-on completion date should be repeated.

Terminology is a special problem. The term *status report* is used interchangeably with *progress report* in some companies. Progress reports submitted at regular intervals are often classified as periodic reports. In some companies a status report is defined as one that briefly summarizes the situation in a given department at a given time, with facts and figures placed first and followed by evaluative comments and recommendations. Sometimes a status report is organized topically: works in progress, materials, inventory on hand, condition of equipment, current production, personnel, and overall status.

The specimen progress report below gives background information in the introduction and then discusses past, present, and future activities.

DATE: February 3, 19—
To: Max Schonbrun, President
FROM: Ann Hart, Chairman, Affirmative Action Committee
SUBJECT: Affirmative Action Guidelines

Background During our telephone conversation on February 2, 19—, you requested a report on the progress made by the Affirmative Action Committee on the revision of our Guidelines. These Guidelines were rejected in November by the Department of Health, Education and Welfare (HEW) because of five specific deficiencies.

Past activities At our December 4 meeting, we strongly recommended that all position descriptions include the statement "Affirmative Action/Equal Opportunity Employer" (deficiency 1). On December 20, committees were appointed to revise the Guidelines statements on the nepotism and maternity leave policies, and on the plan for dissemination of facts (deficiencies 2 and 3). At the January 4 meeting, the committee worked on the revisions. On January 15, the revisions for nepotism and dissemination of information were accepted; the maternity leave policy was tabled.

Present At our meeting today, February 3, we are con-
activities tinuing to discuss the maternity leave policy and
are agreeing to table it again. We are seeking
additional information from the HEW office in
Washington, D.C., before we consider problem
areas by departments and the specific goals and
timetables (deficiencies 4 and 5). Our guest
speaker, the director of employee relations, is
presenting initial data for the revision of these
deficiencies.

Future At the February 19 meeting we hope to have
activities additional data available that will help us identify
problem areas. We assume that we will receive
the additional information from HEW on goals
and timetables by March 1. In March and April
we will rewrite the Guidelines, correcting the
deficiencies related to problem areas and goals
and timetables. In May we will add a grievance
statement and will, hopefully, resubmit the
Guidelines in June, well before the July 1 deadline. We will submit a final report to you on June
25.

The progress report can also be used to reschedule
projects after difficulties have been encountered. After
an introduction that reviews authorization for the
project and previous decisions reached, the report can
include headings such as "Accomplishments,"
"Difficulties," "Cost Schedule," and "Work
Schedule"—as in the following memo.

To: Tom Braford
From: Ralph Stephone
Subject: Bible Call project
Date: October 1, 19—

Operation of the Bible Call telephone tape library containing information on 215 Bible subjects was authorized on
August 1. A 9 a.m. to 10 p.m. daily work schedule that required 24 volunteers working 1- to 2-hour shifts was planned,
and full implementation of the project was scheduled for October 1.

Accomplishments. Three Tele-Dex tape machines and 250
tapes were purchased on September 1 from Tele-Dex Corporation and from Gospel Advocate Publishers. Two desks,
two chairs, and a filing case to store the tapes were installed.
Twelve hundred tracts on subjects related to the tapes were
ordered from the Corinth Publishing House.

Difficulties. The tracts, ordered on September 1, have not
yet arrived, and only 18 volunteers signed up for daily shifts.
When the tapes were delivered on September 28, it was
discovered that each needed an ending and call-back message

added. Holiday, night, and 10-minute-break tapes also needed to be cut. A malfunction in the #1 tape machine caused it to
be returned to the manufacturer.

Cost schedule. Major expenses have been the three Tele-
Dex machines at $600 each, the office remodeling at $300, and
the tapes at $175. Telephone installation was $150, and
monthly billing for phone services will be $115. The price of
the tracts will be $125 upon delivery. Advertising this project
during its first year of operation will cost approximately
$1,000. Thus the Bible Call operation can be funded at a cost
of $3,000 for the first year—only $200 above the original cost
estimates of August 1.

Work schedule. The 9 a.m. to 10 p.m. daily work roster will
have to be rescheduled for October 15. By that date, I plan to
have recruited 6 more volunteers. Corinth Publishing House
assures me that the tracts will arrive by October 10. I will submit a final report to you on October 15.

Laboratory Reports

The purpose of laboratory reports is to tell about
work done on specific experiments—to communicate information gained through laboratory tests. Sometimes
the reports may be very brief ones on the running of
tests. Other times the reports on laboratory work must
also include a discussion of the problems that dictated
the tests made as well as the recommendations.

A set procedure for reporting the results of laboratory
work, as well as other types of short reports, is usually
developed by the individual company. Such precedents
should be followed because the familiar format will
make the report easier to read. If there is no set form
used in the company, the work should be arranged
around the headings listed below.

The basic parts of a laboratory report usually include
(1) a general description of the procedure, (2) the
specific steps, and (3) the results. The introduction may
include the purpose, the theory, and the procedure or
only one or two of these items—depending on the type
of experiment. The body of the laboratory report is
made up of the results, the comments on the results, the
conclusions, the appendix, and the original data or on
any combination of these headings, again depending on
the type of data needed.

Obviously, not all these sections will always be included in every laboratory report. Sometimes the explanation of the theory is not required when the procedure is
standardized. The comment on the results may not be
needed, but if such comments are necessary, sometimes
they can be placed in the "Results" section rather than
in the separate section. Occasionally, the results are the
only conclusions reached, so no "Conclusions" section
is necessary. The appendix is used only if there are materials that are too technical or would take up too much
room to include in the body of the paper. Sometimes
"Original Data" is under "Results" instead of in a
separate section. The above order of headings can be
used or perhaps rearranged with "Conclusions," for instance, coming first.

The short laboratory report may just consist of the title, the procedure, the results, and the conclusions. Others are very detailed, lengthy analyses. In either case, though, accuracy usually depends on the procedure used during testing.

The specimen laboratory report below includes theory and comments as well as the standard procedure, results, and conclusions.

TITLE: Nitration of an Arylamine

THEORY: Aniline in the form of aniline nitrate is nitrated at low temperature with concentrated nitric and sulfuric acids to form *m*-nitroaniline and *p*-nitroaniline. To reduce the oxidation of aniline in the process and to avoid the meta-derivatives, convert the aromatic amine to its acetyl derivative before nitration.

PROCEDURE: *p*-nitroaniline

1. In a 125-ml flask dissolve 0.10 mole (13.5 g) of pure acetanilide in 15 ml of glacial acetic acid. Cool until crystals form; then add slowly 20 ml of cold sulfuric acid. Add a mixture of 0.12 mole (7 ml) of nitric acid and 10 ml of sulfuric acid to the solution and cool.

2. Let the mixture stand for 40 minutes to completion. Pour onto 200 ml of water and ice. Collect the product with suction and dry. Mix the cake with 150 ml of water and continue washing with water and suction.

3. In a 250-ml flask mix the *p*-nitroacetanilide (just prepared) with 30 ml of water and 35 ml of concentrated hydrochloric acid. Heat the mixture slowly with occasional stirring and boil gently for 30–40 minutes. Add 60 ml of cold water and cool to room temperature.

4. Pour the *p*-nitroaniline hydrochloride into a mixture of 40 ml of aq. ammonia, 150 ml of water, and 50–60 g of ice. Ascertain that the mixture is alkaline; then collect the yellow *p*-nitroaniline with suction and wash with water.

RESULTS: The yield of *p*-nitroaniline was 3.99 g of the orange-yellow solid. The melting point was found to be 62°–65°.

COMMENTS: Acetanilide is nitrated in the usual fashion to yield *p*-nitroacetanilide, which is then hydrolized to *p*-nitroaniline.

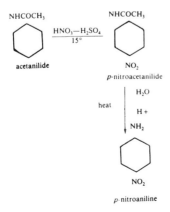

CONCLUSIONS: Nitration of acetanilide at high temperature would probably yield more *o*-nitroacetanilide than para. In electrophilic substitution, aromatic amines are too reactive and substitution occurs at any ortho or the para position. Also nitric acid oxidizes the highly reactive ring. The amine is converted to anilinim ion in acid solution. Substitution is then controlled by the $-NH_3+$ group, which directs to the meta positions.

Biographical and Organization Sketches

Biographies of well-known organizations and their employees are published in appropriate trade journals and in technical periodicals as well as in their own in-house newspapers and pamphlets. An important responsibility of any in-house newspaper is to acquaint employees with others in the organization or sometimes with the organization itself. Biographical sketches with accompanying photographs honor long-time workers, introduce new employees, announce promotions and the winners of cash awards, and present obituaries. When the biography is of a company or institution, it often includes a photograph of the exterior of the building and a drawing of the floor plan of the interior—or perhaps a flow chart showing the corporate structure. Facts can be gathered from company files, public records, and personal interviews. Such articles are brief, rarely over one page, and are often a regular feature.

The purpose of the biographical sketch is to trace the history of a person or of an institution, usually for publication in an in-house organ. Most large organizations have their own newspapers written for the information of the employees and published weekly or at least periodically. Boeing has ''Plane Talk''; Phillips Petroleum, ''Phil News''; Hallmark Cards, ''Marketing World''; the J. C. Penney Company, ''Penney News''; and Farmland Industries, ''Farmland News.''

The basic parts of a biographical sketch for an employee include (1) an explanation of current accomplishments and then (2) a flashback into history. The introduction of any biographical sketch should be an attention-getter that begins with a key fact about that person at a career focal point. Then the primary accomplishments during the public career should be described in several detailed paragraphs that deal with the subject's attainments after becoming prominent. Second comes the flashback into history. Included here are the person's place and date of birth, education, early years in business before becoming prominent, family and/or the development of leisure interests. This briefer section includes facts and figures about the subject's early life that are not directly connected with public life.

In the biographical sketch of an organization, the most outstanding fact about it comes first, then a discussion of its other noteworthy features. The article ends with a brief resumé of the institution's beginning and of its path to national prominence.

Spatial and visual devices used in biographies most often are photographs and sketches of the subject. Headings are sometimes used to label the parts of the sketch so the reader who does not have time to read the whole article may quickly identify the portion he wishes to read.

The specimen biographies below are of an institution and of an individual. The St. Luke's Hospital article begins with the current status of the hospital and its philosophy, followed by paragraphs describing its personnel, reputation, size, and teaching program. The last two paragraphs briefly sketch its history. The George C. Cheek biography begins with a key fact about his current work and then continues with paragraphs about his recent professional accomplishments, honors, and past accomplishments. The final paragraph details his education and community activities.

ABOUT ST. LUKE'S HOSPITAL

Current status— attention- getter

Philosophy

From its modest beginning more than ninety years ago, St. Luke's Hospital has firmly established its reputation as one of the leading community medical centers in the United States. Founded in 1885 as an expression of concern by the Diocese of West Missouri of the Protestant Episcopal Church, it is dedicated to the care of the sick and injured of all faiths and races, regardless of financial circumstances.

Personnel Quality of patient care has been the overriding concern of St. Luke's from its beginning. It is a specialty nonprofit hospital with a distinguished medical staff of more than 300 physicians. The physicians are supported in their care of patients by the most modern medical equipment available, and by a highly trained and competent staff of paramedical and administrative personnel. St. Luke's Hospital is an acute care facility devoted to healing patients with various medical problems.

Reputation It is a major referral center for a wide area of Western Missouri and Eastern Kansas, with over 36 percent of its patients coming to the hospital on referral by their physicians each year.

Size St. Luke's Hospital has grown in size as it has grown in quality and stature. Today it ranks in the top one percent in size among the more than 4,000 private hospitals in the nation. It has 665 beds. There are more than 27,000 admissions annually, and its operating budget of $34 million makes St. Luke's a major economic force in the community. St. Luke's also employs more than 2,200 personnel in various job classifications.

Teaching program St. Luke's is a medical research center of growing importance for Kansas City and has become known nationally as a teaching hospital. More than 450 students are in training here each year in various medical and paramedical programs. St. Luke's is affiliated with the University of Missouri—Kansas City and University of Kansas Schools of Medicine. St. Luke's also operates an accredited School of Nursing which began in 1887. It is currently one of two private hospital schools of nursing in the Kansas City area.

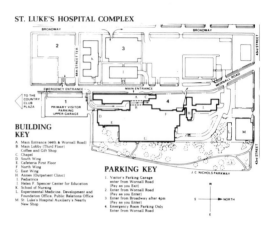

ST. LUKE'S HOSPITAL COMPLEX

History St. Luke's Hospital of Kansas City had its beginning in 1882 when 17 citizens signed Articles of Agreement under the name of "The Church Charity Association of Kansas City." The Bishop of the Diocese of Missouri opened the All Saints Hospital May 10, 1885, in downtown Kansas City, Missouri.

The Church opened St. Luke's Hospital in 1902 in a store building with a 12-bed capacity. By 1906, the hospital had outgrown this facility and moved to another downtown location. On May 16, 1919, the Circuit Court of Jackson County, Missouri, legally changed the name of the hospital to St. Luke's Hospital, a corporation of Kansas City, Missouri.

(Courtesy St. Luke's Hospital [12])

**For his contributions to the
advancement of the wood industry . . .**

WOOD SALUTES

George C. Cheek

*Attention-
getter* FIVE YEARS ago, when George Cheek took charge of the American Forest Institute, its income was only $795,000, it was in deficit financing, and it was not effectively serving its members. Today, after completely reorganizing the group and initiating a unified public education and information effort, Cheek is overseeing a program that will spend close to $3 million in 1975. The fund-raising mechanism he created has not only paid for the rejuvenated communications activities but has also brought in enough money to fund an enlarged program for the future.

*Recent
accomplish-
ments* In addition to becoming a spokesman for the forest products industry, Cheek has multiplied the effectiveness of his program by establishing a network of regional committees to spread the message of industry more effectively. One industry executive commented, "Under the leadership of George Cheek, the American Forest Institute has done more to tell the story of good foresty to the general public than any other single organization."

Honors Evidence of Cheek's success is seen in the awards and honors accumulated by A.F.I. under his leadership: First place, 1974 Forestry Film Festival, presented by the Society of American Foresters; Arbor Day Award, 1974, best of show in all major categories; 1973 International Film and TV Festival of New York; 1973 U.S. Industrial Film Festival, first place Gold Camera Award; and *Environmental Monthly*'s annual award for "making environmental excellence a basic condition in the pursuit of corporate goals."

Not all Cheek's accomplishments have been in the area of public relations. He also brought the Southern Forest Institute, with more than 100 members, into A.F.I. as a division and was instrumental in creating the Forest Industries Council, a group composed of the officers of the major forest products associations, which serves the industry in carrying out its policy directives. Cheek is permanent secretary of the council and is a member of its operations committee.

*Past accom-
plishments* Prior to joining A.F.I., Cheek was director of plans and programs for the National Forest Products Assn., where he carried out a successful educational program with Congress and served as liaison with member associations. Before that, he was with the American Plywood Assn. in a number of public and government relations capacities. He was specifically honored in a speech on the floor of the U.S. Senate for his role in A.P.A.'s flood disaster relief efforts in the Northwest in 1965.

As an authority on reforestation, the environment, and land use, Cheek has appeared before key business, professional, and academic audiences. He has been a guest lecturer at several colleges, and his articles have appeared in professional, technical, and business publications, including *The Wall Street Journal*.

History Cheek received his A.B. degree from Gonzaga University with majors in economics, English, and philosophy and a minor in mathematics. He was elected chairman of the first parish advisory board established in the Roman Catholic archdiocese of Seattle and was president of the Community Association of Vienna, Virginia, for two years. He has been active in the Society of American Foresters and United Good Neighbor, has served on the board of directors of a semi-professional football team, and has belonged to the Chamber of Commerce, Elks Lodge, and the University Club in the District of Columbia, as well as being active in college alumni and fund-raising programs.

(Courtesy *Wood and Wood Products* [13])

SUMMARY

Definition

The short report, regardless of the method of exposition used and of the specific type, can be defined as a communication written in response to a request for specific technical information. It is the writer's responsibility to collect the facts, analyze them, and present them in an organized, impersonal way that will be most helpful to the audience. The short report must catch the attention of the reader and give all the needed information as objectively as possible. It may be presented in the memo form, on a blank form, or in the article-report form.

Methods of Exposition

Several different methods of expository development can be used in short reports. Technical definitions and descriptions are often more briefly developed than are instructions, explanations of processes, and analyses.

Common Types

The short reports described in this chapter serve different purposes. Feasibility, progress, and laboratory reports are usually written as separate, independent reports. Feasibility studies can be very lengthy and represent months of investigation. Biographical and organization sketches are rarely published separately; they appear as features in plant newspapers or in periodicals.

Unclassified Types

The types of short reports presented in this chapter are not all-inclusive. Many varieties of reports do not fit neatly into the standard categories. If you are asked to write a report that is not one of the specific types described here, do not be overly concerned. Simply follow the steps listed below and you will be able to present the necessary information effectively.

1. *Consider* the purpose of your report. This will help you to decide what information should be included and what should be omitted.
2. *Think* about your audience. Organize the details logically so the readers can find the answers they are seeking.
3. *Decide* what kind of style will be most appropriate to your report. Be consistent in using that style throughout.
4. *Use* mechanical devices. Headings that label the parts of a paper, figures and tables that simplify complex ideas, and numbered lists that clarify steps are all helpful to the reader.
5. *Identify* yourself as the writer. You can put your name below the title as in an article, or you can identify yourself in the first paragraph. You can sign your name to the report. If you are writing on behalf of a committee, identify it at the beginning of the report; list the names of the members alphabetically at the end, putting the name of the chairperson last, with that title following the name.

As a beginning writer, you will want to follow carefully the patterns of exposition and the types included in this chapter. However, as you become more skillful and experienced, you will realize that the boundary lines between types of short reports are sometimes not very distinct. It is often impossible to follow rigid specifications. In such cases, an analysis of the reader's needs; a clear, logical organization; and a concise style will help you to write an effective report that does not fit any of the specific types discussed in this chapter.

WRITING ASSIGNMENTS

The following writing assignments cover all the different methods of exposition and types of writing discussed in this chapter. Some of the subjects are highly technical and others can be handled without specialized information. There is a wide range of writing topics calculated to appeal to students in arts and sciences, technology, and education as well as to full-time employees on the job. Most assignments can be handled in one class period to simulate writing under pressure on the job—those developed through technical definition, technical description, instructions, explanations of processes, and analysis. Some assignments, however, for feasibility reports and laboratory reports might be better handled both in class and outside class. For biographical sketches, one period might be spent in interviewing the subject and a second period in actually writing the short biography.

A. Technical Definition

Write an expanded definition of one of the words listed below or of any other comparable term with which you are familiar.
1. histology
2. oscilloscope
3. yeast
4. sunspot
5. electricity
6. transfusion
7. computerized printing
8. raisin
9. new math
10. laser
11. shock absorber
12. geriatrics
13. détente

Write four expanded definitions of a matchbook or of a ball-point pen, each one suitable for a different audience: (1) business executives, (2) third graders, (3) foreign visitors, and (4) students in your class.

B. Technical Description

Write a technical description of one of the following objects or of any other relatively simple object with which you are familiar. Use headings and include at least one figure.
1. stapler
2. matchbook
3. spiral notebook
4. desk calendar
5. pencil
6. ball-point pen
7. thermometer
8. a small electrical appliance
9. microscope
10. flashlight
11. lamp
12. wrench
13. screwdriver
14. a piece of furniture

(Several of these objects should be kept in the room

so writers can look at them as they plan their descriptions.)

C. Instructions and Explanations of Processes

The topics listed below may be developed by either of these methods of exposition.

If you write a set of instructions, use at least one figure and mechanical devices such as headings, numbers, and indentations to help the readers understand what they are expected to do. Keep in mind what your readers already know about the job and how much detail they will need.

If you write an explanation of a process, remember that you want your readers to understand the process in order to judge its efficiency—not to do it. Use at least one figure, headings, and any indentation and numbering that seem necessary.

1. Operating some machine used in your major area or on the job
2. Checking some type of equipment to determine the cause of failure
3. Pre-enrolling
4. Studying for a test
5. Doing some cleaning job around the house
6. Buying some article of clothing
7. Performing some job connected with your major area
8. Taking a picture with a certain type of camera
9. Making an outline
10. Purchasing a used car
11. Planting a tree or shrub
12. Assembling some item of merchandise for Christmas display or for a Christmas gift
13. Giving a shot
14. Cleaning a carpet, tile floor, or discolored concrete
15. Constructing a float for Homecoming
16. Washing a car
17. Painting the exterior of a house
18. Writing a report for Technical Writing
19. Running for an elective office
20. Building a piece of furniture
21. Pouring concrete
22. Checking out a library book
23. Changing a tire on a car
24. Mowing a yard
25. Making some article of clothing
26. Doing the laundry
27. Operating a small hand tool
28. Operating a record player

D. Analysis

Write an analysis of one of the subjects listed below or of a comparable subject about which you can obtain information.

1. Analyze a periodical in your major area or job area concerning the subjects it deals with, the length of articles, the number of articles, the space devoted to advertising, etc.

2. Analyze the cost of using prepared frozen foods in relation to the various benefits.
3. Analyze the nature and advantages of no-fault divorce.
4. Analyze the attitude of college students toward campus politics.
5. Analyze the advantages of minor surgery on an out-patient basis.
6. Analyze the expense of emission control systems in this year's automobiles.

E. Feasibility Reports

As you write one of the feasibility studies called for below, remember to use tables, figures, and headings.

1. You are employed by a small struggling company to operate a certain machine with which you are familiar. The needed repairs for this machine will cost a third of its list price. You have been asked to determine whether or not these repairs should be made or a new machine purchased.
2. The fraternity or sorority house that you live in is now too small for the organization. It has been suggested that an addition be built; that a larger, older house be purchased; and that a larger house be built. As president, you must decide which solution is most economical.
3. You want to build a skating rink in your hometown. There are two alternatives: build it on an expensive lot downtown or on a less expensive lot at the edge of town. You must decide which location will give you the most successful skating rink.

F. Progress Reports

Write a progress report, using the memo form. Remember that you do not use figures or tables in a memo, but you may use headings if you wish.

1. Analyze the progress you have made toward your degree.
2. Report the condition of the car you are driving.
3. Tell your landlord of the progress you have made on a certain improvement project in your room, apartment, or house.
4. Assume you are president of a campus organization. Write a memo to the faculty sponsor analyzing the progress the organization has made on Homecoming preparations.
5. Assume you are president of a campus organization. Write a memo to the faculty sponsor analyzing the progress made on the semester goals of the organization.
6. Report to your Technical Writing instructor the progress you have made in Technical Writing.
7. Report to a friend the progress you have made on some project at home.

8. Report to a classroom instructor the progress you have made on the semester project or paper that has been assigned.

9. Write a progress report on an experiment you are doing in a lab.

G. Laboratory Reports

If your course of study has included a laboratory course to supply you with subject matter, write a laboratory report on some test or experiment you have performed. Include tables, figures, graphs, etc., if necessary. You may report on a test you have made on an engine, on a household appliance, on a chemical substance, etc.

H. Biographical Sketches

Interview someone and then write his or her biography, or research an early-day civic leader in your community at the library and then write his or her biography.

REFERENCES

1. *Co-op Annual Report 1972.* Kansas City, MO: Farmland Industries, Inc., 1972.

2. Donald J. Selby and James King West. *Introduction to the Bible.* New York: Macmillan Publishing Co., 1971.

3. Bob Horwitz, "Safety Belt and Fall Protection," *Mid-America Commerce & Industry,* Sept. 1975, p. 7.

4. William M. Crouse and Donald L. Anglin. *Automotive Engines,* 5th ed. New York: McGraw-Hill Book Co., 1976.

5. William Bloom and Don W. Fawcett. *A Textbook of Histology,* 10th ed. New York: W. B. Saunders Co., 1975.

6. *Writing Papers.* Kansas City, MO: Hallmark Cards, Inc., 1975.

7. Carl Smiley, "Gibbs-Cook, Des Moines: Builds for Efficiency," *Mid-America Commerce & Industry,* Oct. 1975, pp. 12, 14, 15, 30, 31.

8. *The Racine Method for Cleaning Carpets.* Racine, WI: Racine Industrial Plant, Inc., 1975.

9. "Special Rigs Push Trans-Alaska Pipeline through Wilderness," *Construction Methods & Equipment,* Dec. 1975, pp. 36–37. McGraw-Hill, Inc. All rights reserved.

10. Val Hicks, "Would You Enjoy One of Your Rehearsals?" *Music Educators Journal,* Dec. 1975, pp. 49–52.

11. Daryl Rankine and Betty Taylor, "Are Community Nutrition Programs Meeting the Needs of the Elderly?" *Journal of Home Economics,* Nov. 1975, pp. 37–40.

12. *About St. Luke's Hospital.* Kansas City, MO: St. Luke's Hospital, 1976.

13. "Wood Salutes," *Wood and Wood Products,* Sept. 1975, p. 92.

C H A P T E R   5

Formal Reports

THE formal report usually includes (1) a title page, (2) a letter of transmittal, (3) a table of contents, (4) a list of tables and figures, (5) an abstract or a summary, (6) an introduction, (7) conclusions and recommendations, (8) an appendix, and (9) a bibliography as well as the paper itself.

Actually, the formal report is a type of book. The book, too, has a title page, a preface similar to the letter of transmittal, a table of contents and list of tables or illustrations, chapter headings, and a clear footnote and bibliography system. The formal report is distinguished from other reports by the impersonal tone; internal, topical headings of more than one rank; and the clear system of documentation. These features are necessary because it is usually prepared for several people. It becomes a part of the company's permanent files since the subject is of more than temporary interest.

At each step in the preparation of a formal report, the audience must be considered. Are the separate lists of tables and figures, the appendix, and the bibliography absolutely necessary for the readers to understand the report? Can several of the methods of exposition described in Chapter 4 be used effectively in the development of the formal report? Can one or more types of the short reports discussed in Chapter 4 be used in the formal report to communicate technical data clearly and accurately to the readers? Include only those parts of a formal report the audience will need; develop the main ideas by carefully chosen methods of exposition.

There are two basic types of formal reports: the analytical and the informative. The purpose of the analytical report is to obtain and interpret facts: these reports are written as a basis for decision and action. They solve problems and investigate the unknown quantities. The purpose of the informative report is to gather known facts; little interpretation of facts and no recommendations are called for. This report is simply a survey of facts, of progress, and of location. Both types are welcomed for publication in technical journals and periodicals.

PROCESS OF WRITING THE FORMAL REPORT

Writing an effective formal report is not a matter of luck. There is a set procedure that, if followed, will allow you to make efficient use of your time. This recommended procedure will not only help you to avoid false starts but will also help you to envision the finished report early in the writing process. This process, however, should not be followed rigidly; it is offered as a systematic approach to the formal report that may be modified to suit your special circumstances.

Selection of the Topic

The employee of a firm does not ordinarily *choose* a topic. A superior assigns it; a problem already exists and it must be analyzed and solved. Students who must find their own topics can survey the questions currently under discussion in their major fields by examining appropriate periodicals: How effective are nine-week mini-courses in high schools? What is the future of computerized printing? Which automotive emission system is superior? Or perhaps the campus itself will suggest some subject related to the students' major areas: How can the campus parking problem be solved? How can the outdoor lighting of the campus be improved? How can the campus grounds be beautified inexpensively?

Some formal reports are informative rather than analytical. Perhaps students wish to communicate the facts they have learned from special studies instead of solving specific problems. Screen printing, the Wankel engine, and the fermentation process of cheese would be suitable subjects for informative formal reports.

Regardless of which type of formal report is to be written, often the first choice of topic is too broad. "New Heating Methods" may be narrowed to "Limitations of Solar Heating." "Ignition Systems" can be limited to "Electronic Ignition Systems for Motorcycles." Both informative and analytical formal reports are suitable for publication in technical periodicals, especially if the topics are limited so they can be thoroughly explored in a few pages.

Tentative Outline

Before you begin reading, you should list all the points you hope to include in the formal report you will write. You will not have made any investigations on your own yet, and you will not have examined the company records and correspondence; or, in the case of a student, you will not yet have gone to the library, conducted experiments, or taken surveys to gain information about your chosen subject. This brief outline will direct your reading, and you will not scan materials aimlessly. See the tentative outlines below:

Direct filing	Laser beams
Alphabetical organization	Kinds
Subject organization	Ranges
Geographical organization	Receivers
Indirect filing	Communication
Terminal digits	applications
Dewey decimal	Long range
Chronological files	Short range
	Rotation
	Radar

Retrieval of Information

All kinds of information are stored in libraries and learning materials centers: books, newspapers, periodicals, records, tapes, films, microfilms, and microfiche. If these centers do not have the material you need, it can be retrieved from other centers through interlibrary loans and computer hookups.

Of the books, indexes will probably be the most valuable type you can use to begin your search for information. Every specialized field has its own index, which is a record of information connected with that specific field: industrial arts, printing, nursing, art, music, and engineering—to name a few. Abstracts list summaries of articles written by experts in your field—*Biological Abstracts* and *Mathematical Reviews,* for example. Bibliographies are lists of works about specific subjects; there are also bibliographies of bibliographies. Directories list names of people and organizations in your specialized area.

Newspapers record current events, reviews, and editorials. The *New York Times* is usually in every library, a complete record of daily events. The index can help you locate stories in other newspapers across the country.

Periodicals include journals of special groups, technological and business magazines, and various house organs published for internal distribution among employees or for external distribution. The key to many general periodicals is the *Readers' Guide to Periodical Literature.* If you want to find out what newspapers and periodicals are available in other centers, go to the *Ayer Directory of Publications,* to *Ulrich's Periodicals Directory,* or to *Writer's Market.*

Microfilm and microfiche save space in the storage center and can be read by using special reading machines. Microfilm is 35-mm film in rolls; each frame produces in miniature a page or several pages. Microfiche reduces several pages to one card.

If you have selected a subject but have no idea where to look for information, you should start with an encyclopedia to get a general overview: *Encyclopedia Americana, Encyclopaedia Britannica,* or *McGraw-Hill Encyclopedia of Science and Technology.*

Information can also be retrieved from the general public through samples, questionnaires, and polls and from individuals through interviews.

Tentative Bibliography

Sources of information available should be listed: printed materials, interviews, and investigations. An initial survey of the information available will facilitate selection of a suitable subject. If there is a great amount of material on the proposed subject, further limitation is desirable. If, on the other hand, there is little available material on the suggested topic, the topic either should be expanded or discarded and another one found.

General Reading

Reading in the general area outlined and surveying the available materials will suggest various limitations of the topic. If certain companies and institutions must be contacted for further information early in this procedure, there will be time to receive the necessary facts and incorporate them into the report. Interviews to obtain other needed information should be set up.

Note Taking

After some general reading in the field has been done and the material available for the proposed paper evaluated, note taking begins. The Xerox machine has changed note taking in recent years. Often the whole article or selected pages from a book can be Xeroxed, key information underlined, and those facts placed directly in the outline. For the experienced writer Xeroxed pages can be a substitute for the traditional note cards.

However, many writers use note cards because they wish to interpret the facts as well as record them, or the Xerox machine is inaccessible, or the cost is prohibitive. They may realize that the note cards will help them to arrange the facts effectively and to visualize the finished report. In such cases, notes should be taken on 4-by-6-inch or 5-by-7-inch cards. Three types of information must be included on each note card: (1) the source of information consisting of the author's name, page number, and, if a book, the call number; (2) the note itself; and (3) the subject heading.

Recorded in the upper right-hand corner of the card are the author's name, the page number, and the call number if applicable. Only one note should be placed on each card, even if that one note is only four or five words long. Paraphrasing the author's words will be helpful since you will eventually have to put those ideas in your own words anyway. Interpreting the facts in addition to recording them and explaining the reasoning used in your interpretation when that reasoning is not immediately evident will speed the writing of the outline later. When the author says something so well that you cannot improve upon it, those exact words should be copied on the card with quotation marks around them.

In the upper left-hand corner of the card, the subject of the note should be penciled in, a subject that you may want to change as you continue reading and note taking. See Figure 5.1.

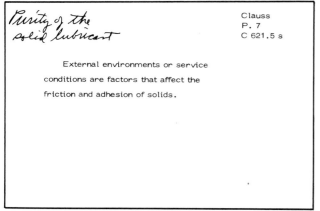

Purity of the solid lubricant

Clauss
P. 7
C 621.5 s

External environments or service conditions are factors that affect the friction and adhesion of solids.

Fig. 5.1. Note card for a book.

As you take notes, you should also prepare the bibliography cards on the smaller 3-by-5-inch cards; then you can tell at a glance whether you are dealing with a note card or with a bibliography card and can save time. The bibliography card for a book includes the author's full name, name of the work, place of publication, publisher, and date. See Figure 5.2. The bibliography card for a periodical includes the author's full name, the title of the article, the name of the periodical, the date of the publication or the volume number, and the page numbers. See Figure 5.3. Remember that information gained from letters of inquiry, interviews, and any experiments and/or polls that you yourself conduct should be recorded on note cards.

Clauss, F. J., _Solid Lubricants and Self-Lubricating Solids_. New York: Academic Press, 1972.

Fig. 5.2. Bibliography card for a book.

Greenberg, Gary, and Timothy Dieffenbacher, "Visual Discrimination in the Mongolian Gerbil (_Meriones Unguiculatus_) as a Function of Age," _The Journal of General Psychology_, January 1976, pp. 31–37.

Fig. 5.3. Bibliography card for a periodical article.

Sorting the Note Cards

After you have read and taken notes on most of the available material, the note cards should be arranged in stacks according to the subject penciled in the left-hand corner. Then close attention should be paid to the arrangement of these stacks; each group will be a roman numeral division of your outline. Next, the cards in each group should be arranged in some suitable order. Putting the cards in a long line will help you to experiment with various types of organization and will help you to visualize the finished paper and to check, early in the process, the accuracy and the logic of the organization. There will be several possible organizations for one set of facts; the one that makes it easiest for the readers to find the answers to their questions should be used. Some note cards that are redundant or do not belong in any of the stacks may have to be thrown away.

Final Outline

The rules for writing an outline as described in Chapter 3 should be followed. Each group of cards should be considered a roman numeral division of the report and arranged in some logical order. Then the outline of each main division is developed, one at a time. An outline consisting of only roman numeral divisions and capital letter divisions is not very helpful; the more subdivision, the easier it will be to develop a report from the finished outline. If you do not have enough notes to fully develop a certain section of a roman numeral division, you will have to leave out that section or do more reading and note taking. Actually, reading and note taking are steps that must be continued throughout the entire writing process. As you develop the outline, you must also decide which figures and tables you will use and where you will put them in the report since these illustrations will affect the text.

Rough Draft

After the outline is developed in detail, the hard work of writing a report is finished. Writing the rough draft should be a pleasant experience. Since you will rarely have time to sit down and write a whole report without interruption, you should plan to write it by sections. You may wish to write section III first, and then I. You should wait until you have finished writing the body of the report before you write the conclusions and recommendations, the introduction, and the abstract.

The tables and figures you intend to use should be checked; if they are closely related to the text, they should be placed right after the first mention of them in the report and the reader told when to look at them. If they are not directly related to the writing but would still be of interest to some of the readers, the tables and figures should be placed in an appendix at the end of the report.

As you write the rough draft, you must decide which information in the report should be documented. Accurate documentation is a courteous way to give due credit to others for their ideas and statistics.

A close examination of the note cards will reveal that

some theories and facts are recorded by several different writers. When the same facts are given in several different works, these facts can be considered *common knowledge* to anyone interested in the field. You may use this information in your report without giving credit to anyone as long as you express this information in your own words. For example, any English major writing a paper on Chaucer will discover in every reference work that Chaucer lived ca 1340–1400. This information is common knowledge to anyone working in the Chaucer area and does not need to be cited in the footnotes and/or bibliography.

However, some information that you have recorded on note cards is *specific information* and the original author must receive credit for it in the bibliography, in a footnote, or in the bibliography/footnote combination:

1. A phrase of more than three or four words copied from a source should be placed in quotations and the reference cited:

> According to Alfred Jones, "A striking concept which appears not only in the natural environment, but in art as well, is symmetry."[1]

2. Statistics must be cited:

> The U.S. Marine Corps claimed that the domes they erected in the Arctic were only 3% of the weight of the conventional housing, 6% of the packaged volume, 14% of the cost, and less than 1% of the erection man-hours.[2]

3. Any idea that has been expressed by only one person, even though you have put it in your own words, must be acknowledged:

> The rising inflationary curve was caused by the embargo.[3]

As you examine the note cards, you should be able to distinguish between *common knowledge* and *specific information*. If you cannot decide to which category your information belongs, you should give credit to the original author through the bibliography and/or footnotes.

You must also give your attention to two other problems as you continue to work on the rough draft: headings and a clear system of documentation. You must decide whether or not you will transfer only the roman numeral and capital letter entries of the outline into the paper as headings or will also include the arabic number entries. Four systems of documentation can be used effectively: (1) the alphabetized bibliography, (2) the numbered list of references, (3) footnotes only, or (4) the footnote/bibliography combination. These systems will be discussed in the Bibliography section appearing later in this chapter.

Concentrate on getting your main ideas down on paper and worry later about word choices, mechanics, and sentence and paragraph structure.

Final Draft

The final draft of a report is typed on 8½-by-11-inch white paper of good quality with a 1–1½-inch margin on the left side and 1-inch margins on the other three sides. The top margin of the first page should be 2–2½ inches down. The paper itself is double-spaced, and the beginning of each paragraph is indented five spaces. Quotations of more than five lines are indented an additional ½ inch on each side and single-spaced. Pages are numbered consistently in the upper right corner or top center or bottom center. Because you have written the rough draft by sections, you will want to add transitional sentences and paragraphs to link together the various parts before beginning the final draft. After you have added and deleted material in various sections of the rough draft, you should reread the whole report to make sure that these changes do not force you to revise other parts of the paper. After the final draft is finished, you should proofread it carefully. Typographical errors can make a difference: "Atlas Industries is now (not) implementing the suggestion of the Washington Bureau."

STYLE

An impersonal style is best for the formal report: *I* and *you*, contractions such as *can't* and *they've*, and technical jargon should all be avoided. Longer, smoother flowing sentences and transitional words, sentences, and paragraphs to connect the various sections of the paper should be used. When this impersonal style is carried too far, it may become stiff, pompous, and vague to the point of "It is believed by this writer that . . ." and "It would appear probable that. . . ." But the formal style, skillfully used, can be dignified, direct, and appropriate when the report is later published in a technical journal.

PARTS OF THE FORMAL REPORT

The parts of the formal report will be described in the order in which they appear in the report, not in the order in which they will be written. The body of the report should be written first; then the parts described below should be added. Occasional repetition is acceptable in the formal report because it is so often read only in part. An important conclusion or recommendation can be stated in the letter of transmittal, in the summary, in the body, and in the conclusion and recommendation sections. Such repetition is not offensive; it simply reinforces a main idea of the report.

Title Page

The title page can be divided into three parts: (1) The title itself appears two or three inches from the top of the page and should be as informative as possible. For example, SCREENING TESTS FOR SICKLE-CELL ANEMIA is more specific than just SICKLE-CELL ANEMIA. (2) "For" and then the name of the course or company and the name of the professor or the superior for whom the report is intended appear in the middle of the page. These two items place emphasis on the upper half of the sheet. (3) At the bottom of the page ''by'' and then your name and the date should be written. All three items are centered. The title of the report is written in capital letters, but only the first letters in the other words on the page are capitalized. See Figure 5.4.

Fig. 5.4. A well-arranged title page for a formal report.

Covering Memo or Letter of Transmittal

A covering memo is usually attached to a formal report that is circulated to persons within the organization. It can be as informal as a brief personal note directed to one person for whom the report is intended. The more formal letter of transmittal is attached to a formal report intended for circulation outside the organization. It does not have to be as impersonal as the report itself: *I* and *you* can be used, and personal opinions may be included.

Several of the following items can be included in a covering memo or in a letter of transmittal: (1) the report may be identified so that the reader will be able to recall the problem that necessitated it, (2) the date on which the report was requested and also the due date may be given, (3) the purpose of the report may be included, (4) the reasons some points were stressed and some de-emphasized may be explained, (5) the advantages or disadvantages faced as you wrote the report may be enumerated, or (6) the report itself may be summarized.

The following specimen memo and letter of transmittal illustrate two different levels of writing. The memo is informal because it is directed to one person, uses *I* and *you,* and includes personal opinion. The letter of transmittal is more formal because it is intended for circulation outside the McMillan Laboratories and is not personalized with *I* and *you.*

To: Bill Daniels   Date: March 15, 19—
From: Steve Soonager
Subject: Solid lubrication

Purpose   Here is the information on the chalcogen family as related to solid lubrication that you requested during our staff meeting of March 1, 19—.

Problem and solution   In writing this report, I encountered some difficulties because of an overabundance of material. I therefore decided to eliminate the applications and film formation areas on which you are already well informed.

Future   If you or any of your staff have further questions, please call me at Ex. 237.

McMillan Laboratories
251 South Lake Avenue
Pasadena, California 91101

April 26, 19—

T. Z. Pierce, Vice-President
Brownell Industries
Newton, MA   02156

Dear Mr. Pierce:

Identification   This is the report on the chalcogen family as related to solid lubrication that you requested in your letter of April 2, 19—.

Procedure   Information was collected from experiments performed in the Utah Laboratories as well as in our own laboratories. The data are presented and analyzed in the following report.

Summary of the report   The significance of the tests on the laminar solids, nonlaminar solids, and soft metals is evaluated. It is concluded that solids do lack the life and the ability to carry away frictional heat that the mobile lubricants have. The ultimate solution to the solid lubricant problem lies in the development of new composite materials that will exhibit low friction and wear.

Future activities   Further experimentation is now under way at the Utah Laboratories to develop a solid lubricant that will have the advantages of the mobile lubricant and none of the disadvantages. I will forward periodic reports from Utah Laboratories as we receive them.

Sincerely,

John J. Jones
Laboratory Supervisor

Table of Contents

Any report more than a few pages long should have a contents page because it helps the readers find the section they wish to read, and it shows the scope and organization of the report. The table of contents should be planned when the final draft of the paper has been finished.

The table of contents functions as an outline of the report. All the following headings and their page numbers should be placed in the table of contents: the summary, introduction, conclusions and recommendations, each roman numeral division, the bibliography, and appendix. All the capital letter headings used within each roman numeral section may be indented beneath the roman numeral entries if appropriate. Any arabic number headings (third-rank headings) may be indented under the appropriate capital letter entry in the table of contents if necessary. The wording of the heading in the report and the entry on the contents page should be exactly the same. But the roman numeral, the capital letter, or the arabic number should not be included alongside each entry. The use of the dotted line in the table of contents to connect the heading with the page number is optional.

If all the figures and tables appear together in the paper, there should be an entry in the table of contents called "Figures and Tables" with the correct page number. If several figures and tables are scattered throughout the report, a separate page should be added after the table of contents called "List of Figures and Tables." All the figures should be arranged in one section, all the tables in another. The number of each figure or table, the title, and the page number should be given.

In the following sample table of contents for an informative type of formal report, the writer decided to list only the roman numeral and capital letter entries used in the body of the paper and to arrange the figures and tables in a separate list.

CONTENTS

LIST OF FIGURES AND TABLES

Abstract or Summary

The terms *abstract* and *summary* are often confusing because there is no widespread agreement on their meanings. It is best to check into the term or variation of the term used in your own school or company. An abstract at the beginning of a periodical article can be one sentence long; in the various professional publications devoted solely to abstracts, each may be four or five paragraphs long.

The informative or scale-model abstract published separately presents the results of research, experiments, and other work in condensed form to colleagues. The method of attack and data used—as well as conclusions reached—should be reported. Generally, the abstract should be an abbreviated version of the conceptual argument of the article—beginning with the thesis, then tracing the major arguments to the conclusions. Some publications limit the abstract to 200 words or less.

The following suggestions should prove helpful in writing the longer, informative abstract suitable for publications devoted solely to abstracts:

1. Reflect the proportions of the original article in the abstract; do not give space to relatively unimportant points.
2. Omit introductory and concluding material, examples, and details.
3. Use transitions that clarify relationships.
4. Keep the wording of the original article when possible.
5. Report the main facts and ideas without such phrases as "the writer reports" and "the article says."
6. Use complete, grammatical sentences. Do not omit verbs and conjunctions, but do avoid excessive use of adjectives and adverbs.

But it is the report abstract that is of major importance here. The term *report abstract* refers to six or eight lines at the beginning of the paper or of the periodical article that state the thesis and list the main points of the report. The summary is longer than an abstract, often reaching 1/10 the length of the total report. It not only states the thesis and lists the main points but also explains the main points.

Both the report abstract and summary are separate

from the paper itself; both are placed at the beginning. Both are most important to reports because they give the readers their initial introduction to and impression of the report. After the readers have read the report, they may reread the summary or abstract again and again at future dates to refresh their memories. The necessary conciseness can be achieved by leaving out the introductory material, the illustrative examples, and the detailed comparisons. The abstract or summary should always be double-checked for accuracy. Any desire for economy should not distort the facts. Since the abstract will be read by more people than will actually read the whole report, technical information and vocabulary should be kept to a minimum; yet the abstract or summary should always be more informative than scanning the table of contents.

The summary should be helpful to the reader who wants the general picture but will not bother to check the highly technical information in tables, figures, and the appendix. It will assist the reader who must make a decision based on the information in the report and who must therefore depend on the overall impression gained from the summary and from the recommendations and conclusions. The summaries that appear at the end of each chapter in this textbook are additional examples. The following typical abstract and summary give the main points of informative types of formal reports.

ABSTRACT

It is the purpose of this report to examine the light-emitting diode and provide information as to its fabrication, material structure, theory, application, and development. A basic understanding of these areas will enhance the reader's knowledge concerning the light-emitting diode as one of the basic opto-electronic devices.

SUMMARY

The Stirling engine started as a large, bulky, and not too efficient engine in 1816 when Robert Stirling applied for its basic patent. Since then it has undergone extensive research and development. Almost all of its operating problems have been eliminated. Its efficiency is 10% higher than even the best diesels, and its size and weight are now comparable to modern passenger car engines.

Its applications range from submarines to space vehicles. The most sought-after application is in the passenger car because of its excellent emissions characteristic, a much desired factor in a pollution-conscious world.

Several companies have completed studies on the applications of the Stirling. Among them are General Motors, Ford, and Phillips Research. Additional studies are now being made with Stirlings powered from stored heat and from hydrogen.

Introduction

Two types of introductions may be found in a formal report. First is the informal introduction of the kind used for briefer memos and reports. This type of introduction gives background information on the subject, defines key terms used in the report, traces the history of the subject to the present time, and/or arouses interest perhaps with direct quotations, startling statistics, or paradoxes. The illustrative informal introduction below provides background information about the structural qualifications of fallout shelters and indicates the organizational pattern. The accompanying outline presents the content of the body of the report.

INTRODUCTION

The nation's buildings represent the primary resource for shelters from natural and man-made hazards. All buildings afford some measure of protection, although the amount of protection can vary substantially from building to building. Certain types of buildings respond favorably when subjected to a particular hazard but provide negligible protection from other hazards.

Background on the subject When construction plans for an existing building are available, the task of evaluating the structural characteristics of floor and roof systems is an easy one. This task, however, can be complicated if plans are not available and the only method of collecting data for a building is by on-site inspection. When designing buildings for human occupancy, architects necessarily devote special attention to covering up many of the structural features that happen to be the object of the survey technician's investigation.

Listing of the main divisions of the paper According to the latest Shelter Survey Technology (SST) information, all buildings qualifying as fallout shelters must have the ability to support themselves structurally and be able to withstand additional loads imposed due to occupancy. The type of construction determines a building's response to the fallout and to the blast of an atomic explosion. New SST regulations require that fallout protection and calculation of shelter spaces be estimated by the Estimating and Analyzing Shelter Yield (EASY) II form. Data must also be collected on the relative blast protection and natural ventilation.

SHELTER SURVEY TECHNOLOGY

  I. Building construction
    A. Light-frame wood construction
      1. Response to fallout
      2. Response to blast
    B. Heavy timber construction
      1. Response to fallout
      2. Response to blast
    C. Steel frame construction
      1. Response to fallout
      2. Response to blast
    D. Regular masonry load-bearing construction
      1. Response to fallout
      2. Response to blast
    E. Reinforced concrete frame construction
      1. Response to fallout
      2. Response to blast
  II. Fallout protection
    A. EASY II
      1. Principles of shielding
      2. Procedure for the use of the form
    B. Protection categories

The second type of introduction is the formal one. This introduction is concerned with the reasons the project was initiated and with the structure of the report itself. It may discuss in detail some of the information briefly mentioned in the covering memo or letter of transmittal: the purpose of the report, the scope of the investigation, any problems encountered during the writing, and the sources of data. This kind of introduction orients the readers so they can better understand and evaluate the report itself. The formal introduction below was written by a technical writing student:

INTRODUCTION

Purpose. This report was written as an assignment in Technical Writing 301. The topic of inertia welding was chosen on the advice of Dr. A. J. Williamson of the School of Technology.

Scope. The report deals with the development of the basic process and some examples of industrial applications. In this particular report machine costs and machine specifications have not been examined.

Sources of information. Most of the information came from booklets published by the Caterpillar Tractor Company and from various metals periodicals such as *Iron Age, Tool and Manufacturing Engineer, Manufacturing Engineer and Management, Metal Progress,* and *American Machinist.* Additional information also came from interviews with area welding experts.

The informal introduction may simply be labeled "Introduction." The formal one also uses the main heading "Introduction," but it often makes use of subheadings too: Purpose (need for the report), Scope (limitation of the subject and/or the level of competence required for the reader), and perhaps Authorization (who requested the report).

Sometimes both types of introduction are used in one paper. The formal introduction should be placed first and labeled "Introduction." Here you can tell the readers what you intend to do in the paper, so they will be better prepared to understand the facts in the paper itself. The informal introduction should be used as a lead-in to the paper and labeled "Background Information" or "Historical Review of (subject)." But regardless of which type or types of introduction you use, you should get right to the point of the report. "Empty" sentences such as "The study of computers is a vital and interesting one" are a waste of time.

Conclusions and Recommendations

Analytical reports lend themselves to a conclusion that consists of beliefs reached on the basis of the evidence presented. These conclusions are based on your interpretation of the facts presented in the report; they should include only information covered in the paper. The conclusion in informative reports can also be a summary of the main points, and these main points may be numbered and indented in a list.

All the conclusions should be arranged together in a single section, not scattered throughout the report. This section can be placed at the end of the report or at the beginning; this is your choice. If it comes at the end of the paper, you can refer to the facts that have led you to your decision; if the conclusion comes first, you may only explain your conclusions. If there are several conclusions, they should be indented and numbered in a list.

When writing the conclusions, you should avoid overstatement. The evidence should be stressed if it is conclusive. Such roundabout statements as "It is believed that . . ." should be avoided.

Recommendations are not always needed in a report since they refer to the actions called for on the basis of the conclusions. You may reach convictions or conclusions without being in the position to recommend that certain actions be taken. However, if you have several recommendations, they should be indented and numbered in a list. When possible, the numbers of the recommendations should be keyed to the numbers of the conclusions.

Writing conclusions and recommendations is a matter of judgment and not a matter of just following rigid rules. The conclusions must stem from the evidence presented in the body of the paper and the recommendations must come from the conclusions. In the illustrative conclusion below, the convictions reached on the basis of the evidence presented are stated. Recommendations are inappropriate since specific actions are not recommended.

CONCLUSIONS

Restatement of the thesis   The catalytic converter, an after-treatment device, is effective in reducing and controlling vehicle emissions because it eliminates some of the extra components that prior systems have used. Some design changes permitted by the use of a catalytic converter are as follows:

Summary of the main points
1. Richer air-fuel mixtures at idle speed can be tolerated.
2. Retarded ignition timing at engine idle speeds is not as critical.
3. A.I.S. (Air Induction Sytems) that utilize an air pump to induce fresh air into the engine's exhaust system near the exhaust ports may be used in conjunction with a converter.

4. Slightly richer mixtures at part throttle operation improve driveability.

In the sample section following, recommendations are included because certain actions must be taken on the basis of the conclusions reached.

CONCLUSIONS

Stressing the importance of the subject The field of arc welding is diverse, highly technical, and still in its infant stages even though its growth has been extensive since World War II. Today our whole society is dependent to some extent on the products or services provided by a particular arc welding process. Several conclusions can be drawn about the future of the arc welding industry:
1. Expansion will be dependent on qualified welding engineers.
2. Recent technological advances will facilitate the building of nuclear energy power plants that will meet higher safety standards.
3. Welds on pipes, components, and reactors necessary for nuclear energy production can now be as strong as the base metals they bond.
4. Construction time and cost can be reduced by new arc welding processes in established production methods.

RECOMMENDATIONS

Premise The arc welding industry can expand significantly in the next decade if the recommendations below are followed:

Actions to be taken (Note that Recommendation No. 1 is based on Conclusion No. 1, etc.)
1. Qualified welding engineers must be trained in greater numbers.
2. Federal funds must be allocated for the building of nuclear energy power plants.
3. Technological experimentation in arc welding must be continued to improve the quality of welds.
4. New arc welding techniques must constantly be incorporated into existing operations.

Appendix

The appendix section of the formal report is optional. If used, it is placed at the end of the report and contains highly technical material, often in the form of tables and figures. Its complex data supplement information presented earlier in the report. These data are not directly connected with the text but often reinforce or add to the material already included. The appendix is usually needed by specialists in the field rather than by the general reader. Sometimes photographs that are too bulky to put in the text are more easily handled here. The material in the appendix should be mentioned in the text if it is closely related to the text or supports statements in the text.

The title "Appendix" may be placed in the middle of a title page that precedes the first page of the appendix or, if the first supplemental item is not a full page in size, "Appendix" can be placed at the top of the first page. If the appendix has main divisions in it, the headings should be treated as headings of the first rank: capitalized, centered, underlined, and entered in the table of contents. Tables and figures in the appendix must be numbered in the same sequence as the other visuals, given titles, and included in the list of tables and figures. The appendix in the student paper at the end of this chapter illustrates some of these general principles.

When there is much supplemental information to be added to a report, several appendixes may be included and numbered A, B, C, etc. In such a case, specific page references to the various appendixes within the text of the report are most valuable—for instance, "See appendix A, p. 72" instead of "See appendix."

Bibliography

The bibliography is a list of sources of information used in writing the report. A list of sources is necessary (1) to indicate the extent of your research, (2) to add authority to startling or controversial statements you wish to make, and (3) to direct the reader to further reading on the subject. There are four basic types of reference systems:

Alphabetized bibliography

Author's last name is first. Indent second and third lines 3–5 spaces beneath first. Give page numbers for periodicals.

Douglas, H., "Telephoning by Light," *Science News,* July 1975, pp. 44–45.

Hawkins, J. W., "Laser Kit Lets You Transmit T.V. Pictures," *Popular Science,* May 1975, p. 144.

Punis, G., and J. O'Donnell, "Build a Laser T.V. System," *Popular Electronics,* November 1974, pp. 32–38.

"Search for Laser Signals from Elsewhere," *Science News,* May 17, 1975, p. 318.

Numbered list of references

Author's name is in normal word order. For book, place period after author's name and after title. For article in periodical, use commas to separate items and include page numbers.

1. Rufus P. Turner. *ABC's of Electronic Power.* Indianapolis, Indiana: Bobbs-Merrill Co., Inc., 1972.

2. Henry V. Hickey and William M. Villines. *Elements of Electronics.* New York: McGraw-Hill Book Co., 1970.

3. Charles L. Alley and Kenneth W. Atwood. *Semiconductor Devices and Circuits.* New York: John Wiley & Sons, Inc., 1971.

4. G. Punis and J. O'Donnell, "Build a Laser T.V. System," *Popular Electronics,* November 1974, pp. 32–38.

Footnotes only

**Indent first
line five
spaces.
Place
footnote
marker
above line.
For book,
place facts of
pulbication
in paren-
theses.**

[1]Matthew Arnold, "Literature and Science," in *The Victorian Mind,* eds. Gerald B. Kauyer and Gerald C. Sorenson (New York: Capricorn Books, 1969), p. 35.
[2]Thomas Babington, Lord Macaulay, "Samuel Johnson," in *Critical and Historical Essays: Thomas Babington, Lord Macaulay,* ed. Hugh Trevor-Roper (New York: McGraw-Hill Book Co., 1965), p. 70.
[3]Arnold, p. 36.

Both footnotes and alphabetized bibliography

**Either
single-space
or double-
space each
entry.
Double-
space
between
entries**

[1]Bertha M. Weeks, *Filing and Records Management* (New York: Ronald Press, 1964), p. 3.
[2]Weeks, p. 20.
[3]Irene Place and Estelle L. Popham, *Filing and Records Management* (Englewood Cliffs, N.J.: Prentice-Hall, Inc., 1966), p. 15.

Place, Irene, and Estelle L. Popham. *Filing and Records Management.* Englewood Cliffs, N.J.: Prentice-Hall, Inc., 1966.

Weeks, Bertha M. *Filing and Records Management.* New York: Ronald Press, 1964.

You should familiarize yourself with the type of bibliography used in the various periodicals of your major area, with the guidelines that prevail in your field, and with the reference system used in other reports prepared by your company or organization. But regardless of the type used, the bibliography entry consists of three kinds of information already recorded on the 3-by-5-inch bibliography card: the author's name, the name of the work, and the facts of publication. For a book, the facts of publication include the place, the name of the publisher, and the date. For a periodical, month/day/year, and page numbers; if the day and month are not given, use the volume number, year in parentheses, and the page number without the page abbreviation, such as 2(1977), 15 or II(1977), 15. In printed bibliographies, titles of books and names of periodicals are placed in italics. But when you are typing a report, underline the words that the printer italicizes.

Alphabetized bibliography. If the report is brief, the list of works used is simply an alphabetized bibliography appearing at the end of the paper. When you wish to verify certain facts or statistics or when you want to add authority to your statements, you can simply mention the source of your information in the text: "According to Thomas G. Tims" or "This theory, as Jonathan J. Smithey explains." This list of references may be expanded to include works that you read in preparation for writing the report but that you did not directly refer to. The alphabetized bibliography may even be expanded to include not only the works specifically referred to in the report and the works read but not mentioned but

also works that would merely be helpful to anyone desiring additional information. Such an expanded list of references would show that you had consulted a number of authoritative, current works before you wrote the report and would thus add weight to your statements.

One standard form for an alphabetized bibliography is shown below. The bibliography entry is either single-spaced or double-spaced, the author's last name comes first, and subsequent lines are indented three to five spaces beneath the first line. In a bibliography entry for a book, periods are ordinarily used to separate the three parts: a period after the author's name, a period after the name of the work, and a period after the facts of publication. Sometimes, however, a comma separates the author's name and the name of the work; then periods are placed after the name of the work and after the facts of publication, as in the student formal report at the end of this chapter. Usually for a periodical, the entry begins with a capital letter and ends with a period; items within the entry are separated by commas. If the periodical is a weekly or monthly publication, the date is given and followed by the page abbreviation and number. For periodicals published less often, the volume number (roman numeral or arabic number) is given, the year in parentheses, and then the page number—omitting "p." or "pp." When more than one title by the same author is listed, a one-half-inch-long solid line is substituted for the author's name in all entries after the first. Whether or not the entry itself is single-spaced or double-spaced, always double-space between each bibliographical entry.

BIBLIOGRAPHY

Able, Henry C. *The Elementary Classroom.* New York: E. P. Dutton & Company, Inc., 1973.

Cornfelt, John Henry, "Activities for the Primary Grades," *Instructor,* March 1976, pp. 25–32.

"Developing Motor Skills," *Teacher in the Primary Grades,* XV (Winter 1976), 53–61.

Jones, Thomas Sylvester, and Samuel A. Brown. *The Open Classroom.* Boston: Houghton Mifflin, 1975.

"Manipulative Skills for Children," *Encyclopaedia Britannica* (1976), XV, 385.

There are several variations to the alphabetized bibliography. The date is often included in parentheses when the author's name is mentioned in the text: "A. Comfort (1964) analyzes the cycle of ageing in great detail." The date is then treated similarly in the bibliography entry:

Comfort, A. (1964). *Ageing: The Biology of Senescence.* London: Routledge & Kegan Paul.

Many scientific journals use the above system since recently published material is vital to the field: "According to Thomas G. Tims (1978)'' or ''This theory, as Jonathan J. Smithey (1977) explains.''

Some psychology, botany, and zoology journals do not mention the name of the original author in the text itself but place both his name and the date of the work in parentheses after the statement in the text: ''This theory (Smithey, 1975).'' Then the usual alphabetized bibliography follows at the end of the report.

Numbered list of references. In several marketing, accounting, and technology publications the entries in the alphabetized bibliography are numbered and the number is placed in parentheses in the text after specific information taken from that work. This system makes the reference system quite explicit without using footnotes; the number is simply inserted into the text. ''A. Comfort analyzes the cycle of ageing in great detail (2).'' Then the bibliography entry could appear as follows:

1. Adams, John Robert. *Biological Factors of Aging.* New York: Little, Brown and Company, 1974.

2. Comfort, A. *Ageing: The Biology of Senescence.* London: Routledge & Kegan Paul, 1964.

In other technical publications, the bibliography number and the page number are placed in parentheses in the text: ''A. Comfort analyzes the cycle of ageing in great detail (2, pp. 28-30).'' This is an even more specific reference and makes it easier for the reader to check when the information is in a lengthy article or in a book.

Another variation of the numbered list of references is sometimes found in home economics and other journals. The bibliography entries are arranged in the order in which they are referred to in the text and then numbered. The author's name is in normal word order and there is no indentation. This variation of the numbered list of references is the system used in many of the specimen reports in this textbook.

1. William Wayne Walker. *Biological Ageing.* Boston: Houghton Mifflin, 1973.

2. A. Comfort. *Ageing: The Biology of Senescence.* London: Routledge & Kegan Paul, 1964.

Since this type of reference system limits you to including only those works that are specifically referred to in the text, you may wish to add a page called ''Additional Works Consulted.'' On this page, all the works you consulted but did not actually cite in the report are recorded.

Footnotes only. In some publications, especially in the fine arts fields, sources are not cited with great frequency and footnotes alone are used. Usually these footnotes are numbered consecutively throughout the report and are placed on a separate sheet at the end. A raised footnote marker is used in the text after the material to be cited—usually a quotation, an idea that belongs to one specific person, or a statement that requires authoritative support. The marker comes after all other punctuation in the sentence. When an idea is paraphrased, the place in the text where the cited material begins should be indicated.

In Chapter 12 of this textbook, ''footnotes only'' are used. The following excerpt also illustrates the basic principles for using only footnotes as documentation.

Thomas Butler died December 29, 1886, but even in the last year of his father's life Samuel seemed to have found a new peace. Jones points out that he could politely thank his father for attempting to help him find a line from Horace, and he could quietly display his learning to his father. He could accept the disappointment of not being named to the Slade Professorship of Fine Arts at Cambridge, and he could speak calmly of Miss Savage again in a letter to Harriet on April 2, 1886.[5]

With less frequency, footnotes are placed at the bottom of each page and the first footnote on each page begins with 1. Footnotes at the bottom of each page are easy for the reader to consult but add to the spacing problems of the typist. Such footnotes are separated from the text with a solid line of about 18 spaces; this line is a double space below the text and a double space above the first footnote. There is a double space between the footnotes, and single spacing or double spacing can be used within each one. The footnote marker is usually raised above the line, but sometimes it is placed on the line with a period after it. The first line of each footnote is indented five spaces. However, if the footnotes are placed together on a separate page, and labeled ''Notes'' or ''End Notes,'' it is easier for the reader to see the full scope of the material cited.

Footnote forms vary widely from one field to another. But a general rule is that the footnote should begin with a capital letter and end with a period. Facts of publication for a book are placed in parentheses. The footnote usually furnishes four types of information: (1) the author's name (in normal word order), (2) the title of the work (underline the name of a book, periodical, or play published separately; use quotes around the title of an article in a periodical, a chapter in a book, and other writings not published separately), (3) facts of publication, and (4) the page number.

It is common practice to include all four types of information in the first footnote to a work and in subsequent footnotes to that work, for clarity and economy, to place only the author's last name and the page number either in parentheses after the cited material in the text or in a footnote at the bottom of the page or at the end of the text. If you refer to several works by the same author, the title of the work (can be in shortened form) as well as the author's last name and the page number should be indicated.

In the excerpt below, a complete footnote is given for the first reference to a work; and for additional references to the same work, the author's name, the volume number when appropriate, and the page number are placed in parentheses in the text.

Many of Samuel Butler's religious judgments can be found in his personal correspondence and papers. As early as January 10, 1861, he said in a letter to Philip Worsley, "Let me recant many religious opinions propounded by me to yourself."[1] When Butler justified his recanting to Worsley, he claimed that his travels had led him to a wider circle of ideas. He was quite aware that he had made a gradual change from his "old narrow bigoted tenets to a far happier present latitudinarianism" (Jones, I, 97). However, even in his negative statements he expressed a fear of going too far. In a letter to Mrs. Philip Worsley, his aunt, dated September 19, 1861, he hoped that he would not over-react against orthodox religion: "The worst of it is that in the total wreck of my own past orthodoxy I fear I may be as much too sceptical as then too orthodox."[2]

[1] Henry Festing Jones, *Samuel Butler: A Memoir* (London: Macmillan, 1919), I, 96. Subsequent page references will be cited parenthetically in the text.

[2] Arnold Silver, ed., *The Family Letters of Samuel Butler, 1841–1886* (Stanford: Stanford University Press, 1962), p. 104. Subsequent page references will be cited parenthetically in the text.

The use of Latin abbreviations in footnotes has decreased in recent years. *Ibid.* means in exactly the same place as previously cited; *Op. cit.* means in the same work already cited and follows the author's name and precedes the page number; *cf.* means "confer" and is used as "compare with" might be used. These Latin expressions often create confusion; assume that you see a footnote marker in the text and find at the bottom of the page only "[5] *Ibid.*" Since *Ibid.* means in exactly the same place as cited in the previous footnote, you may have to turn back to another page to discover the source of the last footnote.

The following sample footnotes will guide you in problems of form. When a roman numeral volume number is included, "p." is not used—only the number itself. A comma is never used before a parenthesis. Additional information on footnote form can be found in *Form and Style: Theses, Reports and Term Papers* by Campbell and Ballou or in *Publication Manual of the American Psychological Association* or in the latest edition of *The MLA Style Sheet* published by the Modern Language Association.

Book with one author

[1] John Jones, *Microbiology* (New York: Thomas Y. Crowell, 1977), p. 160.

Book with several authors

[2] Samuel J. Smith and others, *Woodworking Techniques* (New York: McGraw-Hill Book Co., 1977), p. 23.

Edited book

[3] Sylvia Rose Cooper, ed., *The Home Economist* (New York: John Wiley & Sons, Inc., 1974), p. 16.

Article in an edited book

[4] John Fredricks, "The County Extension Office," in *The Home Economist* ed. by Sylvia Rose Cooper (New York: John Wiley & Sons, Inc., 1974), p. 74.

Unsigned pamphlet

[5] *Dahlgren Dampening System* (Dallas: Dahlgren Manufacturing Company, no date), p. 3.

Signed article in a periodical

[6] A. W. VanderMeer, "Expanding Music Education to All Segments of Society," *Music Educators Journal,* December 1975, p. 54.

Unsigned article in a periodical

[7] "Flying Forms Lift Production, Lower Costs," *Construction Methods & Equipment,* December 1975, p. 46.

Encyclopedia article

[8] "Yam," *Encyclopaedia Britannica* (1970), XXIII, 871.

Signed newspaper article

[9] Bernard Gwertzman, "Turk-Cypriot Settlement Key to Pact," *The Kansas City Times,* March 30, 1976, p. 1, cols. 5–6.

Unsigned newspaper article

[10] "Fabric Workers Settle with the Woolen Jobbers," *The New York Times,* May 6, 1973, Sec. 1, p. 36, cols. 1–2.

Speech

[11] Davis J. Hillhouse, *The BiCentennial Spirit,* a speech given before the Delta Phi chapter of Kappa Gamma Delta, Indianapolis, Indiana, May 21, 1976.

Personal interview

[12] David Vequist, Chairman, Department of Printing, Pittsburg State University, personal interview on continuous feed dampeners, Pittsburg, Kansas, April 12, 1978.

Both Footnotes and Alphabetized Bibliography. The most detailed type of documentation is the footnote/bibliography combination, the type most often used in scholarly writing. The footnote/bibliography combination is particularly valuable when you want to include specific page numbers for all the material cited and when you want to include all the works you have consulted in the alphabetized bibliography—not just those for which you have footnotes.

When footnotes are supplemented by a bibliography, the form of the footnotes is the same as that already illustrated; the form of the alphabetized bibliography is the same as that already illustrated. However, a shortened version of footnotes for books may be used: the publisher and place of publication may be omitted.

A variation of the footnote/bibliography system is often found in technical journals. Footnotes are used for explanatory notes needed throughout the text, and a numbered list of references is placed at the end of the article. This system is used in the sample formal report, "Reported and Revealed Preferences as Determinants of Mode Choice Behavior," at the end of this chapter.

SUMMARY

The formal report is several pages long, is impersonal in style, uses topical headings of more than one rank, and has a clear system of documentation. It usually has a title page, table of contents, and abstract or summary.

There is a recommended procedure for writing a formal report that will help you to avoid false starts and envision the finished report early in the process: (1) choose a topic if one has not been assigned to you, (2) make a tentative outline and bibliography to guide your reading, (3) begin reading and taking notes, (4) write the final outline, (5) write the rough draft, and (6) write the final draft.

The parts of the analytical formal report may be arranged in either of the two ways listed below:

Title page
Letter of transmittal or covering memo
Table of contents
List of tables and figures
Summary or abstract
Introduction
Body
Conclusions and/or recommendations
Appendix
Bibliography

OR

Title page
Letter of transmittal or covering memo
Table of contents
List of tables and figures
Summary or abstract
Conclusions and/or recommendations
Introduction
Body

Appendix
Bibliography

The parts of the informative formal report can be arranged as follows:

Title page
Letter of transmittal or covering memo
Table of contents
List of tables and figures
Summary or abstract
Introduction
Body
    Past
    Present
Appendix
Bibliography

Other formal reports, however, do not include all the parts discussed in this chapter; the audience often determines which parts will be needed and the arrangement of those parts. Remember that the parts are not written in the order in which they appear in the final draft. The body of the paper is written first; the conclusions and recommendations, the abstract, and the introduction are written next; and the title page, table of contents, and list of tables and figures are produced last.

Four systems of documentation can be used in the formal report. (1) The alphabetized bibliography provides sufficient information for the short report. (2) The numbered list of references gives more explicit information without using footnotes; this system seems to be the most widely used in technical writing today. (3) Footnotes alone can be used when sources are not cited with great frequency; this system is generally used in the humanities areas. (4) Both the footnote and alphabetized bibliography are most often used in scholarly writing where many page numbers must be cited and works not specifically referred to in the text must be included in the bibliography.

This chapter is offered as a systematic approach to the formal report, but feel free to modify these suggestions to suit your special circumstances. The periodicals and other publications in your major field will show you what is currently being written and how it is written.

SPECIMEN FORMAL REPORTS

The authors of the following sample formal report made several choices as they planned their paper: they included an abstract between the title and introduction but did not label it; they used explanatory footnotes throughout the report and a numbered list of references at the end; they did not add an appendix, apparently believing that they were writing for a highly specialized audience and all technical information could be included in the report itself.

RICHARD B. WESTIN and PETER L. WATSON*

The relation of attitudes toward transportation system characteristics and
the sensitivity of travelers to perceived differences in these characteristics
is studied. A probabilistic model of choice behavior is used, and effects
of attitudes are studied by examining how estimated elasticities differ among
groups of travelers stratified on the basis of attitude.

Reported and Revealed Preferences as Determinants of Mode Choice Behavior

INTRODUCTION

**Back-
ground**

In recent years, the scope of marketing activities
has become increasingly broad, not only in terms of
what is being marketed but also in terms of who is
undertaking marketing. Thus, it is no longer uncommon
to find social objectives being marketed alongside
detergents; nor is it unusual to find nonbusiness and
public institutions operating alongside private enterprise. The increase in popularity of social marketing
and marketing by nonbusiness institutions leads to
the necessity of considering the activities of such
agencies from the point of view of marketing management. The aim of marketing management is to examine
"the wants, attitudes and behavior of potential customers as this might shed light on designing a desired
product and on merchandising, promoting and distrib-
uting it successfully" [8]. The necessity for such
activities may be clearly seen in the programs of
government and other public agencies aimed at improving the characteristics of transportation modes.
Travel time has received considerable attention in
developments such as the turbo-trains recently introduced by AMTRAK and by European rail services

*Richard Westin is Assistant Professor of Economics, Scar-
borough College, University of Toronto; Peter Watson is with the
Transport Research Division, Transport and Urban Projects
Department, International Bank for Reconstruction and Development. The authors would like to thank Bruce Vavrichek for his
assistance in this research and Professor Frank M. Bass and a
referee for their detailed comments. The views expressed in this
paper are those of the authors and not necessarily those of the
World Bank. A preliminary report on this research appeared in
the *1973 Proceedings of the Business and Economic Statistics
Section,* American Statistical Association.

and, at a global level, in the form of the supersonic
transport. At a more local level, cost characteristics
have been emphasized in fare-free experiments. More
recent developments in urban transportation systems
have emphasized service-oriented characteristics,
such as accessibility in "dial-a-bus" systems and
personal amenity in the "Personal Rapid Transit"
systems. Such developments, and the concomitant
investments, should be made against a background
of the wants, attitudes, and behavior of the traveler.
This article investigates the extent to which the attitudes and behavior of the traveler provide a consistent
basis for marketing management and product development.

Purpose

In addition to the substantive results we report here,
our methodological approach to the problem of analyzing choice behavior should be of interest. The
question we examine is whether the system characteristics that travelers report are most important to
them are in fact the characteristics that travelers reveal
themselves to be most sensitive to in an analysis of
their actual choice behavior. In this sense, our investigation is similar to the current debate in the marketing
literature over the inclusion of importance weights
in the multi-attribute model of attitudes based on the
work of Rosenberg [12] and Fishbein [5] (see [18]
for a discussion of this controversy). Both our model
of choice behavior and our method of investigation
differ from those commonly used, however, and thus
examine this problem from an alternative approach.

*Clarifica-
tion*

Procedure

*Arousal
of interest*

THE MODEL OF CHOICE BEHAVIOR

The model of choice behavior we use is based on
the psychological theory of probabilistic choice surveyed in [9] and extended to an empirical framework

Journal of Marketing Research
Vol. XII (August 1975), 282-9

Explanation of the random utility model

by McFadden [10]. In this model, termed the "random utility" model, each individual in the population faces a finite set of alternatives which he ranks by a utility function of the form:

$$(1) \qquad U = V(\mathbf{X_{ij}}) + \epsilon(\mathbf{X_{ij}})$$

where $\mathbf{X_{ij}}$ is the vector of attributes faced by the *i*th individual for the *j*th alternative, *V* is nonstochastic and summarizes the representative tastes of the population, and ϵ is stochastic and summarizes the idiosyncratic tastes of the individual. Given a determination of the $\epsilon(\mathbf{X_{ij}})$, an individual then chooses the alternative with the highest utility. By specifying a functional form for *V* and a joint distribution for ϵ across all individuals, it is possible to derive the functional relationship between the vectors of attributes $\mathbf{X_{ij}}$ for the alternatives and the probability that an individual selected at random from the population will choose a given alternative. In the special case of two alternatives available to the individual and using the assumptions suggested by McFadden, the selection probabilities can be written as:

$$(2) \qquad P_{i1} = \frac{1}{1 + \exp\{-\alpha - \beta(\mathbf{X_{i1}} - \mathbf{X_{i2}})\}}$$

$$P_{i2} = 1 - P_{i1}$$

where P_{i1} and P_{i2} are *i*th individual's selection probabilities for the first and second alternatives, α is an intercept term, and β is a row vector of constants.[1] Equation (2) is identical to the binary logit model introduced by Berkson [2] for the bio-assay problem, and estimates of the parameters β from observations on observed choices and characteristics of the alternatives can be obtained by the maximum likelihood method or by various iterative regression procedures [14].

Clarification through contrast

To readers unfamiliar with the model described above, the value of this approach over a more familiar technique such as two-group discriminant analysis may need clarification. The random utility model differs both theoretically and empirically from the discriminant approach. Theoretically, the random utility model begins with the assumption that individuals do make choices between alternatives, while discriminant analysis assumes that individuals belong to particular groups that the statistician is seeking to identify in terms of the characteristics of the group. Since ultimately our interest in a marketing analysis is how to induce individuals to change their choices, a model

beginning in a choice framework rather than a classification framework is desirable. Although this theoretical distinction is clear, it would be irrelevant if the models were empirically equivalent; this is not true, however. The random utility model, by focusing on choices, implies that observed choice is the result of a drawing from a Bernoulli random variable with probabilities given by (2); this implies that the estimates chosen for β (under the maximum likelihood criterion) should be those that maximize the function:

$$(3) \qquad L = \prod_{i=1}^{n} (P_{i1})^{y_i} (P_{i2})^{1-y_i}$$

where y_i is a variable taking the value one if the individual chooses alternative one and zero if he chooses alternative two, and *n* is the number of individuals in the sample. The solution of (3) requires iterative maximization techniques. On the other hand, the theory of discriminant analysis such as given in [1] derives the discriminant function on the basis of a Bayesian analysis of classification into one of two known multivariate normal populations. The estimation of the discriminant function is then accomplished by equating sample moments with population moments; in general these estimates differ from those obtained by maximizing (3). Logit and discriminant analysis are sometimes confused because of the well-known property that discriminant analysis yields posterior estimates of the probability that an individual will belong to a given classification which are in the logistic function form (2). In practice, however, these estimates of probabilities will differ between logit and discriminant analysis because of the different estimates of their functional parameters. Since these differences ultimately arise from the distinction between a choice and a classification framework, the model we use here is logit analysis.

Restatement of the purpose

Returning to the problem of reported attitudes, we wish to determine how travelers' attitudes toward the characteristics of the modes affect their choice behavior. The approach we follow is to examine a representative model of mode choice behavior and to seek to determine whether reported attitudes toward characteristics of the modes have a systematic effect on the sensitivity of the choices of travelers to perceived differences in those characteristics.[2] Rather than handling the difficult problem of scaling attitudes, we use a method of paired comparisons between groups of travelers stratified by the attitudes they report.

Procedure

STUDY BACKGROUND AND DATA

The data used to test the relationship between reported attitudes and mode choice behavior are from

---

[1] Another model surveyed by Luce and Suppes, termed the "strict utility" model, assumes that utility does not contain the random $\epsilon(X_{ij})$ component of (1) and that individuals make their choices in a probabilistic manner based on the relative utility of the alternatives. McFadden shows that under certain assumptions, this model yields the same selection probabilities as those given by the random utility model (2).

[2] Our use of the word "attitudes" should not be confused with the different meaning given the word in the multi-attribute model of attitudes mentioned earlier. For studies of mode choice behavior using the multi-attribute attitude model, see [6, 13].

284   JOURNAL OF MARKETING RESEARCH, AUGUST 1975

Table 1
CLASSIFICATION OF FACTORS

	Car	Train
Economic	Journey time	Journey time
	Cost	Cost
Convenience	Freedom to choose starting time	Convenient arrival times
	Freedom to stop or change route	Convenient departure times
	Ability to make several stops	Location of stations
Amenity	Comfort	Comfort
	Safety	Safety
	Scenic beauty	Scenic beauty
	Necessity of carrying luggage/samples	Buffet car facilities
	Size of traveling party	Size of traveling party

Source of data

the Edinburgh-Glasgow Area Modal Split Study, which investigated intercity mode choices between train and car in the central lowlands of Scotland.[3] Travelers by train and automobile were interviewed en route and asked to report the times, costs, and service characteristics of their journeys together with an estimate of these variables by the second-best mode. Thus, the data used are the perceptions of mode characteristics as reported by the travelers. In the case of the cost of the journey by automobile, it is interesting to note that more than 90% of respondents explained (in response to a subsequent question) that the automobile costs reported were made up entirely of the costs of gasoline and oil.

Identification and differentiation of the travelers

In addition to the data discussed above, respondents were also asked to select from a list of alternatives the service characteristic which they had considered to be most important in making their choice of travel mode. For the purpose of analyzing the relationship between reported preferences (i.e., the characteristics reported to be most important) and revealed preferences (i.e., the variables revealed to be most important by statistical analysis), the responses to the "most important characteristic" question were used to group travelers into three classifications which we labeled Economic, Convenience, and Amenity. Table 1 lists the separate factors which formed the bases of these groups. The Economic group was isolated in an attempt to identify those travelers who respond to perceived differences in the traditional policy variables of journey time and cost. The Convenience group represents those travelers who might respond more favorably to service characteristics emphasized by dial-a-bus and

Personal Rapid Transit. The Amenity group is a residual group of travelers who consider factors other than those on the economic and convenience dimensions to be most important.

The basic model of mode choice behavior used is the one which had proved to be the best overall explanation of mode choice behavior in previous analysis. Except for relatively minor differences in definition of variables and variables included, this model is similar to models reported by other investigators [10, 11]. The four independent variables used were:

Criteria

Time: Perceived difference in time between the two modes relative to the average perceived time of the journey.
Cost: Perceived difference in cost between the two modes relative to the average perceived cost of the journey.
Segments: Perceived difference between the number of segments (walking, waiting, and riding) associated with the journey by each mode.
Walk/Wait: Perceived time that would be spent walking and waiting if the journey were to be made by train.

The time and cost variables are common to most mode choice studies; the journey segments and walking/waiting time variables are convenience variables that are easily measured.

Effect of attitudes

Since stratifying groups of travelers by reported attitudes holds the effects of attitudes on choice behavior constant, the sensitivity of choices to attitudes can be determined by testing for differences in the logit models between the groups.[4] If the role of reported attitudes is separate from the four explanatory variables discussed earlier, the effect of attitudes should be reflected in different intercept coefficients across the groups—i.e., equivalent to a dummy variable. On the other hand, if the effect of reported

Table 2
LOGIT COEFFICIENTS AND t-VALUES FOR ATTITUDE GROUPS[a]

Group (Sample size)	Coefficient (t-value)				
	Intercept	Segments	Walk/Wait	Time	Cost
Amenity	1.856	−.192	−.032	−.359	−.643
(442)	(5.74)	(3.40)	(4.31)	(0.89)	(3.64)
Convenience	1.259	−.138	−.032	−.819	−.476
(844)	(5.54)	(3.35)	(6.16)	(2.96)	(3.52)
Economic	2.348	−.149	−.028	−2.777	−1.031
(643)	(7.78)	(2.83)	(4.69)	(7.08)	(5.69)

[a]Numbers in parentheses under coefficients are asymptotic t-ratios (in absolute value).

[3]This study was financed by the British Ministry of Transport (now part of the Department of the Environment) as part of a program of research into the value of time. The results and views expressed in this paper are not to be interpreted as the official position of the D.O.E. For details of the study background, see [15].

[4]Estimation across individuals does implicitly involve interpersonal utility comparisons. On the other hand, the random utility model does make explicit use of unobserved differences between individuals in justifying the probabilistic nature of choices.

Table 3

LIKELIHOOD RATIO TESTS OF EQUALITY OF ALL
COEFFICIENTS

	Convenience	Economic
Amenity	16.9[a]	24.7[a]
Convenience		60.6[a]

[a]Critical value for 1% significance level = 15.1.

Illustration

attitudes is caused by interaction with the measured explanatory variables, we should observe differences in estimated slope coefficients between the groups. For example, travelers who reportedly consider economic variables to be most important should have larger and more significant coefficients on such variables as compared to other attitude groups. The rest of this article discusses the results of our tests on these estimated equations, both in the aggregate and when trip purpose and the spatial configuration of the trip were controlled.

DIFFERENCES ACROSS AGGREGATE ATTITUDE GROUPS

Problem

Our purpose in this section is to test across the aggregate attitude groups to determine whether reported attitudes do affect mode choice behavior and whether this effect is separate from or caused by interactions with the measured explanatory variables. Table 2 gives the estimates of the basic logit model of binary choice for each of the attitudinal groups. A simple examination of this table reveals an important pattern: the coefficients of the time and cost variables are both larger and more significant for the group of travelers who report that they make their mode choice decisions on the basis of economic considerations than for the other two attitudinal groups. In order to make more precise statements about these differences, we performed two hypothesis tests. The first test was the likelihood ratio test of the hypothesis

Method

that the entire vector of coefficients is the same across attitude groups; under the null hypothesis, this test statistic is asymptotically distributed as χ^2 with five degrees of freedom.[5] These tests are given in Table 3, and reveal that there are significant differences in the coefficients between the attitude groups. The second test is more revealing as to the cause of these differences. To focus on the economic characteristics of the modes, we tested whether the coefficients of the time and cost variables are the same across the attitude groups without constraining the intercepts or coefficients of the other two variables to be equal. Table 4 gives the results of this test and clearly reveals that a significant part of the differences between the

---

[5]This test is a generalization to logit analysis of the analysis of covariance test between regressions given in [3].

groups is caused by interaction between reported attitudes and the economic variables. In particular, in testing travelers who ranked economic considerations of the trip most important against travelers who considered either convenience or amenities most important, the coefficients of the time and cost variables differed significantly between the groups, verifying the results of the inspection of coefficients. On the other hand, when the convenience and amenity groups were tested against each other, the coefficients of the economic variables did not differ significantly. This implies that the differences between these latter groups are not caused by interaction with the economic variables but rather are caused by differences in the intercepts or in the coefficients of the two measured convenience variables. We then estimated a logit model that constrained the coefficients of the economic variables to be equal across the amenity and convenience groups and tested whether the intercepts and other coefficients varied across these groups (test statistics not shown here). Although this test verified that significant differences remained between the groups, further tests could not attribute these differences solely either to the intercepts or to interactions with the convenience variables. We therefore conclude that interactions with the convenience variables only imperfectly characterize the differences between the convenience and amenity groups.

Results

Interpretation

In summary, our results demonstrate that reported attitudes are a significant influence on the mode choice behavior represented by our estimated model. Furthermore, in the case of travelers who rated the economic characteristics of the mode most important, significant interaction between reported attitudes and measured time and cost variables is clearly revealed. On the other hand, the evidence indicates that the convenience variables used in this study only imperfectly capture the differences between the amenity and convenience groups.

Summary

RELATIONS WITH TRIP PURPOSE AND ORIGIN/DESTINATION

Although our results of the last section are indicative of the importance of reported attitudes in explaining mode choice behavior, further tests on the stability of these results are necessary before we can accept the findings. In particular, previous researchers have found that trip purpose [11] and the spatial configu-

Further tests

Table 4

LIKELIHOOD RATIO TESTS OF EQUALITY OF TIME AND
COST COEFFICIENTS

	Convenience	Economic
Amenity	1.4	21.6[a]
Convenience		23.5[a]

[a]Critical value for 1% significance level = 6.6.

286

Table 5
LIKELIHOOD RATIO TESTS OF EQUALITY OF ALL COEFFICIENTS

Tests Across Attitude Groups, Trip Purpose Held Constant			
	Trip purpose		
Tested attitude groups	Business	Journey to work	Social/ Recreational
Economic vs. amenity	10.0	14.4[a]	9.6
Economic vs. convenience	31.4[b]	18.6[b]	16.2[b]
Amenity vs. convenience	10.1	9.2	5.4

Tests Across Trip Purposes, Reported Attitudes Held Constant			
	Reported attitudes		
Tested trip purpose groups	Economic	Amenity	Convenience
Journey to work vs business	3.4	17.3[b]	14.3[a]
Journey to work vs. social/recreational	13.7[a]	15.6[b]	9.0
Business vs. social/recreational	6.7	8.0	8.1

[a] Critical value for 5% significance level = 11.1.
[b] Critical value for 1% significance level = 15.1.

ration of the trip [16] cause differences in the estimated model of mode choice behavior. It is possible that our results in the last section using aggregated attitude groups may be caused by differences in trip purposes or spatial configurations between the attitude groups (or conversely, findings of differences by trip purposes and spatial configurations may be a result of failure to disaggregate by attitudes). In this section, we disaggregate our tests of the last section by trip purpose and by spatial configuration to test for this possibility. The basic test we perform is again the likelihood ratio test that the vectors of coefficients of the logit model are the same between different data subgroups.

Journey Purposes

Identification

Journeys for three purposes were identified: travel on company business, journey to or from work, and travel for social, recreational, and other purposes.

Differen-tiation

Table 5 reports the results of the tests for equality of coefficients when trip purposes are held constant and when attitudes are held constant. The most interesting comparisons are those tests where the trip purpose is the same for all travelers but their reported attitudes are different.

Method

In these cases, we reject equality of the coefficients three times out of three for the convenience versus economic attitude groups, one out of three times for the amenity versus economic attitude groups, and never for the amenity versus convenience attitude groups.

Conclusion

We therefore conclude that reported economic attitudes significantly affect mode choice behavior as compared to the amenity and convenience groups, but that distinction between these latter two groups may not be necessary.

We also note from Table 5 that when reported attitudes are the same for all travelers but their trip purpose differs, we reject equality of the coefficients two out of three times for the journey to work versus business groups, two out of three times for the journey to work versus social-recreational groups, and never for the business versus social-recreational groups. These results indicate that a valid distinction exists between the journey to work trip and other trips but that the business and social-recreational trips do not appear to be significantly different.

Interpre-tation

Spatial Characteristics of the Trip

Following Watson and Westin [16], trips that had an origin and/or destination in a city center (central trips) were distinguished from trips that neither began nor ended in a city center (noncentral trips). Results of tests for equality of the logit coefficients across groups are given in Table 6.

Differen-tiation

We find that when spatial characteristics of the trip are held constant, we reject equality of the coefficients two out of two times for the convenience versus economic groups, one out of two times for the amenity versus economic groups, and one out of two times for the convenience versus amenity groups. These results confirm that the observed effect of the reported economic attitudes on choice behavior is not caused by differences in spatial characteristics of the trip. Finally, when attitudes are held constant, we reject equality of the coefficients two out of three times for comparisons between central and noncentral trips, supporting the distinction made between these trips.

Interpre-tation

INDEPENDENCE OF ATTITUDES AND MEASURED CHARACTERISTICS

The results of the last two sections indicate that reported attitudes do have a significant effect in determining how travelers will react to the characteristics of the modes. In this section, we wish to show that reported attitudes are independent of the

Transition and explanation

Table 6
LIKELIHOOD RATIO TESTS OF EQUALITY OF ALL COEFFICIENTS

Tests Across Attitude Groups, Spatial Characteristics of Trips Held Constant		
	Spatial characteristics	
Tested attitude groups	Central	Noncentral
Economic vs. amenity	20.0[b]	7.8
Economic vs. convenience	35.4[b]	27.5[b]
Amenity vs. convenience	5.0	16.5[b]

Tests Across Spatial Groups, Reported Attitudes Held Constant		
	Reported attitudes	
Tested spatial groups	Economic	Amenity	Convenience
Central vs. noncentral	11.8[a]	2.8	16.9[b]

[a] Critical value for 5% significance level = 11.1.
[b] Critical value for 1% significance level = 15.1.

Table 7
LIKELIHOOD RATIO TESTS FOR EQUALITY OF
DISTRIBUTIONS OF EXPLANATORY VARIABLES

Tests Across Attitude Groups, Trip Purpose Held Constant

	Trip purpose		
Tested attitude groups	Business	Journey to work	Social/recreational
Economic vs. amenity	26.4[a]	12.1	23.4
Economic vs. convenience	19.3	20.9	19.2
Amenity vs. convenience	21.8	22.4	17.0

Tests Across Trip Purposes, Reported Attitudes Held Constant

	Reported attitudes		
Tested trip purpose groups	Economic	Amenity	Convenience
Journey to work vs. business	18.5	27.1[a]	26.4[a]
Journey to work vs. social/recreational	101.4[b]	57.9[b]	35.3[b]
Business vs. social/recreational	114.8[b]	69.7[b]	81.3[b]

[a]Critical value for 5% significance level = 23.7.
[b]Critical value for 1% significance level = 29.1.

Procedure

Interpreta-tion

perceived values of the other explanatory variables. This implies that it is not possible to distinguish attitude groups by looking at more commonly measured variables; thus, attitudes must be explicitly sampled along with the other variables if they are going to be controlled for in the analysis.

The procedure for testing whether reported attitudes are independent of the other explanatory variables is to see whether the distribution of the explanatory variables differs significantly by attitude groups. The test we use is the test that would be appropriate if the explanatory variables other than attitudes were drawn from a multivariate normal distribution. Although this assumption is somewhat restrictive in the types of variables that can be tested, it appears reasonable for our data set and reduces the statistical problems involved in testing for equality of a four-dimensional distribution. Therefore, we performed likelihood ratio tests of the hypothesis that the mean and covariance matrices of the explanatory variables used in this analysis are identical across attitude groups.[6] Tables 7 and 8 report the results of this test when the data are divided by trip purpose and by spatial characteristics.

In order to interpret these tables, we note from Table 7 that when trip purpose is held constant and we test across attitude groups, equality of the distributions of explanatory variables is rejected only once in nine tests. When attitude groups are held constant and we test across trip purposes, however, equality of the distributions of explanatory variables is rejected

[6]See [7, p.266] for the exact form of this test statistic. As this test is sensitive to data outliers, the data set was subjected to the BMDX72 test [4] for identification and deletion of outliers before applying the test described in the article.

eight out of nine times. Furthermore, Table 8 shows that when the spatial characteristics of the trips are held constant and we test for equality of the distributions of explanatory variables across attitude groups, equality is weakly rejected only twice in six tests. On the other hand, when attitude groups are held constant and we perform the test between the central and noncentral spatial groups, equality of the distributions of explanatory variables is always strongly rejected. We therefore conclude that trip purpose and origin/destination significantly affect the observed distribution of the explanatory variables but that reported attitudes do not, implying that attitude groupings are independent of the distribution of the other explanatory variables.

IMPLICATIONS FOR MARKETING EFFORT

The marketing implications of the results reported earlier are of importance in a number of respects. First, to the demand analyst, we have shown that there does exist a correspondence between the system attributes that people report as important and the behavior revealed by those travelers. For analysis based on our model, attitudinal groups must be separated before estimation in order to take these attitudes into account. On the other hand, if the demand analyst chooses conventional multi-attribute models of attitudes of the type reviewed by Wilkie and Pessemier, our results imply that importance weights should be included.

First inter-pretation

Second, to the transportation planner considering the implementation of new systems, the results are important in identifying segments of the market that will be responsive to these innovations. For example, the results show that with respect to the important dimension of travel time, there is a segment of the market that is particularly responsive to perceived differences in travel time. This is clearly revealed by examining the aggregate elasticities of population

Second inter-pretation

Illustration

Table 8
LIKELIHOOD RATIO TESTS FOR EQUALITY OF
DISTRIBUTIONS OF EXPLANATORY VARIABLES

Tests Across Attitude Groups, Spatial Characteristics of Trips Held Constant

	Spatial characteristics	
Tested attitude groups	Central	Noncentral
Economic vs. amenity	33.3[b]	19.7
Economic vs. convenience	38.0[b]	17.8
Amenity vs. convenience	17.9	21.9

Tests Across Spatial Groups, Reported Attitudes Held Constant

	Reported attitudes		
Tested spatial groups	Economic	Amenity	Convenience
Central vs. noncentral	237.4[b]	156.1[b]	293.5[b]

[a]Critical value for 5% significance level = 23.7.
[b]Critical value for 1% significance level = 29.1.

288

JOURNAL OF MARKETING RESEARCH, AUGUST 1975

Table 9
AGGREGATE ELASTICITIES

	Variable	
Group	Time	Cost
Amenity	−.04	−.07
Convenience	−.14	−.06
Economic	−.24	−.10

*Explana-
tion*

mode split with respect to time and cost given in Table 9. These elasticities are defined as the percentage of the total population of travelers who would switch modes because of a 1% change in the population mean of the explanatory variable; for a detailed discussion of their computation, see [17]. Looking at Table 9, we find that the elasticity of mode split with respect to changes in perceived travel time is six times greater for the economic group as compared to the amenity group and also double that of the convenience group. Furthermore, for the economic group, aggregate mode choice is almost two and one-half times as responsive to changes in perceived travel time as to changes in perceived cost. This implies that for this segment of the market, which comprised one-third of our sample, reductions in travel time can be accompanied with somewhat higher costs and still increase the demand for the service.

*Third
inter-
pretation*

Finally, our results show the planner that market research efforts should be extended to include attitude surveys toward system characteristics as well as information on journey time, cost, purpose, and destination. Failure to take the attitudinal dimension into account will lead to the use of inappropriate models for demand predictions and hence to transportation investment resources being mis-allocated.

CONCLUSIONS

Thesis

The analysis of this article demonstrates that travelers' attitudes toward the characteristics of transport modes are important in determining their mode choice behavior. We have distinguished at least two separate groups of travelers in terms of how their attitudes influence their choice behavior. These groups are travelers who report the economic characteristics of the transport mode to be most important and travelers who report the convenience or amenity characteristics of the mode to be most important. The importance of traditionally used economic variables in determining mode choice behavior is then found to be critically influenced by the attitudes the travelers report. Travelers concerned about economic characteristics of the modes are shown to be particularly sensitive to differences in the perceived times and costs of the modes. On the other hand, travelers concerned about the convenience and amenity characteristics of the modes are not as responsive to differences in perceived times

*Explana-
tion*

*Summary
of results*

and costs and the use of economic variables in describing their behavior must be questioned. Finally, reported attitudes appear to be independent of our measured explanatory variables.

Studies of mode choice behavior have tended to neglect the role of travelers' attitudes in determining choice behavior because of measurement problems. Difficulty in measuring variables, however, is not a sufficient reason for ignoring them if their effect is important. By directly distinguishing attitude groups, we have been able to demonstrate their importance in determining choices and ultimately their importance in providing answers to important policy questions.

*Restate-
ment of
the thesis*

REFERENCES

*Numbered
list*

1. Anderson, T. W. *Introduction to Multivariate Statistical Analysis.* New York: Wiley, 1958.
2. Berkson, Joseph. "Application of the Logistic Function to Bio-Assay," *Journal of the American Statistical Association*, 39 (September 1944), 357-65.
3. Chow, Gregory C. "Tests of Equality between Sets of Coefficients in Two Linear Regressions," *Econometrica*, 28 (July 1960), 591-605.
4. Dixon, W. J., ed. *Biomedical Computer Programs, X-Series Supplement.* Berkeley: University of California Press, 1970.
5. Fishbein, Martin. "A Behavior Theory Approach to the Relations Between Beliefs about an·Object and the Attitude toward the Object," in Martin Fishbein, ed., *Readings in Attitude Theory and Measurement.* New York: Wiley, 1967, 389-99.
6. Hartgen, David T. and George H. Tanner." Investigations of the Effect of Traveler Attitudes in a Model of Mode-Choice Behavior," *Highway Research Record*, No. 369 (1971), 1-14.
7. Kendall, Maurice G. and Alan Stuart. *The Advanced Theory of Statistics*, Vol. 3. London: Griffen, 1966.
8. Kotler, Philip and Gerald Zaltman. "Social Marketing: An Approach to Planned Social Change," *Journal of Marketing*, 35 (July 1971), 3-12.
9. Luce, R. Duncan and Patrick Suppes. "Preference, Utility, and Subjective Probability," in R. Duncan Luce, Robert R. Bush, and Eugene Galanter, eds., *Handbook of Mathematical Psychology*, Volume III. New York: Wiley, 1965, 249-410.
10. McFadden, Daniel. "Conditional Logit Analysis of Qualitative Choice Behavior," in Paul Zarembka, ed., *Frontiers in Econometrics.* New York: Academic Press, 1974, 105-42.
11. McGillivray, Robert G. "Binary Choice of Urban Transport Mode in the San Francisco Bay Region," *Econometrica*, 40 (September 1972), 827-48.
12. Rosenberg, Milton J. "Cognitive Structure and Attitudinal Affect," *Journal of Abnormal and Social Psychology*, 53 (November 1956), 367-72.
13. Sherret, Alistair and James P. Wallace. "Estimating the Relative Importance of Product Attributes," presented to the Conference on Urban Travel Demand Forecasting, Williamsburg, 1972.
14. Walker, Strother H. and David B. Duncan. "Estimation of the Probability of an Event as a Function of Several

Independent Variables," *Biometrika*, 54 (March 1967), 167-79.

15. Watson, Peter L. *The Value of Time: Behavioral Models of Mode Choice*. Lexington: Heath, 1974.

16. _____ and Richard B. Westin. "Transferability of Disaggregate Mode Choice Models," *Regional Science and Urban Economics*, forthcoming.

17. Westin, Richard B. "Predictions from Binary Choice Models," *Journal of Econometrics*, 2 (May 1974), 1-16.

18. Wilkie, William L. and Edgar A. Pessemier. "Issues in Marketing's Use of Multi-Attribute Attitude Models," *Journal of Marketing Research*, 10 (November 1973), 428-441.

(Courtesy American Marketing Association for *Journal of Marketing Research* [1])

The author of the next formal report includes an unlabeled abstract, introduction, the report itself, conclusions, and a numbered list of references.

E-7B

The Case for Stressing Proposals
in Technical Writing Courses

DOLORES M. LANDREMAN

Columbus Laboratories

Battelle Memorial Institute

Abstract

Many teachers of technical writing apparently do not appreciate the critical role that proposals play in the technical communications cycle. Consequently, in designing their courses they give far too little attention to proposal analysis and preparation. Proposals have a pervasive influence in technical communications; they are the foundation upon which all other technical communications are based. Teachers should help students to (1) appreciate the central significance of proposals in technical communications, (2) form a realistically broad concept of what a proposal is, and (3) develop the insights and skills necessary for preparing effective proposals.

INTRODUCTION

Background of the problem

Many new courses in technical writing are being offered to college students planning careers in science and engineering, and many English faculty members whose previous teaching assignments have been related to literature or general composition are being asked to design and teach such courses. However, if what I've read gives an accurate picture, and if the teachers with whom I've talked are representative, it seems to me that many teachers—even some with considerable experience in the teaching of technical writing—have far too little appreciation of the critical role that proposals play in the technical communications cycle. Consequently, they fail to give appropriate stress to proposals in the design and presentation of their courses.

If there really is a pretty general lack of understanding by technical writing teachers of the pervasive importance of proposals, many students may fail to develop needed insights concerning their future on-the-job technical communication challenges. This article presents some of the reasons for giving greater attention to proposals in college technical writing courses. Examples are given from the business and industrial world of actual proposal preparation requirements, and suggestions are made for class discussions and activities related to proposals.

Purpose statement

Parts of the report

THE PERVASIVE IMPORTANCE OF PROPOSALS

Thesis

Proposals are not just another type of technical document. They are of *central* significance. Their influence is felt throughout the technical communications cycle. They are the springboard for all technical activity, the foundation upon which all other technical documents are based:

reports, manuals, brochures, journal articles, books, patent applications, etc. The teacher of technical writing should relate the proposal to all of these. If this is done competently, students will be helped in acquiring a realistically broad concept of technical communications.

Explanation

Figure 1 illustrates the critical role of proposals in the technical communications cycle. Of course, the individual writer might enter into the cycle at any stage. However, as shown in the figure, from the overall standpoint all technical activity starts with either an idea or a problem. These stimulate the preparation of either a proposal or a request for proposal (RFP). The request for proposal is intended, of course, to stimulate the preparation of a proposal (or several competing proposals).

To illustrate, initially a scientist or an engineer might have an idea that he thinks could benefit mankind if it were properly exploited. But, he needs funds for further research: to support his own additional allocation of time, for needed experimental apparatus and materials, for travel expenses, for salaries of laboratory assistants, and for many other essentials that he himself cannot provide. Before anything can happen, he must prepare a convincing proposal concerning the benefits to be derived from the research project he envisions. Then he must submit this proposal to some individual or organization with both the necessary discretionary funds and a potential interest in bringing the idea to fruition. If the proposal is accepted, work can begin.

Example

On the other hand, an industrial organization or a government agency might have a pressing technical problem for which a solution is needed. In this case, someone must be found who has the appropriate education and experience—and the willingness—to pursue the solution. The needed talent must be identified, either within the organization or somewhere else. Consequently, some type of request for proposal must be prepared and distributed to likely solvers of the problem. The hope is that some individual or group with suitable skills will respond to the request with an acceptable offer to seek the solution—that is, with a proposal.

Example

In any event, work doesn't just start. A technical report doesn't spring from its own base. Nor do any other technical documents.

Even in the case of a single-author professional journal article, there are generally two types of proposals involved. First, the subject matter of the article can be traced back to some idea or problem. Otherwise the article is pointless. Many journal articles represent, essentially, proposals to the world at large. That is true, for example, of this article. But there is also a sort of inbred proposal involved. That is, initially the would-be author proposes to himself that he do the work necessary (e.g., survey the state of the art) to produce something of value (i.e.,

Scope

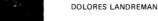

DOLORES LANDREMAN

4455 Kenfield Road
Columbus, OH 43224

Battelle Memorial Institute. Senior Communications Advisor, Proposal Center Columbus Labs.

Member and past sectretary, Central Ohio Chapter, STC. Chairperson, Special Projects Committee.

B.A., English, Lawrence University. M.A., English, University of Minnesota.

Publications: "Technical Writing Style Guide," *Ohio Academy of Science, 1972.* "A New Look at Outlining," *Proceedings, ITCC, 1974.* "English Teachers and Advancement of Science and Engineering," *The English Journal, Mar 1972.*

E-7B

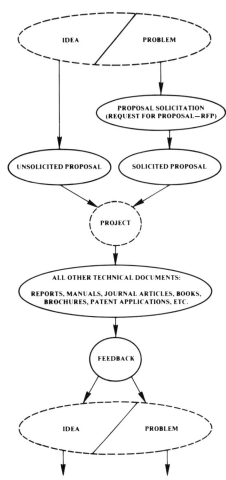

**FIGURE 1. CRITICAL ROLE OF PROPOSALS
IN THE TECHNICAL COMMUNICATIONS CYCLE**

something publishable). He reponds to this proposal to himself with a decision to go ahead, and he implements this decision by allocating part of his time and energies for the needed investigation and writing. Even such a situation involves (mostly by implication, of course) all the essential elements of any proposal. Teachers should insist that proposals written by their students also include all essential proposal elements. These will be discussed later. Students will learn best if they are required to include them explicitly.

It should be pointed out to students that proposals are sometimes presented in disguise—often incorporated, for example, in truncated form as recommendations in reports. That is why it is very important for students to grasp the **concept** of the technical proposal. A proposal with too many layers of disguise might not be able to do its job effectively. Surprisingly, in the "Documentation Pyramid" recently described by Joseph Rice and John Colby in *Technical Communications*[1], the proposal is not included as a separate type of technical document. The authors do make reference to a report that *contains* a proposal, and they also call attention to the need for selling ideas. It is not clear why they did not include the proposal; perhaps this was an oversight? However, teachers should stress, not ignore, proposals as independent, separate documents in designing their courses.

To omit consideration of proposals in a technical communications course seems to me to be presenting a course without a proper rationale. In fact, I believe that it is virtually impossible to design a truly effective course (one that prepares students for successfully meeting their future technical communication challenges) without serious consideration of proposals.

Students should be so sensitized to the ramifications of the proposal situation that they will recognize what is going on when they make proposals—as inevitably they will. Then they will be able to make strong, clear proposals, regardless of format.

HELPING STUDENTS TO FORM AN ACCURATE CONCEPT OF TECHNICAL PROPOSALS

Teachers should help students to form an accurate (therefore, broad) concept of just what technical proposals are. Proposals can be oral or written, formal or informal, solicited or unsolicited, competitive or non-competitive. Although some students may have presented informal oral proposals to some of their science teachers concerning projects they planned to undertake, it is probable that neither these students nor their science teachers gave much thought to the many subtle implications of that communication situation. Probably they just came to a reasonably clear understanding concerning the work entailed and the report to be submitted at the end of the term. In some cases the proposal might have taken a simple written form: a thesis sentence or a hypothesis paragraph. Maybe a brief outline of the planned project work was required. But it's unlikely that great care was taken to ensure that all the essential proposal elements had been incorporated in the sentence, the paragraph, or the outline. *Detailed definition of proposals*

All complete proposals have common elements, either stated or implied. In the business world, the decision maker who authorizes work on the basis of an incomplete (or vague) proposal does so at his peril. The example below of an informal, oral, solicited, noncompetitive proposal incorporates all essential proposal elements either explicitly or by implied reference to the RFP. The informal RFP that stimulated the proposal fulfills all RFP requirements; it stimulated a proposal adequate for decision making. Also shown below is the negotiation/contract aspect of the overall situation.

Request for Proposal:
  Supervisor: "John, do you think you can have this new machine back in working order, at a reasonable cost, before plant start-up next Monday?" *Example*

Proposal:
  Engineer: "I think so, Tom. But we'll have to dismantle the whole back end. I'll need a welder, an electrician, and about $500 of copper tubing and $50 of other supplies. We'll have to work on the weekend. Will you O.K. about 30 hours overtime pay?"

Negotiation/Contract:
  Supervisor: "O.K., go ahead. But when you get in there, if it looks as though cost is going to go much beyond that, call me. Might be better to just ship it back to the manufacturer."

The essential proposal elements included above, directly or indirectly, are statements concerning: the problem, expected results (objectives or benefits), work to be done (approach), responsibilities (management), manpower and material requirements (costs), schedule, and qualifications of the workers. A formal written proposal wouldn't contain much more, although undoubtedly all statements would be elaborated upon considerably. *Elements*

An excellent article on how to prepare good proposals was written by Ernest M. Allen, "Why are Research Grant Applications Disapproved?"[2] Although the article is fairly old, the points it makes are quite valid today. On the basis of a survey that Allen made of organizations having funds available for grants to researchers, he divided the reasons for rejection of applications into four general categories: problem, procedure, personnel, and miscellaneous. The miscellaneous area included, for example, difficulties related to management, budgeting, communications, and other nontechnical considerations.

E-7B

**HELPING STUDENTS TO UNDERSTAND THE
SEVERAL FUNCTIONS OF PROPOSALS**

*Purpose
of
proposals*

Students should also be helped to realize that proposals have several functions. First of all, of course, they are selling documents. This fact is hard for many technical people to accept. They resist the idea that their insights and expertise must be sold and bought, and that technical progress depends to a great extent on effective selling. Nonetheless, this is true. Teachers must present proposals for what they are basically: selling tools. And they ought to stress some of the things that all good salesmen know about what it takes to sell. For example, teachers might do well to discuss with their students the five basic steps in the selling process as given by Percy Whiting: (1) attention, (2) interest, (3) conviction, (4) desire, and (5) close.[3]

A proposal functions as the basis for an agreement, and a written proposal can actually become incorporated into a contractual document by reference. Thus it can function as a record of the understanding reached. In such a case it also has legal significance. The wording of a proposal can assume great importance during the project or at its conclusion if a disagreement should arise concerning such things as the scope of a study, the dates on which reports are due, or authorized expenditures.

*Explana-
tion*

The proposal can and should function as a management tool. It contains a statement of objectives which can be used to keep the entire project on target. It contains a schedule which can be used to assess progress toward goals with respect to time. It gives guidance for allocations of manpower and other resources. It contains a budget. It describes project team organization—usually via an organization chart—which can be used in resolving questions of leadership and specific responsibilities. A proposal can function very well as the touchstone by which supervisors judge individual or group performance. It can reveal when and how corrective action must be taken. Students might well be encouraged to read a book on management techniques as part of their preparation for classroom discussion of proposals.

Restatement

A well-constructed proposal also simplifies report writing. Essentially, a report must provide answers—yes or no— about whether the anticipations or promises of the proposal have been fulfilled. A reasonable report outline is generally inherent in the proposal Table of Contents.

**HELPING STUDENTS TO SEE PROPOSALS
AS REPRESENTING COMMITMENTS**

*Reason
for
importance*

A basic reason that proposals are such important documents is that they represent commitments. Imaginatively directed study of proposals can help students comprehend how seriously the business and scientific worlds regard commitments made. People depend on them. Progress reflects whether they are met or not. Careers can be advanced or damaged by commitments met or commitments disregarded.

Proposals are regular fountains of commitments. They commit to objectives, to schedules, to allocations of resources, to procedures. They commit to submission of reports and other deliverables on time!

Explanation

Teachers should insist that student proposals contain specific schedules that tell how the planned work will be paced and when it will be completed. A special point should be made that the schedule should allow, specifically, for adequate report preparation time (including typing!). Apparently one of the most difficult things that many technical people have to learn on the job is realistic budgeting of time. Some, even if they do learn to make reasonable projections of time required for such things as laboratory tests and construction of prototypes, seem unable to calculate how long it will take to prepare a report. Generally, they grossly underestimate.

Industry and Government are notoriously time conscious because time equates rather conspicuously with money. If needed reports or other documents are not delivered as scheduled, the ripple effect can become a tidal wave effect, knocking dependent activities behind schedule almost *ad infinitum* and causing cost over-runs, loss of customers, and all sorts of frustration and embarrassment.

If student proposals required at the beginning of a technical writing course contain schedules for planned projects, with fixed dates for the submission of reports, the teacher who accepts any late reports without imposing drastic penalties, and without vociferous protests and lectures, is not doing the students any favor. Later on their bosses will be quite positive when they discuss the evils of failure to follow through on commitments, including the meeting of report deadlines. Terminations of employment are known to follow from the breaking of commitments as expressed in proposals.

WRITTEN PROPOSAL FORMAT

Although proposal format depends greatly upon the selling situation involved, some general guidelines for the preparation of written proposals can be given to students. Students might be told that the thesis statement for almost any proposal can be very simple, something like this: "I (we) propose to *(solve a problem or provide a benefit)* and you should support my (our) efforts with *(resources needed—i.e., time/cost)* because *(qualifications for competent work on the problem).*

Organization

Most proposals should be organized on a modified journalistic inverted-pyramid pattern. The intended audience is, like the journalist's, a busy one, and if interest is not captured immediately other duties (or a competing proposal) might get the major share of the limited audience time available. Informal written proposals are often in business letter or interdepartmental memorandum format. Formal written proposals often follow a pattern somewhat like that shown in Figure 2.

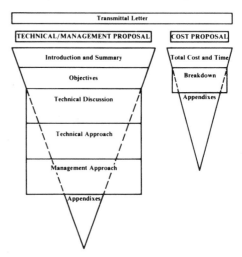

**FIGURE 2. TYPICAL STRUCTURE OF
FORMAL WRITTEN PROPOSALS**

Procedure

Perhaps the greatest technical proposal challenge in America is faced by those responding to RFP's* issued by the Federal Government. Although not many students are likely to be called upon to manage the design and production of such proposals—at least not early in their careers—class analysis of the generally stringent requirements for these proposals can provide many insights. If the teacher could acquire several representatve RFP's (perhaps by writing to some major Government agency that sponsors many research programs, such as the Department of Transportation), class discussions could benefit tremendously. The teacher might also obtain copies of the special Federal Government daily newspaper, the *Commerce Business Daily,* which contains announcements of the planned release of RFP's and other information of interest to those who market to the Government.

Government employees responsible for the writing of RFP's, as well as those who must evaluate the proposals that they stimulate, have learned a great deal over the years about what it takes in an RFP to elicit responsible proposals that are responsive to the needs of the Government. They have also identified some of the things that make proposal evaluation easy or hard. Also, they are strongly motivated to improve their skills in writing RFP's and proposal evaluation criteria, because they know from experience how much frustration and what costly delays can result when Government contract awards are challenged by unsuccessful bidders. They try to be extremely precise in the language they use. To simplify comparative evaluation of competitive proposals, some agencies even include in their RFP's suggested or mandatory

---

*Under some circumstances IFB's (Invitation for Bid) or RFQ's (Request for Quotation) are issued.

E-7B

proposal outlines. The discussion of individual proposal sections that follows is based on a brief analysis of proposal outlines provided in RFP's issued recently by several Government agencies.

Typically, proposals to the Government are transmitted as attachments to formal transmittal letters.* All estimated costs must be isolated in a separable proposal section or a separate volume. This is required so that technical evaluation can be made independently, without cost considerations entering into initial assessment of proposal acceptability. Costs are considered only after the technical and management portions of the proposal have been judged to be "within the zone of consideration". Large proposals are often presented in separate Technical, Management, and Cost Volumes.

In general, each major section of the proposal has a definite function to perform, a specific segment of the overall message to convey. However, teachers should stress that each proposal should be treated as a unique document, with content and organization determined by the selling situation and the information needs of the audience addressed.

The following paragraphs contain highly simplified descriptions of the ordinary contents of the typical major proposal sections as shown in Figure 2. This discussion refers primarily to large Government proposals; however, some large industrial organizations seem to be adopting elements of Federal procurement procedures for their own major programs, and they sometimes make requirements that are almost as stringent.

As stated previously, students probably need not expect to be shouldered with the primary responsibility for a major proposal very early in their professional careers. In fact, they may never enter into the technical communications cycle (Figure 1) at the formal written proposal stage. However, they really should know what proposals are all about. Then they will be able to handle various proposal-type situations intelligently, as Engineer John did in the little dialog we listened to a while back. Engineer John knew what information Decision-Maker Tom needed—and so he put it all into his informal oral proposal.

The following description of some typical major sections in proposals to the Government is offered as a "blast-off pad" for what I hope will be some stimulating class discussions.

Introduction and Summary

Sometimes the Introduction and Summary are treated as separate sections, but they can be combined.

The Introduction must state exactly what is being proposed; that is, what problem is to be attacked and what solution is anticipated. It must also provide any needed general background information, such as results of previous efforts to solve the problem. The qualifications of the proposer to handle the work must be indicated. The Introduction is the primary sales section of the proposal, but every section should be designed to carry some portion of the sales message—or at least to reinforce it.

The Summary gives an overall view of the proposed work—the procedures to be followed, possible difficulties and how they may be handled, alternatives that will be considered, the tasks or phases into which the work will be divided, the bidder's qualifications, the overall management plan, etc. Essentially, it is the proposal in brief.

The busy reader should be able to stop after reading the Introduction and Summary and make at least a tentative decision, with reasonable confidence, concerning what action to take. Together, the Introduction and the Summary should include the technical/management equivalents of the journalist's five W's: Who, What, Where, When, and Why (How).

---

*Government RFP's on competitive procurements include a specified date and time for submission of proposals, and unless there is some mitigating circumstance, late proposals are returned to the senders unopened. Acceptance of a late proposal could be interpreted as an unjustified advantage given to one of the competitors. Teachers can hardly overemphasize the general need for promptness, especially in dealings with Government agencies.

Objectives

The Objectives section should state, in unambiguous language, exactly what the outcome of the proposed project is expected to be (the "deliverables"). What will be supplied after the project has been completed? Will it be a written report? Detailed engineering drawings of some new equipment? A demonstration model? A computer program? Deliverables should be described in the most concrete terms feasible, but language should be carefully chosen because the Objectives section is perhaps the most significant section from a legal standpoint.

Technical Discussion (Background)

The contents of this section and how it is organized depend on the particular technical situation, of course. Assumptions, difficulties foreseen, scope of planned investigations, and other such matters of technical significance should be discussed in suitable detail. For example, if the proposal relates to the design of a new mechanical system, this section might include discussions of possible computer-aided design synthesis, the need for interfacing with other machinery, alternative configurations to be considered, potential safety problems, descriptions of off-the-shelf equipment to be incorporated, weight/cost/reliability tradeoff possibilities, the need for retraining operators, maintenance requirements, and countless other considerations.

Technical Approach (Technical Procedure)

This section tells how things will be done and why they will be done that way. Often the discussion is organized in terms of steps or tasks. If any experimental equipment must be built or purchased, it is described. If specimens are to be examined, their characteristics are discussed and sometimes pictures or sketches are provided. Methods for ensuring quality control or statistical validity are described. Again, the particular situation governs what is included.

Management Approach (Project Control)

This section describes how the project will be managed. Usually three important parts of this section are the team organization chart, the "work breakdown structure" (WBS), and the planned schedule of work.

The organization chart shows who the project manager is; it might also show who the various task leaders are, who will act in an advisory or consultant capacity, who will provide such things as fabrication support.

The WBS—that is, the division of work, the specifics of planned manpower allocations—is of great interest to proposal evaluators, especially for large, complex, long-term projects. It can tell a great deal about the proposer's understanding of the magnitude and complexity of the problem. The WBS is often presented in tabular form.

The schedule might be shown in a very simple form or in great detail. Although student proposals are not likely to be so complicated as to require more than a simple schedule chart, teachers should discuss briefly such broadly used terms as PERT (Program Evaluation and Review Technique), CPM (Critical Path Method), Gantt charts, and milestone charts. These are all devices used in controlling progress, expenditures, etc. Students shouldn't be surprised later by such terms.

An important consideration is how the project manager derives his authority. What access does he have to top management? How will he control quality of performance? What corrective action will he be able to take if work falls behind schedule? How will conflicts be resolved when, for example, needed special equipment is in high demand by managers of other projects?

E-7B

Appendixes

Many different things might be presented in appendixes. There should be specific reference to each appendix in the main text of the proposal. Appendixes might contain, for example, extensive tabulations of laboratory or field data that are summarized in the text, the derivation of equations used in the text, detailed descriptions of procedures or equipment to be used, an elaboration of the proposer's claims about qualifications to do the work proposed, such as resumes of intended project staff members. An excellent class exercise would be the writing of *professional* biographies—from the *sales*, not chronological standpoint. Such biographies should emphasize personal qualifications for handling some specific technical task. A scientist or engineer new on the job could very well be asked to write such an "input" for a large proposal. Students should be encouraged to select appendix material first for their proposals, before they outline the main text. This will cut down on the later need for restructuring and rewriting.[4]

Cost Proposal

The cost proposal does much more than tell what the cost of the proposed project will be: it also reveals (as do, for example, the work schedule and the WBS) a lot about the proposer's understanding of the magnitude and complexity of the problem being addressed.

The cost proposal should include not only a total figure, but also an appropriate breakdown. Major cost elements might be man-hours (separated into professional staff, nonprofessional staff, consultants, etc.), equipment use charges (e.g., computer time), materials for construction, expendable materials, travel expenses, etc.

Costs might also be broken down in terms of project phases or tasks. Sometimes estimated expenditures per month or some other accounting period are shown in graphic form. This enables proposal evaluators to see quickly at what point(s) costs will be greatest.

In Government proposals, cost figures are usually presented on a specified standard form, the text of the proposal being supplementary paragraphs of summary or explanation. Sometimes other miscellaneous information of contractual interest is provided such as statements concerning the firm's compliance with equal employment opportunity regulations, its pertinent safety provisions, or its method of calculating overtime pay.

Again, students need not expect to be given responsibility, immediately, for calculating costs on major projects. But, they should become sensitive to costing problems and prepared to figure costs for any aspects of projects for which they have personal responsibility.

SUMMARY OF THE CASE

Conclusion

The case for stressing proposals in technical writing classes rests squarely on their fundamental importance, as indicated in Figure 1. Technical progress depends on selling, and the proposal is the basic vehicle for the sales message.

The student need not expect, under ordinary circumstances, to be required to write a major formal proposal as soon as he begins his professional career. But he could be asked (or might want to volunteer) to write an informal proposal concerning a project of minor significance. More likely he will be asked to make a contribution—such as a resume describing his personal qualifications for handling some aspect of a proposed task—to a proposal that a senior colleague is responsible for preparing. Then, the insights he gained in his technical writing course will enable him to see his limited contribution as a truly important component in meeting the overall technical communications challenge imposed by his organization's mission or goals. He will be able to write effectively, whatever the contribution requested. And also, because he understands the basic proposal *concept*, he will be skillful in writing disguised proposals, such as the recommendations sections of reports. He will be able to do his part in ensuring that all types of proposals fit neatly into the "Documentation Pyramid"[1] of his organization.

The preparation of major proposals is generally supervised by proposal specialists or by senior people or members of the executive staff because the success or failure of such proposals can have tremendous implications for the success or failure of the whole organization. The preparation of every major proposal (successful or not) represents the expenditure of substantial funds. And, every unsuccessful proposal represents, essentially, unrecoverable costs. (Indirect recovery, as through increased overhead charges distributed to other accounts makes customer services more costly, and if the burden becomes too great, customers can be lost.) Career advancement within an organization can be directly related to an appreciation of the important role of proposals and an ability to produce winners—and not only winners, but winners that represent opportunities to strengthen the organization.

The magnitude of proposal preparation costs on a national basis can be grossly assessed from consideration of costs associated with many of the competitive proposals prepared in response to Government RFP's. Conservatively speaking, the cost of a 100-page (relatively small) proposal would be about $20,000, depending on the technical complexity and the management requirements of the proposed program. If 15 organizations (a reasonable number) respond to an RFP, a total cost of $300,000 is represented. And only one proposal will be selected as the winner!

Teachers of technical writing have a serious responsibility to prepare the aspiring scientists and engineers who come to their classes for effective communication on the job. One of their greatest services can be in stressing the importance of proposals—for the advancement of careers and for the advancement of science and technology.

REFERENCES

(1) Colby, John and Rice, Joseph A., "The Documentation Pyramid: A Better Paper Clip", *Technical Communications*, First Quarter 1978, p. 4.
(2) Allen, Ernest M., "Why Are Research Grant Applications Disapproved?", *Science*, November 1960, p. 1532.
(3) Whiting, Percy H., *The 5 Great Rules of Selling*, McGraw-Hill Book Company, Inc., New York, 1957.
(4) Landreman, Dolores M., "A New Look at Outlining—The LSN/SN Approach", *Proceedings 21st International Technical Communications Conference*, May 15-18, 1974, St. Louis, Mo., p. 88.

Numbered list

(Courtesy Society for Technical Communication [2])

In the following informative formal report, a technical writing student also made several choices. He wrote a title page, memo to his advisor, table of contents that included both roman numerals and capital letter entries, a separate list of figures and tables, and an abstract. He placed the conclusions next, then the introduction, body of the report, appendix, and references.

When you have completed your evaluation, please return this paper to my technical writing instructor who will then grade it for style, format, handling of figures and tables, and the reference system.

PILE DRIVING RIGS AND HAMMERS

For Technical Writing 301

by
Fred Strasser

November 15, 19—

CONTENTS

LIST OF FIGURES AND TABLES

To: Professor Gene Russell, Construction Technology
From: Fred Strasser
Subject: Formal Report for Technical Writing 301
Date: November 15, 19—

Identification   Here is the formal report I prepared in Technical Writing 301. It is the purpose of this *Purpose* paper to present information on the types and uses of pile driving rigs and hammers. The operating procedures for different types of hammers will also be discussed.

Sources of   I have found several sources of information. *information* Some textbooks on foundations have chapters or parts of chapters devoted to explanations of pile driving rigs and hammers. A class in "Fundamentals of Soil Mechanics" gave much information. *The Manual of Structural Design and Engineering Solutions,* which you loaned me on October 28, contained information and tables on the subject; some of the tables I Xeroxed and put into the paper.

Appreciation   I appreciate your approval of my outline on October 28, the advice you gave me on possible sources of information, and your willingness to grade this formal report for technical content.

ABSTRACT

Listing of main points of report   This report explains the different types of pile driving rigs used in driving operations and the driving hammers. Different types of hammers are described; operating procedures are analyzed and some advantages and disadvantages of each are presented. Tables showing different hammer characteristics and selections for a given job are included in the appendix.

CONCLUSIONS

Types   Pile driving equipment, in the form of rigs and hammers, represents a fast-changing and fast-growing field. The rig that carries the lead and hammer is, in most cases, a crane of some type. It is more mobile and any company that does any major construction work usually owns one. The crane is used only on land with made-up steam units mounted on barges for driving in water. Unique rigs are manufactured before the job is begun to fit the particular locale. These are designed by an engineer to meet the specifications of that one specific job.

Acquisition   A lead and hammer of any type can usually be rented by a contractor so he will not have so much money invested in a piece of machinery he will not use that often. This rental system also gives him the option of doing the work himself, thus saving money on a subcontractor and getting the work done on time.

Importance   The reason pile driving is becoming so popular and a trade of the specialist is that the soil stratum is so complex. Little was known previously about how soils reacted to the moisture, weight, and drying out. It has become a very scientific and expensive operation, so now only companies with a large amount of capital to invest in equipment and personnel can afford to enter the pile driving field. The so-called ideal building sites have already been used. Current available sites are those often formerly considered to be poor; foundations must be tailor-made to fit the soil stratum. Thus, a number of different type rigs and hammers have been designed.

INTRODUCTION

Informal introduction
Background information
Indication of organizational pattern

There are several different types of rigs, but the current trend is toward the crane with the lead and hammer connected to it. Pile hammers come in various shapes and forms. The types are either impact or vibratory, and each has various weight categories. The impact group of hammers consists of the drop, single-acting, double-acting, differential, and diesel, with the double-acting and diesel being the most widely used. The vibratory hammer is of one basic type but comes in various sizes. The hammer for each job is selected according to set formulas and tables

Justification   based on existing conditions. Thus, the contractor needs to know and understand each rig and hammer type so he can select the one most feasible for the job.

PILE DRIVING RIGS

Roman numeral entry from the outline

The rig is the apparatus that is the base for the operation of the pile driving work. The rig can consist of some type of crane with a leader, the steel framework for the hammer, and a hammer,

Definition   or it can comprise a framework and platform to support the engine, boiler, air compressor, winches, leader, and hammer. All types of driv-

ing rigs must have sufficient weight and be able to lift several tons in excess of the pile, hammer, and mandrel in case a pile has to be pulled for inspection.

Capital letter entry from the outline

Cost

"The equipment necessary to engage in pile driving operations requires a considerable amount of capital investment by the owner" (1).

Initial investment   The amount of the investment in large equipment and hammers prevents competition from small companies. To make the investment of driving

Operational costs   rigs, hammers, and crews show a profit, the company must contract jobs all over the country and move the operations from site to site. Crews are expensive to maintain but essential for proper setup and operation of driving equipment. Improper setup can create fuller consolidation of packing material in the driving cap, tilting of the driving cap, and nonaxial blows causing head damage and reduced efficiency.

Capital letter entry from the outline

Types

"Spool-roller pile driving rigs roll sideways, backward, and forward with a flanged spool running on two 10-inch longitudinal pipes. Pen-

Technical description of rigs   dulum rigs or batter leader rigs drive piles at an angle as well as vertically and are very often mounted on barges, railroad cars, and trucks" (2). This type of rig is popular in driving piles for trestles or for bridges. The turntable rigs or swiveling rigs are most useful in locations where a considerable number of piles are to be driven in a small area. A pile can be driven anywhere within the area reached by the leads, when the rig swings from side to side, rolls backward, moves forward, or slides sideways. "The tilt rigs are very economical for large compact operations because they can be rolled forward, backward, or slid sideways on long cross-pipe rollers" (2). This movement is accomplished by pulling on cables attached to drums that are hooked to the platform and powered by steam or air.

Description of cranes   Locomotive, caterpillar, and whirley cranes are used for pile driving when they are equipped with a boom for handling pile leads, steam hammers, drums, or winches. The locomotive crane operates off a special flatcar and the steel leads, mounted on a turntable, fold up for railway clearances. The cranes operating as floating pile drivers do so off barges that are towed, then anchored during driving.

PILE DRIVING HAMMERS

Roman numeral entry from the outline

There are various types of hammers available to an owner and more than one type will work on any given pile. Hammers operate on two dif-

Transition paragraph introducing hammer types to be analyzed   ferent methods: one is the impact type that drops on the pile top driving it downward; second is the vibrating type that, with its own weight, vibrates the pile downward.

Capital letter entry

Arabic number entry

Description

Procedure

Evaluation

Impact Hammers

Drop hammers. A drop hammer is a special shaped weight that is hoisted or raised to a predetermined height by a rope or cable connected to a winch driven by a gasoline engine. The winch is trigger released thus tripping the cable and allowing it to unwind, letting the hammer drop freely and strike the top of the pile. Blows are produced as rapidly as the hammer or weight can be raised and released. "The weight or force of the hammer should be about equal to the weight of the pile to be driven" (7). This type of hammer is cheap to operate and is used on very small jobs. This type of hammer can also be used to drive batter piles when the hammer guides are greased or the hammer is put on wheels or rollers to reduce friction and develop greater impact energy.

Notice that the paragraph head is separated from the sentence that follows. The sentence repeats the head and does not refer to it with "it."

Single-Acting Hammer. A single-acting hammer is raised by compressed air or steam injected into a cylinder by a simple system of valves that directs and controls the amount of pressure. See Figure 1.

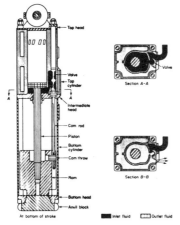

FIG. 1.   Single-acting hammer at bottom of stroke (6).

Description

The ram on the single-acting hammer is made of cast iron. It is called single-acting because the mechanical action on the hammer is in only one direction—up. As the ram reaches the top of its motion, the steam is cut off and the exhaust port in the cylinder is opened, letting the ram fall by gravity until it strikes the pile head. The channel tracks in which the ram travels up and down are part of the hammer.

Procedure

"The average blows per minute for a single-acting hammer are sixty" (5). This can vary from fifty to eighty blows per minute depending on the hammer weight, pressure, and volume of the compressed air or steam. The only time the hammer may exceed sixty blows per minute occurs when the ram weight is below 5,000 pounds and the stroke is shortened. "The average weights for the single-acting hammer are 5,000 to 10,000 pounds with a stroke height of 2 to 3½ feet" (6).

Evaluation

"The steam- or air-powered single-acting hammers can be either open or closed in regard to intake and exhaust" (5). The open hammers work openly with the surrounding atmosphere. The closed hammers use special hoses and port controls for inlet and exhaust. The closed type hammer can be used for driving piles up to 80 feet below the surface of the water.

TABLE 1.   Data for Some Single-Acting Hammers

Specific Hammers	Vulcan No. 3	Vulcan No. 2	Vulcan No. 1	MKT S8	MKT S10	MKT S20
Weight, lb	3,700.0	6,700.00	9,700.0	18,300.0	22,400.0	38,600.00
Length, ft	9.5	11.50	13.0	13.3	13.0	15.40
Stroke, ft	2.0	2.42	3.0	3.5	3.5	3.42
Ram, lb	1,800.0	3,000.00	5,000.0	8,000.0	10,000.0	20,000.00
Energy, ft-lb	3,600.0	7,260.00	15,000.0	26,000.0	32,500.0	60,000.00
Blows/min	80.0	70.00	60.0	55.0	55.0	60.00
PSI	80.0	80.00	80.0	80.0	80.0	150.00
Boiler hp	18.0	25.00	40.0	120.0	130.0	190.00
Air volume cfm	220.0	336.00	565.0	850.0	1,000.0	1,000.00

Source: Day, 1973 [4].

Description

Procedure

Double-acting hammer. The double-acting hammer uses a reciprocating motion. More complicated than the single-acting hammer, the double-acting hammer employs air or steam pressure in both the upstroke and downstroke. This movement is accomplished by the arrangement of the cylinder port holes so that the injection of air or steam pressure at one end of the piston will alternate with air or steam injection at the opposite end. See Figure 2.

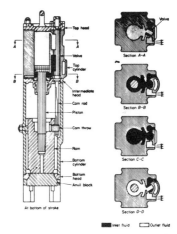

FIG. 2.   Double-Acting Hammer (6).

Thus, pressure in the cylinder is used to raise the ram or piston and the downstroke uses both gravity and pressure acceleration. Pressure being added to both upstrokes and downstrokes causes the stroke to be shorter and the hammer more compact. With a shorter stroke, 6 to 24 inches, blows can be more rapid than that of a single-acting hammer. The double-acting hammer can produce between one hundred and three hundred blows per minute. Because of the rapidity of blows, it keeps the pile in continuous motion during driving and reduces inertia, soil friction, and point resistance.

Evaluation

This type of hammer is most efficient in driving lightweight and average-weight piles or casings in soil of average consistency. "The ram weight can be from 100 to 10,000 pounds depending on the job" (7). "The energy that the hammer can produce is between 1,000 and 20,000 pounds" (5). The hammer can be operated under water if a hose connected to the exhaust manifold is above the water level. It is preferred over other types of hammers for driving off barges because it avoids surging.

TABLE 2.   Data for Some Double-Acting Hammers

Specific Hammer	MKT No. 3	MKT No. 6	MKT 9-B-3	MKT 11-B-3
Weight, lb	675.0	2,900.0	7,000	14,000
Length, in.	58.0	63.0	98	133
Stroke, in.	5.5	8.5	17	19
Ram, lb	68.0	400.0	1,600	5,000
Energy, ft-lb	700.0	2,500.0	8,750	19,150
Blows/min	400.0	275.0	145	95
Boiler hp	15.0	25.0	45	60
Air volume cfm	110.0	400.0	600	900

Source: Day, 1973 [4].

Description   Differential-acting hammers. The differential-acting hammer combines the advantages of both single- and double-acting hammers. It has the same ram weight of a single-acting hammer plus the rapidity or number of blows per minute of a *Procedure*   double-acting hammer. The hammer can be operated by air, steam, or hydraulic fluid pressure. "Hydraulic-operated hammers are not as successful as their counterparts" (4). The differential-acting hammer has upper and lower pressure chambers. The force it adds to the ram can be accounted for by the differential amount of steam pressure between the two chambers. The *Evaluation*   statistics on a differential hammer are comparable to that of the double-acting hammer.

Description   Diesel hammer. "It (the diesel hammer) consists of a cylinder ram, anvil block, and a simple *Procedure*   fuel-injection system" (2). The operation of a diesel hammer begins by raising the ram piston to its top position by a separate crane hoist line. On the upward movement of the piston, fuel and air are drawn into the lower combustion chamber to provide an explosive mixture to be set off by the ram piston. The ram piston is tripped and it falls by gravity, closing the intake and exhaust ports of the lower chamber. The fuel and air trapped in the cylinder are compressed between the lower end of the ram and the anvil. The pressure produced by the falling ram creates enough heat to ignite the explosive mixture. The explosion serves a twofold purpose. First, it adds to the gravity force of the ram on the anvil in driving the pile downward. Second, the explosion drives the ram upward into striking position; on doing so it compresses air at the top of the cylinder that adds to the next downward thrust. The upward movement of the ram piston opens the exhaust ports to release the burned gases and lets new fuel and air enter the lower cylinder for continued operation. The process is discontinued by pulling a rope from the cab of the operator, which opens the

port, not allowing any fuel to enter the lower chamber—a situation that does not allow any explosive force to return the ram upward.

The diesel hammer can either be of the closed-end or open-end type. The closed-end diesel hammer has a housing extending over the cylinder to form a bounce chamber. "Compression rings in the top of the cylinder chamber permit air to be compressed in the bounce chamber by the rising ram" (5). The compressed air acts as a spring that shortens the stroke, adds energy, and accelerates the downstroke. This, in turn, increases the blows per minute. The open-end diesel hammer works on the same fuel injection principle as the closed-end hammer but does not have the bounce chamber to increase the speed and energy of the downstroke.

"The stroke length of the diesel hammer is proportional to the pile resistance; therefore the harsher the driving, the more effective the hammer" (2). The heavier the resistance the slower the hammer speed. "The stroke of a diesel hammer ranges from 6½ to 8½ feet with a ram weight of 3,000 pounds" (4).

Evaluation   Some advantages of the diesel hammer are the elimination of boilers or compressors, supply hoses, greater mobility, easier plumbing of piles, and the hammer can be connected to a single steel section for control guide. The disadvantage of a diesel hammer is that some types stall under easy driving conditions, resulting in frequent restarts.

Vibratory hammer

Description   In contrast to the impact hammer is a vibratory hammer or driver. "The vibrator driver sinks piles by longitudinal vibrations and the weight of the vibrator and not by the forcefulness of distinct blows" (3). An impact hammer may apply one or two blows every second but a vibratory hammer will create 15 to more than 100 load variations every second.

The vibratory hammer destroys soil friction and makes it behave as a viscous medium. "It works on the principle of oscillation so that horizontal components of the centrifugal force cancel, whereas the vertical components are additive.

Procedure   "A vibratory hammer has a series of horizontal shafts with eccentric weights on them" (4). The hammer has a power unit, which may be off to one side with just feeder lines to the moving hammer on the pile. It delivers the power, generally hydraulic or electric, to rotate the weighted shafts at high speed. "The shafts operate in pairs, with one revolving clockwise and the other counterclockwise" (4). The eccentric weights are attached so that their effects add together in the vertical direction but cancel each other horizontally. To be effective, the vibratory hammer must be firmly clamped to the pile being driven. Then the vertical effect of the eccentric weights amounts to either a downward compressive push on the pile or an upward tensile pull. With the lateral effect in the pile due to longitudinal compressive and tensile forces, there will be horizontal movement of the pile side surfaces. "When the pile is in compression, its sides move outward, and when in tension, they move inward" (4). With a high frequency of load variation, the outward-inward movements of the sides are rapid. "It amounts to a vibration of the sides which keeps the soils from getting any friction or grip on the pile" (1). The vibrations from the hammer are isolated from the hoisting crane equipment by a spring support system.

Evaluation   The average weight of a vibratory pile hammer is three to five tons. This creates a bulky machine, its major disadvantage. This hammer is often used in cold regions since no steam or condensate is present. It is less expensive to operate because it reduces the placing time. This reduced placing time cuts back on power consumption and labor costs. The hammer is most effective in water-saturated noncohesive soils that it can keep in a fluid state. Under the right conditions it can put in a pile in one-hundredth the time it takes a single-acting hammer.

HAMMER SELECTION

Criteria for selection   The type of pile and hammer to use on any given job is determined by the time schedule of the job; availability and cost of the hammer; accessibility to the site; headroom clearance; and number, length, spacing, and weight of piles. Other important aspects are soil conditions, presence of batter piles, cribbing, and depth of excavation. No particular hammer type is right for every job, and any job may have two or three suitable types; but usually there is one that is best for the situation.

Characteristics to be considered   The hammer weight should be one-half the total weight of the pile, and the driving energy should be at least one foot-pound for each pound of pile weight. "Hammers that deliver insufficient energy to drive piles to high capacity loads will require a larger number of blows. A high blow count with less penetration per blow will give deceptive and disappointing results" (1). Too high an impact energy may cause pile damage and provide inconclusive results. The ratio of pile weight to ram weight should be given a great amount of consideration to avoid wasting hammer energy. See the appendix for tables that give hammer characteristics and selection for different job requirements.

APPENDIX

Technical information to supplement text   "The most in-depth set of hammer formulas used in America were developed by A. M. Wellington in 1920" (1). These formulas are known as the Engineering News Formula: $L = \dfrac{2WH}{S+C}$.

For drop hammer: $L = \dfrac{2WH}{S+1.0}$

For single-acting hammers: $L = \dfrac{2WH}{S+0.10}$

For double-acting hammers: $L = \dfrac{2E}{S+0.10}$

L = Safe load bearing.
W = Weight of ram or striking parts, in pounds.
H = Height of stroke, in feet.
S = Set penetration per blow, in inches.
E = Rated energy as listed by manufacturer of hammer, in foot-pounds.
C = Constant derived from laboratory experiments.

In calculating the load-bearing capacity of a pile at least (S) must be an average from the last ten blows.

The Modified Engineering News Formula looks like this:

$L = \dfrac{2WH}{S+(C \times \frac{P}{W})}$ where P = weight of pile in pounds.

TABLE 3.   Pile Hammer Data and Characteristics (1)

Page 9044   MANUAL OF STRUCTURAL DESIGN AND ENGINEERING SOLUTIONS

TABLE: Pile hammer data and characteristics						9.4.6
MANUFACTURER OR TRADE NAME	NUMBER OR MODEL	TYPE OF ACTION	RATED ENERGY IN FOOT POUNDS	RAM SPEED BLOWS PER MIN.	WEIGHT OF RAM IN LBS.	W S Z E I Z
	020	SINGLE	60,000	60	20,000	1
	200-C	DOUBLE	50,000	98	20,000	2
	014	SINGLE	42,000	60	14,000	3
	140-C	DOUBLE	36,000	103	14,000	4
	010	SINGLE	32,500	50	10,000	5
	08	SINGLE	26,000	50	8,000	6
VULCAN IRON WORKS	80-C	DOUBLE	24,450	111	8,000	7
	06	SINGLE	19,500	60	6,500	8
	65-C	DOUBLE	19,200	117	6,500	9
	50-C	DOUBLE	15,100	120	5,000	10
	1	SINGLE	15,000	60	5,000	11
	30-C	DOUBLE	7,260	133	3,000	12
	2	SINGLE	7,260	70	3,000	13
	DGH-900	DOUBLE	4,000	238	900	14
	S-20	SINGLE	60,000	60	20,000	15
	S-14	SINGLE	37,500	60	14,000	16
	DA-35	SINGLE	35,500	48	2,800	17
	DA-35	DOUBLE	21,000	82	2,800	18
	S-10	SINGLE	32,500	55	10,000	19
	DE-40	DIESEL	32,000	50	4,000	20
	S-8	SINGLE	26,000	55	8,000	21
	C-8	DOUBLE	26,000	78	8,000	22
	DE-30	DIESEL	22,400	50	2,800	23
	11-B-3	DOUBLE	19,150	95	5,000	24
McKIERNAN-TERRY	S-5	SINGLE	16,250	60	5,000	25
	D1-20	SINGLE	16,000	50	2,000	26
	C-5	DOUBLE	16,000	100	5,000	27
	10-B-3	DOUBLE	13,100	105	3,000	28
	C-3	DOUBLE	9,000	135	3,000	29
	S-3	SINGLE	9,000	65	3,000	30
	DE-10	DIESEL	8,800	50	1,100	31
	9-B-3	DOUBLE	8,750	145	1,600	32
	7	DOUBLE	4,150	225	800	33
	6.5	DOUBLE	3,200	280	600	34
	6	DOUBLE	2,500	275	400	35
	5	DOUBLE	1,000	300	200	36
	3	DOUBLE	585	400	68	37
	520	DIESEL	30,000	82	5,070	38
	440	DIESEL	18,200	90	4,000	39
LINK-BELT CORP.	312	DIESEL	18,000	100	3,855	40
	180	DIESEL	8,100	95	1,725	41
	105	DIESEL	7,500	95	1,445	42
	D-30	DIESEL	54,250	45		43
DELMAG-GERMANY	D-22	DIESEL	39,700	48	4,850	44
	D-12	DIESEL	22,500	51	2,750	45
	D-5	DIESEL	9,100	56	1,100	46
	MB-70	DIESEL	155,50T	60	15,840	47
	MB-40	DIESEL	91,135	60	9,039	48
	MB-22	DIESEL	42,674	60	4,840	49
MITSUBISHI-JAPAN	M-43	DIESEL	92,580	60	9,460	50
	M-33	DIESEL	61,840	60	7,260	51
	M-23	DIESEL	44,000	60	5,060	52
	M-145	DIESEL	26,000	60	2,970	53

TABLE 3 (Continued)

PILE DRIVING AND DOCK FENDERING Page 9045

TABLE: Pile hammer data and characteristics, continued 9.4.6

MATCH LINES	RAM STROKE HEIGHT IN FT. OR IN.	CAPACITY BOILER H.P.	OPERATING PRESSURE P.S.I.	GROSS W'T. HAMMER IN LBS.	HOSE DIA. INLET IN INCHES	TOTAL LENGTH OF HAMMER FEET + INCHES	REMARKS OR GENERAL USE	MATCH LINES
1	36.0"	278	120	39,000	3.00	15'-0"		1
2	15.5"	260	142	39,050	4.00	13'-2"	DIFFERENTIAL	2
3	36.0"	200	110	27,500	3.00	14'-6"		3
4	15.5"	210	140	27,985	3.00	12'-3"	DIFFERENTIAL	4
5	39.0"	157	105	18,750	2.50	15'-0"		5
6	39.0"	127	83	16,750	2.50	15'-0"		6
7	16.5"	180	120	17,885	2.50	12'-2"	DIFFERENTIAL	7
8	36.0"	94	100	11,200	2.00	13'-0"		8
9	15.5"	152	150	14,885	2.00	12'-2"	DIFFERENTIAL	9
10	15.5"	125	120	11,780	2.00	11'-0"	DIFFERENTIAL	10
11	36.0"	85	80	9,700	2.00	13'-0"		11
12	12.5"	70	120	7,050	1.50	9'-8"	DIFFERENTIAL	12
13	29.0"	50	80	6,700	1.50	11'-6"		13
14	10.0"	75	78	5,000	1.50	6'-9"	EXTRACTOR	14
15	36.0"	280	150	38,650	3.00	15'-5"		15
16	32.0"	155	100	31,100	3.00	13'-7"		16
17	8'-0"	---	---	10,000	---	17'-0"		17
18	5'-10"	---	---	10,000	---	17'-0"		18
19	39.0"	130	80	22,380	2.50	13'-0"		19
20	8'-0"	---	---	9,900	---	14'-2"		20
21	39.0"	120	80	18,300	2.50	13'-3"		21
22	20.0"	110	100	18,750	2.50	9'-9"		22
23	8'-0"	---	---	8,125	---	14'-0"		23
24	19.0"	126	100	14,000	2.50	11'-1½"	NO CUSHIONS	24
25	39.0"	85	80	12,460	2.00	12'-2"		25
26	8'-0"	---	---	5,500	---	12'-2"	DIESEL	26
27	18.0"	80	100	11,880	2.50	8'-9"		27
28	19.0"	104	100	10,850	2.50	9'-2"	NO CUSHIONS	28
29	16.0"	60	100	8,500	2.00	7'-9½		29
30	36.0"	57	80	9,030	1.50	11'-4"		30
31	8'-0"	---	---	2,900	---	11'-3"		31
32	17.0"	85	100	7,000	2.00	8'-4"	NO CUSHIONS	32
33	9.5"	65	100	5,000	1.50	6'-1"	EXTRACTIONS	33
34	8.375"	65	100	4,550	1.50	6'-2"	EXTRACTIONS	34
35	8.75"	45	100	2,900	1.25	5'-3"	EXTRACTIONS	35
36	7.0"	35	100	1,500	1.25	4'-9"	EXTRACTIONS	36
37	5.75"	25	100	675	1.00	4'-10"	EXTRACTIONS	37
38	43.17"	---	---	12,545	---	13'-6"	RECIPROCATING	38
39	48.55"	---	---	10,300	---	14'-6"	RECIPROCATING	39
40	30.89"	---	---	10,375	---	10'-9"	RECIPROCATING	40
41	37.60"	---	---	4,550	---	11'-3"	RECIPROCATING	41
42	35.23"	---	---	3,885	---	10'-3"	RECIPROCATING	42
43	NOT LISTED	---	---	NOT AVAIL.	---	NOT AVAILABLE		43
44	VISIBLE	---	---	10,055	---	12'-10½"		44
45	VISIBLE	---	---	5,440	---	12'-7½		45
46	VISIBLE	---	---	2,400	---	11'-2½"		46
47	9'-6"	---	---	40,700	---	18'-8⅛"	FOR STEEL PILES	47
48	8'-2"	---	---	24,030	---	18'-5¼"	FOR STEEL PILES	48
49	8'-2"	---	---	11,660	---	16-0¼"		49
50	NOT LISTED	---	---	22,660	---	15'-4⅜"	FOR STEEL PILES	50
51	NOT LISTED	---	---	16,940	---	14'-8⅛"		51
52	NOT LISTED	---	---	11,220	---	13'-3¼"		52
53	NOT LISTED	---	---	7,260	---	13'-4"		53

TABLE 4. Hammer Blows per Foot for Safe Pile Load (1)

PILE DRIVING AND DOCK FENDERING Page 9065

TABLE: Hammer blows per foot for safe pile load 9.6.6

MANUFACTURER OF HAMMER OR TRADE NAME	TYPE OF ACTION	HAMMER MODEL OR NO.	BLOWS PER MINUTE	RATED ENERGY IN FT. LBS.	LOAD IN TONS					MATCH LINES
					5	10	15	20	25	
VULCAN IRON WORKS	SINGLE	18-C	150	3,600	19.5	46.2	85.7			1
VULCAN IRON WORKS	DOUBLE	NO. 3	80	3,600	19.5	46.2	85.7			2
UNION IRON WORKS	DOUBLE	NO. 3	160	3,660	19.0	45.2	83.3	145.0		3
UNION IRON WORKS	DOUBLE	NO. 3A	150	4,390	15.5	35.4	62.3	100.0	160.0	4
UNION IRON WORKS	DOUBLE	NO. 2	145	5,755	11.5	25.3	42.3	64.0	92.5	5
VULCAN IRON WORKS	DOUBLE	30-C	135	7,260	8.9	19.2	31.3	45.7	63.3	6
VULCAN IRON WORKS	SINGLE	NO. 2	70	7,260	8.9	19.2	31.3	45.7	63.3	7
UNION IRON WORKS	DOUBLE	1½A	125	8,680	7.4	15.6	25.0	36.0	48.5	8
McKIERNAN-TERRY	DOUBLE	9-B-3	145	8,750	7.3	15.5	24.8	35.5	48.0	9
McKIERNAN-TERRY	SINGLE	S-3	65	9,000	7.0	15.0	24.0	34.3	46.0	10
BROWN INDUSTRIAL	DOUBLE	1	110	9,650		14.0	22.0	31.5	42.0	11
UNION IRON WORKS	DOUBLE	1A	120	10,020		13.3	21.0	30.0	40.0	12
UNION IRON WORKS	DOUBLE	NO. 1	130	13,100		10.0	15.5	21.6	28.3	13
McKIERNAN-TERRY	DOUBLE	10-B-3	105	13,100		10.0	15.5	21.6	28.3	14
VULCAN IRON WORKS	SINGLE	NO. 1	60	15,000		10.0	13.4	18.5	24.0	15
VULCAN IRON WORKS	DOUBLE	50-C	120	15,000			13.2	18.4	23.8	16
McKIERNAN-TERRY	SINGLE	S-5	60	16,250			11.0	16.8	22.0	17
McKIERNAN-TERRY	DOUBLE	11-B-3	95	19,150			10.2	14.0	18.0	18
UNION IRON WORKS	DOUBLE	OA	90	22,050				12.0	15.4	19
VULCAN IRON WORKS	SINGLE	O	50	24,375				11.0	14.0	20
VULCAN IRON WORKS	DOUBLE	80-C	111	24,450				11.0	13.6	21
McKIERNAN-TERRY	SINGLE	S-8	55	26,000				10.0	12.8	22
VULCAN IRON WORKS	SINGLE	OR	50	30,225					10.8	23
McKIERNAN-TERRY	SINGLE	S-10	55	32,500					10.0	24
RAYMOND INTERNAT'L.		00	50	32,500					10.0	25
VULCAN IRON WORKS	DOUBLE	140-C	103	36,000						26
McKIERNAN-TERRY	SINGLE	S-14	60	37,500						27
RAYMOND INTERNAT'L.		000		40,600						28
VULCAN IRON WORKS	DOUBLE	200-C	98	50,200						29
UNION IRON WORKS	DOUBLE	00	85	54,900						30
McKIERNAN-TERRY	DIESEL	DE-20	48-52	16,000		10.9	17.1	20.0	31.6	31
McKIERNAN-TERRY	DIESEL	DE-30	48-52	22,400		7.2	11.8	16.2	20.8	32
McKIERNAN-TERRY	DIESEL	DE-40	48-52	32,000						33
DELMAG-GERMANY	DIESEL	D-5	56	9,100	9.5	20.6	34.0	50.0	70.0	34
DELMAG-GERMANY	DIESEL	D-12	51	22,500			12.0	16.3	21.0	35
DELMAG-GERMANY	DIESEL	D-22	48	39,700				8.7	11.0	36
DELMAG-GERMANY	DIESEL	D-30	45	54,250						37
MITSUBISHI-JAPAN	DIESEL	M-14S	60	26,000			10.0	13.7	17.7	38
MITSUBISHI-JAPAN	DIESEL	M-23	60	44,000					12.0	39
MITSUBISHI-JAPAN	DIESEL	M-33	60	61,840						40
MITSUBISHI-JAPAN	DIESEL	M-43	60	92,580						41
MITSUBISHI-JAPAN	DIESEL	MB-22	60	42,674						42
MITSUBISHI-JAPAN	DIESEL	MB-40	60	91,135						43
MITSUBISHI-JAPAN	DIESEL	MB-70	60	155,507						44

TABLE 4 (Continued)

Page 9066 MANUAL OF STRUCTURAL DESIGN AND ENGINEERING SOLUTIONS

TABLE: Hammer blows per foot for safe pile load, continued 9.6.6

MATCH LINES	SAFE LOAD CAPACITY IN U.S. TONS																	
	30	35	40	45	50	55	60	65	70	75	80	85	90	95	100	105	110	115
1																		
2																		
3																		
4																		
5	131.0																	
6	84.6	112.0	147.0															
7	84.6	112.0	147.0															
8	63.5	81.0																
9	62.6	80.0	101.0	128.0														
10	60.0	76.2	96.0	120.0	150.0													
11	54.0	68.2	85.0	105.0	129.0	159.0												
12	51.3	64.4	79.6	98.0	120.0	146.0	180.0											
13	35.7	48.8	52.8	62.8	74.0	87.0	101.5											
14	35.7	48.8	52.8	62.8	74.0	87.0	101.5	118.0	138.0									
15	30.0	36.5	43.6	51.5	60.0	69.5	80.0	92.0	105.0	120.0								
16	30.0	36.2	43.3	50.0	59.5	68.8	79.2	91.0	104.0	118.5	136.5	155.5	177.0	203.0				
17	27.2	33.0	39.2	46.0	53.4	61.4	70.0	80.0	91.0	103.0	116.5	131.5	149.0	169.0	192.0			
18	22.3	26.8	31.7	37.0	42.5	48.5	55.0	62.0	69.2	79.2	87.0	96.0	106.5	118.2	131.0	145.5	162.0	180.0
19	19.0	22.6	26.6	30.8	35.2	40.0	44.8	50.0	56.0	62.0	68.3	75.4	82.8	91.0	99.5	104.5	120.0	131.0
20	16.8	20.0	23.6	27.3	31.2	35.0	39.3	43.7	48.5	53.5	58.8	64.4	70.5	76.7	83.6	91.6	100.0	107.5
21	16.7	20.0	23.5	27.7	30.9	35.2	39.1	43.4	48.3	53.3	58.4	64.0	69.9	76.3	83.0	90.4	98.2	106.5
22	15.7	18.7	21.8	25.8	28.6	32.3	36.0	40.0	44.3	48.7	53.4	58.4	65.5	69.0	75.0	81.4	88.0	95.3
23	13.2	16.0	18.3	21.0	23.8	26.8	30.0	33.0	36.2	39.6	43.3	47.0	51.0	55.0	59.5	64.0	68.6	73.6
24	12.2	14.5	16.9	19.3	21.9	24.5	27.2	30.0	32.6	36.0	39.2	42.5	46.5	49.6	53.4	57.3	61.4	65.6
25	12.2	14.5	16.9	19.3	21.9	24.5	27.2	30.0	32.6	36.0	39.2	42.5	46.5	49.6	53.4	57.3	61.4	65.6
26	11.0	13.0	15.0	17.2	19.4	21.4	24.0	26.4	29.0	31.6	34.3	37.1	40.0	43.0	46.2	49.4	52.8	56.2
27		12.4	14.3	16.4	18.5	20.6	23.0	25.2	27.6	30.0	32.6	35.2	37.9	40.8	43.6	46.7	50.0	53.2
28		11.3	13.1	15.0	16.9	18.9	21.0	22.9	25.0	27.2	29.4	31.8	34.2	36.7	39.2	42.0	44.6	47.4
29			10.4	11.9	13.3	14.8	16.3	17.8	19.5	21.3	22.8	24.5	26.2	27.0	29.9	32.0	33.8	35.6
30			10.0	10.7	12.0	13.4	14.7	16.1	17.6	19.0	20.5	22.2	23.6	25.1	26.8	28.4	30.3	31.8
31	40.0	49.4	60.0	72.1	85.7	101.5	120.0											
32	26.1	32.3	37.5	43.8	50.8	58.7	66.7	75.7	85.7	96.7	109.0	122.8	138.5	156.0	176.5			
33	15.0	20.5	24.0	27.7	31.6	35.7	40.0	44.6	49.5	54.3	60.0	65.7	72.0	78.6	85.7	93.3	101.5	110.5
34	95.0	126.4	170.0															
35	26.0	32.0	37.4	46.0	51.0	58.2	66.5	75.4	85.0	96.0	108.0	122.0						
36	13.5	16.0	18.6	21.6	24.2	27.0	30.3	33.4	38.0	40.5	44.3	48.5	52.0	56.2	61.0	65.5	70.5	75.5
37					16.8	19.0	21.0	22.8	25.0	27.0	29.4	32.0	34.0	36.5	39.0	42.0	44.5	47.3
38	21.8	26.3	31.0	36.0	41.4	47.2	53.3	60.0	67.0	75.0	83.3	92.7	102.5	114.0	126.0	140.0	155.0	172.5
39	12.0	14.5	16.5	18.9	21.1	24.0	26.7	29.5	32.3	35.5	38.4	41.6	45.0	48.5	52.2	56.0	60.0	64.2
40	8.3	9.8	11.3	12.9	14.5	16.2	17.8	19.5	21.3	23.2	25.0	26.9	28.9	30.9	33.0	35.1	37.3	39.6
41								12.4	13.4	14.6	15.5	16.7	17.8	19.0	20.8	21.4	22.6	23.2
42	12.4	14.7	17.2	19.7	22.2	25.4	27.7	30.6	33.6	36.8	40.0	43.4	47.0	50.6	54.6	58.6	62.8	67.3
43										14.8	15.9	17.0	18.2	19.4	20.6	21.8	23.9	24.3
44															11.3	11.8	12.5	13.1

TABLE 4 (Continued)

PILE DRIVING AND DOCK FENDERING Page 9067

MATCH LINES	SAFE LOAD CAPACITY IN U.S. TONS																	MATCH LINES
	120	125	130	135	140	145	150	155	160	165	170	175	180	185	190	195	200	
1																		1
2																		2
3																		3
4																		4
5																		5
6																		6
7																		7
8																		8
9																		9
10																		10
11																		11
12																		12
13																		13
14																		14
15																		15
16																		16
17																		17
18	202.0																	18
19	143.4	157.0	175.0	189.0														19
20	116.5	125.5	137.5	149.3	162.0	176.0	192.0											20
21	115.5	125.4	136.4	148.0	160.5	175.0	190.5	207.8	227.0									21
22	103.3	111.0	120.0	129.5	140.0	151.3	165.5	177.0	192.0	208.0								22
23	79.0	84.5	90.8	97.0	103.6	110.5	118.0	126.3	135.0	144.0	155.0	165.0	176.5	190.0				23
24	70.3	75.0	80.0	85.3	90.8	96.6	102.6	109.3	116.4	124.0	132.0	140.0	149.0	159.0	170.0	180.0	192.0	24
25	70.3	75.0	80.0	85.3	90.8	96.6	102.6	109.3	116.4	124.0	132.0	140.0	149.0	159.0	170.0	180.0	192.0	25
26	60.0	63.8	67.8	72.0	76.3	80.8	85.7	90.8	96.0	101.5	107.5	113.5	120.0	126.5	134.5	141.5	150.0	26
27	56.5	60.0	63.7	67.5	71.5	75.6	80.0	84.5	88.3	94.3	99.5	105.0	111.0	116.6	123.5	130.0	137.0	27
28	50.3	53.3	56.5	60.0	64.2	66.6	70.3	74.0	78.0	82.0	86.5	91.0	95.6	100.0	105.5	110.8	116.5	28
29	37.9	39.8	42.0	44.2	46.4	48.8	50.1	53.6	56.3	58.8	61.8	64.3	67.3	70.0	73.3	76.3	79.5	29
30	33.8	35.4	37.2	39.0	41.1	43.3	45.0	47.2	49.3	51.0	54.0	56.2	58.5	61.0	63.6	66.2	68.8	30
31																		31
32																		32
33	120.0	130.5	141.7	154.0	168.0	183.0	200.0											33
34																		34
35																		35
36	81.2	87.0	93.2	100.0	107.0	114.0	122.0	130.5	139.5	145.0	160.0	171.3	183.6	197.0	212.0	229.0	246.0	36
37	50.2	53.2	56.5	60.0	64.0	66.5	70.2	74.0	77.8	82.0	86.5	91	95.5	100.0	105.3	111.0	116.2	37
38	192.0	214.0																38
39	68.5	73.2	78.0	83.0	88.5	94.0	100.0	106.2	113.0	120.0	127.5	135.5	144.0	153.0	163.0	173.5	184.5	39
40	41.8	44.3	46.8	49.2	51.9	54.6	57.4	60.3	63.2	66.3	69.5	72.7	76.2	79.6	86.5	87.3	91.0	40
41	24.2	26.3	27.6	28.9	29.4	31.6	33.0	34.4	35.9	37.4	38.8	40.3	42.0	43.5	45.2	46.8	48.5	41
42	72.0	77.0	82.2	87.5	93.2	99.4	105.8	115.5	120.0	127.7	136.0	145.0	154.5	164.5	175.5	187.0	200.0	42
43	25.5	26.9	28.2	29.5	30.9	32.3	33.7	35.2	36.7	38.1	39.8	41.3	43.2	44.5	46.2	47.8	49.6	43
44	13.7	14.4	15.0	15.7	16.4	17.0	17.7	18.4	19.1	19.7	20.5	21.1	21.4	22.6	23.3	24.1	25.0	44

COMPUTATIONS BASED ON ENGINEERING-NEWS RECORD WORK

FORMULAS: $L = \frac{2E}{S + 0.10}$ AND $L = \frac{(2WH) + (AP)}{S + 0.10}$

NUMBER OF BLOWS PER FOOT $= \frac{120\,L}{(20E) - L}$ = AVERAGE 10 FINAL.

NUMBER OF BLOWS PER INCH $= \frac{n}{12}$ AND SET $= S = \frac{1.00}{n}$

1 U.S. TON = 2000 LBS. 1 BRITISH TON = 2240 LBS.

- L = SAFE LOAD CAPACITY IN POUNDS.
- E = MANUFACTURES RATED HAMMER ENERGY, IN FOOT LBS.
- W = WEIGHT OF STRIKING RAM, IN POUNDS.
- H = HEIGHT OF RAM'S FALL, IN FEET.
- A = AREA OF PISTON, IN SQUARE INCHES. $A = 0.7854\,D^2$
- P = STEAM PRESSURE AT HAMMER, IN LBS. SQ. IN. (P.S.I.)
- S = SET PENETRATION PER BLOW, IN INCHES.

NOTE:
HAMMER BLOWS FOR DIESEL HAMMER LISTED ARE BASED ON 75 PERCENT OF RATED ENERGY.

REFERENCES

Numbered list   1. Maurice E. Walmer and Baron L. Stephen, *Manual*
of references   *of Structural Design and Engineering Solutions.*
                    Englewood Cliffs, N.J.: Prentice-Hall, 1972.
2. Robert D. Chellis, *Pile Foundations.* New York:
   McGraw-Hill, 1961.
3. Gregory P. Tschebotarioff, *Foundations, Retaining
   and Earth Structures.* New York: McGraw-Hill,
   1973.
4. David A. Day, *Construction Equipment Guide.* New
   York: John Wiley & Sons, 1973.
5. Ralph B. Peck, *Foundation Engineering.* New York:
   John Wiley & Sons, 1974.
6. Wayne C. Teng, *Foundation Design.* Englewood
   Cliffs, N.J.: Prentice-Hall, 1962.
7. M. J. Tomlinson, *Foundation Design and Construction.* New York: John Wiley & Sons, 1963.

WRITING ASSIGNMENTS

The writing assignments listed below can be used to produce formal reports suitable for publication in the various technical periodicals and journals. These topics will encourage you to report the results of your own surveys and/or experiments as well as information from other sources, and they lend themselves to development through the use of tables and figures. Most of them are more technical than the topics used for brief assignments written in a limited amount of time.

A. Topics suitable for the analytical type of formal report.
   1. How can an auto salvage yard be operated more efficiently?
   2. Which emission control device is most effective?
   3. How does modular housing compare economically to conventional types?
   4. What is the teacher's role in the open classroom?
   5. How can high school music festivals be organized to best advantage?
   6. How can secondary social studies be taught innovatively?
   7. What is the most effective treatment for the emotional problems related to advanced alcoholism?
   8. How will the industrial draftsperson be affected by the metric system?

   9. Why are antiskid braking systems advantageous?
   10. Would an artificial snow skiing area in your state be a profitable venture?

B. Topics suitable for the informative type of formal report.
   1. Advantages of continuous feed dampeners
   2. Method of intersections for isometric axonometric projection
   3. Automotive refinishing
   4. Ford's EGR system
   5. Rotary power
   6. Virtual storage access methods
   7. Light-emitting diode
   8. Reinforced fiberglass building components
   9. COBOL language
   10. Techniques in electric arc welding
   11. Types of cutting tool materials for machining metals
   12. Theory and operation of an FM receiver
   13. Problems of using lithographic ink
   14. The fermentation process of cheeses

C. Limit the general topics below to some specific local situation that you know about or can learn about.
   1. Adequacy of fire protection in a campus building
   2. Location of a new shopping mall
   3. Air pollution caused by a local industry
   4. Speeding up the U.S. mail deliveries
   5. Revitalizing the downtown shopping area
   6. Effects of the Buckley Amendment on written recommendations
   7. Campus changes to accommodate the physically handicapped

D. Prepare a questionnaire to get information from the general public on a college or industry problem.

REFERENCES

1. Richard B. Westin and Peter L. Watson, "Reported and Revealed Preferences as Determinants of Mode Choice Behavior," *Journal of Marketing Research,* Aug. 1975, pp. 282–89.
2. Dolores Landreman, "The Case for Stressing Proposals in Technical Writing Courses," *25th International Technical Communication Conference Proceedings,* May 1978, pp. 398–402.
3. Fred Strasser. *Pile Driving Rigs and Hammers.* Pittsburg State University, 1976.

CHAPTER 6

Proposals

A PROPOSAL is a suggestion that some action be taken. Usually an individual, a firm, or an organization wants to do a job or solve a problem for another for payment. Proposals are a necessity in the everyday world. They bring about changes in existing conditions and they start new projects. They deserve special attention because they are different from other types of technical writing: most technical writing deals with projects completed; proposals are concerned with the future. Instead of describing what exists, the proposal describes an idea. Some organizations produce proposals so seldom that each one is carefully tailored to fit a specific situation; others turn out proposals for new projects daily by filling out standardized forms.

AUDIENCE

The audience dictates the information placed in any proposal; generally it must be customer oriented. If the customers already have specified the way they want their problem solved, their way must be followed. If they are most interested in the length of time the implementation of the proposal will take, this point must be stressed. If they have told you which other companies are also bidding for their business, they will be interested in a comparison of your proposal with those of the competition. Why is your price, quality of work, and equipment better than theirs? But not all proposals are formal, customer-oriented ones. Brief, informal interoffice proposals to management can range from proposing the purchase of a single hand tool to the reorganization of an entire business.

The proposal must be easy for the readers to understand; it should move from the major points to the details. Headings, especially in the longer formal proposal, should be used so it can be read only in part.

STYLE

The first rule for successful proposal writing is that clear language must be used; ordinarily the biggest fault of proposals is vagueness. If the idea cannot be understood, it cannot be approved.

Often the same proposal must serve managing, engineering, purchasing, and operating staffs, so remember to use simple language—especially in the technical sections—that can be understood by people of different backgrounds. Words that reflect your genuine interest in doing the job should be chosen—words that will suggest that you are eager to provide complete satisfaction. *Advantages* and *superiority* imply greater interest and confidence than do *feasibility* and *methods*.

FORMAL PROPOSALS

The formal technical proposal is an elaborate communication written to prove that a certain organization has the ability to solve a problem or provide a service. It requires extensive knowledge and subtle selling ability.

Solicited Proposal

When the proposal is asked for, the points the customer is most interested in are given to you. These points of concern must be translated into the proposal as detailed sections. When the proposal is solicited, it is easy to determine how much freedom you will have in solving the problem. Have the customers specified how they want the problem solved, or can you solve it in any way possible? If the clients are most concerned with cost, cost must be stressed; if they are interested in durability or appearance, these must be emphasized in the proposal.

Government contracts initiate a chain of proposal writing. When the prime contractor wins a government contract, he solicits other contracts from various subcontractors. The winner is determined by cost, quality of the product, qualifications of personnel, financial status of the company, and its demonstrated ability to meet deadlines.

Unsolicited Proposal

Although it is a more efficient use of your time to contact a potential customer or agency first to get permission to submit a proposal, sometimes it is necessary to give a potential customer one that has not been requested. There are four steps in getting such an unsolicited proposal accepted: (1) your preliminary exploration, (2) the writing of the proposal, (3) the study of the proposal by the potential customer or agency, and (4) the awarding of the contract or grant. Some workers have trained themselves to find out about available contracts and grants and then to write proposals applying for those contracts or grants, as the two described and interviewed in Figure 6.1.

JAMES WALSH
. . . county juvenile director

Two in the Know Who Win the Dough

The two top federal grant writers in Jackson County government have been instrumental in channeling more than $4 million in federal money into departments they direct.

James Walsh, county juvenile director and one-time jail director, and Jim Bergfalk, current corrections director, say obtaining federal law enforcement grants involves contacts in the right places and some delicate phraseology in proposed contracts. "Grantsmanship," they say, has evolved into an intricate art that becomes easier with practice.

As a recent U.S. Commission on Intergovernmental Advisory Relations study noted: "Those who are best organized and most skilled in this art of grantsmanship have tended to prevail."

Both men have been sought after for their expertise in assembling proposals for spending somebody else's money. Most of their practice has come from writing contracts for spending the millions of dollars available annually from the Law Enforcement Assistance Administration.

"I've got the contacts in the right places where the money comes from," said Walsh, who also serves on the regional Missouri Council on Criminal Justice, which dispenses LEAA money in the Kansas City area. "And Bergfalk knows how to take care of the technicalities that go into making a grant look attractive."

Both men agree that grant-writing is a time-consuming process that involves keeping up to date with sources of available money and extensive knowledge of the operation of the applying agency.

"When you know both those processes the rest becomes a matter of setting up procedures to meet the stated objective of the grant," Bergfalk said. "The grant application process is a cut and paste job that means a lot of Xeroxing and Scotch tape.

"You have to draw upon the best ideas of people knowledgeable in their fields. The only creative writing involved is matching good ideas to the county's needs."

Mike White, county executive, has asked Bergfalk to study the possibility of a full-time grantsman position in county government. At the moment Bergfalk said he favors an increase in co-operation between county department directors and grant writers rather than a permanent grantsman.

"Sure, we could pull together five people in the county and get half a million dollars in federal grants for human welfare," Bergfalk said. "But what would happen when the grants run out?"

Bergfalk has also been asked to study ways the county can be more selective in pursuing federal grants. The county administration has expressed concern about the effects expiration of grants has on the county budget.

"The county would like to be sure it is not losing some grants it should be receiving," Bergfalk said. "We'd like to do it in some form or fashion so we don't just muddle along."

JIM BERGFALK
. . . county corrections director

Fig. 6.1.   Writing the unsolicited proposal.
(Courtesy *The Kansas City Star* [1])

An unsolicited formal proposal is a lot of work, and it runs the risk of not being accepted. To give the proposal a greater chance of acceptance, attention is focused on the introductory material. At the very beginning, the reasons the customers should be interested are stressed; they should be convinced that a problem exists. The one aspect that is most likely to persuade them is emphasized. You must also impress them with the competence and dependability of your organization and with the fact that your proposal will be better than any others they may receive.

Types of Formal Proposals

There are four main types of formal proposals: research, research and development, sales, and planning. These can range from a four- or five-page brochure suggesting a minor change in procedure to a 500-page proposal for supplying a certain number of new ships to another country.

The research proposal is written to secure funds for study. Such proposals are submitted to some funding agency, to philanthropic foundations such as Carnegie Institute or Rockefeller Foundation, or to various governmental agencies.

The research and development proposal is often written in industry. Here, the goal is to develop a project or a new process of some kind. These can be sent to the Department of Defense; the Department of Agriculture; the Department of Health, Education and Welfare; or to various drug and chemical companies. The funding body often supplies a clear format to be followed, but within each segment is the problem of exactly what information to include.

The sales proposal is the ultimate outcome of the whole sales effort. It must persuade the customer that the product or service is needed and is more desirable than similar products or services on the market. Each sales proposal should be specifically tailored to meet each customer's needs.

The planning proposal is most often seen as a bond issue proposal for a new school or as one for new procedures or divisions within a business. One kind of planning proposal is the capital expenditure type proposing that funds be spent for additions or improvements to plant or equipment.

Organization of Formal Proposals

All types of formal proposals contain similar information and are compiled by the same general rules. The various sections can be grouped into the following areas: *what* is proposed, *how* it can be done, *why* this way will get the best results, and *who* can implement the proposal most efficiently in regard to cost and time schedules.

Similarities between the formal proposal and the formal report discussed in Chapter 5 are many. The title page includes the same information: the word *proposal* should appear along with some reference to the client's request (date of the letter, project number, etc.). If this is a solicited proposal, the client himself will supply the title for you. The letter of transmittal is similar, with a strong sales message and expression of confidence. The table of contents, like that of the formal report, indicates the thoroughness of the study and permits the reader to examine only certain parts of it.

The introduction provides background: it gives the history of the problem, describes its present magnitude, and perhaps includes previous attempts at solutions and their shortcomings. The statement describing the existing problem is especially important because it assures the client that you understand the situation and it puts the problem in the proper perspective. The introduction also states the scope of the proposal by listing the major sections and clarifying the organization. You must not make yourself accountable for more than you intend to do; a clear statement of scope in the introduction will assure a good working relationship during the entire project.

The summary, when the proposal deals with a noncontroversial subject, can be a part of the introduction or can be placed right below the introduction. It sums up the work to be done, the cost, and qualifications of the company desiring to do the work. A request for action can be included here, although in more complex proposals it is separate. Usually, however, it is better to place the summary at the end of the proposal so the customer will be encouraged to read the whole report first and then can better understand it.

The conclusion is also similar to that of a formal report. It encourages the client to act on your proposal by stressing the advantages honestly. Listing all the advantages allows you to summarize the whole project. Listing the resulting products, side benefits, improved methods of production, savings, or knowledge accumulated will help you to avoid having an unhappy customer. The extent to which you believe the proposal will solve the customer's problem should be shown in percentages. The proposal should end on a positive note with an offer of further information if needed, appreciation for the opportunity to submit the proposal, and anticipation of working for the potential customer. The expiration date of the proposal should be clearly stated so the customer will not keep it two years before acting on your suggestion.

The appendix, like that of the formal report, can include blueprints, detailed drawings, catalogs, and price lists. Any analyses, security clearances, physical location, and setting of your company would also be helpful as well as organizational charts, records of previous projects, and letters of recommendation from satisfied customers. Items in the appendix include factual information; propagandistic brochures and pamphlets should be avoided.

The methodology, found in the body of the proposal, is most important and most detailed because it tells how the work will be done. The most comprehensive methodology usually gets the job. Standard methods can be briefly identified, but innovative ones are described step by step. It is the methodology that distinguishes the formal proposal from the formal report; this section includes the plan of attack, the method of operation, and a systematic breakdown of planned procedures intended for technical readers, for managers, and for financial advisors.

The technical part includes a detailed discussion of the problem itself and the technical aspects of the solution, of the approach, or of the design for the product.

Managerial sections deal with (1) the schedule for the project, (2) facilities available, and (3) personnel requirements. The schedule for the project must allow for disruptions such as those due to bad weather or interrupted delivery of materials. It estimates the time required for each phase of work and itemizes the periodic reports and the final report that will be written—including the dates for each, the names of the employees who will write them, and the form they will take. This section describes how quality, costs, and schedules will be controlled.

The section on facility requirements can be divided into facilities supplied by the customer, those provided by your company, and those contracted for with a third party. A facility requirement can mean anything from a typewriter to a technical library to the use of a light aircraft. If the facilities capabilities of the customer must be expanded, this expansion must be specified. This facilities section is important to the success of the whole proposal because it shows that you realize the extent of the project, that you have the means to implement the solution, and that you will assign top priority to it.

The personnel section should list the names of key personnel in your company who will be working on the project and give their credentials briefly. Complete biographical sketches that list their publications and the chain of command can be included in the appendix. Any necessary retraining of the customer's personnel should be explained. While it is better to implement a proposal without expensive outside help, any personnel needed to complete the project and the personnel needed to continue the project after it is completed must be detailed. Levels of education and experience for those to be hired should be listed and the part-time personnel to be used itemized. However, a discussion of the cost of any extra personnel should be deferred until the cost section. By then, the reader may be persuaded of the worth of the proposal in spite of cost.

The cost section is usually the last; sometimes it is even presented as an addendum or rider to the proposal. It gives a complete breakdown of labor, parts, and material costs and allows for unexpected expenses. In industry expensive cost overruns are rarely allowed. This section itemizes expenses under headings such as salaries, capital equipment, expendable equipment, miscellany, and overhead and explains how the money will be recovered through profit potential and/or time to recover.

As you plan the proposal, you should remember that you will write it part by part and that transitional sentences to link the various sections together smoothly will be added later. But only very long and comprehensive proposals will include all the sections described above. When appropriate, sections should be condensed or combined. The material dictates the pattern of the proposal; a rigid pattern should not be forced on the material.

The following brief specimen formal proposal begins with an introductory section that states the immediate problem of the coming special bond election. The methodology in the body of the proposal explains the need for the new school, the desirability of the Middle School, and the fifty-acre site already owned by the Board of Education; it anticipates objections concerning additional busing expenses and includes a detailed drawing. Next comes the cost section in tabular form and the summary. This proposal ends with a separate request-for-action section.

**CRAWFORD COUNTY
UNIFIED SCHOOL DISTRICT NO. 250
PITTSBURG, KANSAS**

Information on a Bond Election for Better Education

Be Informed!!

**IT IS IMPORTANT THAT YOU VOTE!
DATE OF BOND ELECTION – TUESDAY, APRIL 3, 19___
POLLS OPEN, 7:00 A.M. TO 7:00 P.M.**

CRAWFORD COUNTY UNIFIED SCHOOL DISTRICT No. 250
PITTSBURG, KANSAS

Introduction that states the proposal

The Special Bond Election will be held Tuesday, April 3, 19—, to vote on the issuance of General Obligation School Improvement Bonds for a new High School Building. The ballot will be substantially in the following form:

**UNIFIED SCHOOL DISTRICT No. 250,
CRAWFORD COUNTY, STATE OF KANSAS
OFFICIAL BALLOT
SPECIAL BOND ELECTION
APRIL 3, 19—**

Shall the following be adopted:

Shall Unified School District No. 250, Crawford County, State of Kansas, issue its general obligation bonds pursuant to the provisions of K.S.A. 72-6761 in the amount of $4,250,000 for the purpose of constructing, furnishing and equipping a new High School Building in and for said District?

To vote in favor of the bonds make a cross (X) mark in the square after the word "YES".

To vote against the bonds make a cross (X) mark in the square after the word "NO".

YES ☐

NO ☐

VOTERS WILL VOTE AT THEIR REGULAR VOTING PLACES

A NEED

Advantages of the plan (salesmanship)

The one major need of Pittsburg is a building program that will solve the space problem of the entire district. This need has been described as the Pittsburg "Master Plan for Facilities." This plan provides for the proper atmosphere for the learning process from Kindergarten through Grade 12. Unlike many building programs that provide new facilities for just one area, the Pittsburg Master Plan has developed a plan that allows modern instructional programing from Kindergarten through Grade 12 and adult education as well, with the addition of just one new building, a proposed new four year high school, ninth through the twelfth grades. One Middle School, sixth through eighth would then be established in the existing high school building, and all the present elementary buildings would then be used for kindergarten through the fifth grade. Lakeside would not only house the elementary school but would have space for present special education programs that are now in real need of additional space.

The Master Plan means more space in the elementary schools for special programs without additional construction except some remodeling which would be done through regular capital outlay expenditures.

This would provide space for library media centers at each building which local educators feel should be the center of learning in any modern school. The construction of a new high school will provide space for such centers in all the elementary buildings and the Middle School.

The present high school building is being utilized at 100% capacity and the construction of the rooms is such that no new programs or teaching methods can be incorporated. Some of the following are reasons for space needs and program needs that can be improved with the construction of a new high school.

    a. Modern instructional programs that involve media such as closed-circuit television, overhead projectors, film-loops, programmed teaching aids, and learning a u d i o tapes can be utilized by students in all schools.

    b. Expanded programs to maintain the comprehensive accreditation rating now enjoyed by our present students, such as a third year of f o r e i g n languages, improved electives in girls' physical education, career education concepts of exposure to many fields of interest, and comprehensive library-media centers.

c. Expanded vocational programs for students desiring educational experiences.
d. Space needs to meet additional state required special education programs.
e. General improvement of teaching in areas of developmental reading, instrumental music, physical education and speech development. These programs now meet in hallways, back stage of auditoriums and sometimes are shifted from one area to another as space will permit.

THE MIDDLE SCHOOL

Contrast between existing and proposed schools

The Middle School which will include grades 6-7-8 is a new way of putting young people and teachers together in creative and satisfying interaction. Today's youth are far different from the youth of previous generations. We are certain that educational needs of 6-7-8 grades are different, too, and that a new organization is required to care for these needs. Following is a comparison of a typical junior high arrangement with the elements of a Middle School as envisioned for Pittsburg:

Middle School
1. Grades 6-7-8.
2. Exploratory curriculum.
3. Purpose is to prepare for continuous learning.
4. Interdisciplinary teaming approach to instruction.
5. Key decisions on grouping and scheduling made by teaching staff.
6. Individualized instruction.
7. Teams of teachers focus on individual student needs and interests.
8. Modular scheduling varying daily.
9. Flexibility prevails.
10. Increased opportunities for independent study.

Junior High School
1. Grades 7-8-9.
2. Curriculum is predetermined.
3. Purpose is to prepare for high school.
4. Departmental organization prevails.
5. Key decisions on grouping and scheduling made by administrators and guidance counselors.
6. More fixed teaching and grouping practices.
7. Individual teachers focus on subject matter mastery.
8. 42 or 45 minute classes each day.
9. Rigidity prevails.
10. Limited opportunity for independent study.

THE SITE

Location

The site chosen by the Board of Education is a 50-acre tract of land located on the southwest quadrant of the intersection of Fourth and Free King Highway, adjacent to the city limits in the extreme eastern part of the City of Pittsburg. The site was chosen after careful study by members of the Board of Education and recommendations from specialists in the field of education. This site was considered the best location of all those considered due to space, utilities, parking, and location within the School District.

A school site must provide space, not only for the building, landscaping and grassed areas, and possible future expansion of the building, but also for sidewalks, driveways, bus loading, and other informal play areas, and for such outdoor instructional areas as may be desired for the natural sciences. Parking is and has been a problem at the present location of the high school building; and the new area would alleviate that particular problem.

Cost of the land

The Board of Education purchased the 50 acre tract of land in 19   at a cost of $2,000 per acre, for a total of $100,000. The cost of the land was paid from the Capital Outlay Fund.

TRANSPORTATION OF STUDENTS

Anticipated objections

Very little increase in cost for pupil transportation is anticipated although transportation will be made available to high school students. Most students will travel to school by personal auto, just as they are presently doing. Those who desire to be bused will be transported by using the same "pick-up patterns" which cover the elementary schools, then Lakeside, then PHS-Roosevelt. All high school students who ride buses will then be taken from the PHS-Roosevelt site to the new high school in three or four buses.

No additional buses will have to be purchased and no additional drivers will be hired. Some buses will travel a few more miles each day thereby causing some increase in daily operational costs but the increase will be minor.

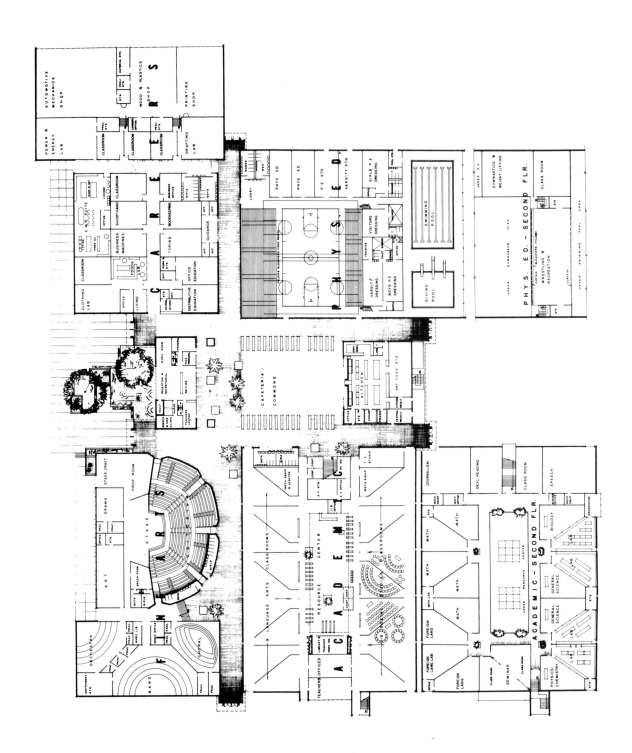

THE USE OF BOND PROCEEDS

ESTIMATED BUILDING AREAS AND COST FOR THE NEW HIGH SCHOOL FACILITY

Area	Square Feet
Academic Area	56,600
Career Development	38,000
Physical Education	34,500
Fine Arts (auditorium, music, art)	25,000
Commons — Lunch Room	21,500
Secondary corridors	6,400
Administration	3,000
TOTAL	185,000

Costs for school

Estimated Building Cost (185,000 sq. ft. at $20.00 per sq. ft.)	$3,700,000
Furnishings	113,000
Equipment	100,000
Parking Area (30,000 sq. yds. at $3.00)	90,000
Curb and gutter (3,000 linear ft. at $5.60)	17,000
Fees — architects, bond attorney (approximate)	230,000
TOTAL	$4,250,000

RESULTING TAX COSTS

At the present assessed valuation of Unified School District No. 250 in the amount of $32,311,381 one mill would raise $32,311. A building program will require a bond levy. Figures show that on the present school district valuation that an approximate mill levy would not exceed nine (9) mills. A nine (9) mill levy is a total tax of $9.00 per year for each $1,000 of tangible taxable assessed valuation in the school district. Depending upon the assessed valuation of a property and home, the following annual costs would apply to the taxpayer in the school district based upon a levy of nine (9) mills:

Examples of Annual and Monthly Tax Cost Based on a 9 Mill Levy

Actual Value of Home	Assessed Value at 30% Assessment Ratio	Annual Increase in Property Tax	Additional Amount on Monthly House Payment
$ 5,000	$ 1,500	13.50	1.13
7,500	2,250	20.25	1.69
10,000	3,000	27.00	2.25
12,500	3,750	33.75	2.81
15,000	4,500	40.50	3.37
17,500	5,250	47.25	3.94
20,000	6,000	54.00	4.50
25,000	7,500	67.50	5.63
30,000	9,000	81.00	6.75
40,000	12,000	108.00	9.00

Costs to taxpayer

It must be remembered that this valuation is the school district's assessed value and not real property value based upon real estate or property sales.

In the event that the assessed valuation increases each year, the mill levy would decrease in proportion. This mill levy is for construction of a building, equipping, and furnishing the building and for the payment of principal and interest of the $4,250,000 but does not include the cost of maintenance and operation.

SUMMARY

Key arguments for the proposal

A. The present High School Building was constructed 50 years ago.

B. The new High School Building would house grades nine through twelve. The present High School facilities would house grades six through eight.

C. Elementary buildings would house kindergarten through fifth grade students. Lakeside would house elementary school and have additional space for present special education programs.

D. Present High School is being utilized at 100% capacity with no room for expansion, new programs or teaching methods.

E. New High School facilities would provide:
   (1) Modern instruction
   (2) Expanded programs
   (3) Expanded vocational programs
   (4) Special Education programs
   (5) Improvement in teaching areas for developmental reading, music, physical education, and speech development.

F. The site selected and purchased by the Board of Education is a 50 acre tract of land located in the eastern portion of the city of Pittsburg. The site selection was determined to comply with recommendations from the State Department of Public Instruction.

G. A $4,250,000 School Building Program will require an average annual mill levy of 9 mills, over a 20 year period.

H. The target date for occupancy of the new High School Building is for September 1, 19__.

YOUR VOTE IS NEEDED!!!

Persuasion

A student's attitude toward education is often determined by the physical condition of the school facilities in which he attends classes. The outcome of this Election is of importance to the young people of this Unified School District. A student skillfully trained and educated becomes an American trained to earn a living and accept his responsibilities.

**EVERY QUALIFIED ELECTOR IN UNIFIED SCHOOL DISTRICT No. 250
SHOULD VOTE TUESDAY, APRIL 3, 19__**

This information is prepared and distributed by the Board of Education of Unified School District No. 250, Crawford County, Kansas. The program has been thoroughly investigated and the proposed school facilities are needed.

FIRST SECURITIES COMPANY
SCHWEITER BLDG.   WICHITA, KANSAS
INCORPORATED
OF KANSAS

WICHITA OFFICE   KANSAS CITY OFFICE
200 SCHWEITER BLDG.   1000 INS. EXCHANGE BLDG.
TEL. AMherst 2-4411   TEL. HArrison 1-3870

(Courtesy Unified School District [2])

INFORMAL PROPOSALS

From the very outset of your career you will write brief, informal proposals that will help you to advance faster in your job. Also, the informal proposal can be the first step in producing a formal report. At a great saving of time and money, it can be submitted first to find out if there is a possibility of acceptance for a longer, more detailed statement.

The specimen informal proposal below was written by a student to his major advisor to secure approval for the subject of his formal report.

To:	Dr. Brownell
From:	Jerry Villmauro
Subject:	Formal report for Technical Writing 301
Date:	September 10, 19—

Problem Changes in the SST Program. Last June the federal government updated the SST Program. It now differs considerably from the SST information presented by Dr. J. L. Jamison in the Workshop last May.

Solution New procedures. It is now necessary to analyze and evaluate the changes made in the existing SST Program. EASY II specifically outlines the principles of shielding, the shelter area, and the floor area usability factors required.

Request Subject for the formal report. I was employed in the Corps of Engineers' SST Program from June to August this year and became quite familiar with these new federal regulations. I would appreciate the opportunity to identify and to interpret the recent changes and request your approval of "Changes in the SST Program" as the subject of my formal report.

Solicited Proposal

Most informal interoffice proposals are requested by a superior. They may range from proposing the purchase of new equipment to changing an accepted procedure to improving the operation of a certain department. Such informal proposals are usually in memo form; sometimes the company supplies employees with a standardized form to make the task of proposal writing easier. The following specimen form asks for details of the problem to be solved, the proposed solution, and the date of the idea.

IDEA RECORD

Title for the proposed idea _____

File number _____

Problem to be solved by this idea _____

_____

_____

_____

_____

Your solution to this problem (Supply a sketch or flow sheet to assist in this explanation; if possible, make a sketch on the back of this sheet.) _____

_____

_____

_____

_____

_____

_____

_____

_____

This idea occurred to me (or us) first on _____

A written verification of this date can be found in my (or our) _____

Signature of Inventor or Inventors   Date_____

_____

_____

_____

Unsolicited Proposal

Producing the unsolicited proposal is a sign of initiative. The one who looks for extra work is usually promoted faster than the worker who does only the minimum. It is wise, however, to check orally with your supervisor before writing the unsolicited proposal. Then approval of the memo will be assured, and it will be sent on to others in the company. You may want to solve the problems of high phone bills, delays in invoicing and shipping, strained customer relations, or unproductive advertising. If you are not an employee of the company for which you would like to perform the service, you should send a letter. But whether you send a memo or a letter, whether it is short or long, headings should be used and the parts labeled so your informal proposal will be easy to read.

Organization of Informal Proposals

There are three parts to an informal proposal: (1) a review of the existing problem, (2) your solution, and (3) the justification/request. These parts may be arranged in any effective order; if the subject is not controversial, you can begin with the request, briefly explain the problem, and give information about your solution. Regardless of how you arrange these three parts, when you review the problem, its development over the years should be described and the reader should be impressed with its importance. Your proposed solution should be described in great detail, perhaps with figures and tables included. In the justification/request part of the informal proposal, the time and/or money your solution will save the company should be stressed as well as other advantages such as the ease with which your proposal can be implemented. You should end with a specific request since it is unwise to leave a reader wondering what you want him to do about this proposal. You may request permission to conduct certain tests to resolve the problem or to get information from company files that will ultimately solve the problem. The memo below illustrates the organizaion of the informal proposal.

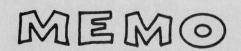

TO: John Olivet, Vice-President
FROM: Jim Haywood, Director of Maintenance
SUBJECT: Facility Improvement
DATE: April 30, 19—

Problem   Faulty valves. The controls of the steam heating system in Plant No. 2 are inoperable. When this building was constructed in 1929, all equipment was designed for hand coal firing and hand operated controls. Air control units were installed on radiator valves but, due to the lack of insulation on steam lines, controls were inefficient. Through the years, the air lines that were installed in concrete floors have broken from floor shifting. Hand operated valves were installed in 1951, but now these valves have rusted out.

Solution   Electrically operated valves. Individual electrically operated control valves should be installed in each room of Plant No. 2. These valves would be controlled by an electric thermostat also installed in each room.

Persuasion Increased productivity at minimum cost. The cost for installation of Amsterdam controls would be $5,000. This project could be paid for from next year's capital outlay budget, and installation could be completed before next fall.

The manager of Plant No. 2 estimates that more comfortable working conditions will increase productivity in each department concerned by approximately 8%.

Request   Please act on this proposal at the May 5 board meeting.

SPECIAL PROBLEMS

Sometimes a customer will ask that you submit a proposal solving a problem in an inefficient way. In this case, it is better to submit two proposals: one for the customer's way and another for the way that you consider better. You should include a detailed justification of the method you believe is superior and stress that the second proposal is in the best interests of all and will not cost any more. If the alternate proposal is more expensive and time-consuming, it will be difficult to submit and justify.

Another pitfall of proposal writing is the temptation to promise more than you can do. You should be sure that you have the time, work force, and capital and check the adequacy of your facilities and technical competence.

To avoid difficulties, any specifications for proposals that some companies and agencies demand should be investigated. Some insist on proposals of a certain length, on specific headings, on a stated number of copies, and on a particular arrangement of the contents. Finding out how the proposal will be judged will also help you to write it more effectively.

SUMMARY

The goal for any interoffice or outside-the-company proposal is to obtain some sort of privilege for the writer or for the company he represents. In commercial proposals, the primary consideration is cost, then performance, reliability, economy of operation, and date of delivery.

The longer formal proposal contains the following parts:

Title page
Letter of transmittal
Table of contents
List of tables and figures
Introduction
    Purpose
    Definition of the problem
    Scope
Methodology sections
    Background information on the problem
    Technical phases of the project
    Schedule for the project
    Facility requirements
    Personnel requirements
    Cost
Conclusion/Summary
Appendix

However, all the above parts are not included in every formal proposal. Proposals are tailored to meet the demands of specific situations, and only the sections relevant to a particular problem and solution are included.

The brief informal proposal includes the analysis of the problem, a detailed account of the solution, and a specific request. These three parts are usually found in every informal proposal, but they may be rearranged in any order that seems most effective.

The proposal is a special type of technical writing because it is concerned with the future and involves much selling ability. But as in all kinds of technical writing, a good idea effectively communicated—whether in proposal form or not—gains recognition for you and for your organization.

SPECIMEN PROPOSALS

The following informal sales proposal illustrates the brevity that is possible when the customer has already decided to advertise:

```
63,100 Watts Audio          KOAM-TV          316,000 Watts Video
NBC Affiliate                                     Channel 7
                           Pittsburg, Kansas

To   Proposal for Carter Drug              Date  February 9, 19_____

From            Tom Freeman                No._____

          Subject:   Spot Schedule beginning in February
_____

Budget of $1200 a month              30 second video-taped spots

13 Prime Class "AA" Spots during month @ $60 each          $780.00

13 Fringe or Class "A" Spots during month @ $25 each        325.00

Production charges – 2 VTR sessions per month @ $45          90.00

                     Artwork and/or slides                    5.00
                                                          _____
                     Average monthly charge               $1200.00
```

(Courtesy KOAM-TV [3])

The next proposal is a formal one that includes a title page, letter of transmittal, introduction giving background on the company, and a complete methodology describing how the insurance plan will operate and what it will cost.

Title page

```
                    A

              MASSACHUSETTS

                 MUTUAL

            GROUP  INSURANCE

              PRESENTATION



  DESIGNED FOR ........................

                    _____

                    _____




  SUBMITTED BY ........................




                        MASSACHUSETTS MUTUAL
                        LIFE INSURANCE COMPANY
                        Springfield, Massachusetts / organized 1851

  IP 801 474 Series I or III
```

Massachusetts Mutual Life Insurance Company

Springfield, Massachusetts

Scope

A plan of employee benefits is an important segment of your employer-employee relations program. As such, it should be designed to meet your company's objectives and the needs of the people it is intended to protect.

Advantages of plan

The benefits proposed in these pages are, in our estimation, the best suited for your company and your employees, having been determined after a careful study of the data gathered at a preliminary meeting with your management. Yet, the plan is flexible enough to permit changes that may be deemed necessary after consultation between you and the Massachusetts Mutual Group Representative.

Cost

The cost estimate is calculated on the latest employee data and benefit provisions made available to us, and is based on the lowest rates consistent with sound underwriting. Not shown in the cost is our pledge of continued service to your full satisfaction and an efficient administration of your plan in return for your confidence in Massachusetts Mutual.

Thank you for the opportunity to be of service.

C. G. HILL, VICE PRESIDENT

The Company

Behind the Plan

Background

OVER A CENTURY OF EXPERIENCE

Organized in 1851, the Massachusetts Mutual is proud of its service to over one million policy owners and their beneficiaries and more than 1 million Group certificate holders with their dependents.

NATIONWIDE SERVICE

The Massachusetts Mutual is licensed to do business in all 50 states and the District of Columbia and Puerto Rico. It has 133 general agencies in over 100 cities across the nation, and operates 375 district offices, 50 group insurance offices, and 16 Group Claim offices.

HAS PAID BILLIONS

The Massachusetts Mutual has paid to policyholders and beneficiaries over $3.5 billion, which, with reserves and surplus held by the Company for the benefit of the policyholders, substantially exceeds the premiums received.

COSTS ARE LOW

Massachusetts Mutual's liberal dividend practice has placed the Company among the very foremost "low net cost" companies in America. As a mutual company, Massachusetts Mutual has no stockholders. It is wholly owned by, and operated exclusively for, the benefit of its policyholders. All income over and above the costs of doing business and maintaining adequate surplus is returned annually to the policyholders in the form of dividends.

$24 BILLION IN FORCE

Of more than 1,700 life insurance companies in the United States, the Massachusetts Mutual ranked among the top 1% in size with over $24 billion of life insurance in force.

STRENGTH

Since its founding in 1851, Massachusetts Mutual has been tested by wars, epidemics, panics, and depressions and has emerged from them all with a constant growth in assets and general strength of position in the life insurance field.

ASSETS AND SURPLUS

The Company has assets of over $5,100,000,000 and surplus in excess of $244,000,000. Both represent substantial increases in recent years.

LEADERSHIP

Massachusetts Mutual specializes in the finest Group Insurance contracts. Offering complete Life Insurance, Disability, and Pension benefits, the Company has long been a leader in the Individual Life and Group Insurance field, and a Pioneer in the introduction of many of the strong points of policyholder protection.

PROGRESSIVE

Massachusetts Mutual, from its very beginning, has had the prestige of being one of the leaders in the life insurance industry of America. It initiated many of the improvements in life insurance that are now regular features in the contracts of other companies. The Company has established a distinguished record of "firsts" in making available new types of coverage and more liberal policy provisions.

Management and Operation . . . .

The company, now in its 122nd year of operation, is purely mutual and is particularly a policyholders' institution. It has long been most ably managed. It ranks very highly and enjoys a most excellent reputation in all areas of its activities. It currently stands as the seventh largest mutual life insurance company in the nation as measured by both assets and insurance in force. Many important benefits and privileges which the company has given to new policyholders has been given to old policyholders on the same terms, except when expressly forbidden by state or other laws.

(Quoted from "Best's Life Insurance Reports" 1973 edition.)

IP 303 774 Series I or III

How the Plan Operates

General explanation of plan

ELIGIBILITY OF EMPLOYEES . . .

Employees are required to complete a period of service before becoming eligible under the plan. Generally one to three months is an adequate period.

It is customary to waive this "waiting period" when plans are first adopted, making it applicable only to employees hired after the effective date of the plan.

There is no age limit for Massachusetts Mutual Group Insurance.

NO MEDICAL EXAMINATION . . .

No medical examination is required of any employee if he applies promptly.

WHEN AN EMPLOYEE'S INSURANCE IS DISCONTINUED . . .

The insurance on an employee is discontinued when he terminates employment or requests discontinuance of his contributions.

When employment terminates there is 31 days extended insurance coverage, without premium charge, under Group Life Insurance, and extended benefits in the event of total disability are provided under most of the other coverages.

For lay-offs, leaves of absence, retirement, or absence on disability, a fixed practice regarding any continuation of coverage, applicable to all employees without discrimination, is provided.

DIVISION OF COST OF PLAN . . .

The Employer may pay the entire cost of the plan or the cost may be divided between the Employer and the employees, except that in the latter instance there are certain maximums applicable to the employee's contribution. The employee's share is deducted from his pay by automatic payroll deduction authorized by the employee on his application card.

MASTER POLICY FOR EMPLOYER — CERTIFICATE FOR EMPLOYEES . . .

The policy is issued to the Employer. The entire contract is between the Employer and the Massachusetts Mutual. A certificate of insurance is provided for each insured employee describing the benefits to which he is entitled, to whom benefits are payable and other provisions of the plan.

HOW PREMIUMS ARE PAID . . .

Premiums may be paid either monthly, quarterly, semi-annually or annually, to suit the convenience of the Employer.

GROUP SERVICE BY MASSACHUSETTS MUTUAL . . .

Service in connection with Massachusetts Mutual Group Insurance plans is provided through a staff of Group Managers and Home Office Representatives located in key cities throughout the country. These men are trained in all phases of Employee Welfare Plans and have a definite interest in the smooth operation of your Group Insurance program.

SIMPLE ACCOUNTING METHODS USED . . .

The accounting methods used in the administration of Massachusetts Mutual Group Insurance plans are the result of careful study of all methods used, and were designed with simplicity of operation for the Employer, a basic consideration. All administrative systems are based on the extensive use of high-speed electronic data processing equipment. They will be found to be simple, effective, and to keep to a minimum the number of forms to be completed by the policyholder and his employees. It will not require a great amount of clerical time to administer Group Insurance under a Massachusetts Mutual plan since only three basic forms are used in the streamlined system of accounting.

IP 301 474 Series I or III

Your Premium Rates

Advantages

THREE-YEAR RATE GUARANTEE

The proposed group insurance program outlined in the pages that follow offers you and your employees a financially stabilized plan in which all coverage rates are guaranteed for three full years from the effective date. When a change in plan takes place during the rate guarantee period, the benefits and the premium rate will be changed but the guarantee period will not be altered.

Among the many advantages because of such guarantee are the following:

1. You are better able to budget for group insurance costs since you can better anticipate your group insurance outlays for employee benefits over a longer time range.

2. Your administrative details are curtailed because of eliminating the necessity for time consuming plan study and review each and every year.

3. Group Insurance benefits are safeguarded from erosion occasioned by cutbacks necessary to maintain contributions at a reasonable level as would be the case if you were insured under a plan where renewals were negotiated each year.

It follows that your employees' sense of security will be greatly enhanced because of the three-year rate guarantee as well.

IP 806 474 Series III

L
I
F
E

LIFE INSURANCE BENEFIT

Scope of plan In the event of his death, regardless of the cause, the amount for which an employee is insured will be paid to his beneficiary. The employee names his own beneficiary and may change the beneficiary at any time by making written request.

IN THE EVENT OF TOTAL DISABILITY

The Plan proposed would provide for continued protection as indicated.

CONTINUED INSURANCE

If the employee becomes totally disabled prior to his 60th birthday, his Life Insurance will be continued in force without payment of premiums as long as he remains disabled, provided he submits proof of the continuance of total disability at intervals of one year each.

EXTENDED DEATH BENEFIT

If an employee's Life Insurance is discontinued while he is totally disabled and if he remains disabled, the death benefit will be paid if he dies before his 65th birthday and within a period of discontinuance equal to the lesser of twelve months or the length of time for which he had been insured.

RIGHT TO AN INDIVIDUAL POLICY OF LIFE INSURANCE UPON TERMINATION OF EMPLOYMENT

In the event his employment terminates, the employee may obtain a policy of Life Insurance on any of the forms of policy customarily issued by the Massachusetts Mutual Life Insurance Company (except Term Insurance) in an amount equal to, or at his option less than, the amount of his Group Life Insurance Certificate. The employee may elect that this policy shall include Single Premium Term Insurance for the first year. No evidence of insurability or medical examination will be required.

This right must be exercised and the required premium paid within 31 days following termination of employment.

The premium for the individual policy will be based on the employee's age and occupational classification at the time his insurance is converted.

If the employee dies within 31 days after termination of employment, the amount which he could have converted will be paid as a death benefit, whether or not he has actually applied for conversion.

IP 320 474 Series I or III

Accidental Death and Dismemberment Insurance

Scope of benefits

WHEN BENEFIT IS PAYABLE

If, as a result of accidental bodily injury occurring while insured, an employee suffers any of the losses listed below within 90 days of the date of the accident, the benefit shown below will be payable.

The Principal Sum (the amount for which the employee is insured) is Payable for Loss of:

One Hand and One Foot

One Hand and the Sight of One Eye

One Foot and the Sight of One Eye

Life

Two Hands or Two Feet

Sight of Two Eyes

Twice the Principal Sum is payable for loss of life due to injury suffered while the employee is a passenger in a vehicle operated by a common carrier.

One-half the Principal Sum is Payable for Loss of:

One Hand or One Foot

Sight of One Eye

Loss of hands or feet means loss by severance at or above the wrist or ankle joints. Loss of sight means total and irrecoverable loss of sight beyond remedy by surgical or other means.

The total amount payable for all losses sustained in any one accident may not exceed the Principal Sum for which the employee is insured, but payment is made for losses due to each accident without regard to any prior accident.

Payment for any dismemberment loss will be made to the employee. Payment for accidental death will be made to his beneficiary. The employee names his own beneficiary and may change the beneficiary at any time by making written request.

Losses for Which No Benefits Are Payable

Benefits are not payable for losses resulting from or caused directly, wholly or partly by:

A. Disease or bodily or mental infirmity or medical or surgical treatment thereof; or

B. Ptomaines, or bacterial infections, except pyogenic infections occurring with and through an accidental wound; and

C. Suicide or intentionally self-inflicted injury, while sane or insane; or

D. Participation in or in consequence of having participated in the committing of a felony; or

E. War or any act of war, whether declared or undeclared.

☐ This plan covers non-occupational injuries only.

☒ This plan covers occupational and non-occupational injuries.

IP 340 474 Series I or III

Proposed Benefits AND Cost Estimate

EMPLOYEE ONLY

Class	Life Insurance	Accidental Death	Accidental Death on Common Carrier
I	$ 50,000	$ 150,000	$ 250,000
II	$ 30,000	$ 90,000	$ 150,000
III	$ 22,500	$ 67,500	$ 112,500
IV	$ 20,000	$ 60,000	$ 100,000
V	$ 10,000	$ 30,000	$ 50,000
VI	$ 2,500	$ 7,500	$ 12,500

ESTIMATED MONTHLY COST

	Volume	Rate per $ 1,000	Premium
Life Insurance	$ 771,250	$ .70	$ 539.88
Accidental Death	$ 1,542,500	$ .07	$ 107.98

The premium rates shown herein are illustrative, based upon census data and information as furnished for preparation of this proposal. Premium rates as of the effective date of the Plan will be determined from census data then applicable.

IP 464 474 Series I or III

BENEFIT ANALYSIS

Class	Basis of Classification	Present Plan		Recommended Plan	
		Life	AD&D	Life	AD&D
I	President	$ 50,000	$ 50,000	$ 50,000	$ 150,000
II	Vice-President	$ 30,000	$ 30,000	$ 30,000	$ 90,000
III	Store Manager, Sales Manager Field Sales Manager	$ 22,500	$ 22,500	$ 22,500	$ 67,500
IV	Treasurer, Assistant Vice-President, Assistant Treasurer, Credit Manager, Warehouse Manager	$ 20,000	$ 20,000	$ 20,000	$ 60,000
V	Secretary, Assistant Store Manager, Salesman	$ 10,000	$ 10,000	$ 10,000	$ 30,000
VI	Any Other Employee	$ 2,500	$ 2,500	$ 2,500	$ 7,500

Dependent | Group Life Insurance

DEFINITION OF DEPENDENT
The term "dependent" means

(a) an employee's wife who is not eligible for benefits as an employee, who is not legally separated from the employee and who is not a member of the armed forces, and

(b) an employee's unmarried child (including any stepchild, legally adopted child and foster child) over seven days of age but under twenty-three* years of age who is not eligible for benefits as an employee and who is not a member of the armed forces, provided that any child over 19 but less than 23* years of age shall be considered as a dependent only if he is not employed and has the same home address as the employee.

The definition of dependent may be extended to include the husband of an insured employee provided he is not eligible as an employee or a member of the armed forces.

If a husband and wife are both insured as employees, only the husband will be eligible for Group Term Life Insurance on the lives of any children they may have.

*The limiting age in California and Ohio is 21.

BENEFICIARY
The beneficiary is the employee. There is no right of election or change.

OPTIONAL METHODS OF SETTLEMENT AND TOTAL DISABILITY
These provisions are not available under Group Term Life Insurance for Dependents.

CONVERSION PRIVILEGE
Upon discontinuance of insurance due to (a) termination of the employee's employment in an eligible class or (b) death of the employee or (c) attainment of the limiting age for a dependent child or (d) discontinuance of the group policy, each insured spouse and child may convert his or her insurance without evidence of insurability subject to the same rules governing the employees conversion privilege, including the extended death benefit.

DEPENDENT GROUP LIFE INSURANCE
In the event of death of your insured dependent from any cause, the amount payable to you is the amount for which the dependent was insured on the date of his death.

Proposed Benefits

Spouse $ 1,000

Age at death of child		
	5 years but less than 23 years	$ 1,000
	4 years but less than 5 years	$ 800
	3 years but less than 4 years	$ 600
	2 years but less than 3 years	$ 400
	6 months but less than 2 years	$ 200
	8 days but less than 6 months	$ 100

Proposed Benefits AND **Cost Estimate**

DEPENDENT ONLY

Spouse $ 1,000

Age at Death of Child

8 Days but less than 6 months $ 100

6 Months but less than 2 years $ 200

2 Years but less than 3 years $ 400

3 Years but less than 4 years $ 600

4 Years but less than 5 years $ 800

5 Years but less than 23 years $ 1,000

ESTIMATED MONTHLY COST

Cost per Dependent	Number	Premium
$ .58	54	$ 31.32

The premium rates shown herein are illustrative, based upon census data and information as furnished for preparation of this proposal. Premium rates as of the effective date of the Plan will be determined from census data then applicable.

IP 464 474 Series I or III

(Courtesy Massachusetts Mutual [4])

WRITING ASSIGNMENTS

A. For one of the topics listed below, write an unsolicited informal proposal using the memo or letter form.

1. Suggest a repair or remodeling job for the classroom.
2. Recommend the purchase of a piece of equipment to be used in a certain class.
3. Suggest a change in procedure for the firm that employs you part time.
4. Suggest to the editor of a periodical in your major area that you do research and write an article on a specific subject.
5. Propose a solution to some current problem at your school or firm: parking, vandalism, loss of library books or other equipment, etc.

B. Write a formal proposal for one of the topics listed below:

1. Your hometown community would like to be the site of a new recreational facility that will be located in the area. You represent the Chamber of Commerce and have been invited by the recreational concern to prove the suitability of your city and to offer incentives that will induce the organization to come there.

2. Your hometown community would like to be the site of a new industrial plant that will be located in the area. You represent the Chamber of Commerce and have been invited to submit a proposal proving the suitability of your city.
3. Your county needs a new jail facility. Write an unsolicited proposal to the county commissioners in which you prove that the facility should be located in a certain area.
4. Suggest in an unsolicited proposal to the local school board that a certain course be added to the high school curriculum.
5. Propose a change in required courses for your major. Assume that you have not been asked to submit this proposal.
6. A large local firm has announced its intention to expand its parking facilities. Convince the members of the firm that your company should do the work.

REFERENCES
1. "Two in the Know Who Win the Dough," *The Kansas City Star,* Mar. 18, 1976, p. 8, cols. 1–2.
2. Unified School District 250, Pittsburg, KS.
3. KOAM-TV. Pittsburg, KS.
4. Massachusetts Mutual. Springfield, MA.

Writing for Publication

EACH of you, regardless of your field, should seriously consider writing technical articles for publication. Writing for publication adds to your professional prestige by making your name well known, it improves your chances for advancement within your company, it allows you to communicate your innovative methods and techniques, and it encourages an exchange of ideas with others in your field. Journals in many areas need articles and will often accept your initial attempts. Some actively solicit additional articles.

Many benefits of publishing contribute to personal satisfaction. Writing articles trains you in orderly thinking and adds to your knowledge. Most publications pay for articles so there are financial rewards as well as the satisfaction of seeing your name in print. Sometimes when you are not paid for an article, your employer reimburses you for your writing time because your publication is good publicity for the company. You can also have the satisfaction of performing a service for your profession since progress often depends on a free, unrestricted exchange of fact and theory.

The formal technical report and the article published in a technical journal are similar: both usually include tables of contents, abstracts, headings of more than one rank, and clear systems of documentation. Both are impersonal in tone—avoiding *I* and *you*—and employ an extensive technical vocabulary.

The difference in the formal report and the technical article suitable for publication lies mainly in audience and purpose. Unlike a formal technical report, which must be read by the person or persons to whom it is addressed, the technical article has to capture the readers' interest at the outset and make them want to read the whole article. It appeals, ordinarily, to a much larger audience. The formal report is often written at the request of a superior; the technical article is usually un-

solicited. Because the technical article is written for a larger potential audience and because it is unsolicited, effective phraseology, emphatic headings, and attractive and informative visuals are more important than those in the formal report.

TYPES OF PERIODICALS

As you examine the periodicals in your field, it soon becomes obvious that they vary widely in tone, style, length, and type. However, there are basically three types: the technical periodicals that print highly specialized articles for fellow professionals, the semitechnical periodicals for specialists in other fields, and the nontechnical or popular periodicals that present interesting and informative articles for the general public. The entire range of articles makes a valid contribution to the field. An exchange of ideas is important whether those ideas are complicated, innovative theories or whether they involve basic information already widely accepted in the field.

Technical Periodicals

The technical periodical includes articles written by those whose professions are directly related to their subjects and who are therefore specialists. These articles are clearly organized and calculated to appeal to others professionally interested in the field. The restrained tone is the result of an extensive vocabulary and of avoiding *I* and *you*:

RESTRAINED TONE	INFORMAL TONE
Initially, the function of	In the beginning, the purpose of
One should always inspect the equipment	You should always check your machine
The protean aspects of preventive medicine	The changing concepts of periodic checkups

Such technical articles report on theory and on research developments. Since they are addressed to colleagues with similar interests, training, knowledge, and experience, they make little attempt to attract attention and stimulate interest in the introduction; they often do not explain highly technical information. Data are considered objectively. Examples of technical periodicals are *Journal of the Optical Society of Ameria, Physiological Psychology, Comparative Education Review, Publications of the Modern Language Association, Reviews of Modern Physics, Journal of Finance, Environmental Science & Technology, Journal of Library Automation,* and *Public Administration Review.*

Semitechnical Periodicals

The semitechnical periodical reports the practical side of the subject and the industrial applications in an easy, informal, readable style. Its articles are aimed at the general professional readers who have only a slight advance interest in the discussion but are usually competent in the field, have a wide variety of interests, and are highly intelligent. They are not, however, sufficiently familiar with the field to follow all the language peculiar to it. Because it is necessary first to gain the readers' interest, special attention should be given to the introductions of these articles: a device with which the readers will be familiar should be used. A direct thesis statement early in the discussion should be avoided. The body of the semitechnical article is as logical, precise, and accurate as the technical one, but it requires more clarification: technical terms you have to use should be explained and interpreted; mathematical treatments should be avoided. The primary objective should be restated often, and more visuals should be used. A formal bibliography is not always included at the end of each article. Semitechnical periodicals include *Scientific American, RN, Music Educators Journal, Wood & Wood Products, Industrial Education, Woodwind World—Brass & Percussion, Plastics Technology, Journal of Home Economics,* and *Teaching Exceptional Children.*

Other types of semitechnical publications are the trade journals, association magazines, and newsletters. Each of the technological specialties seems to have at least one trade journal and some have several: construction, air conditioning, automotive technology, electronics, and metals. Most national and international professional organizations and interest groups publish their own association magazines; for example, *AAUP Bulletin* for the American Association of University Professors and *Technical Communication* for the Society for Technical Communication. There are also thousands of newsletters, house organs that publish semitechnical articles for internal distribution among employees or for external distribution or for both audiences.

Nontechnical or Popular Periodicals

The nontechnical periodical presents informative articles written by the professional journalist for the general reading public. The journalist presents the material in a colorful way to entertain the nonprofessional readers. Such periodicals include *National Geographic Magazine, Popular Mechanics, Reader's Digest,* and *Popular Science Monthly* and are beyond the scope of this chapter since their articles are produced by writers who are not experts in the subject matter.

TYPES OF ARTICLES

Several different types of articles appear in technical and semitechnical periodicals. Some articles introduce a new subject; new products, processes, experiments, and theories may be discussed. Examples would be "Rat Strain Differences in Pilocarpine-Induced Mouse Killing" in *Physiological Psychology* and "New Ten-Station Foam Molder Makes Its Debut" in *Plastics Technology.*

Another type is a new analysis of a subject that has already been written about in great detail. New procedures or new equipment to perform a well-known process would be appropriate. Examples of such articles would be "Positive Attitudes: A Must for Special Programs in Public Schools" in *Teaching Exceptional Children* and "Newest Treatment for Cancer: Immunotherapy" in *RN.*

A third type of article deals with a subject made timely by a recent event. Destructive floods, hurricanes, or earthquakes generate a flurry of articles on early detection of, protection from, and aftermath of natural disasters. The death of a Howard Hughes brings about studies of corporate interests, of early flight records, and of distinctive life-styles. The Bicentennial encouraged such articles as "Manpower in the Age of Jackson" in *Worklife.*

A fourth type of article is written to express a strong conviction or defend a controversial viewpoint related either to an old or new subject. Every profession must constantly reexamine its concepts and performance. If you do not agree with every idea currently held in your professional area, you may already have the basis for a technical article. "A Theory of Inflation and Recession: Monopoly Power and Resource Immobility" in *Wage-Price Law & Economics Review;* "Changing Sex Roles—Concepts, Values, and Tasks" in *Social Casework;* and "Are Community Nutrition Programs Meeting the Needs of the Elderly?" in *Journal of Home Economics* all illustrate this type of article.

STEPS IN WRITING THE TECHNICAL ARTICLE

There are four steps in producing a technical article: (1) finding the idea itself, (2) selecting a suitable periodical for publication, (3) writing the article, and (4) submitting the article.

Finding a Subject

There are definite guidelines for selecting a subject. You should be aware of specific applications or processes in your company that others might be interested in and should communicate the way you have solved problems in your organization. Perhaps other companies are searching for solutions to the same problem. Conversations with fellow employees may suggest controversial topics. But you should always choose a subject with which you are quite familiar and limit yourself to one operation or to one problem and its solution.

You should not be discouraged if others have written on your subject. A fresh point of view can be developed or something new can be stressed. You may decide to write several articles all on the same subject.

Selecting the Periodical

You should examine the technical and semitechnical periodicals in your field. Sometimes editorial policy is stated on the inside cover. Here you can find out if the journal for which you want to write accepts unsolicited manuscripts and if the authors are paid. Is the accepted length of articles mentioned? If so, you must keep in mind the desired length and be sure you can develop your idea fully in the space available. Often editors mail, at your request, an editorial statement that describes the purpose of the periodical and the types of subject matter accepted.

Editorial policies vary in length and detail. *Phycologia* uses both the inside front and back covers for detailed instructions on acceptable subjects, length, and preparation of the manuscripts. *Social Casework* makes the following brief statement on the inside front cover:

Social Casework is directed primarily to the interests of social work practitioners and educators. Preference is given to articles that illuminate a facet of social work theory or practice, that report professional experimentation or research, or that are relevant to the social problems of the day and to the professional concerns of social workers. Manuscripts by members of related professions or disciplines are welcome.

Manuscripts submitted for publication should be between 16 and 20 double-spaced typed pages, with margins of at least one inch. Three copies are requested, one of which should be an original on nonerasable bond paper. References should be typed double-spaced at the bottom of the page on which they are cited and should be numbered.

(Courtesy Family Service Association of America for *Social Casework* [1])

Additional examples of statements of editorial policy are found below:

PUBLICATIONS OF THE MODERN LANGUAGE ASSOCIATION

Editor:	WILLIAM D. SCHAEFER
Managing Editor:	JUDY GOULDING

Promotion and Production Manager:	JEFFREY HOWITT
Assistant to Managing Editor:	MARGOT RABINER
Editorial Assistant:	Jean Park

A STATEMENT OF EDITORIAL POLICY

PMLA publishes articles on the modern languages and literatures that are of significant interest to the entire membership of the Association. Articles should therefore normally: (1) employ a widely applicable approach or methodology; or (2) use an interdisciplinary approach of importance to the interpretation of literature; or (3) treat a broad subject or theme; or (4) treat a major author or work; or (5) discuss a minor author or work in such a way as to bring insight to a major author, work, genre, period, or critical method. Articles of fewer than 2,500 or more than 12,500 words are not normally considered for publication.

Only members of the Association may submit articles to *PMLA.* Each article submitted will be sent to at least one consultant reader and one member of the Advisory Committee. If recommended by these readers it will then be sent to the members of the Editorial Board, who meet every three months to discuss such articles and assist the Editor in making final decisions.

Submissions, prepared according to the second edition of the *MLA Style Sheet,* should be addressed to the Editor of *PMLA,* 62 Fifth Avenue, New York, New York 10011. Only an original typescript, not a photocopy or carbon, should be submitted.

(Courtesy Modern Language Association of America for *PMLA* [2])

PUBLIC ADMINISTRATION REVIEW

Editorial Goals and Manuscript Procedures

The aim of PUBLIC ADMINISTRATION REVIEW is that of the Society—to advance the science, processes and art of public administration. It seeks to do this by fostering understanding among practitioners, teachers, researchers, and students of public administration. The aim of the editors is to publish material representative of all interests and opinions across the broad spectrum of public administration. The aim of all contributors should be to *communicate* across this broad spectrum. Opinions expressed are those of the authors and do not necessarily reflect the outlook of the organizations in which they work, of ASPA, or of the editors.

For contributions to all departments, clarity is prized and relative brevity necessary. Article manuscripts submitted for consideration should not exceed 4,000 words, and those ranging from 2,000 to 3,000 words are particularly welcome. Four copies of manuscripts should be submitted, three to the Managing Editor and one to the Editor-in-Chief, with the first page having only the title of the article and with a cover page to show title, author and position. All material should be double spaced, on one side of the page and with margins of one and a half inches. Footnotes, if any, should be double spaced on separate sheets following the end of the text. In general, the style (especially with regard to citations) should be that of recent issues of the REVIEW. An abstract of not more than 150 words and a brief biographical paragraph should accompany article manuscripts.

Communication and Routing

General articles, Professional Stream, and Communications:
Frank Marini, Managing Editor, School of Public Ad-

ministration and Urban Studies, San Diego State University, San Diego, California 92182.

Developments in Public Administration: Fremont J. Lyden, Feature Editor, Institute for Administrative Research, Graduate School of Public Affairs, University of Washington, Seattle, Washington 98105.

Book Reviews and Notes: Thad L. Beyle, Book Review Editor, Department of Political Science, University of North Carolina, Chapel Hill, North Carolina 27514.

Research and Reports: H. George Frederickson, Feature Editor, College of Public and Community Services, University of Missouri–Columbia, Columbia, Missouri 65201.

Business matters: Barbara Byers Judd, Production Editor, American Society for Public Administration, 1225 Connecticut Avenue, N.W., Washington, D.C. 20036.

Review policies and symposia: Dwight Waldo, Editor-in-Chief, The Maxwell School, Syracuse University, Syracuse, New York 13210.

(From *Public Administration Review*. Published by the American Society for Public Administration. Reprinted by permission.)

When there is no editorial policy statement in the periodical, you should closely examine the articles published in a few of the issues. Does the periodical favor controversial subjects or does it accept scholarly studies of generally held opinions? Sample issues should be checked for style, length of sentences, paragraphs, and vocabulary. Does the periodical include an introductory summary, a biographical sketch, references, and drawings and photographs for each article? Are headings used frequently?

Writing the Article

The writing process for the technical article is no different from that for any other type of writing: (1) official approval of the subject when appropriate, (2) reading and personal investigation, (3) note taking and outlining, (4) rough draft, and (5) final draft.

Official approval is necessary before submitting the article when you are writing about specific applications or problems solved in your organization. This approval will avoid leaking confidential information. And it also acquaints your superior with your desire for personal growth as well as for good public relations within the firm.

Researching is an important first step to find out whether or not the subject has already been fully explored by other writers and to find out how others have approached similar problems. Many corporations today have their own libraries; an examination of the appropriate index will reveal the scope of articles connected with the subject. The research that precedes the actual organization, writing, and revision is all-important. Your laboratory and shop training may make you want to attack the job of physical experimentation and scientific observation, but you should not slight the reading.

Note taking and outlining follow the preliminary research and reading. The same procedures described in the chapter on formal reports should be followed, and the temptation to include everything you know about the subject should be avoided. The finished technical article must be complete but also concise.

The rough draft of a technical article should be written quickly; a strong style and smoothness of ideas result. The rough draft includes the same parts described in the formal report and formal proposal chapters.

Although the title is usually written last, it is the first part of the article that the reader sees. As in other types of technical writing, the title of the highly specialized article simply indicates the subject of the report: "Development of the Tapetum in *Pinus banksiana* Preceding Sporogenesis," "Blowing Agents for Structural-Foam Molding," "Effects of Membrane Potential on the Capacitance of Skeletal Muscle Fibers," and "Test Performance and Socioeconomic Status in Uganda." But when writing a semitechnical article, use a title that also attracts attention and suggests your point of view: "High Efficiency Motors: An Energy-Saving Approach," "Purchasing Managers Will Play Even Greater Role in Fighting Inflation," "Design Safety into Your Shops and Labs," and "Shaping Lathe Headrig Will Stretch Shrinking Timber Supply."

A table of contents for the technical article is sometimes required by very scholarly publications. Here, again, is a part of the rough draft usually written last but seen by the reader first. When there is a separate title page, the table of contents follows. In the example below, there is not a separate title page, so the table of contents follows the abstract and precedes the introduction.

Recent advances in nonlinear optics

Y. R. Shen

Department of Physics, University of California and Inorganic Materials Research Division, Lawrence Berkeley Laboratory, Berkeley, California 94720

We present here a survey on the progress of nonlinear optics in recent years. Emphasis is on physical ideas, basic principles, and important experimental results.

CONTENTS

(Courtesy American Institute of Physics for *Reviews of Modern Physics* [4])

An abstract or summary is often placed at the beginning of the technical article. It gives the main facts and ideas and can be as short as a single sentence or as long as 5% of the entire article. This kind of abstract is called the report type. Review the rules for writing such an abstract as well as the informative (scale model) abstract in Chapter 5. A sample abstract follows:

Purpose The influence of infection with *Septoria nodorum* of leaves below the flag leaf on the translocation of ^{14}C-labeled assimilates in wheat was followed. In the vegetative phase, export of *Summary* assimilates from a single infected leaf was *of effects in* reduced, but export from a healthy leaf on a *each phase* heavily infected plant was increased. During the reproductive phase, export from leaves was not affected by disease. Heavy leaf infection had little effect on the patterns of distribution of export, especially during reproductive growth when only changes in the proportion of assimilates in leaf sheaths and tiller stumps were found. Distribution of export from a healthy flag leaf on an otherwise heavily infected plant was unaltered. During vegetative growth, changes in the distribution of assimilates were more marked, the greatest changes occurring when a single infected leaf on a healthy plant was exposed to $^{14}CO_2$.

(Courtesy *Annals of Botany* [5])

The abstract for an article in a semitechnical periodical can be considerably less formal and designed to attract attention:

Thesis With a trend developing in surgical ICUs to move their post-op heart-surgery patients out sooner than ever, floor nurses will have to master some new skills and knowledge. An ICU nurse *Organiza-* points the way through three main areas of *tional plan* observation and care.

(Courtesy *RN* [6])

Introductions to articles vary greatly, depending on whether the article is written for a technical periodical or a semitechnical one. Both types of introductions usually state the purpose of the article. But the technical introduction includes a historical review or definitions or a cause-and-effect analysis:

Problem Mining and milling of copper, lead, zinc, and nickel in Canada involves a nationwide accumulation of at least a half million tons of waste material each day and requires approximately 250 million gallons of process water per day. The *Scope* waste management considerations with which the industry must be concerned in order to handle such large volumes in an economic and environmentally acceptable manner are far-ranging and

Solutions complex. In Canada the past three to four years have represented a period of particular environmental awareness to the industry and have led to the application of several innovative programs and the development of new regulatory requirements in many jurisdictions.

(Courtesy *Environmental Science & Technology* [7])

Background In his thesis and published work, Kuehn discussed the possible connection between consumer brand buying behavior and a stochastic model of learning, developed by Bush and Mosteller in the field of mathematical psychology. Many authors in the consumer behavior and marketing science literature have since referred to the linear learning model.

Methods This article first examines critically the Bush-Mosteller methods and assumptions. The learning model proves to take the form of a well-known forecasting device, the exponentially weighted moving average. It is then shown that the same model can be generated by treating consumer panel data as a time series, with the advantage that Box-Jenkins methods of time-series analysis can be applied to problems of model identification, parameter estimation and inter-*Causes and* pretation, forecast updating, and so on. The Box-*effects* Jenkins stochastic models assume only one input, regarded as the driving force which produces change in processes giving rise to time-series data. This input is white noise, or a series of uncorrelated random shocks. The shocks are presumed to have a known mean and variance but are otherwise unexplained. Such causal factors are *Purpose* hardly consistent with "learning," but time series analysis permits a number of conclusions to be drawn about the stochastic element in brand-buying behavior.

(Courtesy American Marketing Association for the *Journal of Marketing Research* [8])

The semitechnical introduction makes use of anecdotes, surprising statements, narratives, or simple comparisons:

Question Are you consciously aware of your pulse or your heartbeat, as long as they remain steady and normal? Probably not. Yet both nature and life *Comparison* itself are controlled by pulses like these, the steady and normal repetitions of events that we too often take for granted and thus become insensitive to—breathing and walking, the passing of day into night, the coming and going of the sea-*Contrasting* sons. Are we lulled by this repetitiveness, this *questions* constancy, this universality? Or are we awakened by the realization that in repetitiveness lies movement, and in movement lies growth, and in growth lies the inexhaustible variety of experiences that give life its meaning? *Definitions* Experience is actually living through an event, and that event then makes a direct and personal impression on our judgments and our feelings.

Experiences with music are direct and personal involvements with sounds and their relationships. Through these experiences, we become increasingly aware of and sensitive to sounds, so that we are able to make judgments about them and be aware of the feelings they produce. Since the es- *Thesis* sence of music experience and music expression is in the relationships of sounds to each other, we must continually develop for ourselves and our students an awareness and a sensitivity to these relationships.

(Courtesy Music Educators National Conference
for *Music Educators Journal* [9])

Anecdote "Oh, no!" said the junior in the Group Discussion class, slumping lower in his chair. "If I said anything to my mother, I'd be hearing about it for a month—the same thing—over and over." He shook his head firmly and the whole class nodded in agreement and sympathy.

Explanation Among all the anxiety-producing problems in *of the* daily life, listening to people insistently repeating *problem* themselves may not seem very significant. Irritating repetition may not be a relationship-wrecker or a people-isolator, but it is annoying, both to speaker and listener. The speaker feels incapable of expressing himself clearly. The listener may feel that the speaker thinks he is stupid, or he may merely be annoyed by having his time and attention wasted with redundant information.

Analysis As a problem, insistent repetition has at least *of the* two good features: it is easy to recognize on both *problem* sides; it can, in some cases, be resolved. Usually there is an easy flow of conversation and then a budding sense of irritation. The conversation is not "going anywhere." One or both parties may realize that one person is repeating himself for no apparent reason. However, either one can turn the stalemate to greater understanding if he knows and uses certain clear principles.

Thesis The crucial question to be explored is "Why *question* does a person repeat himself?" If the reader will consult his experience, chances are he knows that he does sometimes repeat himself, even though no one has asked him to do so. The repetition seems necessary to him although no one has asked to hear again what he has already clearly *Answer* stated. I believe I have identified two principles of repetition.

(Courtesy National Council of Teachers of English
for *English Journal* [10])

Background The term *four-wheel drive* brings to mind the F.W.D. and the Nash Quad vehicles of World War I. Some were not only four-wheel drives but also had four-wheel steering. They were used mostly as ammunition carriers, and though they had solid slick tires, they usually got the job done.

They played a very important part in our defeat of the enemy, and so did the small F.W.D. Jeep in World War II.

Thesis Suppose we talk about one of today's models of these unique vehicles, for instance the Chevrolet light duty F.W.D. truck.

(Courtesy W. R. C. Smith Publishing Company for
Southern Automotive Journal [11])

The body of an informational article includes the facts enhanced by headings, tables, and figures. The facts may be clarified by many of the same devices used in the introduction: definitions, explanations of principles if necessary, examples, and citation of authority. The old may be compared with the new, the main idea repeated often, definite data and figures given, and functional visuals used. The relationship of the main ideas should be clearly shown and they should be arranged in some effective order, perhaps in the order of occurrence or of ascending or descending importance.

The conclusion must tie up all the loose ends and leave the reader with a feeling of satisfaction and accomplishment. Here a summary of the main points, a projection of the thesis into the future, specific proposals, a restatement of the thesis, or an evaluation of the implications of the work are appropriate. The conclusion should be short; sometimes it is not even needed because the discussion terminates itself smoothly at the end of the body of the paper and it is unnecessary to stress the implications of the work.

The following conclusion includes a restatement of the thesis, a summary of the main points, and an interpretation of the factors that determined the success of the program.

CONCLUSIONS

Restatement The results of data analysis indicate that the *of thesis* counseling technique was successful in teaching principles of a balanced diet and principles of caries prevention. Although the increase in *Summary* knowledge was equal for both groups, sample B *of results* adolescents, from a public school, had greater knowledge before and after counseling than did sample A participants from a private dental practice. The counseling method did motivate a high proportion of the participants to desire diet improvement and to practice some change in diet. Of the two samples of adolescents, those in group A demonstrated higher response in terms of actual change, as measured by the diet record, possibly because of less restricted financial circumstances.

Interpreta- These findings suggest that several factors *tion of* function in determining the success of the pro- *results* gram. First, the participant must feel he has some control over his diet. This involves either the ability to purchase desirable foods or the ability to influence the family's food buyer. Second, adolescents who receive preventive dental care are probably more receptive to dietary change. Third, and possibly most important, is the attitude of the family. Group A adolescents, whose parents encouraged dental care, showed greater improvements than did group B adolescents, whose parents indicated little or no interest.

(Courtesy American Dental Association for *Journal of the American Dental Association* [12])

The final draft is the product of several revisions of the rough draft. It should include only the necessary information stated in clear, concise language; vague expressions such as *a number of, in such cases, in connection with, considerable,* and *very* should be eliminated. Action verbs and a positive tone telling the reader what to do instead of what not to do are also important to the final draft. A clearly stated topic sentence in each paragraph and transitional expressions to link the sentences and paragraphs together are sometimes added during the revision process.

A neat, clean final copy should be mailed to the editor of the appropriate periodical. It should be typewritten, double-spaced with wide margins on good quality paper, the pages not stapled but left flat, and mailed in a 9-by-12-inch mailing folder or envelope. A letter of transmittal summarizing the article, giving your qualifications, and stressing current reader interest in the subject should be included. A copy of the manuscript should always be kept because the original might get lost or misplaced even though reputable publishers do return manuscripts.

Some editors give very specific directions for preparation of the final copy. Sometimes they limit you to only two paragraphs per page and to no more than two visuals per page. Often they ask you to submit an abstract of 150 words before you mail the article. *Reviews of Modern Physics* gives specific directions on the form for footnotes and references on the inside back cover. *Comparative Education Review* asks that all articles be submitted in triplicate, that footnotes be placed on a separate page at the end of the manuscript, and that *A Manual of Style* be followed.

SUMMARY

Writing technical articles for publication can both advance your career and give you personal satisfaction. There are three types of periodicals to which you may submit articles: the technical periodicals that print highly specialized articles for fellow professionals, the semitechnical periodicals for specialists in other fields, and the nontechnical periodicals that present interesting and informative articles for the general public. Technical and semitechnical periodicals are of primary interest here because they publish articles written by experts in the field; nontechnical periodicals print articles written by professional journalists. Articles in technical journals are restrained and impersonal in tone; the abstracts, introductions, conclusions, appendixes, and references are clearly labeled; and mathematical treatments are used frequently. Articles in semitechnical journals have a more informal style, the introduction is calculat-

ed to arouse interest, technical terms are used sparingly and clearly explained, many visuals are used, and often a formal bibliography is not included at the end of the article.

Four steps are involved in writing a technical article: (1) finding the idea itself, perhaps through an awareness of the applications and processes used in your own organization; (2) selecting a suitable periodical for publication by checking the editorial statement or the work itself; (3) writing the article and including the title, abstract, table of contents, appropriate introduction, well-documented body, conclusions, appendixes, and bibliography; and (4) submitting the article to a potential publisher in the required form.

Samuel Johnson's advice in the eighteenth century on writing is still helpful today to those who wish to write for publication: "What is written without effort is in general read without pleasure." The revisions of the rough draft are all-important to the success of the completed article.

SPECIMEN TECHNICAL ARTICLES

The first specimen technical article is representative of those found in technical periodicals. Notice that the abstract, introduction, parts of the body of the report, conclusions, acknowledgments, and bibliography are all clearly labeled. *Radome* is not defined because this report is written for other specialists. The impersonal tone, mathematical treatments, and lengthy bibliography are all indicative of the technical article. Placing all the figures and tables at the end of the article is standard practice for many technical periodicals.

The second article illustrates the type published in semitechnical periodicals because it defines terms, includes fewer statistics, and uses photographs to illustrate the subject. The personal tone, simple comparisons, and examples are all indicative of the semitechnical article.

INVESTIGATION OF REINFORCED
PLASTICS FOR NAVAL
AIRCRAFT ELECTROMAGNETIC
(E-M) WINDOWS

Vance A. Chase*
Maxwell Stander**

*WRD, A Division of Whittaker Corporation
3540 Aero Court, San Diego, California 92123
**Naval Air Systems Command, Code AIR-52032D
Washington, D.C. 20361

INVESTIGATION OF REINFORCED PLASTICS
FOR NAVAL AIRCRAFT ELECTROMAGNETIC
(E-M) WINDOWS

Vance A. Chase
Whittaker Corporation
Research and Development Division
and
Maxwell Stander
Naval Air Systems Command

ABSTRACT

Purpose Polymer and fiber materials for naval radome applications were investigated. The investigation was concerned with materials having low and stable dielectric constant and loss tangent properties. Primary emphasis was on polybutadiene polymers. A survey was conducted on the availability of polybutadiene polymers and a characterization study performed on 14 different resins from three manufacturers. Promising candidate resins in unreinforced form were evaluated for resistance to thermal and humid aging. Dielectric constant and loss tangent measurements were made at 8.5, 17, and 24 GHz, versus temperature, and both before and after humid aging. Certain materials (for example, polyimide and Kevlar 49) which had previously been considered to be good dielectric materials were found to be severely degraded after humidity exposure. A study was conducted into the type of contaminants contained in polybutadiene resins and their effect on electrical properties.

Procedure Composite processing studies were conducted for the more promising resin candidate materials. Primary candidate fiber reinforcement materials were Astroquartz and Kevlar 49. Investigations were conducted into fiber finishes and surface treatments compatible with the polybutadiene resin for both fiber reinforcements. Efforts toward upgrading the toughness and adhesion characteristics of the polybutadiene were performed. Mechanical and electrical properties of the composite materials were determined both before and after humid aging and versus temperature. Leading edge specimens were fabricated from the more promising composite materials and evaluated for rain erosion resistance at 500 m/hr and 2 in./hr rainfall.

INTRODUCTION

Background Historically one of the most critical and demanding aircraft and missile applications for reinforced plastics has been the radome. Typically the radome makes up the forward portion of the vehicle where it is subjected to the severest aerodynamic heating and rain erosion environment. In addition to the environmental problem, the material is required to have satisfactory dielectric properties which are stable over the temperature and frequency range at which the radome is required to operate. In recent years the development of improved, high frequency radar systems and requirements for all-weather operation have created problems in the successful utilization of conventional reinforced plastic radome materials.

Explanation of investigation This program was concerned with the investigation of radome materials for utilization at frequencies up to 35 GHz. The physical thickness of a radome wall is a function of the frequency and the dielectric constant. [1] Higher frequencies and higher dielectric constants can result in a reduction of the physical wall thickness where it is no longer structurally adequate. Therefore, at the higher frequencies it is highly desirable that the radome material have a low dielectric constant. In addition, it

was the objective of this program that the material have other desirable characteristics such as rain erosion resistance, stable dielectric constant versus temperature and frequency as well as after humid conditioning, simplified processing requirements, and low material cost.

Result of investigation Of the various materials investigated, the polybutadiene resins were found to provide the most desirable combination of properties and characteristics.

PRIMARY RESIN CANDIDATES

Desirable characteristics Earlier investigations had demonstrated that polybutadiene resins, through their all-hydrocarbon nature, have a very unique combination of electrical properties and environmental resistance, which made them primary candidates for investigation under this program. [2,3,4] Commercially available polybutadiene resins typically consist of a mixture of 1,2-polybutadiene and 1,4-polybutadiene microstructure.

For fiber reinforced composite materials, a high percentage of the 1,2 structure (vinyl) is desirable due to the high reactivity and resultant simplified cure which proceeds via the pendulant vinyl group located on every second carbon atom in the polymer chain. The 1,4 material has the double bond reactive site in the main polymer chain, which results in a much lower reactivity and increased difficulty in achieving cure.

Other important considerations in a polybutadiene resin include a high molecular weight in order to be amenable to prepreg preparation and a narrow molecular weight distribution for faster curing. A variety of polybutadiene resins were available from Firestone's Synthetic Rubber and Latex Company, Colorado Chemical Specialties Company, and Dynachem Corporation, under the trade names of Dienite, Ricon, and Hystl, respectively.

INITIAL RESIN SCREENING

Explanation of first test When considering a resin for radome application the first concern must be with the basic dielectric properties of the material. Therefore the initial evaluation for a number of the candidate resins involved measurement of dielectric constant and loss tangent at 24 GHz. Also included in this evaluation was a study on the effect of postcure on dielectric properties. Test data as shown in Table 1 illustrate the very low dielectric constant and loss tangent values for the various polybutadienes. The most noticeable effect of a high temperature postcure was a slight reduction in loss tangent for the polybutadiene resins.

A second area of concern in selecting a polymer for radome applications involves the stability of the materials under high humidity conditions.

Explanation of second test A Du Pont 941 thermal mechanical analyzer was used to evaluate the degradation of mechanical properties of resins after humidity exposure. The TMA basically provides a deflection or expansion curve versus temperature for a polymer specimen under a constant compression load from a weighted cylindrical probe. Figure 1 shows the type of curve which was obtained on ERLA 4617 epoxy resin cured with metaphenylenediamine. When the resin is dry, a normal thermal expansion curve is obtained up to the T_g, at which point a deflection is obtained. As temperature continues to increase, the expansion rate exceeds any deflection which may be occurring and a thermal expansion curve is again obtained. As is typical of polymers, a much higher thermal expansion rate above the T_g is evident. The effect of moisture is to initiate deformation of the specimen under load at a much lower temperature, as may be seen for the 1-hour and 4-hour water boil curves. Table 2 shows the difference in deformation temperature for a number of the candidate resins before and after a 24-hour water boil. Also shown in the table is the amount of water absorbed by the specimens during the 24-hour water boil. As expected, the polybutadienes absorb a very small amount of water and show no difference in the TMA deflection temperature before and after water boil. All other candidate materials showed substantially greater water absorption, lower deflection temperatures, and a tendency to foam due to the internal pressure created by the water vapor at elevated temperature. The heating rate for the TMA was ~30°F/min.

COMPOSITE STUDIES

Analysis of first candidate   The candidate fiber reinforcements investigated were Astroquartz (J. P. Stevens) and Kevlar 49 (Du Pont). The Astroquartz reinforcement is well established as a radome material which results in composites having low dielectric constant and loss tangent and excellent stability versus temperature and frequency. Electrical properties for epoxy/Kevlar 49 composites at X-band are reported in the Du Pont literature, which indicated that this material is potentially a promising material for radome applications.

Analysis of second candidate   After fabrication of the initial Kevlar/Dienite PM-502 polybutadiene composite, a problem area was obvious in that mechanical properties were quite a bit lower than those reported for epoxy-based laminates. This was attributed primarily to poor adhesion between the fiber and matrix material. Kevlar 49 presents some difficulty in the fiber/resin adhesion even for epoxy materials.

Problems   The nonpolar nature of the polybutadiene, which results in outstanding electrical properties, detracts from its adhesive properties. It has been well established with glass reinforcement that satisfactory fiber matrix adhesion requires a vinyl silane type finish. This type finish allows crosslinking between the vinyl groups of the finish and those of the polybutadiene polymer. The lack of a suitable bond between the resin and fiber is readily obvious by the fuzzy nature of a Kevlar laminate after machining or after failure in a mechanical test. The first step toward increasing the resin/fiber bond involves a thorough drying of the Kevlar prior to resin impregnation. Du Pont recommends drying Kevlar fabric at 250°F for a minimum of 16 hours. Since we were working with Kevlar roving, it was decided to investigate drying approaches involving passing the roving through a heated zone prior to resin impregnation. In order to accelerate the rate of drying, a higher temperature of 550°F was arbitrarily selected for a starting point. At a normal rate of winding the roving was exposed to this temperature for approximately 1 second. During this initial fabrication of NOL rings the laboratory technician mistakenly set the drying oven at 550°C instead of at the specified 550°F. The roving emerged from this drying oven having a dark brown color and showed much greater resin wet-out than the fibers dried in accordance with Du Pont's recommendations. It was anticipated that this severe oxidation treatment would result in degradation of the strength properties of the fiber. A study was conducted involving fabrication and testing of NOL rings based on roving exposed to different heat treatment/drying conditions. Surprisingly, there was a trend for increase in hoop tensile strength with increase in temperature of fiber treatment. Further testing was conducted involving impregnation, curing, and testing for tensile properties of single roving strands. The Kevlar was pretreated at 800°F for 10 minutes. The strand tensile test indicated a 40% reduction in tensile strength and a slight increase in modulus after the heat treatment.

It is obvious that the oxidative treatment enhances wetting and adhesion of the matrix to the fiber. However, under the conditions utilized, this is at some sacrifice of tensile properties of the fiber. This fiber degradation was not evident in the hoop tensile properties obtained on the NOL composite rings which were exposed to even higher temperatures but for a shorter period of time. Even with the fiber degradation experienced at the 800°F treatment, it was felt there may be overriding benefits due to the improved fiber-matrix bond, which would be reflected by increase of other composite properties including rain erosion resistance.

Astroquartz fabric was finished with Union Carbide's A-172 vinyl silane finish and polybutadiene laminates were prepared. Wetting of the reinforcement was excellent, and the laminates produced were highly translucent in nature.

ELECTRICAL PROPERTY EVALUATION

Results of tests   Early in the program preliminary dielectric property measurements were performed on various PBD resins at 17 to 18 GHz for the purpose of studying the effects of cure conditions, catalyst concentrations, resin impurities, and general characterization. In general, the variables studied had minor effects on the electrical properties, with all of the materials showing dielectric constant values of <2.5 and loss tangent values of <.002.

Further testing was conducted on laminates and candidate resins at 8.5 GHz over a temperature range of room temperature to 500°F. The materials tested at 8.5 GHz included Dienite PM-502 polybutadiene/Kevlar composite, Dienite PM-502 polybutadiene/Astroquartz, polyphenylquinoxaline PPQ 401 resin, and cyanurate ester XSR-10500 resin. The PBD/Kevlar showed an initial dielectric constant on the order of 3.2 at room temperature, decreasing to 3.06 at 515°F, and maintaining the 3.06 reading at room temperature after the elevated temperature test. The initial loss tangent was .015, peaking at .026 at 211°F, and dropping to .016 at 515°F. At room temperature after the elevated temperature run, the loss tangent was measured to be .005. This behavior involving lower dielectric properties after the temperature cycle indicated that the specimen had absorbed moisture at ambient room temperature conditions which was removed during elevated temperature testing.

The PBD/Astroquartz laminate showed an initial dielectric constant value of 3.10 at room temperature, decreasing to 3.04 at 516°F. After the elevated temperature test, the room temperature dielectric constant was measured to be 3.09, or essentially identical to what was measured initially. The loss tangent for the PBD/Astroquartz laminate was .002 initially at room temperature, decreasing to .001 at 516°F. At room temperature after the elevated temperature cycle, the loss tangent was measured to be .002, identical to the initial measurement.

At this point laminates and candidate resins were subjected to a 30-day exposure at 120°F and 99% relative humidity. Dielectric constant and loss tangent were measured at 24 GHz before and after humidity aging. This was considered a particularly important environmental test in that significant changes in dielectric properties of the radome due to moisture absorption would result in a serious performance degradation of the radar system. The PBD/Astroquartz laminate showed the minimum change in electrical properties of all the laminate materials evaluated. All of the Kevlar reinforced laminates showed levels of increase in dielectric constant and loss tangent which are considered prohibitive for radome applications. The least change of any of the PBD/Kevlar laminates was obtained on Kevlar fabric which was oxidized 10 minutes at 800°F and sized with a Kerimid 601 finish. In this case the dielectric constant and loss tangent changed from 3.33 and .006 in a dry condition to 3.47 and .036 after humid aging. The largest change on the Kevlar composite was experienced when the fabric was only dried at 250°F. In this case the dielectric constant and loss tangent for the material in a dry state was 3.52 and .033, increasing after humid aging to 4.06 and .138. The polyphenylquinoxaline (PPQ 401) and polyimide (PBI 373)/Astroquartz laminates both suffered serious degradation in electrical properties after humid aging, with the polyimide being the most seriously degraded. The dielectric constant and loss tangent for the PPQ/Astroquartz laminate changed from 3.19 and .004 in a dry condition to 3.53 and .045 after humid aging. The polyimide/Astroquartz laminate's dielectric constant and loss tangent was 3.35 and .004 dry, and 3.85 and .092 after humid aging. Changes of this magnitude in the dielectric properties of a radome material would be prohibitive for most high performance radomes.

This problem of susceptibility of the polyimides to dielectric property degradation due to moisture pickup has apparently not been recognized in this country; however, earlier work by the British Aircraft Company showed this problem to exist at X-band frequencies. [5] The dielectric constant and loss tangent of polyimide composites were found to increase from 3.9 and .006 in a dry condition to 4.45 and .035 after moisture pickup at *normal atmospheric conditions*. While this earlier work identified a substantial problem at X-band for polyimide composites, it is apparently much more severe at the higher frequencies.

Evaluation The PBD/Astroquartz laminate showed excellent properties and good stability versus temperature, having an initial dielectric constant at room temperature of 3.09 and .006. After the temperature cycle to 500°F, the specimen was again measured at room temperature and gave dielectric constant and loss tangent values of 3.07 and .003.

RAIN EROSION STUDY

A major consideration in the selection of a material for radome applications is resistance to rain erosion. In order to determine the performance of the materials under study, a number of leading edge specimens were fabricated and submitted to the Air Force Materials Laboratory for evaluation in their whirling-arm facility. Testing was performed at the standard conditions of 500 m/hr and 1 in./hr of rainfall. Leading edge specimens after rain erosion testing are show in Figure 2. From left to right, specimens are identified as follows:

Materials tested
1. PBD PD-753/Kevlar 49, with the Kevlar dried at 250°F
2. PBD PD-753/Kevlar 49, with the Kevlar dried at 800°F
3. PBD PD-753/Astroquartz
4. Narmco 587 epoxy/E glass (standard)
5. PPQ 401 resin molding
6. PPQ 401/Astroquartz

7. PPQ 401/Kevlar 49, with the Kevlar dried at 250°F
8. PPQ 401/Kevlar 49, with the Kevlar dried at 800°F.

Results All of the Kevlar reinforced composites showed severe erosion after a 2-minute exposure and were eliminated from further testing. Unlike conventional glass reinforced composites, the resin is removed and the fractured Kevlar fibers are retained to produce a fuzzy surface. The degree of erosion for the PBD/Astroquartz, epoxy/E glass, and PPQ/Astroquartz specimens after 10-minute exposure were of the same order of magnitude. The unreinforced PPQ resin molding gave excellent performance, with negligible material being removed after the 10-minute exposure.

CONCLUSIONS

Conclusions arranged in descending order of importance— general to particular
1. The polybutadiene/Astroquartz material was superior, from an overall standpoint, for radome applications of any of the materials investigated. Particularly impressive were dielectric properties and their stability versus frequency, temperature, and after humid aging.
2. Continued efforts are required to optimize the polybutadiene composite material in terms of mechanical properties. This is presently being performed under an ongoing program through approaches involving resin modification and processing and postcure optimization studies.
3. The low dielectric properties of the PBD/Astroquartz composite will allow design of radomes having performance over a broader frequency range, and sandwich walls for high frequency applications with physically thicker skins to resist rain erosion. Due to the low dielectric constant, the allowable wall thickness tolerances of the manufactured radome will be increased. Also, the costly test range fine tuning of the finished radome by localized addition and removal of material should be substantially reduced.
4. The PBD resins provide superior resistance to degradation by moisture. A PBD (PD-753)/Astroquartz laminate gave a dielectric constant of 3.08 and a loss tangent of .006 at 24 GHz prior to humid aging. After the 30-day humidity exposure, the dielectric constant and loss tangent for the same specimen was measured as 3.09 and .007.
5. The use of a fiber surface treatment on Kevlar when used with PBD resin is highly desirable if good wetting and adhesion is to be obtained. The oxidation treatment involving exposure of the fiber for 10 minutes at 800°F (with or without the Kerimid 601 size) provided improved fiber wetting and enhancement of certain mechanical properties in the composite. However, this oxidative treatment did result in a degradation of the tensile strength of the fiber. To optimize this surface treatment approach, lower temperatures and/or exposure times should be investigated.
6. For compatibility with the PBD resin, a vinyl silane type finish is required on the Astroquartz reinforcement. Union Carbide's A-172 finish was found to perform satisfactorily.
7. The Kevlar reinforced composites proved disappointing for radome applications due to dielectric property changes after humid aging and poor rain erosion resistance.
8. Of the materials evaluated for rain erosion resistance, the Kevlar 49 composites (PBD and PPQ) gave the poorest performance. The Astroquartz laminate (PBD and PPQ) showed initiation of erosion damage earlier than the epoxy/E glass standard. However, after 10 minutes exposure, the weight losses for the Astroquartz laminates were in the same general

area as those of the epoxy/glass. The unreinforced PPQ molding showed exceptional resistance to rain erosion.

ACKNOWLEDGMENTS

Acknowledgment is given to the Naval Air Systems Command for financial support of this program. Further acknowledgment is given to Mr. George Schmitt of the Air Force Materials Laboratory for rain erosion testing, and to Mr. William Westphal of the MIT Laboratory for Insulation for dielectric property measurements.

BIBLIOGRAPHY

1. Chase, Vance A., "Investigation of Reinforced Plastics for Naval Aircraft Electromagnetic (EM) Windows," Final Report, U.S. Navy Contract N00019-74-C-0055, January 1975.
2. Clark, H. and Vanderbilt, B. M., "A Hydrocarbon Thermoset Resin for Reinforced Plastics," SPI 14th Annual Meeting of Reinforced Plastics Division, February 1959.
3. Lewis, Theodore and Howlett, R. M., "Buton Hydrocarbon Resin Laminates," SPI 19th Annual Meeting of the Reinforced Plastics Division, February 1964.
4. Bianchi, M. P. and Dorman, E. N., "New High Performance Versatile Polybutadiene Systems for Electrical and RP Applications," SPI 26th Annual Technical Conference, February 1970.
5. Cray, M. C., "Polyimides in Advanced Composites for Aerospace Applications," British Aircraft Corporation Ltd.

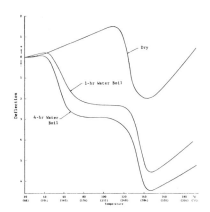

Figure 1. Thermal Mechanical Analysis (TMA) of ERLA-4617/MDA Casting After Different Environmental Exposures.

Figure 2. Rain Erosion Specimens After Testing

Table 1. Dielectric Properties for Candidate Resins at 24 GHz

Resin	Core	Dielectric Constant K'	Loss Tangent δ
Dienite PD-702 (90% 1,2-vinyl polybutadiene)	350°F–36 hr	2.34	.0026
	*450°F–22 hr	2.34	.0019
Dienite PM-502 (PM-702 polybutadiene + 30 wt% vinyl toluene)	350°F–36 hr	2.37	.0031
	*450°F–22 hr	2.37	.0025
Dienite X-545 (PM-502 resin in a purified form)	350°F–36 hr	2.36	.0030
	*450°F–22 hr	2.37	.0020
Dienite PD-701 (70% 1,2-polybutadiene/ styrene copolymer)	350°F–36 hr	—	—
	*450°F–92 hr	2.37	.0024
Ricon 100 (70% 1,2-polybutadiene/styrene polymer)	350°F–23 hr	2.40	.0036
	*450°F–24 hr	2.40	.0014
PPQ 401 (polyphenyl-quinoxaline)	700°F	3.18	.0059
XSR-10500 (cyanurate ester)	450°F	3.15	.0070

*Postcure

Table 2. Effect of 24-Hour Water Boil on Resin Candidates

Resin	Water Absorption (%)	TMA ~Failure Temp. Dry (°F)	TMA ~Failure Temp. 24-hr H$_2$O Boil (°F)
Hystl B-1000 polybutadiene	.14	662	—
Hystl B-2000 polybutadiene	.185	671	671
Hystl B-3000 polybutadiene	.22	—	671
Ricon 100 polybutadiene	.125	—	725
Ricon 150 polybutadiene/styrene copolymer	.155	671	671
NR-150A thermoplastic polyimide	2.015	536	441*
Torlon 2000 amide-imide	2.435	509*	396*
Torlon 4000 amide-imide	2.06	482	356 432*
Torlon 4000 amide-imide	1.86	—	446
PPQ 401 polyphenyl-quinoxaline	1.67	509	465*
ICI 200P poly-ethersulfone	1.69	347	347*
ICI 300P polyethersulfone	1.81	410	356 410*

*Specimen foamed

(From *Pacific Technical Conference and Technical Displays,* sponsored by the Western Sections of the Society of Plastics Engineers, Inc., PACTEC '75.)

Photographs to illustrate the topic

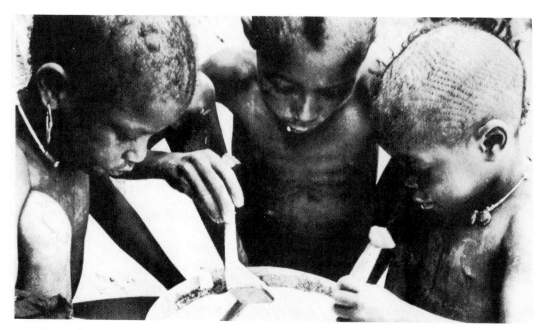

Starvation

Purpose

In this article, Dr. Parham describes the physiological, psychological, and social effects of hunger. She draws on records of three kinds:
- **the accounts of those who have personally experienced starvation**
- **the experiences of those who have worked in hunger-relief efforts, and**
- **research reports of the limited number of controlled studies available (1).**

Definitions

Throughout her article, she uses the words "hunger" and "starvation" interchangeably to indicate acute and extreme deprivation of food with accompanying loss of weight.

Personal tone

For most of us in the western world, real hunger is beyond our experience or imagination. It is difficult for us to relate hunger statistics—often tabulated for us in highly impersonal form—and predictions of future famines to our experience of life.

General-ization

Hunger: Physiological Effects

When there is a calorie deficit, the body adjusts to or compensates for that deficit by breaking down adipose (fatty) tissue to satisfy

the body's primary need for energy.

In most adults of normal weight, this breakdown of adipose tissue can continue for from 45 to 50 days before death ensues. A healthy nonobese adult can lose up to 25 percent of body weight without endangering life, and some persons have survived losses of 50 percent of their initial weight (2). Greater losses than this are likely to cause death.

Although most of the body's cells can use fat (or fat's metabolic products, ketones) for energy, certain bodily processes require glucose. Because the body's carbohydrate stores are depleted after only a few hours without food, body proteins become the main source of glucose and eventually of energy.

Because the body's fat supply cannot last forever, eventually all the adipose tissue is lost and the skin hangs loosely over a gaunt frame. Because of the protein loss described, vital body tissues atrophy: the heart of a starved person is about one-half normal size (2). Circulatory difficulties develop and heart failure may cause death. The endocrine glands also atrophy, producing a deficiency of their

By Ellen S. Parham

Explanation

Dr. Parham has frequently written and lectured on the effects of chronic hunger and starvation on the human body.

A registered dietitian and an AHEA member, Dr. Parham is an associate professor in the Department of Home Economics, Northern Illinois University, DeKalb, where she teaches courses on world, community, and child nutrition. She is the current chairman of the Illinois Nutrition Committee.

Simple comparison

hormones. Only the brain is spared in the body's relentless search for energy.

The lining of the intestinal tract changes from a lush, velvety surface of tremendous absorptive capacity to a paper-thin tissue resembling pigskin. As it is this surface that absorbs nutrients, what little food is available may not be absorbed by this pigskin-like tissue in a starving individual. Often, the result is a devastating diarrhea that frequently accompanies death, especially in infants and children.

The photograph on the preceding page is of children in the refugee camp at Tchin Tabaraden, Niger, dipping into their daily bowl of high-protein porridge. They also get a daily ration of milk.

On the other hand, that same pigskin-like intestinal surface can also cause extreme constipation. Both the diarrhea and the constipation are frequently worsened by the nature of the foods that *are* available.

Many starved persons also suffer from fluid retention (edema) because of upsets in the body's balance of proteins, fluids, and electrolytes. This edema, which may mask tissue atrophy, is responsible for the classic protruding abdomen of a starving child. Sometimes, however, in contrast to edema, there is extreme dehydration, especially in children with diarrhea.

Explanation

As the system's energy supply decreases, the body begins to make certain adjustments to compensate for the loss. In early starvation, there may even be improved efficiency of nutrient absorption and decreased excretion of nutrients. As body weight is lost, the rate slows at which cells use energy, thus decreasing calorie needs and lowering the body temperature.

A starving person is therefore very sensitive to cold. The lowered body temperature of the starving may then mask fever symptoms of the diseases that frequently accompany famine—malaria, tuberculosis, and infective gangrene of the mouth.

Sexual Function and Reproduction

General-ization

Starvation undoubtedly depresses sexual function and reproduction. The extent and nature of its depressive effect is difficult to determine exactly, however, because of the lack of controlled studies and because sociological factors frequently complicate observations of famines.

Explanation

Although the chronically undernourished usually have high birthrates in comparison to well-fed populations that practice family planning, acute starvation reduces the number of conceptions and live births. As many as 60 to 70 percent of young women in a famine have amenorrhea (absence, or abnormal stoppage, of menstruation) *(1)*.

Example

The Minnesota Experiment, a controlled observation of young men living under semistarvation conditions, reported a decrease

in the men's sperm viability and in their excretion of 17-ketosteroid—an indicator of the extent of male sex hormone production *(1)*.

Example

During World War II, a number of American men in Japanese prison camps who had been underfed developed breast enlargement, apparently because their diets had caused failure of the liver to inactivate the estrogens also normally produced by males. This phenomenon has not been reported in other famine conditions.

Females usually survive famine better than males, perhaps because of lower calorie needs, freedom from heavy work, adaptation resulting from amenorrhea, their favored position in society, or, for those with children, from some maternal instinct to survive.

Babies conceived and delivered by undernourished mothers frequently have low birthweight and a reduced chance for survival. The prognosis for these babies is highly related both to their mothers' prepregnant condition and to the severity and duration of their mothers' starvation.

Example

A comprehensive follow-up study *(3)* of children born or conceived during the Dutch famine winter of 1944-45 found that the fetus was most vulnerable during the third trimester.

The milk produced by undernourished mothers is of generally high quality but, after the infants are about 6 months old, it is seldom of adequate quantity *(4)*. Because little other food is available, the infant slowly starves as the mother's milk production dwindles. Too weak to cry and barely able to suck, the infants can only lie quietly, without movement.

Growth and Development

General-ization

Growth requires energy—but so does survival, which takes precedence. When the body has only enough energy to survive, physical growth is severely retarded and sexual development is delayed.

Explanation

There is some evidence that "catch-up" growth can occur when a liberal food intake is again available. On the other hand, after the first 2 years of life, the brain loses nearly all of its capacity to grow in size.

For babies to have a normal number of brain cells, not only must they have received adequate nourishment during their first few postnatal months, but their mothers also must have had adequate nutrients during their pregnancies. Infants who die of undernutrition during their first year of life may have as few as 40 percent of the normal number of brain cells *(5)*. Undernourished infants who survive do not acquire normal brain size even when they receive normal nourishment again.

The relationship of reduced brain size to intelligence is not entirely clear. Although malnourished children frequently have reduced mental capacity, it has not so far been possible to separate nutrition effects from those of heredity, infection, and sensory deprivation.

Example

The 20-year study of the Dutch famine in the winter of 1944-45 showed that the hunger had been without effect on the mental performance, physical stature, or general health of the young men whose prenatal life included that period (3)—with one exception.

That exception was the increased frequency of central nervous system anomalies—including spina bifida (a defect in the bone surrounding the spinal cord), hydrocephalus, and cerebral palsy. This effect had apparently been the result of nutritional deprivation plus some other stress—possibly infection.

The numbers affected were small. The investigators believed that prenatal brain-cell depletion had probably occurred but had not resulted in mental dysfunction. The human body is remarkably resilient. It usually gives the brain top priority in satisfying its energy needs over all other bodily systems.

Right: ". . . Too weak to cry and barely able to suck, [starving] infants can only lie quietly, without movement. . . ."

Those at greatest risk in famines are young children and old persons. Children have the combined needs for growth and maintenance and have limited body stores. Unlike the aged, however, they are often given high priority in food distribution.

The starved appear to age at an accelerated rate. A 35-year-old man may look 80; he feels and acts old. His loss of adipose tissue is largely responsible for his aged appearance, and the slowing of his body processes and metabolism causes him to feel and behave as an aged man. There is no evidence of a real change in the aging process.

The Importance of Nutrient Stores

General-ization

People survive famines by using the nutrient stores in their bodies to eke out the little food available. Body tissues are consumed as energy "fuel," but vitamins and minerals are made available to the body in the process. Because these substances are already in the blood, the normal digestion and absorption processes are not required.

Explanation

The most likely famine victims are those who, for most of their lives, have had inadequate diets; they seldom have significant nutrient stores. Those who survive seem to do so because their bodies have had a long adjustment to low nutrient intakes and because they have developed immunity to the many infectious diseases usually accompanying famine.

Although the nutrient-deficiency diseases of scurvy, rickets, and beri-beri have been associated with some famines, vitamin and

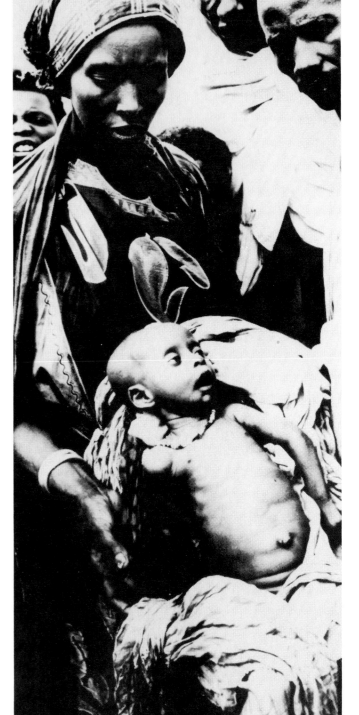

mineral deficiencies are usually minor problems for the food-relief administrator compared with the population's energy deficit.

Behavioral Effects

Generalization

When well-fed Americans imagine how starvation feels, we imagine extreme hunger pangs. Indeed, in starvation's early stages, there is extreme hunger, and food becomes an overwhelming preoccupation.

Example

A study *(6)* of the 16 survivors of the 1972 Andes crash relates the young men's planning of a fantastic restaurant, their contest for the best original menu, their extensive list of their favorite eating places. Food completely replaced sex as a conversational topic. However, they finally had to outlaw all food-related conversation because it had increased their discomfort.

Example

Children of the African Ik tribe, which has suffered slow starvation for years, play very elaborate games involving mud food *(7)*. The children often end their game by eating their mud concoctions or small pebbles as make-believe food.

Explanation

Usually, however, appetite maintenance depends on food consumption. As starvation proceeds and large amounts of body weight are lost, appetite dwindles and the starving person may even reject food. When near death from starvation, some become euphoric and feel they no longer need food.

Example

The starving move as little as possible, an adaptive behavior that seems to conserve energy. The young men in the Minnesota Experiment found even routine exertion extremely taxing *(1)*. There is dizziness or fainting when a starving person moves quickly to a vertical position, but this becomes less of a problem as starvation continues because the person can no longer make rapid movements.

Most persons experience unpleasant personality changes after enduring hunger for some time. They are no longer rational or objective, and their moods oscillate from high to low without recognizable cause. They lose interest in sexual activity.

In spite of their apparent lack of response to their environment, their senses seem to be sharpened. They have increased sensitivity to sound. Although their intelligence remains the same, they lose the ability to concentrate and their motivation to learn.

There seems to be wide variation among individuals in the will to survive. Members of the Donner expedition, stranded in a high pass of the Sierra Nevadas during the winter of 1846–47, are examples of this. Sturdy (but unattached) young men took to their beds—not even rising to remove their companions when they died—and surrendered to death.

Photography Credit
The photographs that illustrate this article are from the Agency for International Development, Washington, D.C.

But the parents of young children struggled for miles on frozen bleeding feet in a desperate effort to find help. Histories of famines include some remarkable tales of heroism. These are the exceptions, however; most people respond to hunger in far less noble fashion.

Social Effects

Generalization

These behavioral changes among individuals naturally bring about changes in social relationships. As the weight losses of the Minnesota volunteers approached 20 percent, a very serious degree of civil disorder and strife developed *(1)*. Weight losses beyond the 20 percent level, however, usually produce a decline in such behavior as the weakened individual slips into a state of apathy.

Example

The basic human response to starvation seems to be survival at all costs. There is an initial attempt to protect the weak, but as conditions worsen, social behavior deteriorates and family ties break.

Example

This phenomenon is dramatically demonstrated by members of the Ik tribe. The tribe once had the usual ties within families and villages to support the young and old. After several years of starvation, however, the "survival of the fittest" has become the major behavioral guideline. At the age of 3, children are turned out of the family hut to fend for themselves. The hunters who would once have brought their catch home to share with pride now gorge themselves in hiding. It is quite acceptable Ik social behavior to take food away from weaker Iks, even from their mouths.

Explanation

Hunger sends human beings tumbling down Maslow's hierarchy of human needs to the very bottom level—physiological survival *(8)*. Humanity's higher needs—for security, a sense of belonging, status or esteem, and self-realization—have little relevance.

We have even seen this effect among well-fed Americans. Remember the response to the rumor of a beef shortage a year or so ago?

Starvation Is a Slow Process

Generalization

The threat of a food shortage causes people to engage in an activity that will obtain food—prostitution, theft, selling their children, or migration *(4)*.

Solutions in chronological order

When people are hungry, they are forced to slaughter their domestic animals, which for a short time provide a high-protein diet, usually of more animal protein than the family has ever had before. When this abundance comes to an end, not only is the meat gone but also the source of milk or eggs or the cash those bring. The family pets are usually the next to be sacrificed.

Persons able to do so roam far in search of food. Although that reduces the number to be fed in a famine area, it also uses up calories, spreads diseases, interferes with crop planting, and causes the abandonment of the sick or immobile.

In the past, some food relief measures have taken the form of work programs, which encourage self-help but also increase calorie expenditures and benefit only those strong enough to work. Workers often must walk miles to the work location.

Throughout human history, famine has been accompanied by cannibalism, although not all starving people have resorted to such measures to assuage hunger. It is most likely to occur in an acute, rather than a chronic, starvation situation and where it is clear that there are no alternatives if one is to survive. The taboo against eating human flesh is probably the strongest dietary taboo in most cultures, and it is not easily overcome. People in Western societies who have survived starvation by eating their dead companions have met extreme public criticism after their rescue.

Hunger Is Rarely the Only Burden

General-
ization
Explanation

Seldom is deprivation of food the only stress the starving person has to bear. Famine is a sibling of war. Famine also brings too little of everything else besides food—too little water, soap, heat, or shelter. Donner expedition diaries, for example, tell of being in the bitter cold for 3 weeks without dry clothing—clothing in which lice and fleas flourished to torment the wearers and their babies.

The body's need for water is more acute than its need for food, and precious human energy must often be expended in famines in obtaining a safe supply, scarce even—or perhaps especially—in flood situations.

Relocation centers for the starving, with barely room to move and few or no sanitary facilities, are seldom much of a haven and are often breeding grounds for famine's companions—bubonic plague, cholera, smallpox, and the like. The relocated are often bewildered, floundering helplessly without the sustaining ties of the extended family or a means of livelihood. Many try to return to their homeland, even though the famine continues there.

Implications

Chronic hunger has profound effects on all aspects of a people's existence. Hungry people cannot be expected to behave as though they are well fed. This is especially true with regard to rational and objective planning and to working for their own future. By necessity, their concern is with surviving this day. Any famine relief programs must cope with the realities of immobility, apathy, and resentment.

Hunger is ugly. The well-fed world would prefer to ignore its existence. However, the next few decades will involve a mighty struggle between the world's population and its resources. Hunger will be there. Perhaps in understanding the personal side of hunger, home economists will be better prepared to take an active role in the battle.

References

1. Keys, A.; Brozek, J.; Henschel, A.; Michelsen, O.; and Taylor, H. L. *The Biology of Human Starvation.* Vols. I and II. Minneapolis: University of Minnesota Press, 1950.
2. Davidson, S.; Passmore, R.; and Brock, J. F. *Human Nutrition and Dietetics.* Baltimore, Md.: Wilkins and Wilkins, 1972, p. 235.
3. Stein, Z.; Susser, M.; Saenger, G.; and Marolla, F. *Family and Human Development: The Dutch Hunger Winter of 1944-45.* New York: Oxford University Press, 1975.
4. Jelliffe, D. B., and Jelliffe, E. F. P. "Famine and the Family." *Journal of Tropical Pediatrics* 16: 91; 1970.
5. Winick, M., and Rossee, P. "The Effect of Severe Early Malnutrition on Cellular Growth of the Human Brain." *Pediatric Research* 3: 181; 1969.
6. Read, P. P. *Alive: The Story of the Andes Survivors.* Philadelphia: Lippincott, 1974.
7. Turnbull, C. M. *The Mountain People.* New York: Simon and Schuster, 1972.
8. Maslow, A. H. *Motivation and Personality.* New York: Harper and Row, 1954.

J. Home Economics/November 1975. Reprinted with permission.

WRITING ASSIGNMENTS

1. Select a periodical to which you might reasonably submit an article. Make a detailed analysis of it. Suitable headings might be the table of contents; types of subjects accepted; length, style, and tone of the articles; use of visuals; use of references; and biographical sketches.

2. Evaluate five periodicals in your major area as to the type and scope of articles printed. Examine the titles used, types of introductions and conclusions, and the techniques used to develop the bodies of representative articles.

3. Assume you have written a letter of inquiry to the editor of a technical periodical suggesting that you do research and write an article—as assigned in Chapter 6. Your idea has been approved by the editor. Now write the article.

4. Examine the papers you have already written in this course. Select one that would be suitable for publication in a certain technical or semitechnical periodical you have examined. Rework the paper so that it meets the standards of the periodical you have in mind.

5. Again, examine the papers you have already written in this course. For each, write an abstract 6 to 8 lines long that gives the main ideas of the paper, uses the same wording as is used in the paper when possible, and reflects the proportions of the paper itself.

6. Study an article in a technical periodical in your major area. Rewrite the article so it will be suitable for publication in the departmental newsletter or in some other school publication.

REFERENCES

1. *Social Casework.* New York: Family Service Association of America, 1978.
2. *PMLA.* New York: Modern Language Association of America, 1978.
3. *Public Administration Review.* Washington, DC: American Society for Public Administration, 1978.
4. Y. R. Shen, "Recent Advances in Nonlinear Optics," *Reviews of Modern Physics,* Jan. 1976, p. 1.
5. J. D. Wafford and R. Whitbread, "Effects of Leaf Infections by *Septoria nodorum* Berk. on the Translocation of ^{14}C-labeled Assimilates in Spring Wheat," *Annals of Botany,* Jan. 1976, p. 83.
6. Diana Forbes, "Early Post-Operative Heart Patients," *RN,* Apr. 1976, p. 59.
7. Alan V. Bell, "Waste Controls at Base Metal Mines," *Environmental Science & Technology,* Feb. 1976, p. 130.
8. Raymond J. Lawrence, "Consumer Brand Choices—A Random Walk?" *Journal of Marketing Research,* Aug. 1975, p. 314.
9. Robert M. Boberg, "Ear Opening Experiences with Rhythm and Pitch," *Music Educators Journal,* Dec. 1975, p. 32.
10. Julia Hurley Goelz, "Repetition and Frustration," *English Journal,* Dec. 1974, p. 45.
11. "Servicing Chevy's Four," *Southern Automotive Journal,* 1976, p. 21.
12. S. E. Shank and H. A. Guthrie, "Nutritional Counseling for Prevention of Dental Caries in Adolescents," *Journal of the American Dental Association,* Feb. 1976, p. 382.

CHAPTER 8

Oral Reports

MUCH writing goes into an oral report. The oral presentation is merely the final step in a procedure that involves writing during every phase of the preparation because the same process must be followed in researching a speech as in researching a paper. Possible subjects must be listed, the chosen subject must be limited and adapted to the potential audience, material must be collected and organized into an outline, and alternate material must be recorded to be used if needed—depending on the audience reaction.

Often the written outline or report leads to an invitation to make a formal oral presentation. Sometimes, on the other hand, the report is delivered orally and later, upon request, it is published. Being able to express ideas well orally is an accomplishment that brings career advancement and personal satisfaction. The greater the importance and responsibility of your job, the more time you will probably spend in oral communication.

TYPES

Skill in formal presentations, in conference and group discussions, and in job and informational interviews can help you make a sizable contribution to your organization and to your profession. Rules for effective oral communication with groups are equally applicable to communication with individuals.

Report That Is Read

The most formal type of oral presentation is the report that is read aloud to the audience. Several of the technical articles cited in Chapter 7 were first read at professional meetings before they were published. A read speech, however, is never as effective as a spoken one. It often bores the audience because it does not require the speaker to establish any communication with the listeners. But there are two situations in which it is necessary to read a speech: (1) when there are many statistics involved and an accurate statement is absolutely necessary, and (2) when a time limit must be rigidly observed.

Certain techniques, however, can guarantee some degree of success for the report that is read. Check the pronunciation of unfamiliar words ahead of time. Practice reading your speech at home, and train yourself to read slowly. Plan the pauses used to emphasize the main ideas, and practice the speech so many times that you can look at the audience for long periods of time while you are reading.

Impromptu Report

At the other end of the scale is a most informal type of oral report—the impromptu one. This is the kind of report you give when you are asked to "say a few words" on the spur of the moment about the work of a certain committee or about the operation of a new machine. This situation demands that you quickly gather your thoughts, organize them in the easiest way for the audience to understand, and compose your sentences as you stand before the group. The impromptu report does not require the preparation discussed in this chapter.

Memorized Speech

The riskiest type of speech to give is the memorized one simply because a lapse of memory can ruin the whole presentation. Once you memorize a report, there is no way you can adjust it to suit the needs of the audience; you are committed to reciting the whole thing. As you recite, you may be afraid to look at the audience for fear of being distracted from the memorized material. Therefore, the memorized speech is seldom successful. Some speakers memorize the beginnings and endings of their speeches to assure a smooth entrance and exit—with varying degrees of success.

Extemporaneous Report

The most successful type of oral presentation is the extemporaneous report. It is a well-organized speech delivered in a conversational, spontaneous way. Knowledge of the subject is essential, but chances are that you will know so much about your topic that your presentation may be rambling without proper organization. You must always take time to outline your speech, then familiarize yourself with it, and compose sentences as you stand before the audience.

The big advantage to speaking extemporaneously is that you can look directly at your audience. You can adjust your talk to suit the listeners. If you see from their reactions that they do not understand a major point, you can explain it in greater detail. If they warmly receive an idea, you can expand on it. If they are hostile to your approach, you can diplomatically win them over. If they are bored and restless, you can omit some of your examples.

Just remember that the speech, as you actually deliver it, will be different from the ways you have practiced. The flexibility of this type of speaking will allow you to personalize your remarks by mentioning the previous speaker, the one who has introduced you, or some other detail of the program. You will be adapting your planned oral presentation as you go along so that it will suit your audience.

The oral presentation delivered extemporaneously is appropriate for any type of technical speaking situation. It can be effectively adapted to the large audience, the smaller group, the panel discussion, the committee meeting, and the interview.

TECHNICAL SPEAKING SITUATIONS

All of you, regardless of your areas of specialization, will have many opportunities for making oral presentations. Technical speaking situations can range from a formal report before hundreds of people to a job or informational interview between only two people.

Large Audience Presentation

Informative and critical reports are often delivered formally to the large audience. The informative or historical report simply and briefly presents the facts about past happenings. The critical report presents facts gained by investigation or interpretation. It is more difficult to prepare because it is concerned with analyses, recommendations, and bases for future action. Both the informative and critical report are often submitted in written form and then the main points are given orally. If a written report does not accompany the oral report, the oral presentation must be complete. Vital data should usually be presented in order of importance.

Because of the large audience, it is especially important to maintain eye contact and to repeat the main ideas often. Using shorter sentences and simpler constructions than in written communications will aid understanding. Transitions will help your audience remember the connection between one idea and another.

Committees, Conferences, and Group Discussions

Committees, conferences, and group discussions all present similar technical speaking situations. All involve an informal exchange with a limited number of participants. Early in your career, you will be more likely to speak as a chairperson of a committee or as a member of a group than to make a public address. The employee who takes part in discussions clarifies the issues, gains more from the contributions of others, and has greater chances for professional recognition and advancement.

The chairperson. As the chairperson of a committee or conference or as the leader of a discussion group, you will have many responsibilities. An agenda that clearly defines the topics to be discussed must be written ahead of time. For example, the agenda of a grievance committee may include (1) rights of the grievant and the charged party, (2) taping of the testimony of each, and (3) makeup of the Discrimination Grievance Committee. When the meeting begins, someone must be appointed to take minutes. A statement of purpose at the outset will guide the discussion of the participants and keep them on the subject. If one member keeps returning to the problem of specific instances of on-the-job discrimination, a tactful reminder of the topic to be discussed will be necessary. An exchange of opinions can be encouraged by avoiding any show of bias, by rephrasing ideas for clarity, and by conveying needed information clearly and concisely. *Robert's Rules of Order* can help you decide procedural questions about motions and the recognition of speakers. Conflicts can often be resolved by delaying an early vote so all members have time to express their thoughts. You should record the conclusions reached so you can summarize them at the end of the discussion. It is not your job to entertain the group; you should always direct the discussion toward an intelligent solution of the problem because productive use of time contributes to practical results and improves the morale of busy committee members.

The member. As the member of a committee, conference, or discussion group, you will also have the responsibility of knowing your group, knowing your subject, having a desire to communicate, and being considerate of others. You should have a quick mind and speak up but should also remember to listen, not to interrupt, and not to monopolize the conversation. It may be necessary for you to jot down the key points made by other committee members so you can readily remember them.

Interviews

An interview usually consists of questions and answers about a specific subject between two or more people who are not of the same status.

The job interview. In the job interview, the applicant is asked questions about the services being offered. The interviewer can accept or reject the services. Sometimes the applicant will get the job because of the favorable impression created during the interview. Three parts of an interview need to be considered: preparation for it, the interview itself, and the follow-up.

Both participants must prepare ahead of time. The interviewer must allot enough time for a fair and complete appraisal of the job seeker, study the credentials to gain a better perspective, maintain a comfortable atmosphere, and list the points to be investigated. The applicant must be familiar with the potential employer and the job opening, with the general organization, training programs, research facilities, insurance and retirement plans, and promotion policies. This information can be obtained from the Chamber of Commerce, trade organizations, local newspapers, and company publications. The placement and the cooperative education offices of your school may keep informational brochures of the companies that usually hire its graduates. The *you* attitude is important for the applicant who should try to visualize the type of worker the employer is likely to want: one with training; one who has a real interest in the company; one who is dependable; one who is interested in long-range opportunities; one who can work well with superiors, equals, and subordinates; one who will effectively represent the company. The applicant, too, must outline ahead of time the probable points of discussion.

    I. My primary qualifications
        A. Education
        B. Experience
        C. Enthusiasm
   II. Reasons for leaving other jobs
        A. E. E. Milne
            1. Equipment
            2. Morale
            3. Pay
        B. Richardson Tool Company
            1. Management
            2. Opportunity for advancement
  III. Career goals
        A. Short term
            1. Job preference
            2. Salary (If money is not a determining factor, you may wish to let the interviewer introduce it.)
        B. Long range
            1. Job preference
            2. Salary

The applicant can offer personal information and introduce such subjects as leisure interests if he or she wishes to do so, but the interviewer is limited to questions directly related to the job itself. Finally, the applicant must plan on making a good impression at the interview by dressing appropriately, arriving on time, being friendly but businesslike, and listening carefully.

When the interview begins, the interviewer has the responsibility of inviting comments from the applicant beyond mere yes and no answers with such questions as the following:

What type of position interests you most?
What do you know about our company?
What can you tell me about yourself?
What kind of boss do you prefer?

Any interviewer must phrase such questions carefully so that unintentional discrimination will not occur. A good rule of thumb is to discuss only subjects related directly to the job; personal subjects should be avoided unless the applicant brings them up. Any personal information needed for postemployment purposes can be obtained

after the applicant has been selected for employment. Current sensitive areas are those involving age, marital status, number and age of children, availability for Saturday or Sunday work (since the answer may reveal the applicant's religion), credit and court records, and citizenship. Some traditional inquiries are now legally questionable:

What is the lowest salary for which you will work?
Do any of your friends and relatives work for this company?
Do you think you will "fit in" with our other employees?

It is also the interviewer's responsibility to end the meeting gracefully.

The applicant, too, has some responsibilities: answering questions honestly and directly; mentioning particular abilities; and explaining educational background, skills, experience, and relevant personality traits. An obvious display of desire for the job and ambition is acceptable, but also any lack of knowledge must be admitted. Asking questions about the company is appropriate:

How will my goals fit into the company's plans?
What opportunities for advancement will there be?
Will it be necessary for me to continue my education?
What kind of insurance and retirement plans does the company offer?

It is wise for the applicant not to introduce any new points into the discussion that have not been carefully considered. When the interviewer looks at his watch or begins to gather up papers, the applicant may assume that the interview is ended and this is the time to express appreciation and, if no decision has been reached on employment, ask for a time to call back and leave immediately.

The job application interview is a controlled conversation between two human beings. Its success depends on vitality, earnestness, alertness, enthusiasm, and a sensitivity to the moods and attitudes of the other person.

Writing a follow-up letter after the interview or making a follow-up telephone call is good business manners for the applicant. In any brief contact, the applicant should thank the interviewer for the appointment and look forward to future contact with the company. The thoughts below could be expressed either in writing or orally and, in any case, would create a good impression.

Thank you for the interview yesterday. I learned a great deal during our discussion of Crowelton's recently awarded government contracts, and I am eager to contribute to the coming expansion.

Again, I appreciate the opportunity of talking with you and look forward to hearing from you soon.

Informational interview. An exchange with some other person for the purpose of gaining needed facts is called an informational interview. It may be a letter of inquiry, direct interview, telephone call, or questionnaire. The purpose determines the medium and form to be used, but an in-depth interview can produce specific details that a questionnaire distributed to many different persons cannot produce. If you have asked for the interview to further your own knowledge or work by drawing on the experience of the other person, you are under greater obligation because you are the one being accommodated. In asking for the meeting, you should state what information is needed and how it will be used. Perhaps you wish to find out about the cooperative education program at a nearby liberal arts college to judge the desirability of a similar program proposed at your school. Before the meeting you should list your questions, wording them so the answers can be brief—sometimes requiring no more than yes or no.

1. Do you have both the alternate and parallel programs? What are the advantages of each?
2. What are the advantages for the student who participates in a cooperative education program?
3. How do you find jobs for liberal arts students?
4. What kinds of jobs can they do?
5. How do you evaluate their on-the-job performance?
6. How much credit does the student receive for his job experience?
7. What federal funds are available for the implementation of cooperative education programs?

Your approach during the interview is particularly important. You must take the initiative yet should maintain a pleasant, courteous, and appreciative attitude. While taking notes on what is said, you should read back some of the important facts to check for accuracy: "Did you say that the applications for Title IV-D funds must be submitted by November 1?" The questions should be brief, and leading questions or opinionated ones should be avoided.

Close by thanking the person or persons who granted the interview. Here, again, a follow-up letter or telephone call is necessary to express your appreciation. If you use the person's information in an article or speech or in your work, you should give credit to the source. It is always wise to give the respondent an opportunity to review your analysis of the interview before you use it.

PREPARATION OF THE SPEECH

Preparation of a speech involves adapting the material to the audience and arranging that material in the most effective order. Planning a presentation to a committee or conference will take as much time as planning something for a larger group.

Audience Adaptation

You should consider the audience as you plan your presentation. What interest do they already have in the subject? Will they be receptive or hostile? How can they best understand the information that you want to give them? Do they know you and accept you as an authority or will you have to give detailed support for every statement? The best talks seem to come from personal experience or first-hand observation. Experience can give you self-confidence, and it prepares the audience to accept your views. But your vocabulary and style should be adapted to the audience and to their level of knowledge. How will they be using this information? Since the audience needs your information in some way, clarity and accuracy are more essential than gimmicks and entertainment. How long should your presentation be? What has preceded your talk and what will follow it? If you are the last of several speakers, your talk should be lively, to the point, and brief.

Arrangement of Material

The same process is used for gathering information for both oral and written communications. There are primarily three sources of data: data available from interviews and reading, data discovered by first-hand observation, and data discovered in laboratory research. Crediting sources of information is just as important in a speech as in a written report.

Although the process of gathering data is the same for both oral and written presentations, the material in a speech must be organized differently. The listener has only one chance to grasp the facts, and there are no headings to label the sections of special interest. This circumstance forces you, as the speaker, to give close attention to the four parts of your oral presentation—the opening, discussion, supporting proof, and the closing.

The opening is very important because listeners pay closest attention at the beginning and ending of a talk. It can be developed in a number of different ways. You can make a broad statement, then narrow it down. Quotations, questions, analogies, comparisons, and contrasts are all effective. The most obvious device is a statement of your purpose and a list of the main parts of the speech so the audience will know what to expect. If you stress the purpose, sources of information, and procedures followed, they can accept the report as accurate and significant.

In the following introduction to an address before a business group in Texas, Mayo J. Thompson states the main idea of his speech and lists his three conclusions that will form the three main divisions. Notice how he refers to his experience in Washington to persuade the audience that he is competent and knowledgeable enough to present an accurate analysis.

Speaker's background After spending two years in Washington as a card-carrying member of the federal bureaucracy, I've arrived at a number of conclusions about where the country is heading and why. I have to *Thesis* tell you that I don't like the direction I think we're headed in and I like the reasons for it even less. My principal conclusions are these:

Conclusions 1. Free enterprise, the most democratic and productive economic system the world has ever seen, is being systematically eroded.

2. Socialism, the most undemocratic and least productive economic system the world has ever seen, is slowly but surely taking over.

3. And it's all happening because we're beginning to lose, it seems to me, our sense of personal responsibility, our willingness to work, and particularly our national pride in being the workshop of the world.

(Courtesy *Wage-Price Law & Economics Review* [1])

The next introduction, part of a paper presented by Florence Turnbull Hall before the Western Regional Conference on Home Management and Family Economics in 1974, begins with a general statement that she then narrows down. Mrs. Hall stresses the relevance of her topic for home economists, describes a sample case, and states the purpose of her oral presentation.

General statement To the bereaved, the death of a family member is an immeasurable loss.

Limitation When that person has been wife, mother, and homemaker, the emotional strains on the family can be devastating. But the financial hardship in a family that has lost a woman's work contributions is severe, too—and is often overlooked by those caught up in the tragedy of her death.

Explanation In court cases dealing with death or disability, however, this financial issue must be faced. Home economists in family economics or home management are occasionally asked to testify in these cases as expert witnesses.

The number of hours spent by homemakers in household tasks and the current weekly or yearly dollar value of those tasks must figure in court testimony. The expert witness must calculate the financial loss to the family for some years into the future, and then discount this loss to present value. For homemakers who were employed outside the home, the expert witness must also calculate the present value of the loss of her future earnings.

But how are we to arrive at the present value of these financial losses? What is essential is that we draw on economic data from various sources and take a comprehensive approach in our calculations.

In the cases for which I have prepared court testimony, some have involved only the financial loss resulting from the loss of homemaking services; others have involved this loss plus loss of future earnings.

Example In a recent case involving both kinds of financial loss, the court award for the financial loss to a family as a result of the homemaker's death was $353,000. (This homemaker had planned to return to work as a high school home economics teacher but was not working outside the home at the time of her death.)

I have prepared sample court testimony . . . to show the financial loss to a family resulting from the death in 1973 of the 32-year-old wife (employed full time), who was the mother of one

child. I will call this homemaker Mrs. Smith. In Mrs. Smith's case, the total financial loss to her family on her death would be $355,399. The way *Purpose statement* of arriving at this figure will now be explained. . . .

(Courtesy American Home Economics Association for the *Journal of Home Economics* [2])

The discussion part of an oral presentation clarifies the one major point that every good speaker should make. Limiting the subject allows you to explain and illustrate each of the subpoints thoroughly, to plan your time so you can indicate the importance of the subpoints by the amount of time you spend on them, and to repeat them with carefully planned variations.

Various devices will keep the audience listening to the discussion part of the talk:

1. Number the points you wish to stress.
2. Simplify your ideas as much as possible; when giving statistics, round numbers are usually easier to understand.
3. Consider the questions the audience may raise. Try to anticipate their objections and incorporate your responses into the presentation.
4. Appeal to the audience's needs—economic, social, personal, professional, or physical—in your discussion.

The supporting proof section can consist of statistics, testimonies, examples of experience with the product or service, and other supporting data. In substantiating the main points of the discussion section, you will find that visuals are especially valuable.

The closing must be carefully planned because the audience is again paying close attention; take full advantage of their interest. If you have arranged your main points in the increasing order of importance, you can conclude with the most important thought. Or you may want to stress the advantages of your plan and urge action. Sometimes a powerful conclusion gives a summary and interpretation of data and a list of conclusions and recommendations. You can also end with an anecdote stressing the main point of the speech, or you can ask a question. But remember that a positive ending is best: you should ask your customers which model of overhead projector they prefer or ask the board members when they can implement your plan. Regardless of which type of conclusion you use, the current trend in oral presentations is to leave the audience with a final idea rather than with "I thank you."

Florence Turnbull Hall, in her address already mentioned in this chapter, ends with a summary and interpretation of data:

Summary Clearly, those of us who are called upon to be expert witnesses in court cases of this nature must be both familiar and comfortable with the economic analyses described. . . . Economists and home economists who specialize in family economics and home management are, of course, likely candidates for this role.

Implications   But whether or not we will actually be called upon to testify, the issue affects us all. For women who are homemakers, wage earners, or some combination of both, the figures are not only revealing but are also essential to an understanding of women's role and valuation in contemporary society.

(Courtesy American Home Economics Association for the *Journal of Home Economics* [2])

DELIVERY OF THE SPEECH

Skill in delivery determines the success of an oral presentation. The carefully thought-out report that is haltingly presented is often rated lower than the mediocre report that is effectively presented. Your attitude is reflected in that of your audience. If you are bored, they will be bored; if you feel superior, they will be resentful; if you are excessively nervous, they will be uneasy. Therefore, make such a thorough preparation that your confidence is obvious. Your positive attitude will arouse an affirmative response in your listeners.

General Suggestions

1. Dress suitably, and wear clothes you are used to so you will not have to think about your appearance.
2. Stand comfortably and naturally with your weight distributed evenly on both feet.
3. Look over the audience before you begin to speak; draw a few deep breaths.
4. Speak clearly and distinctly at a rate slower than that of your normal conversation; most beginning speakers speak too rapidly.
5. Be friendly and enthusiastic.
6. Do not draw attention to your own shortcomings or those of the room.
7. Move around if you are not limited by space or a microphone. Movement can release your nervous tension, get the attention of the audience, and make you feel more forceful.
8. Time gestures and bodily movements to coincide with the content of the speech.
9. Indicate important ideas by varying the pitch and volume of your voice; also vary the rate of speed.
10. Do not be afraid of silence. Pause to emphasize key statements and to create suspense.
11. Know when to stop talking.

Practicing beforehand. Practicing in front of a mirror can help you to notice any irritating mannerisms such as teetering back and forth on your feet or precariously balancing on the edge of a table or desk. You may jingle loose change in your pocket, play with your glasses or pencil, or scratch your head.

If you tape the speech, you can identify any words or expressions that you use too much and can hear vocalized pauses in which you fill the space between words with *ah, uh,* or *you know.* Voices usually sound higher and thinner on a tape recorder. Controlled breathing and a relaxed throat can give you a fuller, deeper, more musical voice. With additional training, concentration, and practice it is possible to lower the voice. It is a mistake to try to speak louder by raising the pitch of your voice. Using a recorder can also help you to check pronunciation; carelessness in pronunciation suggests carelessness in the more fundamental matters of data and procedures.

Checking the microphone. It is wise to practice with the microphone before you use it. Microphones range from the small pencil type to the large boom. They are a mixed blessing since they emphasize the speaker's faults as well as pleasing qualities. The pencil microphone must be held an inch or two from your mouth. You should stand about a foot from the round microphone, speak directly into it, and avoid moving about or turning your head. The boom microphone picks up sound from a large area and thus allows you freedom of movement.

There are several rules for the effective use of a microphone. Use your normal tone of voice. When you reach any emotional climax of the talk, take a step back to avoid undue magnification. If you need to cough or clear your throat, turn your head away. Avoid brushing against the microphone, hitting it with your hand, or handling your notes close to it. Do not let the microphone distract you or cause you to lose eye contact with your audience.

Visual Aids

There are three types of visual aids: (1) projective materials, (2) nonprojective materials such as maps, flip charts, and blackboards, and (3) physical exhibits. Projectives are best when the subject contains movement and when the group is large. But the equipment is bulky, and slides and films require a dark room. Nonprojective materials are inexpensive and good for small groups. You usually need no assistance with them; you do not need to break eye contact with the audience, but they must be large enough to be seen. Physical exhibits are good for a small group. However, some are cumbersome and are not very effective when passed around among the audience because they distract from the message. Visuals are good at the beginning of an oral presentation because they are dramatic enough to attract attention, and they focus attention away from you when you may be most nervous. They can be used in the supporting proof section and in the summary at the end. When you are using visuals, you should not concentrate on them rather than on the audience but should know them so well that you can talk about them without giving them your full attention. You should not read aloud the wording on the visual aid but should incorporate the idea into your talk, slowing your rate of speaking as you use the visual aid. When finished with a visual, you should remove it from sight so you do not have to compete with it for the attention of the audience.

Use of Notes

The outline is the most effective type of reminder you can use in an oral presentation. If you are an experienced speaker, the outline can be a topic one that just gives a key word to suggest an idea. However, a key phrase outline can be more helpful because it gives you a start on your sentences. And if you are a nervous, beginning speaker, the complete sentence outline—which takes longer to prepare—will give the most help because each sentence is a topic sentence for a paragraph. See the following examples of the three kinds of outlines.

THE TOPIC OUTLINE

DESIGNING SAFETY INTO SHOPS AND LABS

I. Goals
   A. Methods
   B. Sources
   C. Equipment
   D. Administrative support
II. Initial planning
   A. Written study
      1. Philosophy
      2. Aims
      3. Objectives
      4. Operations and materials
   B. Continual supervision
      1. Laboratory layout
      2. Lighting
      3. Ventilation
      4. Housekeeping
      5. Storage
      6. Sound
III. People protection
   A. Eye safety programs
   B. Reliable manufacturers
   C. Compliance with recognized standards
IV. Fire prevention and suppression
   A. Removing hazards
      1. Smoking
      2. Flammables
      3. Waste disposal
      4. Housekeeping
   B. Suppressing a fire
V. Accident control
   A. Handling of a casualty
   B. Investigating the accident

THE KEY PHRASE OUTLINE

DESIGNING SAFETY INTO SHOPS AND LABS

I. Goals that should be achieved
   A. Elimination of hazardous methods
   B. Identification of the sources of various hazards
   C. Protection through the use of equipment
   D. Administrative support that permits the program to

operate systematically and to be integrated into all laboratory operations
II. Initial planning before the construction or remodeling of the shop or lab
   A. A detailed written study of the instructional program of the lab
      1. Philosophy of the proposed project
      2. Periodic and final aims of the project
      3. Short-term and long-term objectives
      4. An analysis of the mechanical operations and materials to be used
   B. Continual supervision, planning, and revision of activities
      1. Flow chart for materials, traffic, storage, and supervision potential
      2. Lighting in the form of intensity and brightness
      3. Fresh air, temperature, and exhaust systems
      4. Arrangement of equipment, storage, supplies, and waste
      5. Storage adjacent to where materials are needed
      6. Noise exposure as a function of time, frequency, and sound level
III. People protection through the use of protective devices
   A. Eye safety programs under professional supervision
   B. Purchase of safety devices from long-established manufacturers
   C. Insistence on proof of compliance with recognized standards
IV. Fire prevention and suppression measures to be taken in the lab
   A. Inexpensive removal of fire hazards
      1. Identification of smoking and nonsmoking areas
      2. Storage of flammables
      3. Periodic cleanup and disposal of wastes
      4. Orderly arrangement of tools and materials
   B. Sprinklers, fire extinguishers, standpipe, and hose
V. Accident control when the prevention program breaks down
   A. First-aid procedures and transportation of the victim
   B. Investigation of the accident leading to modification of equipment, methods, and materials

THE SENTENCE OUTLINE

DESIGNING SAFETY INTO SHOPS AND LABS

I. The following goals that should be achieved are listed in order of effectiveness and preference.
   A. Eliminate the hazards from the methods, machines, materials, or environments.
   B. Guard against, or otherwise eliminate, the hazards at their sources.
   C. If the hazards cannot be eliminated at their sources, protect those who are exposed by use of personal protective equipment.
   D. Seek administrative support for the systematic operation of the safety program and for its integration into all industrial laboratory operations.
II. Initial planning before the construction or remodeling of the shop or lab is the best time to eliminate hazards inherent in laboratory design.
   A. A detailed written study of the proposed operations, facilities, and materials of the lab should be finished before construction begins.
      1. Philosophy of the project should be clearly stated.

2. Periodic and final aims of the project should be agreed upon by management and workers.
3. Short-term and long-term objectives should be listed with the accompanying dates.
4. All mechanical operations and materials to be used in the project should be listed and described.

B. Continual supervision, planning, and revision of activities are necessary to achieve a safe atmosphere in the industrial lab.
1. Laboratory layout must facilitate the flow of materials to machine, traffic patterns, storage, and supervision potential.
2. Intensity and brightness of lighting can eliminate fatigue and accidents.
3. Fresh air, comfortable temperature, and adequate exhaust systems can increase alertness.
4. The orderly arrangement of tools, equipment, operations, storage facilities, materials, and supplies is vital to safety.
5. Storage adjacent to the point where materials are needed expedites the smooth flow of materials.
6. Noise exposure is a function of time, frequency, and sound level that can cause a loss of hearing.

III. People should be protected through the use of various personal devices only after every attempt has been made to eliminate the hazard.
A. All eye safety programs should be under the supervision of an ophthalmologist.
B. Safety devices should be purchased from long-established manufacturers with a proven record in industrial safety devices.
C. Proof of compliance with recognized state and federal standards must be provided.

IV. Fire prevention and suppression measures in the lab are cheaper than controlling a fire and restoring a damaged lab.
A. Obvious fire hazards can easily be removed.
1. Identify smoking and nonsmoking areas and insist on their use.
2. Store flammables in safe, supervised areas and post rules for their use.
3. Be conscientious about the cleanup and disposal of wastes.
4. Arrange tools and materials in separate, labeled areas and insist on their return to the proper place.
B. Use sprinklers, fire extinguishers, standpipe, hose, and other equipment to control and suppress fires.

V. Accident control in the form of an emergency plan on paper is needed for the time when the prevention program breaks down.
A. First aid must be administered in the lab, and then the victim must be transported by city ambulance to Mt. Carmel Hospital.
B. The safety supervisor must investigate the accident immediately and suggest modification of any lab equipment, methods, and materials that contributed to the accident.

Writing the outline on 3-by-5-inch note cards that fit easily in the palm of your hand is helpful, and you do not have to make a special effort to conceal such cards since audiences expect you to use notes of some type. Familiarizing yourself with your notes ahead of time will allow you to give full attention to the listeners and to glance at the cards only occasionally. If you must read an address, you should avoid pages of notebook paper that may rattle in nervous fingers and certainly should not turn the pages close to the microphone.

SUMMARY

You must be familiar with several different types of oral presentation: the report that is read, the impromptu talk, and the extemporaneous speech. Of these three, the extemporaneous speech is most adaptable to all kinds of technical speaking situations. The more formal the situation, the harder you will have to work to get and keep the audience's attention. Repeating, simplifying the technical aspects, and covering points more thoroughly will help retain interest.

Arrangement of material is most important. The same devices used in a written report can also help attract the audience's attention at the very beginning of a speech: a question, a startling statement, a quotation, or a story. Any device used, though, must be clearly connected to the subject of the speech. After you have clearly indicated the main parts so the audience will know what to expect, the development of each main point begins. These main points can be substantiated by citing authority in testimonies, statistics, examples, and supporting data—using visuals for emphasis and explanation. A summary of the main points, a repetition of the conclusions reached, a final fact, or a simple "Are there any questions?" can make an effective conclusion. It is vital that the ending be planned.

Delivery of the speech is important, too. Looking at the audience as you speak, noting their reaction to the various parts of your presentation, adjusting the speech as you go along to suit their needs, and speaking in a natural, conversational tone to your audience instead of *reading* or *reciting* all contribute to an effective speech. It is better to speak from an outline and make up the sentences as you proceed than to memorize; but if you do memorize the ending, you should speak naturally. Coordinating gestures with the content of the speech, practicing speaking from your notes, using the microphone, and handling the visual aids will determine the success of your talk.

Thus there are five steps in preparing an effective oral presentation:

1. Analyze the needs and interests of the audience.
2. Be well informed on your subject.
3. Arrange the material to satisfy the needs of the audience.
4. Plan a method of presentation with which you feel comfortable, as long as it does not involve memorizing the whole speech. You may want to speak from a topic, phrase, or sentence outline.
5. Prepare visual aids.

SPECIMEN SPEECH

Julian Goodman, chairman of the board of the National Broadcasting Company, spoke on "Freedom:

The First Priority'' at the Anti-Defamation League Dinner in Atlanta, Georgia, on December 6, 1975. He first clearly stated and clarified the thesis, traced the history of the Fairness Doctrine and defined and evaluated it, and then considered judicial interpretations and public attitudes.

Appreciation   I appreciate your inviting me to be with you tonight. For me, this is really the week of the An-
Purpose   ti-Defamation League. Next Wednesday I'll be attending a dinner in New York at which ADL honors Tex James, publisher of the *New York Daily News,* with its First Amendment Freedom Award.

Thesis   I'm pleased to be part of events like these, but it troubles me that—as we prepare to celebrate the 200th birthday of our country—we still must honor those who fight to keep America free; and that we still have to fight to make sure the First Amendment is respected for what it says. But that's a subject I've spoken on too often, I suppose, since the last time I did *Broadcasting* magazine, with something of a visible yawn, headlined it, ''Goodman Hammers on Government Intrusion.''

Limited   I regret that hammering is necessary. So let me
purpose   just say, at least for the moment, how glad I am to join you in honoring Elmo Ellis, and how glad I am to be associated with him in this sometimes strange and always wonderful world we call broadcasting.

Explanation   Broadcasters don't make things, or dig them from the ground and sell them. Our product is news, information, entertainment—enlightenment where we can find it—and a key ingredient in that endeavor is trust. The kind of trust that makes the public believe in and depend upon what it hears and sees. The kind of trust that makes the advertiser and the community leader believe in and depend upon what a broadcaster says when he gives his word. No one exemplifies this better than Elmo Ellis.

Elmo's station, WSB, is there when you need it—and he's there when you need him. And, fortunately for broadcasting, he has also been in the forefront of those of us committed to free expression, and to determined efforts to keep broadcasting free.

Restatement   As I have said, one thing that bothers me more
of thesis   than most things is that broadcasters must still explain how it happens that they are not as free as they should be and why it is in the best interest of the public for them to want to be.

Background   Our system of commercial broadcasting was consciously designed by private enterprise and built by private investment. It didn't cost the taxpayers a cent. Other countries have done this differently, some with government-chartered noncommercial systems, others with systems owned and operated by the government. Such systems may be effective in other nations, but they are not the kind of systems that serve the needs of most Americans.

History   There is and always has been a certain amount of Government control over American broad-
casters. The number of broadcast frequencies is limited, and they are not available to just anybody who might want one. To give the system order, the Government, quite correctly, took on the job of assigning frequencies and licensing stations, and the holders of those licenses are required to show that they operate in the public interest.

This is most fitting and proper. But since the Federal Communications Act, which governs broadcasting, was written—more than 40 years ago—succeeding generations of politicians and public officials have had their say about its application and interpretation. A great many regulatory actions have been applied in its name, especially in the area of news and information, and over the years broadcasters have found themselves removed from the protection that other media enjoy under the First Amendment to the Constitution.

Definition of   Broadcasters have their own amend-
Fairness   ment—Section 315 of the Communications Act—
Doctrine   which saddles them with the Fairness Doctrine and the equal-time rule. The purpose of the Fairness Doctrine is to expand public discussion of significant issues. The equal-time rule requires any station providing broadcast time to one candidate for public office to grant equal time to all of his opponents, no matter how serious their candidacies might be.

The intent of these provisions is admirable. But their effect is not.

Effects of   The Fairness Doctrine has discouraged the very
Fairness   type of discussion it purports to foster. It has
Doctrine   done this by giving Government the right to intervene as a frequently partisan editor in the process of broadcast journalism.

The equal-time rule, by forcing broadcasters to provide time to fringe and sometimes even frivolous candidates, has impaired the ability of broadcasting to deal with the major candidates and the campaign issues they develop.

There are bills in Congress to repeal the Fairness Doctrine. And the FCC has made some new exemptions in the equal-time law. But people in Government are not easily moved to change Government policies.

Congressman Torbert Macdonald, chairman of the House Subcommittee on Communications and a man for whom I have great respect, wrote to the *Washington Post* recently that without the Fairness Doctrine and equal-time protection, broadcasters—in his words—''would be left as the final arbiters as to what views are presented to the American people. . . .'' I can only ask, even if that were so, what alternative does the Fairness Doctrine offer?

The alternative—it seems to many of us who are concerned about these things—is the Government substituting a government official's news judgment for that of a trained journalist. And that is something that must be avoided if the First Amendment's guarantee of a free press means what it says to the American people.

Just how far that guarantee extends, even for newspapers and magazines, is a matter of grave concern today in light of a growing number of judicial rulings that severely restrict the reporting of court trials.

Other restrictions on press

Acting on one such "gag" order imposed by a judge in a Nebraska murder case, U.S. Supreme Court Justice Harry Blackmun ruled last month that a court may decide what information is and is not permissible for the press to report. He also ruled that "voluntary guidelines" devised for the reporting of criminal cases could be made mandatory and binding on the press.

If Justice Blackmun's ruling should stand—and it is one of the most restrictive ever handed down on the right of the press to report freely—it could be taken as a guide in other cases. Only this week, for example, the Nebraska Supreme Court held that in all future Nebraska criminal cases, pretrial proceedings may be partly or entirely closed to the public and the press.

Actions such as this will greatly weaken the ability of the public to keep a check on Government, including the administration of justice. And more than ever I am reminded of what David Brinkley once remarked: "If over the last generation," he said, "the politicians and the bureaucrats in Washington have made such a mess of things with the press keeping some kind of watch over them, what would they have done with nobody watching?"

Without the press, there is nobody to do the watching. And to those who see in an uninhibited press any danger to the public interest, Brinkley has this to say: "There are numerous countries in the world where politicians have seized absolute power and muzzled the press. There is no country in the world where the press had seized absolute power and muzzled the politicians."

The Fairness Doctrine has been a muzzle on broadcast journalism's pursuit of stories and issues the public should know about, and it has enabled the Government to stand at the broadcaster's shoulder and ask him to justify or amend his journalistic effort.

Judicial interpretation of Fairness Doctrine

Several years ago the FCC held that an NBC News documentary on private pension plans was unfair. We maintained that it wasn't and appealed the FCC's verdict in court. The U.S. Court of Appeals reversed the FCC. But if the FCC's intervention had been upheld, the Fairness Doctrine, I am sure, would have been invoked to cover more subjects than pensions.

The Court handed down an opinion I believe should be the controlling principle here. The opinion of Judge Harold Leventhal stated that—I'm quoting—". . . the evils of communications controlled by a nerve center of Government loom larger than the evils of editorial abuse by multiple licensees, who are not only governed by the standards of their profession but are aware that their interest lies in long-term confidence."

There are, however, ramifications to all this that concern me beyond the scope of broad-casting. And it is a concern I think many of us share.

Effects

I am concerned about the condition we find ourselves in, as a nation, after we have discovered the mistakes of our recent past. I am concerned about whether we have the strength and determination to recognize the reasons for those mistakes and to correct them. I am concerned by the low esteem so many people have for the leadership and institutions which are supposed to serve them. And I am concerned about whether that leadership and those institutions have the will to recognize their weaknesses and to overcome them on behalf of the people.

Attitudes toward government

As the *New York Times* has said editorially, "In the wake of Watergate and the more recent revelations by the Senate committee on intelligence, it has become increasingly difficult for Americans to hold the mirror up to their own country's behavior without the painful discovery of a devastating resemblance to the worst features of Governmental systems they have always properly detested and spurned."

Public attitudes appear to support this feeling. A Louis Harris poll taken two months ago reveals something that should trouble all of us. To a cross-section of 1,500 Americans, the Harris Survey asked: "As far as people in charge of running (our key institutions) are concerned, would you say you have a great deal of confidence, only some confidence, or hardly any confidence at all . . . ?" The results showed that among those who voted a great deal of confidence, only four groups registered more than 30 percent. Medicine led with 43 percent; colleges had 36 percent; television news, 35 percent; organized religion, 32 percent. At the bottom were Congress and the Executive Branch of Government—tied at 13 percent each. Major companies were at 19 percent.

Attitudes toward television news

It gives us no comfort that television news ranks high on the list in public confidence. *All* the percentages are *much* too low. In television and radio news, we try as hard as we can to recognize many of our imperfections, and our audience is alert in pointing out others to us, almost daily. We do, quite seriously, have a decided benefit in living the visible public life we do, being tested each day by our reports that are seen and heard in practically every American home.

Still, there is no escaping today's realities and the uneasiness we feel about our national condition as we prepare to observe our country's 200th anniversary. Remedies do not come easily. Perhaps the stability we seek will come with the election of a President 11 months from now—but that will be at the end of a road that includes more than 30 primaries, two national conventions, and a 10-week campaign. We can fervently hope that the victorious candidate and the exhausted electorate will emerge with a feeling of unity, and a program that will work for the benefit of the people. But what seems to be missing—and sometimes lost in the midst of political rhetoric—is a national sense of priorities that disregards politics.

Possible solution to problem of attitudes

Narrative of past goals Fifteen years ago last week, a Presidential Commission on National Goals—appointed by President Eisenhower and financed by eight foundations—reported its conclusions. They were formed under the shadow of what was called "the great dangers . . . of Sino-Soviet threat . . . the Soviet Union's great and swiftly growing strength, (and) the industrial and military progress and potential of Red China." Its conclusions might strike us today as simplistic: "We must have more doctors, nurses, and other medical personnel. . . . We must remedy slum conditions (and) reverse the process of decay in the larger cities. . . . Disarmament should be our ultimate goal."

That the Commission's findings now gather dust on library shelves may be the result of its failure to provide a plan for reaching the goals it agreed on; but its very existence made us examine our national purpose and establish priorities to realize it. It was a useful endeavor that we ought to go at again.

With today's détente with Russia, tenuous though it may be, and with the President of the United States having completed a friendly visit to China, the nature of the strains and pressures upon us has changed. Today, they may be more internal than external.

Restatement of thesis There should be no doubt in anybody's mind, here or abroad, that America has the capacity to face its problems and to solve them. But we need to have our national priorities examined by a group of qualified Americans who do not have to concern themselves with the pressures of partisan politics. That such an examination was made 15 years ago without a visible improvement in our national direction should not stop us from trying again; and the occasion of our country's 200th birthday is a good time to do that.

As we grapple with those things that concern us, broadcasting's chief responsibility is to keep the public informed, to cover events and issues and expose them to the greatest number of people. And to let the people make up their own mind. Anything that interferes with this can only dilute and distort the quality of broadcast service, and that is the ultimate in public disservice.

Example to support thesis Several years ago, Elmo Ellis wrote a book called "Happiness Is Worth the Effort." And he concluded that the path of true happiness lies in service to one's fellowman. Elmo lives by that belief, as a person and as a broadcaster. He has used broadcasting to serve the needs of his audience and to build public trust. He knows, as all broadcasters do, that if he breaches that trust,

people will know it, or sense it, and they will not believe him any longer.

Restatement of thesis This is something that lies at the heart of our system of broadcasting and I believe it is something that has made it work so well. Broadcasting is one of the strongest and most dependable voices in our society, and any attempt to silence it or divert it from its free course must be fought—for freedom is, to all of us, our most prized and fragile possession.

(Reprinted with permission of National Broadcasting Company, Inc. [3])

SPEECH ACTIVITIES

1. Make an oral presentation of the formal report that you have already written during the term. The speech should be extemporaneous and five to ten minutes long. To prepare for the presentation, outline the speech, plan the visuals, and practice ahead of time. A question and answer session with other students in the class should follow your talk.

2. Present orally to a small group an informal proposal. Your goal will be to secure permission from the class members in the group to proceed with the project you are proposing. Use a nonprojective visual aid.

3. Focus on some problem at your school: parking, cafeteria facilities, study space at the library, student apathy, student evaluation of faculty, lower tuition rates, etc. Set up a committee to deal with it; assign one student the role of chairperson. Discuss the problem, reach a conclusion or conclusions, and write a brief letter of recommendation to an administrative officer of your school or of your student body.

4. Assume that you are being interviewed for a job for which you will be qualified after graduation. Appoint one student in the class to interview you or two or three to act as an interview committee.

5. Read a written report aloud to a group.

REFERENCES
1. Mayo J. Thompson, "Inflation and the Labor Unions: 'Redistributing' Income from the Non-Union Workers to Union Members," *Wage-Price Law & Economics Review,* vol. I, no. 2 (1975), 53–54.
2. Florence Turnbull Hall, "The Case of the Late Mrs. Smith, Homemaker: Preparing Testimony for Court," *Journal of Home Economics,* Nov. 1975, pp. 30, 33.
3. Julian Goodman. *Freedom: The First Priority.* New York: National Broadcasting Co., 1976.

CHAPTER 9

General Principles of Business Correspondence

BUSINESS CORRESPONDENCE is the most common type of writing done by men and women in technical fields. Letters, if written effectively, will advance you in your chosen career, but all the technical training you have received is of little value if you cannot express yourself in forceful written language. It is through letters that you most often influence the actions of others.

Most of the basic principles for good report writing are equally applicable to business correspondence. Thought and analysis must precede writing; wasted words mean wasted time and money in the business world. There are three levels of technicality for all correspondence: direct technical letters to someone completely familiar with your area of specialization, semitechnical to the person who is knowledgeable in the field but not expert in your area of specialization, and nontechnical to the educated layman who is not expert in the field and in your area of specialization. When in doubt, use the less technical level because clarity and conciseness come first.

There are no shortcuts in achieving clarity in letters. For the most important letters on complex subjects you must prepare, research, organize, write, and revise. For very brief letters on noncontroversial subjects, just jot down the main points and arrange them in a logical order. The lengthier process, however, can save your employer the expense of misunderstandings.

There is a difference, though, between the usual reports and the letters: most kinds of technical writing deal with things; business correspondence deals with people, so different techniques are needed. Tone and word choice merit special attention in letters of inquiry, request, acknowledgment, instruction, sales, complaint, adjustment, and application. All these kinds of letters (1) give information, (2) secure action, and (3) create goodwill among people of very different backgrounds, training, and attitudes.

The purpose of a business letter is to influence the ac-
tion or attitude of the one who receives it, and the letter is judged by the results it gets. To achieve this purpose, you must first give close attention to the content of the letter.

CONTENT OF THE LETTER

The content of a business letter is all-important. Even a routine one represents a personal contact for your organization, and you should take full advantage of that contact. It should do more than just communicate the facts clearly and inoffensively. You want to affect the actions of the reader in some way, so the attitudes expressed and the techniques used are of prime importance.

Reader as the Focus

The reader is the focus of attention. Concern for that reader should be expressed, questions answered, and the action to be taken explained in easily understood language.

FOCUS ON THE WRITER:
Thanks for the order for five dozen Betty Crocker cookbooks. We will ship them immediately.

FOCUS ON THE READER:
Thank you for your order for five dozen Betty Crocker cookbooks. It was shipped to you on October 16.

The reader must be convinced that whatever you are suggesting will be advantageous and that some reward can be anticipated. Promise of this reward will encourage greater attentiveness and perhaps a favorable response:

FOCUS ON THE BROCHURE:
The enclosed brochure, *London Adventureland,* gives all the facts on ten exciting days in this fun-filled city, a vacation priced at only $595 per person.

FOCUS ON THE READER AND REWARDS:
You will feel that you're already in London when you read the enclosed brochure. Imagine that you are hearing

the chimes of Big Ben, wandering amid the history of Westminster Abbey, and sailing down the Thames. All these adventures can be yours for as little as $595.

FOCUS ON THE WRITER:
The Futuramatic Micro-Wave Oven is the best on the market today. We're making a special introductory offer October 10–15. Come see us at Brown Appliance Company now.

FOCUS ON THE READER AND REWARDS:
Save yourself time! Give yourself the pleasure of perfectly prepared meals! As the owner of a Futuramatic Micro-Wave Oven you will be the best cook in your neighborhood—and the thriftiest too. Do yourself a favor. Take advantage of our sale October 10–15.

Reader's Point of View

Linking the message directly to the reader's interest will stimulate a favorable response. A review of past correspondence or an analysis of the style of writing may give clues to the reader's interests and personality and help you to anticipate possible reactions. You will find that there are many different responses to any given situation.

Usually, a letter written to appeal to all types of readers appeals to none. The same letter cannot appeal to a midwestern farmer and an eastern lawyer or to a Minnesota teacher and a Los Angeles student.

Motivation. Persuasion calculated to motivate the reader depends on how believable the writer is. You must recognize the desires that will motivate your reader so your message can reflect them. The urge to be *told* by an authority figure, the desire for security, or the desire for some type of acceptance may predominate.

Sometimes the writer is considered an authority figure, and you, as the writer, can cause the reader to accept the new product or service without regard to the content of the letter—just on the strength of your endorsement. Occasionally a reader may feel a greater desire for newness and variety. Sometimes the desire for prestige can lead to some positive action merely on the strength of the writer's recommendation: "The only logical conclusion that I can reach, based on my twenty-five years as president of this company, is that you should immediately purchase the outstanding shares of stock and join other community leaders on our board of directors."

Other readers desire security. They may be more susceptible to the peer-figure approach (common man) than to the authority figure. You can offer hope or encouragement: "Your Century Hospitalization is still in force because of the thirty-day grace period; you have the full benefits." Another motivation for insecure individuals is group conformity. Especially for a member of a stable socioeconomic group, such as the middle class, the future may be envisioned as being much like the present and any persuasion should reflect immediate use of whatever the message proposes.

The rational or logical approach successfully motivates the psychologically mature person who is most susceptible to a presentation that respects intelligence and discretion: "This report presents consolidated financial statements that show sales have climbed to $752.7 million, an increase of 9.8% over the previous year." Some experts advise you to develop the emotional appeals for action first and then to reinforce them with rational ones because the emotional appeals cause your reader to do what you want and the logical appeals merely rationalize the emotional desires. There are always some readers, however, who do not respond to either appeal and do not react in any predictable fashion.

Postive Approach. You should consider the situation, treat the reader as you would like to be treated, and be guided by what is convenient and appropriate. You must appear to be a fair, impartial observer who has the customer's best interests in mind. Your consistent friendliness will make refusal difficult. In a business letter you want to influence actions; you can best do that in an atmosphere of concern and cooperation. You must never ridicule the reader. It is more important for your firm to retain the goodwill of a customer than for you to win an argument or vindicate your position.

All readers respond favorably to positive ideas; positive thoughts give a sense of well-being and negative ones a sense of failure.

NEGATIVE:
The refrigerator, model No. 372, which you ordered has not been shipped from the factory. It should be here by February 15.

POSITIVE:
The refrigerator you ordered, model No. 372, should arrive by February 15. Our shipping invoice indicates that you will be sent your first choice of color, Fire Gold.

The beginning of a letter should include some point on which you can agree. If you are so at odds with the reader that friendliness would be hypocritical, the beginning can at least be courteous. A negative beginning is offensive because it communicates distrust and dislike, and the neutral one merely reports the facts. Courtesy, sincerity, and friendliness are necessary ingredients of the positive beginning.

NEGATIVE:
We have received your letter complaining about the supposedly damaged merchandise.

NEUTRAL:
We have received your letter about the damaged merchandise.

POSITIVE:
Thank you for your letter about the merchandise shipped on August 10.

Rewrite the following beginning sentences, improving the content and word choice. Add facts if necessary.

1. I have received your letter complaining about "the damned fertilizer plant."
2. I am sorry to inform you that brake realignment on your new Chrysler Newport is not covered by the warranty.
3. I know that you receive requests from many organizations for contributions, but I hope that you won't throw this one away before you read it.
4. I hope that you won't be offended if I object to your mowing your lawn each Saturday morning at 7 a.m.

A positive ending will gain the reader's future goodwill. If you have to refuse something, there should be no reminder of this unpleasantness at the end of the letter. Better relations in the future should be stressed. "I believe you will agree that our decision is a responsible one; we now look forward to your continued business" is a better ending than "I'm sorry I cannot grant your request at this time but look forward to doing business with you in the future." If some action is desired, a specific statement in the last paragraph should explain what action you want taken. This request for action should imply that you are doing a favor for the reader: "If you will let us know, at your earliest convenience, whether or not you can speak to us on October 23, we can make hotel reservations and arrange publicity immediately." The reader will continue thinking about anything mentioned in the ending. "Let me again express my regret for the damaged merchandise" merely reminds the reader of the complaint. A better ending would be "We appreciate your business and look forward to serving you in the future."

Rewrite the following concluding sentences, improving the content and word choice. Add facts if necessary.

1. I believe that all the repairs have been made to your watch and am sorry that it took so long.
2. We regret the aggravation caused you by the failure of your Champion power mower to start, but look forward to doing business again with you next year.
3. Please let us know as soon as possible whether or not you will be able to serve on the committee so we will still have time to get someone else if necessary.

Arrangement of the Parts of the Letter. Always arrange the parts of a business letter with the reader's point of view clearly in mind. It is easiest to write a letter saying yes. Give the good news immediately: (1) say yes, (2) explain why you have said yes, and (3) look to future dealings with the organization or individual. The following specimen letter saying yes illustrates this type of arrangement.

September 15, 19—

H. A. Borthwick
1716 Moffit
Joplin, MO 64801

Dear Mr. Borthwick:

Positive beginning Thank you for your letter of September 12 which referred to the playing of the National Anthem on September 9. I appreciate your concern on a matter such as this. I wish you to know that no disrespect for the flag was intended and that we *Saying yes* will change our pregame maneuvers to prevent any further misunderstanding.

You may wish to know, however, that the passage in the Flag Code to which you refer does not pertain to the musicians who are performing the National Anthem.

Explanations There are no stipulations either written or traditionally understood on this matter. Symphony orchestras, for example, that perform the anthem before a concert are not facing the flag, nor are they standing; the same is true for the many pianists and organists who perform the anthem for various ceremonies and games throughout the country.

Band members who perform the anthem cannot remove their hats or salute the colors while playing. Their respect for the flag is shown in their playing of the anthem itself. In our case, the logistic simplicity necessary for the preparation of a performance despite limited rehearsal required that our formation face south.

Repeating the yes For the next game, this can be very easily changed, and I will be most happy to make the necessary adjustments so that the patriotism of our band and its conductor is not called into question.

Future I am confident that your concern is sincere and appreciate your taking the time to write to me. I hope that by making the change you requested we will have your needed encouragement and support.

Sincerely,

Gary Corcoran
Director of Bands

When saying no, do not say it immediately; the reader may be too angered to read the rest of the letter. (1) Begin on a positive note by finding some point on which you can agree, (2) explain the circumstances or give background information that will force you to say no,

(3) say no, and then (4) look to the future. If you have both good and bad news to give, always give the good news first. See the following specimen letter.

Professional Building
Glendale, IL 62937
September 16, 19—

Mr. John M. Johnson
Gross Manufacturing, Inc.
Shiloh, NC 27974

Dear Mr. Johnson:

Positive beginning   Thank you for the invitation to speak to your investment club on November 11. I have long admired the leadership that Gross Manufacturing has given the wood products industry and was much impressed with your organization during my inspection trip shortly before my retirement last March.

Explanation saying no   However, I have already agreed to participate in a federally funded seminar planned for Munich, Germany, the week of November 8 through 12. This appointment will make it impossible for me to speak to your group on November 11.

Alternate suggestion   I do have an article scheduled for publication in the December issue of Wood and Wood Products. If you like, I can edit it and send my former associate, Paul V. Jones, to read it.

Future   I wish you every success at your meeting.

Sincerely,

G. H. Grandle

G. H. Grandle

GHG/sa

Tone

The overall tone of a business letter must be one of honesty, sincerity, and courtesy. You must believe that your product or service is the best and communicate that thought to your reader in a natural, conversational tone.

Honesty. Is your letter merely a delaying action promising the customer delivery in two weeks when you know that it will take six weeks? Remember that the integrity and reputation of your company rest upon your words. Instead of writing "Your order will be filled as soon as possible," say "Your order will be filled as soon as we receive the shipment from the factory—about May 10."

If you cannot pay a bill on time, honestly present the facts and give the assurance that you are not avoiding payment deliberately. This admission can save the company the expense of sending you additional letters that may cost as much as $6 apiece for stationery, stamp, secretarial time, and use of equipment. See the brief letter below.

Request   Please give me an extension of one month on my thirty-day revolving charge account. My in-
Explanation   come tax refund has not arrived, but I expect it any day.
Assurance   I will be able to pay my bill in full at least by May 1.

Sincerity. Be sure that your letter "rings true." The relationship between the writer and the reader can suffer if there is a lack of integrity; never exaggerate. A form letter sent to thousands of people "personally" inviting them to take advantage of a special offer is an example of insincerity.

Courtesy. Economy of word choice is no reason for omission of *please, thank you, I am sorry,* and *I apologize.* These important words can dissolve a customer's anger and win goodwill. Notice the difference that a courteous tone makes in the following sentences:

Abrupt: We received your order of January 5.
Courteous: Thank you for your order of January 5.

WORD CHOICE

Your business letters should sound like you at your best. Directness, economy, and simplicity should characterize the style. Always be courteous. Avoid sarcasm and profanity even when the letter you are answering has made liberal use of substandard English, slang, sarcasm, or profanity.

Negative Words

Eliminate any basically negative words that, in turn, produce a negative outlook:

Negative: We regret that we will not be able to hire a cooperative education student until next February.

Positive: We look forward to hiring a cooperative education student next February.

Negative: My experience has been limited to only two months of writing press releases for a local political organization.

Positive: I was most fortunate to spend two months writing press releases and newspaper ads for the Skubitz for Congress campaign.

Overuse of *I* and *we* instead of *you* also produces an unfavorable reaction. Always emphasize the reader's interests and needs first:

Negative emphasis on the writer:
I must have the payment of $61 immediately or I will have to remove the color television set from your home.

POSITIVE EMPHASIS ON THE READER:
Immediate payment of the $61 will allow you to keep the color television set in your home, and it will also protect your good credit rating.

Old-fashioned Terms

Flowery, old-fashioned terms popular in letters for the last hundred years are now out of date: *I remain your humble servant, I beg leave to inform you, Enclosed please find a copy of, Kindly advise us as to your wishes in this matter, Thanking you in advance,* and *Awaiting your reply, I remain.* The best way to avoid trite, old-fashioned language in business correspondence is to ask yourself, Would I use these words in a personal conversation? Correct the out-of-date language in the sentences below:

1. Your letter of recent date informs us of your decision.
2. Kindly reply at your earliest convenience.
3. I beg leave to inform you of a change in our meeting date.
4. Thanking you in advance, I remain your humble servant.

Trite Business Jargon

Overused business jargon must be avoided. Natural, relaxed, specific English should replace the following worn-out phrases:

attached herewith	we are attaching
enclosed herewith is our check in the amount of	we enclose our check for
please be advised that	(omit)
with reference to	about
at an early date	soon
in the event that	if
due to the fact that	because
we should like to have benefit of	we would appreciate
in lieu of	instead of

Correct the trite business jargon in the following sentences:

1. Fill out application and return same to us.
2. We sincerely desire to have the benefit of your expertise in this area.
3. Enclosed please find your copy of the proposed agreement.
4. Attached herewith is the daily schedule in lieu of the usual progress report.
5. Please be advised that we would welcome your remittance at an early date.

Words with Unflattering Connotations

Words with unflattering connotations can keep you from achieving the desired result. *Allege, we contend that, although you assert that, claim, error, fail, complain,* and *neglect* all have a belligerent tone. Expressions such as *we refuse* and *you have failed* may so offend the reader that the action you suggest will not be taken. Correct the words with unflattering connotations in the sentences below:

1. We are extremely touched by your sad story. However, our tests do not substantiate your claims.
2. There is no way that we're ever going to replace what you refer to as "damaged merchandise."
3. In the event that you insist on continuing to allege that you have been treated unfairly, our legal advisors will be forced to take decisive action to refute your claims.

SENTENCES AND PARAGRAPHS

Selecting the most effective words is only the first step in writing business letters. To communicate ideas to your reader, you must combine words into sentences and then into paragraphs.

Sentences

Sentences should be appropriate for the message you are communicating. They will determine the kind of impression you will make on your reader, so length and structure should be varied to make them more interesting. Using action verbs and specific words will give them more vitality.

Sentences rarely meet all the requirements the first time you write them. The important thing is to get your thoughts down on paper, then go back over the sentences and rearrange them for greater clarity. Add transitions to improve the flow of thought and vary sentence length and structure.

Placement. Usually the first and last sentences in a letter, though they are brief, are the most important ones. The first sentence states the purpose, refers to any past correspondence, and establishes a friendly tone. The last states some specific action to be taken and looks to future contacts. Sentences in the middle of the letter can be longer and usually explain or justify the main idea. Note the placement of sentences below.

Friendly tone and purpose Thank you for your recent inquiry regarding employment with the Standford Company.
Decision We have studied your qualifications with respect to our present needs, but at this time it does not appear that we have a suitable position. We do appreciate your desire, however, to be a part of our growing organization and will add your correspondence to our active files.
Future We will contact you should a suitable opening develop.

Place important ideas in independent clauses and less important ideas in single words, phrases, and subordinate clauses.

Transitions. One type of transition is the word repeated from one sentence to another. Using the same subject in sentences throughout the paragraph can impart a certain unity that causes the ideas to flow. Transitional words that indicate a time sequence and stress the relationship of one sentence to another also make the letter easier to read:

Control procedures on our paper machine can be improved.

Time *As* the finished paper leaves the calender stack at
sequence the dry end, it is wound on a reel. *When* the reel is
transitions full, the continuous sheet is broken and the new
are italicized end of paper is fed to another reel. The paper on
this first reel is wound off, slit to the proper
widths, and wound onto a core in its final roll
form *while* the second reel is being filled. *By the
time* the second reel is full, the first reel is *again*
ready to receive paper.

Notice the A sample strip of paper across the width of the
repetition of machine can be taken when there is a reel change.
"reel" and This cut sample of paper can be sent to the lab
"paper" where it is measured for weight, bursting
strength, tensile strength in both machine and
cross-machine directions, tearing strength in both
directions, folding endurance, porosity, and absorbency.

Length. Flowing thoughts and vitality of presentation usually call for variety in sentence length. Most sentences, however, will be quite short; for instance, the first sentence should be short enough to immediately attract your reader's attention and get the message across before he loses interest. But do not sacrifice clarity for brevity; use all the words you need to make your meaning clear. Longer complex and compound sentences are appropriate for the body of the letter because they allow you to qualify and clarify the initial brief statement. But remember that even a well-written longer sentence can be self-defeating when it requires rereading.

Complexity. There are four basic kinds of sentences. The *declarative* sentence makes a statement: "The invoice was sent." The *interrogative* sentence asks a question: "Did you send the invoice?" The *imperative* gives a command: "Please send the invoice." The *exclamatory* expresses some type of emotion: "Sending the invoice was a mistake!"

Sentences can be arranged in several ways. A simple sentence contains one main clause that has a subject and a verb and makes sense by itself: "I want to apply for the position of architect." The compound sentence has two or more main clauses: "I want to apply for the position of architect; I believe that I am well qualified." The complex sentence has one main clause and one or more subordinate clauses: "Because I have a degree in architectural engineering, I would like to apply for the position."

Each sentence type has its usefulness. The simple sentence has greater impact and clarity and is especially effective at the beginning and end of a business letter. But when overused, as in the excerpt below, it seems abrupt and repetitious:

Direct filing is the easiest way to file. This system is simple. There are no code numbers to remember. An index or cross reference file is not necessary. Three areas of direct filing are alphabetic, subject, and geographic.

There are several advantages to this system. Direct reference to filed materials is possible. The dictionary arrangement is simple to operate. Cross-referencing is not difficult. Misfiling is easy to check. The alphabetic sequence makes checking easy.

Compound sentences clarify meaning and make for easy, smooth reading in the middle of the letter; but they can become monotonous, as in the following example:

Direct filing is the easiest way to file, and this system is simple. There are no code numbers to remember, and an index or cross-reference file is not necessary. Three areas of direct filing are alphabetic, subject, and geographic.

There are several advantages to this system, and direct reference to filed materials is possible. The dictionary arrangement is simple to operate, so cross-referencing is not difficult. Misfiling is easy to check, and the alphabetic sequence makes checking easy.

Notice the variety of sentence types used in the version below and their overall effectiveness. Key ideas are expressed in coordinate clauses, and less important thoughts in subordinate clauses. The usual subject-verb-complement sentence pattern is rearranged:

Direct filing is the easiest way to file. This simple system encompasses only three areas: alphabetical, subject, and geographic. Since there are no code numbers to remember, an index or cross-reference file is not necessary.

Advantages to this system are (1) direct reference to filed materials and (2) a dictionary arrangement that makes cross-referencing simple. Because of the alphabetic reference, any misfiling is easy to check.

Paragraphs

In the first paragraph of a business letter, the purpose of the letter should be clearly stated. A participial phrase such as "Referring to your letter of May 1" can be confusing. A more emphatic beginning would be "Thank you for your order of May 1." A one-sentence first paragraph is usual.

Paragraphs in the body of the letter usually run from two to four sentences in length, and each includes a topic sentence that is developed in sufficient detail. These details should be arranged in the best psychological sequence. Will the reader react more favorably to a descending scale (most important items first and least important last) or an ascending scale? Different arrangements are better in different situations, but the essential point is for the effect to be calculated. If you use several long paragraphs, you can place a heading at the beginning of each to guide the reader. But for most letter writers, long paragraphs are not the problem. Usually you have to guard against the tendency to begin every sentence with a new paragraph. The letter will then sound like a telegram and perceived rudeness will be the end result, especially when you are refusing something.

The last paragraph, again often a single sentence,

should make it easy for the reader to take the action or accept the point of view that you want him to take. If you enclose self-addressed envelopes or postcards for the reader's reply, refer to them in the last paragraph to get him to take action. Remember that the ending sentence may determine not only the reader's reaction to the whole situation but also your future relationship with him.

Observe these principles of paragraphing in the following letter:

Positive note Thank you for your resumé.
Descending scale We are indeed impressed with your qualifications, but we do not have any openings for which we might be able to consider you at the present time. We will, however, retain your resumé in our files for review in the future if an opportunity arises.
Positive note We appreciate your interest in Edmundon Consolidated.

STANDARDS OF NEATNESS

After you have given close attention to the content, word choice, sentence structure, and paragraphing of a business letter, you must next understand the basic rules for neatness, acceptable forms, and various parts of the letter. Whether you intend to handle your correspondence personally or to supervise the work of a secretary, you must meet high standards in these areas.

A neat, attractive letter creates a favorable impression for your firm. A good format will suggest that the message is well organized and clear; a messy, inaccurate letter implies that your work will be below par, or the service that you offer will be carelessly done. The reputation of a company rests partly on its letters to customers: proofread carefully and ask the secretary to retype if there is awkwardness of phrasing, strikeovers, erasures, or misspelled words. Neatness is more important than the particular form you select for the letter.

Stationery

The stationery should be good quality bond paper, preferably white, 8½ by 11 inches in size. Any smaller size paper makes filing difficult. Business letters are seldom more than one page but when they are longer, the first page should be typed on printed letterhead paper and subsequent pages on blank paper of equal quality.

Placement on the Page

Type the letter with more white space at the bottom than at the top of the page. Side margins should be 1 to 2 inches and the top and bottom margins should be 1½ to 2½ inches. When using letterhead paper, arrange the full-page letter so it begins with the date line a double space beneath the letterhead and the inside address a double space beneath the date line. The salutation is a double space below the inside address. Single-space within the paragraphs of a business letter and double-space between the paragraphs. Place the complimentary closing a double space below the body of the letter. Allow four spaces for the handwritten signature and then type the name of the sender.

The short letter requires special handling. Place the date a double space below the letterhead and then type the inside address perhaps three inches beneath the date. Center the short letter on the page and use wider side margins. If there are less than nine or ten lines in the body of the letter, double-space within the paragraphs.

Accuracy

Any time you dictate a letter to a secretary, you are responsible for its final form. You must have mastered the basic principles of good writing so that you can intelligently proofread the letter before you sign it. Be on the alert for wrong words that change the whole meaning: "I am not (now) sending the information to you." "The meeting will be Monday, May 4" (when May 4 is on Tuesday). Such inaccuracies create ill will, cause confusion, and often necessitate another exchange of letters—an expensive proposition at today's inflationary prices.

Continuation Pages

Try to express your ideas in only one page, but when it is necessary to use a second sheet, label it. There is no generally accepted form for the heading of the second and subsequent pages of a letter, but often the name of the person to whom the letter is written, the date, and the page number are typed on the upper left margin, single spaced.

John Jones Jowett
September 10, 19—
p. 2

An alternate, less popular form arranges this information across the width of the page on a single line:

John Jones Jowett   September 10, 19—   p. 2

Any page after the first should include at least a paragraph of the text. If you have only the complimentary closing and signature left, use wider margins to make the letter longer so you will have a sentence or two in the final paragraph. Or you can shorten the content of the letter so it can all be typed on one page.

FORMS OF THE LETTER

There are three basic forms of the business letter: the block, the indented, and the semiblock. Any departure from these generally accepted forms may result in attention being given to the unusual arrangement of the letter on the page rather than to its content.

The block form is the easiest to use and to type because all parts of the letter are arranged on the left-hand margin. The first line of each paragraph also begins on the left margin. This is the form that is growing most rapidly in popularity.

The indented form places the date (if you are using letterhead paper) or the complete heading (if you are using blank paper) on the right side of the page. The lines of the inside address and the salutation begin on the left margin. The beginning of each paragraph is indented five spaces. The complimentary closing and signature are placed on the right side directly beneath the heading.

The semiblock form refers to any compromise between the block and indented forms: (1) it may be the same as the block except that the beginning of each paragraph is indented five spaces or (2) it may deviate from the block by placing the heading and complimentary closing in the center of the page or to the right of center.

The following letters illustrate the block format, the indented format, and the semiblock format.

Specialty Projects Corp.

206 S. Broadway ▪ P. O. Box 663 ▪ Pittsburg, Kansas 66762
Phone 316-231-8060

September 16, 19—

John R. Richards
1000 S. Broadway
Miami, FL 33100

Dear Mr. Richards:

Thank you for your letter and resumé of September 9, 19—. Your interest in our corporation is appreciated.

The expansion experienced by Specialty Projects over the last two or three years has resulted in the addition of several levels of specialists, running from the office areas to the production shops. In most instances, the greatest needs have been for skilled persons to operate machinery and assemble the finished product.

Your resumé reflects a varied background of education and work experience that would certainly prove useful to the right company. Unfortunately, at this time our work force is relatively stable and we do not foresee further increase in the near future.

I will review your qualifications with other members of our management team in our Tulsa Division and should an opening occur where your abilities can be utilized to mutual advantage, you will be contacted.

Yours very truly,

SPECIALTY PROJECTS CORP.

G. D. Gollander
Personnel Manager

GDG/jj

THE KANSAS POWER AND LIGHT COMPANY
818 KANSAS AVENUE, TOPEKA, KANSAS 66601

July 24, 19—

Adams J. Abee
1715 James Avenue
Overland Park, KS 66204

Dear Mr. Abee:

I appreciated your taking the time to come for a personal interview on your campus this past week.

After further review of your application we have decided not to make you an offer of employment at this time. We will keep your application in our active files. I thought you would want to know of our decision as soon as possible for I am sure you have other opportunities to consider.

We wish you well in whatever you undertake to do. Thank you for your interest.

Sincerely,

John Hede
Staff Assistant

JH:cmm

Kim-Tam® Designs
A Division of the S.P.C. Corporation

Cheerleader Uniforms & Supplies

September 8, 19—

Angus M. McIlvaine
1016 S. Platt
St. Joseph, MO 64500

Dear Mr. McIlvaine:

We appreciate your letter of application and resumé and look forward to an interview with you during the week of October 3.

Our personnel manager, Mary R. Snyder, is presently in New York but will return to her office by September 29. She will call you at that time and set the interview on a date convenient for both of you.

We believe that your education and work experience can prove useful to Kim-Tam Designs, and we look forward to discussing employment opportunities with you.

Sincerely,

Agnes Mary Kope

AGK:bsb

PARTS OF THE LETTER

There are five basic parts to a letter in addition to the body of the letter itself: the heading, inside address, salutation, complimentary closing, and the signature.

Heading

Many firms use specially printed letterhead stationery. A printed letterhead should be simple in design and include the name of the firm, address, telephone number, and sometimes the cable address as well as the names of executive officers. The heading to be typed on letterhead paper consists only of the date, and it can be placed on the right side, in the center, or on the left side. Sometimes the printed letterhead is designed to provide a natural space for the date line. Use letterhead paper whenever possible because it adds an air of authenticity that will gain acceptance for the content of the letter.

The following letterheads illustrate a variety of types both in design and in information included.

On plain paper the heading consists of three or four lines: the first, and second line if necessary, gives the local address from which you wrote the letter; the next line gives the city, state, and zip code; and the final line gives the date. The heading is typed 1½ to 2½ inches from the top of the page. If you use the indented form, arrange the heading slightly to the right of center or so the longest line ends at the right margin. The zip code is typed a double space after the abbreviation of the state. Notice that your name does not appear anywhere in the heading.

Avoid abbreviations except for the abbreviations of states. Write out the names of companies and the names of months. Always use March 22, 19—, not 22 March 19— as is common in some areas of the government and the military, and certainly not 3/22/78. Spell out *Street, Boulevard, Avenue, North, South, East,* and *West.* If the name of the street is a number that consists of only two words, write it out: *Fifty-first Street.* But if the number is longer than one or two words, use figures: *121st Street.* There is a growing tendency to express any street number in figures if *North, South, East,* or *West* appears between the number of the house and the number of the street. The house number is always written as figures.

SPECIMEN TYPED HEADINGS

Arrow Merchandising
1123 Mesa Avenue
Tucson, AZ 85700
July 1, 19—

229 Hughes Street
Chula Vista, CA 92010
May 17, 19—

815 Twenty-third Street
El Paso, TX 79900
June 7, 19—

116 East 49th Street
Joplin, MO 64801
August 10, 19—

Inside Address

Include the same information in the inside address that you will place on the outside of the envelope. When the letter is addressed to an individual, always give some title or the equivalent: the reader may be addressed by the abbreviations Mr., Ms., or Dr. or by Professor or Reverend fully written out before the name. The Honorable is used before the name of an important government official. It is acceptable to place the reader's degree after his name instead of placing a title before the name. Either "Dr. Timothy T. Titus" or "Timothy T. Titus, M.D." would be appropriate, but not "Dr. Timothy T. Titus, M.D."

Ms. is an appropriate form for addressing a woman regardless of her marital status and is now almost universally accepted. The modern tendency is not to specify marital status, even when that status is known. If the woman, however, expresses a preference for Miss or Mrs., that preference should be honored. An academic or professional title such as Dr., Professor, or Capt. should take precedence over Ms., Mrs., or Miss.

When writing an official's name, follow his name with a title. You are allowed considerable flexibility so the lines will not become too long. If his title is very long, place it on the second line beneath his name. It is always better to address a letter to an individual rather than to a company or organization, but when you do write the name of a company, type it exactly as they do—using the same abbreviations.

Dr. Gerald H. Kramer
Director of Employee Relations
Pittsburg State University
Pittsburg, KS 66762

Salutation

The salutation is placed a double space below the inside address and is followed by a colon. Some firms omit the colon after the salutation, but this is not a widely established practice. The salutation must be addressed to the same person or persons to whom the letter is addressed. Always use *Dear* and the person's last name instead of *Dear Sir* unless you do not know the name of the one who will be reading the letter. Then *Dear Sir* is appropriate. If you do not know the name of the woman who will read the letter, *Dear Madam* is acceptable although rather formal. If you do know the woman's name, *Dear Ms. Smith* is widely used. If the person to whom you are writing is of high rank, the more ceremonious *My dear Sir* is appropriate; notice that only the initial letters of the first and last words in the very formal salutation are capitalized. On the other hand, if you call the reader of the letter by his first name in conversation, address him as *Dear Bill* or her as *Dear Mary*. If the salutation must address several people, *Gentlemen* or *Ladies* is acceptable.

The following inside addresses and salutations illustrate the proper procedure for a variety of circumstances:

Dr. Mary Ellen Greer
Director of Student Services
University of Colorado
Boulder, CO 80301

Dear Dr. Greer:

———

Mr. Charles H. Pillard, President
International Brotherhood of Electrical Workers
1125 Fifteenth Street, Northwest
Washington, DC 20005

Dear Mr. Pillard:

———

The Delta Kappa Gamma Society
International Headquarters
416 West Twelfth Street
Austin, TX 78767

Ladies:

———

The Honorable Joe Skubitz
The House of Representatives
Washington, DC 20515

Dear Mr. Skubitz:
    (or the more formal *My dear Mr. Skubitz:*)

———

Southern Electric Laboratories
Professional Building
1025 Dupont Boulevard
New Orleans, LA 70100

Gentlemen/Ladies:

———

The Reverend William Mapes
First Baptist Church
Ames, IA 50010

Dear Bill:

———

Complimentary Closing

The complimentary closing is placed a double space below the last line of the body of the letter. It begins on the left margin in the block and semiblock style and in the center or to the right of center in the indented style. The complimentary closing is followed by a comma and only the first word is capitalized. There has been a tendency in recent years to omit the comma after the complimentary closing when the colon is omitted after the salutation, but this practice is not widespread yet. The most frequently used complimentary closing is *Sincerely. Sincerely yours* and *Respectfully yours* are close seconds. A friendlier closing is *Cordially yours* or *With warmest regards*. A more formal closing is *Very respectfully* or *Yours truly*.

The tone of the complimentary closing must coincide with that of the salutation. If the salutation is *My dear Mr. Skubitz, Respectfully yours* would be suitable. If the salutation is *Dear Bill, With warmest regards* would be appropriate. If the salutation is *Dear Dr. Greer, Sincerely* would be best.

Signature

The signature must be placed a double space below the complimentary closing and the typewritten name a double space beneath the signature. The signature and typed name should agree unless the salutation, body of the letter, and the complimentary closing are very informal; then you may sign your first name. When the letter comes from a committee or an organization, sometimes the name of that committee or organization is typed in capital letters a double space below the complimentary closing. Then the writer signs his name a double space below the name of the organization, with his typed name underneath.

If you believe that the recipient of the letter needs some guidance in how to address you, put your title in parentheses before your name. This is especially helpful for a woman. For a single woman, *Susan A.*

Jones is sufficient; for a divorcee, (*Mrs.* or *Ms.*) *Susan A. Jones;* for a married woman, *Susan A. Jones* with *(Mrs. Stephen S. Jones)* on the line underneath and single spaced; and for a professional woman, for example, one with a doctorate, *(Dr.) Susan A. Jones.*

The following complimentary closings and signatures show the proper procedure for a wide range of situations:

Very sincerely,

(Mrs.) Susan A. Jones

———

Respectfully yours,

THE AFFIRMATIVE ACTION COMMITTEE

(Dr.) Steffann Piorot, Chairman

———

Sincerely yours,

BEECH AIRCRAFT CORPORATION

J. L. Sheldon, Supervisor
Management Development

———

With warmest regards,

Mary Alice Johnson

Change the following inside addresses, salutations, and complimentary closings so they conform to the usage discussed. Do not change anything that is already correct.

(1)
Amyx Printing Company
Box 733
DeKalb, MS   39328

Dear Sir;

Cordially yours,

(2)
Dr. Annie Lou Jackson, M.D.
Medical Building
Fort Lauderdale, Florida 33300

Dear Dr. Jackson,

Sincerely Yours

(3)
John R. Cox, Jr., president
ABC Block Company
Cedar Springs, Georgia 31732

My Dear Mr. Cox:

Yours truly

(4)
Jacob E. Smith
The House of Representatives
Washington, D.C. 20515

Dear Honorable Mr. Smith,

Sincerely,

Five additional parts are occasionally included in a business letter: attention line, subject line, stenographic references, enclosures, carbon copies, or distribution. The envelope should also be given careful attention.

Attention Line

When a letter is addressed to an organization, sometimes an attention line is included in addition to the inside address. It names a certain official in the firm who may expedite your business even though the letter is addressed to the company. If the person named is ill or out of town, the correspondence process is still speeded up because the letter is to the firm and not to the absent employee. An attention line, however, is seldom included when a person's name is a part of the inside address. And regardless of the attention line, the salutation must always match the inside address.

The attention line is placed a double space below the inside address and a double space above the salutation. It usually begins at the left margin and does not extend beyond the middle of the page. On rare occasions it is centered and then there are no limits to the length.

Subject Line

The subject line is especially helpful in letters that must identify an insurance policy number or an order number—even though the information in the subject line may be repeated in the opening sentence. Such a line is often considered a courtesy to the one who receives the letter and an aid to filing. When used, it is usually placed to the right of the salutation following the word *Subject,* but it can also be placed a double space below the salutation and a double space above the first line of the letter. Specimen subject lines follow.

Mr. Richard J. Walker
Box 6
El Dorado Springs, MO 64744

Dear Mr. Walker: Subject: Order #785

Thank you for Order #785 dated . . .

Ms. Sally Jane Howells
2536 Agnes Avenue
Cincinnati, OH 45200

Dear Ms. Howells:

Subject: Policy No. 7218–562

We have settled your claim for . . .

Stenographic References

When a business letter has been dictated by a company employee and transcribed by a stenographer, it is wise to keep a record of the initials of both in case there is some question about the letter in the future. The initials of the one who dictated the letter are placed on the left margin in capital letters a double space below the typed signature line. These are followed by a slash mark or colon and the stenographer's initials in lower case letters (WWW/vf; WWW:vf).

Enclosures

If enclosures are sent along with the letter, this is indicated a double space beneath the initials. The word *Enclosure* can be written out or it can be abbreviated *Encl.* followed by a colon. Either indicate the number of enclosures or list them in full.

Enclosures: 3   or   Encl.: Publicity brochure
                                               8-by-10-in. glossy
                                               Data sheet

Always refer to the enclosures in the last paragraph of the letter.

Carbon Copies

The carbon copy line is a double space below the enclosure. Abbreviate it *CC:* or *cc:* and then list, single

spaced, the names of others in the company who are receiving carbon copies of your letter. If space is limited, list all the names across the width of the page on one line. If copies of your letter will be sent to departments instead of individuals, label it *Distribution:* instead of *cc:*

cc: Mary N. Brownlow   or   Distribution: Photography Dept.
    Kevin E. Deramus   Art Dept.
    Bruce Broderick   Printing Dept.

The examples below illustrate the placement of these additional parts of a business letter.

MFA Insurance Companies
1615 South Aspen
Columbia, MO 65201

Attention of Mr. Henry A. Schulz

Gentlemen: Subject: Claim No. 15-1-128840

American Association of University Women
1532 Handover
Dover, MI 49323

Ladies:

Subject: Order No. 273

On June 23 the Eagle chapter placed an order with the Dover office . . .

Sincerely,

John J. Jerome

John J. Jerome

JJJ/sl

Enclosure

cc: Ann Tillyard, Samuel A. Smith, and Walter Wickware

Respectfully yours,

Mary Lorene Anthony

Mary Lorene Anthony

MLA/dl

Enclosures: 2

cc: Benjamin Shillmer
    William Nonnaman
    Audrey Allan

Cordially yours,

Douglas Anderson

Douglas Anderson

DA/bab

Enclosures: Employment memo
            Job description
            Form A

Envelope

The two parts of the envelope are the *outside address* and the *return address*. The outside address is identical to the inside address in the letter. If it consists of three lines or less, double-space it. If it has more than three lines, single-space. The outside address is placed slightly above and left of center. The return address is in the upper left corner of the envelope and includes your name without Mr., Mrs., or Dr. and your address as it appears in the heading of the letter. Do not type the return address on the back on the flap.

The Optical Character Reader (OCR) is a machine used by the Post Office to read over 40,000 addresses an hour. If the OCR is to scan your envelopes, you must follow specific rules for typing the inside address on the envelope:

1. All lines of the envelope address must begin on the same left margin. The address must not be more than 6 inches wide and five typed lines in height. There must be a ½-inch margin at the bottom and on the right side of the envelope.
2. The street-address line must appear immediately below the name.
3. Room, suite, or apartment must be typed on the same line after the street address.
    (809 Lakeview Drive, Apartment 2A)
4. City, state abbreviation, and zip code line must be placed below the street address. The name of the state should not be typed out; instead, the authorized abbreviations listed below should be used.

Alabama	AL	Kansas	KS	
Alaska	AK	Kentucky	KY	
Arizona	AZ	Louisiana	LA	
Arkansas	AR	Maine	ME	
California	CA	Maryland	MD	
Colorado	CO	Massachusetts	MA	
Connecticut	CT	Michigan	MI	
Delaware	DE	Minnesota	MN	
District of Columbia	DC	Mississippi	MS	
Florida	FL	Missouri	MO	
Georgia	GA	Montana	MT	
Hawaii	HI	Nebraska	NE	
Idaho	ID	Nevada	NV	
Illinois	IL	New Hampshire	NH	
Indiana	IN	New Jersey	NJ	
Iowa	IA	New Mexico	NM	
New York	NY	Tennessee	TN	
North Carolina	NC	Texas	TX	
North Dakota	ND	Utah	UT	
Ohio	OH	Vermont	VT	
Oklahoma	OK	Virginia	VA	
Oregon	OR	Washington	WA	
Pennsylvania	PA	West Virginia	WV	
Rhode Island	RI	Wisconsin	WI	
South Carolina	SC	Wyoming	WY	
South Dakota	SD			

In addition to the two regular parts of the envelope, an *Attention* line can be added a double space below and 1 inch to the left of the outside address; it is often underlined. The wording should be the same as the attention line in the letter. It is used when the letter is addressed to a company. A *Personal* or *Confidential* line may also be added to the envelope. It is capitalized, usually underlined, and indicates that only the addressee is to read the letter. This line usually appears to the left of the last line of the outside address. *Personal* or *Confidential* must also appear in the letter itself, usually a double space above the inside address.

The following examples show the outside address of three lines and the outside address of more than three lines.

Jonathan Jellcoe
1513 Mead Street
Newark, NJ 07100

                          Mr. Stewart Steinle

                          2630 Glencoe

<u>Personal</u>   Provo, UT 84601

Frances Mary Still
506 East Ninth Street
Broomall, PA 19008

                 The Epler Institute
                 Science and Technology Complex
                 7582 Brownington
                 Montpelier, VT 05601

          <u>Attention: Dr. James L. Walter</u>

Postal regulations specify envelope sizes and color codes. A first-class mail envelope must not exceed 100 inches in combined length and width and should not be smaller than 3 inches by 4¼ inches. Almost 90% of all envelopes are either (1) the 4⅛ inches by 9½ inches standard business stationery size, called the No. 10, or (2) the 3⅝ inches by 6½ inches standard business statement size, with or without a window, called the No. 6¾. Special computer envelopes have become popular in recent years and they vary greatly in size. In the next few years strict postal regulations are anticipated that will dictate a given size for all first-class letters. Then all first-class letters can be sorted by machine. Since all first-class mail now goes by air or surface carrier, there is no longer the distinction between air mail and regular mail.

Color codes, although not required by postal regulation, do assure the sender that the mail will be sent first class. Green *half diamond* or *saw tooth* borders (or red and blue parallelograms) printed on both front and back edges of envelopes indicate first-class mail. Green borders on manila envelopes and/or mailing labels help the clerks sort mail accurately.

DICTATION

Dictation is a quick, efficient way to handle correspondence, but you must learn the proper technique. It involves both preparation and the actual dictation.

Preparation

Purpose. First, determine the primary purpose of the letter. Do you wish to thank a board member, register a complaint concerning defective merchandise, or request information on a new product? Should you build goodwill, acknowledge some action, make or adjust a claim, or supply information? If you are answering a letter, be sure to reread it.

Then decide on any secondary purpose. A letter usually accomplishes several things. Do you wish to create goodwill and request that a specific action be taken even though your primary purpose is to complain about poor service?

Audience. After you have decided on the purpose of the letter, consider whether or not your reader is a long-time employee who is familiar with the technical aspects of the situation and who has the authority to solve the problem or to take the action that you request. Or is your reader a recently hired employee? These considerations will set the tone of the letter and will help you decide on the best approach.

Outline. Write an outline of the points you wish to include in the letter. Express each point as a single word, a phrase, or complete sentence—depending on how much help you will need as you compose your sentences. Vary the beginnings of your sentences. Always recheck the completed outline for (1) unnecessary information, (2) omission of vital information, and (3) the logical arrangement of the necessary facts. Have clearly in mind the beginning and ending that you will probably use so

you can avoid the most common fault of dictation—wordiness.

Procedure

Secretary. Meet with your secretary and agree on the dictation procedure. Will you give the secretary instructions on format and layout before you dictate the letter itself? Or will you permit these decisions to be made without further consultation? Will you be able to spell each name accurately? Are you aware of the transcribing speed of your secretary? Remember to help by including all the necessary little words such as *a, an,* and *the*.

Dictating Machine. Familiarize yourself with the machine you will use. Locate the erase button and use it for necessary changes. Always listen to your first few tapes: Are you speaking clearly and distinctly? Have you omitted the vocalized pause of *er, and uh,* and *the uh*?

SUMMARY

Business correspondence makes up a large percentage of the technical writing done each day by employees in supervisory positions. The rules for writing effective reports also apply to business correspondence. The letter must be planned, it must be written on a level appropriate for the reader, and it must be clear and concise. Its purpose is to influence the action or attitude of the one who receives it.

To achieve this purpose, you must first give close attention to the content of the letter and focus upon the reader's well-being, point of view, and emotional and intellectual needs. Desirable actions will be motivated by your friendly concern expressed honestly, sincerely, and courteously. Positive beginnings and endings determine the initial impression of your letter and the impression of your company that will linger long after the letter has been read.

You can arrange the text of a business letter in two different ways, depending on whether you are communicating good news or bad. When saying yes, communicate the yes first, explain it, and look to the future. When saying no, begin on a pleasant note, give reasons for saying no, say no, and then look to the future.

Word choice often determines the success of the letter. Use of *you* gives it the desired informal tone and puts the reader first. Avoid old-fashioned terms, jargon, and words with unflattering connotations. Be so specific that the reader cannot misunderstand. Do not write a memo stating, "The pieces of furniture in the lobby which show signs of wear should be replaced immediately," and then discover that all the furniture in the lobby has been replaced when you meant that only those pieces showing signs of wear should be replaced. Since your letter or memo will become part of a company's files, it should be self-explanatory and complete.

To communicate ideas to your reader, you must combine words into sentences and paragraphs. Place important ideas in main clauses and less important ideas in single words, phrases, and subordinate clauses. Add transitions to improve the flow of thought and vary their length and structure. Use declarative, interrogative, imperative, and exclamatory sentences; use a combination of simple, complex, and compound sentences. First and last paragraphs in a business letter can be single sentences, but do not paragraph every sentence. Develop some ideas in greater detail.

The neat letter suggests a clearly organized message. It must be typed on standard size, white paper. There must be uniform margins on all sides, and each part is separated from the others by a double space; the lines within each paragraph are single spaced. Most business letters should be one page long; but if a second page is necessary, it should be labeled in the upper left-hand corner.

Three basic forms for the letter are block, indented, and semiblock. In the block, all lines begin on the left margin. In the indented, the heading and complimentary closing are on the right side and the beginning of each paragraph is indented five spaces. The semiblock is any modification of the block: the heading and complimentary closing may be placed on the right side *or* the beginning of each paragraph may be indented five spaces.

The basic parts of the letter, in addition to the text itself, are the heading, inside address, salutation, complimentary closing, and the signature. Some additional parts can also be included when necessary: the attention line, subject line, stenographic reference, enclosures, carbon copy, or distribution.

Two main parts of the envelope are the outside address, which is the same as the inside address in the letter, and the return address. There is additional space for an *Attention* line or a *Confidential* or *Private* line.

Dictation is an efficient way to handle correspondence, and it involves preparation as well as the actual dictation. Decide on the purpose of your letter, consider the knowledge and authority of your reader, and outline the main points you want to include. After you check your outline and begin the dictation, try to give the person who will transcribe the tape as much help as possible: give directions on form and layout if necessary; spell names; include *a, an,* and *the;* avoid vocalized pauses; and speak distinctly.

A well-written letter, both in content and form, contributes to the good reputation of your organization. And remember that it is less expensive to write a good letter than a poor one because the vague one requires further correspondence to clarify the situation.

EXERCISES

A. Evaluate the form and content of the following letter. Rewrite.

October 1, 10—

Dear Customer,

The portraits that were taken at The Food Mart in The Mall on September 2 and 3, 1975, in St. Louis, Missouri, were no good due to a malfunction in the camera.

We have arranged with the help of The Food Mart to have one of our finest photographers return on October 22 and 23 from 10:00 a.m. until 6:00 p.m. each day. For the inconvenience caused you, we are enclosing a certificate entitling you to a 5-by-7 portrait in lieu of the original offer.

Would you please arrange to have your portraits retaken during the above stated times, retaining your coupon until our representative returns to the store to allow you to select your portrait pose?

We hope that you will continue your fine patronage of The Food Mart, and we are sorry for the inconvenience caused you.

With Warmest Regards,

PERFECT PORTRAITS

ER/dk

B. Collect five business letters of various types. As you evaluate them, answer the following questions about each:

1. What kind of letterhead is used?
2. What form is used?
3. Is the letter neat and attractive in appearance?
4. What special parts of the business letter are used?
5. Does the letter have the *you attitude?* Give evidence.
6. Does it have a positive tone?
7. Does the letter use clear, concise language?

WRITING ASSIGNMENTS

1. Assume that an official at the high school from which you were graduated has invited you to return to judge some contest. Write a letter saying yes to the invitation; then write a letter saying no. You are not using letterhead paper.
2. Assume that you are working for a company that would logically employ you after graduation. A client has made a request of your company, and you must answer and refuse the request. Use letterhead paper.

3. A certain organization has asked you for a cash contribution. Write a letter saying yes. Do not use letterhead paper.

4. The radio campaign for your company urges customers to apply for a charge account and enjoy its greater convenience. Some applicants, after investigation, must be turned down. Write such a letter of refusal. Assume that you are using letterhead paper.

5. The homecoming committee of the local university has asked you, as the Oldsmobile dealer, to provide three sedans for transportation of state officials in the parade. Say yes on the letterhead stationery of your company.

6. A class of college students wants to tour your plant, which produces highly classified electronics components. Say yes to the tour, but refuse to allow foreign students to participate because of federal security regulations. Assume that you are using letterhead paper.

7. You have been asked by the local junior chamber of commerce organization to present the February program on ways to attract new industry to the community. You will be out of the country during February but would be willing to present a program at the April or May meeting on the new federal regulations on employment practices. Do not use letterhead paper.

8. You have been invited to serve on the state board of directors of an organization to which you belong. This is a non-paying post; it will involve much travel and attending many social events; it is for a two-year period. Write a letter saying yes; then write one saying no. Do not use letterhead paper.

9. A college student has written to your company asking for information for a term paper she is writing. The information she is requesting is classified and you cannot give it to her. Say no on letterhead paper.

10. A local civic club has asked permission to use your bank's social rooms for their October meeting. Using letterhead paper, write one letter saying yes; then write another saying no.

11. A customer bought a $25 blouse at your dress shop and has returned it today because when she sent it to the cleaners it shrank; she can no longer wear it. She wants a full refund, but your laboratory tests reveal it has been washed. A tag sewn in the blouse says "dry clean only." Refuse her claim. Assume that you are not using letterhead paper.

12. You own an apartment house in another city. One of your long-time tenants has requested that you recarpet her entryway and living room. Say yes; do not use letterhead paper.

DICTATION ASSIGNMENTS

1. Workers from the water company dug down to the sewer line that runs along the boundary of your property. They damaged valuable shrubs and trees on your lot and on the one next to you. Dictate one letter to the water department and one to the out-of-town owner of the adjoining lot. Assume that you will let your secretary decide on form and layout.

    a. Decide on the primary purpose of each letter.
    b. Identify any secondary purposes in each.
    c. Set the tone by careful consideration of the recipient of each letter.
    d. List the points you want to include in each letter.
    e. Recheck each list before you begin dictation.

2. Dictate letters to two different companies asking for information on new products. You have already done business with the vice-president of one company and he has recently invited you to contact him. You have had no previous contact with anyone in the other organization.

    a. Decide on the primary purpose of each letter.
    b. Identify any secondary purposes in each.
    c. Set the tone by careful consideration of the recipient of each letter.
    d. List the points you want to include in each letter.
    e. Recheck each list.
    f. Dictate to the secretary the instructions on form and layout before you begin each letter. As you dictate include "paragraph," "period," and "comma."

Special Types of Business Letters

ALTHOUGH it is sometimes difficult to classify every type of letter, a familiarity with the basic kinds of letters will make it easier for you to deal with business correspondence. Many professionals, from the beginnings of their careers, will be called upon to write the types of letters described in this chapter. There are set rules to follow in arranging the content of the letters discussed here. If you adhere to the general principles of business correspondence and if you arrange the parts of a letter in accordance with recognized rules, you will be able to handle competently all correspondence.

COMPLAINT

The number of items that most firms handle today is greater than a few years ago. Because billing, inventory, handling, and shipping procedures are more complex, there are greater possibilities for error. Usually a favorable adjustment can be secured if the claim letter is complete, clear, and specific.

But the claim or complaint letter is most often poorly written, perhaps because tempers are involved. You will be tempted to give full vent to your anger or to prove that your position is the only correct one. You may feel free to express anger, sarcasm, or other emotions because you are not face to face with your reader. But remember that the purpose of a business letter is to affect the conduct or attitude of that reader. Therefore, anger will be self-defeating; it is more important to retain goodwill and business than to prove yourself right.

Tone

The tone of the letter of complaint will often determine the future relationship between your company and the reader. Courtesy is essential because your letter represents the firm. Assume that the reader is a responsible, fair person. Give all the facts needed to reach a proper decision. If you can go a step further and use a friendly tone, so much the better. *An error was made* is a more tactful statement than *You made an error.* Always avoid the implication that you are totally guiltless and that the reader is absolutely at fault. Even when the situation is so serious that you must issue a warning, express it so that you appear to have only the reader's best interests at heart. After you have clearly stated the facts of the case, politely ask that some specific action be taken, implying that it is the only reasonable solution to the problem. Never vaguely ask that *something* be done about the situation.

Parts

There are usually five parts to a letter of complaint:

1. The pleasant beginning in which you find something on which to agree with the reader or in which you refer specifically to the transaction
2. The complaint
3. The facts of the case as you see them
4. A specific request for action
5. A friendly close that will motivate favorable action

The well-written letter of complaint below clearly illustrates these five parts: It begins on a pleasant note, states the complaint at the beginning of the second paragraph and gives the facts, makes a specific request in the brief third paragraph, and ends with a friendly anticipation of continued good programming.

Gentlemen:

Pleasant note I am a loyal viewer of KATV.

Complaint However, I protest the substitution of "Nashville Music" for "Police Woman" at 8 p.m. on Tuesday, May 25. I was late getting off work on that day, and my husband and I were so eager to see "Police Woman" that we gave up a pleasant dinner in a restaurant, grabbed hamburgers and malts at a drive-in, and hurried home to watch our favorite show. You can imagine our disappointment when "Nashville Music" came on.

Explanation

Request Such program changes are a great inconvenience and aggravation. Please avoid any more substitutions for shows listed in *TV Guide.*

Future Over the years, programming at KATV has been quite dependable and I look forward to a continuation of your high standards.

Sincerely,

The next letter of complaint also begins with a pleasant reference to a specific transaction, clearly states the complaint and gives the facts of the case, makes a specific request in the third paragraph, and ends on a friendly note.

Dear Mr. Ruddent:

Facts My order #615 was delivered to my home this morning by your No. 3 delivery van.

Complaint All the items I bought arrived in excellent condition with one exception. There is a deep, 6-inch scratch on the left side of the Broyhill coffee table, a defect that I did not immediately notice. It cannot be concealed either by placement against the wall or by indirect lighting.

Request Will you please pick up this coffee table and substitute an undamaged one for it? I am at home on Monday, Tuesday, and Friday mornings from 8 a.m. to 12 noon.

Appreciation I would appreciate your delivering another Broyhill #2801 coffee table by April 10 because I will be doing a great deal of entertaining after that date.

Sincerely,

You should be aware, however, that there is some question about the arrangement of information in a letter saying yes to a letter of complaint. If you say yes first, the reader may never read on to the explanation; so if the explanation is important, you may wish to explain first and then grant the claim. On the other hand, if the explanation may cause the reader to lose confidence in your firm, it is best to omit it altogether. One item not open to question, though, is the apology. It is always a plus for your letter and does more to win over the reader than any other single part. Observe the difference in a grudging assent and an apology:

Thank you for your letter of March 15 telling us that an "account overdue" notice was sent to you on March 10. A careful check of our records reveals the truth of your statement.

Grudging assent It is correct that your account No. 1692 is fully paid up.

We appreciate your business here at Don Key Chemical Company.

Sincerely,

Thank you for your letter of March 15. The "account overdue" notice you received was intended for another of our customers.

You are absolutely correct that your account No. 1692 is fully paid up.

Apology I'm very sorry that you received this notice and will try to see that it doesn't happen again. Your business is appreciated here at Don Key Chemical Company.

Sincerely,

ANSWER TO A LETTER OF COMPLAINT

When answering a letter of complaint, keep your reader in mind. Give a definite answer. Try not to rely on vague, unsatisfactory statements such as "Please be assured that we will look into the matter and try to settle it to our mutual advantage" or "It is our feeling that perhaps the loss might have taken place on. . . ."

Answers to claim letters follow the general rules for letters saying yes and those saying no. It is, of course, easier to say yes.

Letter Saying Yes

If your company is at fault, the most important rule for saying yes is to say yes immediately and cheerfully instead of grudgingly. The reader will be more willing to listen to your explanation after you have granted the request. The usual parts for this type of letter are:

1. A pleasant acknowledgment of the letter and yes
2. An expression of regret
3. The explanation
4. The emphasis on future dealings

Following is a letter saying yes to the complaint about programming from the loyal television viewer. Notice the acknowledgment of the complaint and an expression of regret in the first paragraph, the explanation in the second paragraph, and the emphasis on future support in the last paragraph.

Dear Mrs. Constantine:

Acknowledgment and regret I appreciate your letter of May 27 and am sorry that we were not able to telecast "Police Woman" at the advertised time.

Explanation "Police Woman" was not available to us to telecast on Tuesday night as we normally do because of preemptions on the network due to broadcasts of political specials. I'm sure that you realize that sometimes there is nothing the local station can do about preemptions on the network.

Future Thank you for your interest in KATV, and I look forward to your continued support as a loyal viewer.

Sincerely,

Letter Saying No

The most important point about a letter saying no is to delay the actual no until a complete explanation can be made. This procedure implies that the writer is a fair person who has examined all the facts and then has been forced to refuse the request. And it also keeps the reader in a receptive mood while reading the reasons for refusing. There are usually four parts to such a letter, which should be written promptly.

1. A courteous acknowledgment of the letter of complaint and a clear statement of the problem to show the reader that you understand the situation
2. The facts that justify your decision
3. No
4. The future relationship and a friendly close

Avoid embarrassing your reader; do not put more blame on him or her than necessary. Do not use words with unflattering connotations such as *refuse* and *claim*. Try to hold resentment to a minimum so you will have retained a customer. Yet, do not be so tactful that your answer is unclear. Once the refusal is made, do not refer to it again and do not apologize. As in other types of technical writing, the middle ground is desirable. End on a cheerful, looking-to-the-future note.

The recipient of the letter below bought a pair of shoes for the list price six weeks previously. She now wishes to return the shoes and get back her money. However, the shoes have meanwhile been put on sale for half price. The manager of the shoe store must refuse to refund the full purchase price.

Dear Mrs. Attwood:

Courteous acknowledgment and statement of problem   Thank you for your letter of May 10 requesting a full refund of $24.95 for your Togwear Capri shoes purchased in this store April 4. I agree that shoes of the wrong shade can ruin the looks of an outfit.

Explanation   It has long been the policy of this store to give a full refund on returned merchandise as long as that merchandise has not been placed on sale.

Decision   Since all Togwear Capris were put on the half-price rack May 8, I can return $12.50 of the purchase price.

Future   We hope to see you in our store soon so you can take advantage of our spring sale. You are a

Friendly close   valued customer of The Shoe Emporium, and we look forward to continuing to serve you in the future.

Respectfully,

LETTER GRANTING CREDIT

The letter granting credit goes a little further than just saying yes. It should also build sales and goodwill. It explains the credit terms clearly to avoid later misunderstandings concerning dates of payments.

The usual pattern for this type of letter includes:

1. Friendly opening
2. Granting of credit
3. Explanation of company credit policies
4. Other services designed to build goodwill
5. Friendly closing

See the sample letter granting credit below:

Dear Mrs. Clark:

Friendly granting of credit   We are happy to add your name to our list of credit customers.

Explanation of procedure and policies   Your two charge plates are enclosed: one for you and one for another member of your family. The next time you make a purchase at Klein's Appliances, just select your merchandise, ask that it be charged, and give your charge plate to the salesperson. That is all there is to it!

You will receive your bill between the tenth and twelfth of each month; payments are due by the twenty-fifth of the same month.

Other services to build goodwill   We know you will enjoy shopping in our store. Remember that our prime interest is customer satisfaction and we will make every effort to merit your confidence. We look forward to serving you in the years to come.

Yours,

LETTER REFUSING CREDIT

The letter refusing credit is similar to other letters saying no; but it is wise to explain the reason for denying credit before you actually refuse the request. Sometimes it is unwise to explain too specifically why credit is refused because this negative information may arouse antagonism. Often the private individual is quicker to take offense at refusal than is the business client. Retaining the reader's goodwill is necessary because in a few years he or she may be an excellent credit risk. Sometimes the reader can be won over with the *you* attitude; it may be to the customer's best interest to buy c.o.d. or on a cash basis. See the following letter:

Dear Miss Baker:

Friendly opening   Thank you for your credit application.

We have thoroughly analyzed the information you gave us and are impressed with your

Explanation and tactful refusal   references. However, we suggest that you continue your purchases on a cash basis while the ratio of your assets to your liabilities is below the minimum level.

"You" attitude   Remember that there are many advantages to cash buying. You will have an immediate 2% discount, faster service, and no bookkeeping problems at the end of the month.

Other I'm enclosing a brochure describing our special
services October sale for preferred customers. Many of
these items will be perfect for Christmas giving.

Future We look forward to serving you during this sale
and future ones too.

Sincerely,

COLLECTION LETTER

There is wide variation in collection letters. Private
individual or consumer accounts that become delinquent need a different kind of letter than do the
wholesale or commercial accounts. The content of a collection letter sent to a good risk is very different from
that sent to a poor risk. There is a difference in tone of
the first collection letter and the sixth one.

The collection communications can be divided into
form reminders, personal letters, and letters from collection agencies. The good risk receives more form
reminders and personal letters before the court action
than does the poor risk. The most popular form
reminders are colored stickers, rubber stamps, or brief
written notes on duplicate invoices that say *Please, Past
Due, Perhaps You've Overlooked This Bill,* or *Don't
Forget Us.* If no action is forthcoming, two or three personal letters may get action. The poor risk will rate a
more insistent tone; the good risk will be addressed in a
more lenient tone. Appeals to fear or self-interest can
move the poor risk; appeals to pride and community
status or to credit reputation may be more effective for
good risk cases. All collection letters, though, should
stress the ways the debtor benefits from paying the bill.

The first letter below is designed for the poor risk, the
second for the good risk.

Dear Mr. Catzin:

Courteous   We can't understand what has happened to
reminder   your check for $327.50. You have been sent
of amount   two reminders and two letters, and still you
due   have sent no remittance.

Date of   Legal action will be started on May 20 if the
court action   past due balance of $327.50 is not received.
Benefit of
paying   But won't you keep us from taking this
Request   drastic step? Send in your check immediately.

Yours sincerely,

Dear Mr. Dover:

Pleasant   Because you've paid your account promptly
reminder   during the last ten-year period, your present past
Amount due   due balance of $327.50 worries us. We know you
Benefit   want to maintain your excellent credit rating.
of paying
Date of   If there is some reason you haven't paid your
next action   account, please let us know about it by May 20.
Advantage
of paying   We value you as a customer and want you to
preserve your good credit reputation so we can
serve you for many years to come.

Sincerely,

The collection message, regardless of its purpose and
tone, should include the following information:

1. A courteous, restrained reminder
2. Specific dates concerning future actions
3. The exact amount due
4. Emphasis on how the debtor will benefit from
   paying the bill

INQUIRY

The easiest type of inquiry to write is the one that
promises some reward, such as an increase in sales, if
the answer is forthcoming. It is also easy to get an inquiry answered if it is sent to a bureau whose sole job is
answering requests for information. But the inquiry that
requires the most tact on the writer's part is the one sent
to an organization or company that is under no obligation to answer except for the goodwill involved. The
secret to getting a satisfactory and prompt reply is
threefold: (1) clearly state the information you need, (2)
make the answer as easy as possible to write, and (3) encourage the reader to be helpful.

There can be six parts to a letter of inquiry:

1. Clear statement of purpose
2. Reason the information is needed
3. Reason this organization was chosen
4. Questions that may be numbered, indented, or
   underlined to call attention to them
5. Some return for the favor if possible
6. Appreciation and suggestion for action

The most important part of the inquiry is the list of
questions. Be as brief as possible. Arrange them in some
logical order. Encourage the reader to answer them in
the margin or at the bottom of the letter and enclose a
stamped, self-addressed envelope. Invite the reader to
include additional comments.

Dear Mr. Compton:

Purpose   For my senior thesis I have selected the topic
"Marketing the Automobile of the Future." I
Reason Ford   would like some information from Ford Motor
was selected   Company since you are a recognized leader in the
automobile industry.

Questions   1. What kind of demand will there be for the
car of the future?

2. What type of car will be most desired?

3. How will federal regulations affect cars of
   the future?

4. What are Ford's sales projections for the
   future?

Request   Please feel free to answer the question in the
for action   space below each and return this sheet to me in
the enclosed, self-addressed envelope.

Appreciation   I will also appreciate any additional information
you can give me about your marketing plans for
the future.

Very truly yours,

ANSWER TO A LETTER OF INQUIRY

Again, the same principles for letters saying yes and no apply to answers to letters of request. If, however, you must say no, it is diplomatic to offer other information instead. The first letter below illustrates an answer to an inquiry that provides the needed information; the second represents the situation in which a request cannot be granted.

Dear Mr. Heath:

Pleasant acknowledg- ment Thank you for your recent inquiry concerning Ford's marketing plans projected toward the year 2000.

Analysis of request You have selected a rather profound subject for your senior thesis—"Marketing the Automobile of the Future." It is not only profound but also quite complex, especially in the ever-changing market in which our industry finds itself.

Explanation and answers Our product plans are based on consumer needs and demands for transportation. In the past several years, revolutionary changes in the marketplace have required a rethinking of the type and size of cars we should design and build. In the height of the energy crisis, we couldn't build small cars fast enough. Today, the pendulum has shifted in the opposite direction—large cars are in vogue again. If gasoline prices increase more, there could be a swing back to small cars.

With the change in attitudes of consumers about what they want in a vehicle, obviously, the marketing strategy to get the consumer interested in our product has shifted as rapidly as the demand for small vs. large cars.

All this points up the difficulty in projecting too far into the future. Federal regulations also preclude long-range planning because many of the mandates from Washington have an impact on our future product plans, which include designing, building, and marketing cars. There are many other factors too numerous to mention here.

Additional material Enclosed is some material that will acquaint you with several company positions. We hope it will add to your research.

Pleasant ending We appreciate your inquiry and your interest in Ford.

Very sincerely,

Dear Mr. Keith:

Pleasant acknowledg- ment I appreciate your interest in Ford and your May 5 request for a tour of the Physical Testing Laboratory for the Yale, Michigan, high school physics class.

Explanation A great deal of proprietary research is being conducted at this time, and that laboratory, along with the many other laboratories in the Scientific Research Building, is classified as a

Refusal restricted area. While I sympathize with your desire to look at this facility, I must tell you that the Physical Testing Laboratory is not open for public touring.

Alternate suggestion As you perhaps know, Ford has reopened its tour operations for the Rouge area. This always is of interest to high school groups, and if your class has not been on one of these tours, we would recommend it highly. These tours originate from the Ford Guest Center on Village Road opposite the Henry Ford Museum in Dearborn.

Sincerely,

(Courtesy Ford Motor Company [1])

INVITATION

As the representative of a professional group or of the chamber of commerce or civic club, you may often need to invite people to attend or participate in meetings and activities. Letters of invitation require great skill and tact because (1) you are usually asking for a favor and (2) you must state the facts so clearly that your reader can decide whether or not to accept the invitation without another exchange of letters.

There are six parts to a letter of invitation:

1. Purpose and an attention-getter—perhaps a reference to something the reader has said or done recently
2. Justification of the expenditure of time involved by explaining the reputation of the organization and the number and importance of the people who will be present
3. Benefits the reader will enjoy if the invitation is accepted—publicity, goodwill, and the opportunity to learn or to renew old acquaintances
4. Facts of the invitation—time, date, place, type of presentation, length of presentation, and suggested subjects
5. Request for a decision (If you must have the answer by a certain date, include some reason that will be to the reader's self-interest such as publicity or printing programs or airline and motel reservations.)
6. Hospitable or complimentary ending

Not all invitations will include all the above parts. You may wish to omit the benefits to the reader, or to combine the request for action and the hospitality. Use only those devices that will be most effective in persuading the reader to accept the invitation. Then you can supply additional information later.

The following letter of invitation illustrates these general principles: The purpose of the letter is clearly stated at the beginning, the reader's accomplishments are noted, the facts of the invitation are given, and valid reasons are included for requesting action.

Dear Mr. Snyder:

Purpose I want to invite you to have lunch with sixteen state legislators and with the Lincoln University *Why reader* administrative officers. As president of the alum-*is invited* ni association, you can be helpful in presenting our budgetary needs to the people who will be determining the funds our school will get for the next fiscal year.

Facts of We will meet in the Heritage Room of the Student *invitation* Union at 1 p.m. on Saturday, December 11. Just plan on informal conversations with the visiting lawmakers. You may wish to review the enclosed fact sheet listing our budgetary requirements for 19—.

The spouses of the legislators and of the administration are invited to come if they wish and then go Christmas shopping at the local mall during our meeting. I extend the same invitation to your wife.

Request for Please complete the enclosed postcard and mail it *action* back to me so I can turn in the luncheon reserva-*Benefit to* tions and plan the shopping trip. I look forward *reader* to seeing you December 11.

Sincerely,

INSTRUCTIONS

The successful letter giving instructions should not only tell the reader how to do something but also tell why it should be done. Clarity, mechanical devices, and a pleasant tone will all contribute to the style.

Style

Clarity involves the judicious use of detail as well as word choice. You must analyze the subject, think of everything that can possibly be misunderstood or go wrong, and deal with it in as few words as possible. The first step in achieving clarity is to explain the overall purpose of the operation or the reasons for performing the task. If the reader understands why something should be done, your directions will probably be followed carefully. However, be sure your explanation does not overshadow the instructions themselves.

Numbers, headings, and indentations are mechanical devices that can call attention to the steps in the instructions. Since your letter will be short, you will not be able to use too many such devices. But take the time to use a few that will add clarity, especially when the letter is sent to a number of people.

Tone is most important in instructions. If you are courteous, the reader will be more likely to follow your directions and to implement your suggestions.

Parts

The parts in a letter of instruction are the same as in other forms of instructions:

1. Explanation of the purpose of the instructions and also a definition of the process if necessary

2. A list of the equipment, skills, preparations, and conditions necessary for carrying out the directions successfully

3. A list and explanation of the steps in the process, including warnings when necessary

4. Explanation of the time or money saved or the pleasure that following these steps will give the reader

The following letter gives instructions. After beginning on a pleasant note, the writer makes the request, gives instructions for filming each segment, and stresses the economy of the filming.

Dear Mr. Miller:

Pleasant Thank you for submitting your August 9–13 *acknowledg-* schedule for filming the Yoster Realty commer-*ment* cial properties. It looks fine, but please add the *Request* filming of a one-minute segment that can be divided into 4 fifteen-second parts.

If you will follow the suggestions below, the additional film will satisfy all our requirements.

Explanation 1. 905 East Jefferson. Show the office and *of each part* the large storage and work building adjoining the rear as well as the large, fenced-in parking lot. Take pictures from the south to show its best side.

2. 101–103 South Broadway. Show these two Glick properties that front on Broadway. Pan the two-story brick buildings and the loading areas on the alley to the rear. Remember to film the undeveloped half city block to the rear of the property because it has great potential value since it is near the downtown area.

3. 215 Latham. Film the former Calhoon Putnam Lumber Company building in Frontenac, highlighting the new office area and the two huge storage buildings.

4. 1615 North Main. Picture the former Calhoon Putnam Lumber Company building in Arma, featuring the railroad siding and the two new storage buildings.

Money This film segment can be reused several times in *saved* the next few weeks in various promotions for Yoster Realty.

Sincerely,

FORM LETTER

The form letter has a message that is appropriate for many people and it is reproduced in quantity. Some organizations, such as some divisions of Ford Motor Company, pride themselves on never using form letters but on answering individually each piece of correspondence that comes to the firm. Other companies, however, make extensive use of the form letter. It is possible to devote more time to the preparation of such a letter than to individual ones, so the form letter is usually more smoothly written than those dictated as a part of the daily routine.

The greatest weakness of the form letter is its impersonality. To counteract this weakness, individual addresses and salutations can be inserted by typewriter. Sometimes it is difficult to recognize the additions. Occasionally the inside address is omitted and the salutation becomes the first part of the letter: Dear Sir, Madam, Dear Friend, Fellow Citizen, Dear Occupant, Dear Subscriber, Dear Customer, or Dear Member can be used. Another device is to replace the salutation with a line like "To All Users of Olympia Typewriters." The body of the letter can be highlighted by the use of indentation, underlining, and numbering. The contents should be appropriate for every reader: geographical or seasonal allusions must be omitted and the phraseology must be easily understood. The writer's handwritten signature can be reproduced for that personal touch. It can be typed on a good quality stationery and sent in a sealed envelope as first-class mail.

The following form letter illustrates the friendly tone, "you" attitude, and the indention and variations in type that can be used to stress information in the body of the letter. Another form letter is (4) on page 178.

Administrative Center
BENTON HARBOR, MICHIGAN 49022

Dear Customer:

Good performance. That's what this letter is all about. We know that you expect good performance from your WHIRLPOOL® automatic washer, and we aim to see that you get it. Here's how its performance is protected.

YOUR FULL ONE YEAR WARRANTY

During your first year of ownership, all parts of the appliance (except light bulbs) which we find are defective in materials or workmanship will be repaired or replaced by Whirlpool free of charge, and we will pay any labor charges. Service under this full one year warranty must be provided by a TECH-CARE® service company franchised by Whirlpool to service this WHIRLPOOL product.

PLUS
YOUR ADDITIONAL LIMITED WARRANTY

During the second through fifth years of ownership, any parts in the gear case assembly as shown on the back of this letter will be repaired or replaced if found defective by us. We'll assume responsibility for parts. You pay any labor charges. The use of a TECH-CARE service company franchised by Whirlpool to service this product is recommended for fulfilling the limited warranty.

These warranties cover your home use of the appliance. Naturally, they do not cover damage by accident, misuse, fire, flood or acts of God, nor do they cover damage to your appliance caused by the use of products not manufactured by Whirlpool. But they do cover you wherever you live in the United States . . . even if you move. Furthermore, this same protection applies to any subsequent owner during the applicable warranty period based on the original owner's purchase date.

Now, about installation and operation. We know you expect to have your appliance properly installed. You also expect to be fully knowledgeable in the operation of the appliance. Printed instructions are furnished by Whirlpool on how to use your new WHIRLPOOL appliance. You'll want to work out all details with your selling dealer, including any costs to you that may be involved.

And, about servicing. Let's face it. Sometimes even the best products need service. So if that's ever true of your WHIRLPOOL automatic washer, there is a way to get action fast. Just call your Whirlpool franchised TECH-CARE service company representative. He's trained to make whatever's wrong right. **Check the Yellow Pages of your telephone directory under Washers, Dryers — Repairing or Servicing.** You can also obtain his name and number by dialing, free, within the continental United States, the Whirlpool COOL-LINE® service (800) 253-1301 [when calling from Michigan, dial (800) 632-2243]. Our COOL-LINE service is a unique telephone information service to assist you with questions about operating, maintaining, or servicing your WHIRLPOOL product.

The model number and serial number of your WHIRLPOOL automatic washer are available from the plate shown in the illustration on the cover of this warranty. We suggest you record the information in the spaces provided and you keep this letter with your sales slip. It's nice to know you have protection, even though you may never need it.

Sincerely,
WHIRLPOOL CORPORATION

(Courtesy Whirlpool Corporation [2])

LETTER OF EMPLOYMENT

The employment process varies from year to year depending on the current job market. Sometimes you will be interviewed on campus by a representative of the company and you will fill out an application blank right there. Perhaps you will read of a suitable job opening in the placement office of your school or in local publications and will decide to send your resumé with the accompanying letter. You may mail an unsolicited letter of application to a company you are especially interested in, not knowing if they have any job openings in your area.

The circumstance determines the type of communication you will send to the company. If you have already been interviewed on campus and have filled out an application blank for the interviewer, you will need to send only a follow-up letter thanking the interviewer and expressing your interest in the company. If you are sending a solicited or an unsolicited application, you will write (1) the traditional letter of application that includes education, experience, personal information, and references or (2) the shorter, covering letter that points out the most important facts on the accompanying resumé. At the present time the short letter and resumé are more widely used. The longer, traditional letter is most appropriate for the individual who lacks some qualifications for the job but is anxious to get an interview. The better qualified applicant can include all the details of his background in the resumé and short letter.

Regardless of the situation or the type of correspondence you use, personalize your letter so the reader will feel that you have written it solely for him. Your letter represents you, so if it is carelessly written the reader will assume that you may be a careless worker. Remember that you want the reader to say, "This person has put together a simple, clear statement of what he has done. He, also, must be well organized and effective." You can send the same resumé sheet to most potential employers, but have it reproduced professionally. No one likes to get the eightieth copy of a dittomaster or the sixth carbon copy.

Traditional Letter of Application

Opening. The first paragraph must clearly identify the letter as one of application for employment, and it can also identify you if necessary. Try to include some fact, if possible, that will set your application apart from all the others that the personnel officer will probably receive. Maybe you know a long-time employee of the company or you have worked there as a summer fill-in or you learned about the opening in an unusual way.

The main part of the letter will deal with education, experience, personal information, and references. There is no set order for these items, but usually the most important is presented first—either education or experience. References are usually last.

Education. The amount of detail in the education section is determined by the closeness of the relationship between your schooling and the work you will do on the job. At least name the institutions from which you have diplomas or degrees and give the year of graduation. As in other parts of the letter of application, begin with the most important item, which is usually the most recent education you have received; then arrange other educational facts in a reverse order of importance or in a reverse chronological order. Always mention academic honors and extracurricular activities since they give some impression of the type of person you are.

Experience. All previous work experience is important, regardless of how closely it is connected with the job for which you are applying, because it suggests your sense of responsibility, dependability, and successful interaction with others. Try to include all your experience and not leave gaps in your record that the potential employer would wonder about.

Personal information. It is no longer necessary to include personal information about yourself. Age, place of birth, height, weight, health, and marital status are not required unless directly related to job performance. You may, however, choose to include these facts as well as those connected with your leisure interests if you believe that such information would help you to get the job.

References. Include the names of three or four references who can affirm the facts that you have included in the application. At least one should be an instructor and one a previous employer; the others can be community leaders, ministers, or friends who can attest to your character. It is wise to include a title for each so your reader will know why you have included that person and why he should know of your fitness for the job. Always ask permission of the reference before you use his or her name in your letter.

Ending. Because a list of references usually makes dull reading, it is necessary to give your letter some kind of *lift* at the end. This may be a brief summary of your qualifications, of your interest in the company, or of your desire to work for the organization. This lift may be a suggestion for action, which can take the form of a request for the job itself or at least for an interview, or an offer to supply additional information. Sometimes you can get the company to act on your letter if you include some dates suitable for interviews or if you give the reason that you must have an answer by a certain date: "Since I must report to the national guard for my annual two weeks training on July 1, I would appreciate an interview before that date." Be positive without being overly aggressive; always stress what you can contribute to the future success of the company. Leave the mention of salary up to the employer. If it is absolutely necessary for you to inquire about the salary, do so at the end of the letter—after you have convinced the reader that your services will be needed.

Resumé and the Covering Letter

The resumé is especially valuable when you have not filled out an application blank for the company. It is a list of facts; and because more facts can be placed in a resumé than in the traditional letter of application, you can include your full record. For each entry use words and phrases, not complete sentences. Place at the top of the page your name and the position for which you are applying, if you are applying for the same position at several different companies. Use the same four headings as in the traditional letter of application: Personal Information, Education, Experience, and References. On the resumé sheet, personal information—if you decide to include any facts about yourself—usually comes first. Use as many subheadings as necessary and arrange the information in the education and experience sections in reverse chronological order. Be sure that the whole page has an attractive appearance.

The purpose of the resumé is to free the covering letter from the routine information that is necessary for completeness but not especially interesting. The accompanying letter can then be brief. It can create a personal interest and can repeat the most significant facts from the resumé.

The following traditional letter of application and the shorter covering letter with a resumé or data sheet illustrate the general principles described in this chapter. But remember that these letters are merely specimens and phraseology should not be borrowed from them when you write your own letter of application. You may, however, adapt the resumé to your needs since it is merely a tabulation of facts and not a personal communication.

1313 State Street
Vista, CA   92083
March 3, 19—

Dr. John Hullman
Assistant Personnel Officer
Tulsa Public Schools
Box 298
Tulsa, OK   74100

Dear Dr. Hullman:

Purpose

On June 28 I shall be discharged from the United States Marine Corps and ready to become a junior or senior high school science teacher. My Bachelor of Science in Education degree, my willingness to accept responsibility, and my eagerness to settle down should qualify me for such a position in the Tulsa Public School system if that type of opening exists.

Summary of qualifications and "you" attitude

Next four paragraphs arranged in order of importance to job performance

I was graduated with honors in 19— from Illinois State University with a degree in biology. My academic background includes 55 hours in biology, 14 hours in chemistry, and 10 hours in physics with an overall GPA of 3.7 on a 4.0 scale. Mr. Charles Chalange, my supervising teacher at Superior High School in Superior, Illinois, gave me an excellent rating in student teaching. I am certified to teach science in grades six through twelve. My extracurricular activities included Phi Theta Kappa Honor Society and Beta Beta Beta Biological Honor Society.

In the service I acted as Hydrologic Officer and held the rank of lieutenant. Since July 19—, forty-five men under my direction have collected and analyzed water samples in our off-shore operations.

As for personal information, I am 27 years old, married, and have a three-year-old daughter. My health is excellent and my leisure interests are hunting and fishing. My family lives in

Oklahoma and my wife's family lives in East Texas, so we are eager to return to the Midwest.

My references, named by permission, are as follows: (1) Col. Charles L. Whately, Commanding Officer, Camp Pendleton Marine Base, CA 92084; (2) Dr. Alvin J. Huntington, Chairman, Department of Biology, Illinois State University, Normal, IL 61761; and (3) Mr. Jonathan A. Moran, Pastor, First Methodist Church, Vista, CA   92083.

Request for interview and "you" attitude

I believe that I can make a real contribution to the Tulsa Public Schools. I would certainly appreciate an interview with you during the week of April 1 so I can more fully discuss how my educational background and my practical job experience can be of value to your school system.

Sincerely,

Gerald J. Hamilton

Gerald J. Hamilton

Box 572
Chapman, KS 67431
September 2, 19—

Mr. Harry A. Johnson
Federal Bureau of Investigation
Federal Building
Kansas City, MO   64100

Dear Mr. Johnson:

Mutual acquaintance

During a recent visit with John F. Joneton of the Dallas FBI Office, I learned that you have two openings for Special Agents. I would like to apply for one of these positions.

Purpose

Most important facts from resumé

My qualifications consist, in brief, of a Bachelor of Business Administration degree from Marshall University and of almost five years as an officer in the United States Army. While at Marshall University, I concentrated on the accounting and economics areas. In the army, as a captain in the 1st Infantry Division, I am a Flight Platoon Leader and direct the work of a dozen men. I am a skilled helicopter pilot and have an expert rating with firearms.

"You" attitude

I shall be glad to fill out an application blank if you will send one; but in order that much of the information such a blank would call for will be available to you immediately, I am enclosing a resumé.

Request for interview and information

"You" attitude

I would welcome the opportunity to come to Kansas City for an interview before my army service ends, which will be on January 5, 19—, and would appreciate any information that you can send me about my prospects. I would like to make law enforcement my permanent occupation and believe that as a Special Agent I could be a real asset to the Bureau.

Sincerely,

Thomas D. Williams

Thomas D. Williams

QUALIFICATIONS OF THOMAS D. WILLIAMS

Address Box 572   Date   February 2, 19—
         Chapman, KS 67431
Phone   (913) 922-6673

PERSONAL INFORMATION

Age—26   Leisure interests—Hunting,
Birth date—December   fishing, skiing, flying
  30, 19—   (Commercial helicopter
Weight—162   pilot license with instru-
Height—5 feet 9½ inches   ment rating)
Health—Excellent   Community activities—
Marital status—Married, no   Masonic Lodge No. 13,
  children   Church of Christ

EDUCATION

Kansas State University, 19— to 19—, six hours graduate
  study
Marshall University, 19— to 19— (Huntington, West
  Virginia)
  Degree: Bachelor of Business Administration
             Double Major—Accounting and ROTC
             Minor—Economics
  Academic record: Grade Point Average 3.2
             Dean's List, 19— to 19—
             Distinguished Military Science
               Graduate, 19—
             Alpha Kappa Psi
               (Honorary Business Fraternity)
               19— to 19—
Barboursville High School, Barboursville, West Virginia,
  Graduated 19—
  Activities: Future Engineers, French Club, Eagle Scout,
             Jr. Assistant Scout Master

EXPERIENCE

Experience—Military
United States Army   Present Rank: Captain
  May 19— to the present: 1st Aviation Company, 1st In-
    fantry Division, Fort Riley, Kansas
  November 19— to April 19—: U.S. Army Helicopter
    School, Fort Rucker, Alabama
  August 19— to November 19—: U.S. Army Primary
    Helicopter School, Fort Walters, Texas. Commandant's
    List
  July 19— to July 19—: 12th Battalion, 5th Training
    Brigade, Fort Knox, Kentucky. Training officer for 230
    men
  April 19— to June 19—: Ranger School, Fort Benning,
    Georgia
  March 19— to April 19—: Airborne School, Fort Benning,
    Georgia
  January 19— to March 19—: Infantry Officer Basic Train-
    ing, Fort Benning, Georgia. Commandant's List
Experience—General
  April 19— to December 19—: Big Bear Stores, Inc., Hunt-
    ington, West Virginia. Part time. Cashier—Front
    Manager

REFERENCES

Lt. Col. F. G. Topemans   Charleton L. Bridvell
Commander   Professor of Accounting
1st Aviation Company   Marshall University
1st Infantry Division   Huntington, WV   25700
Fort Riley, KS   66441

Emory A. Thornton   Carleton Ohm, Minister
First State Bank   Church of Christ
Barboursville, WV   25504   Junction City, KS   66441

            Allen Alexander Jones
            Scoutmaster, Troop 62
            Wilkinson Drive
            Huntington, WV   25700

Tone

Just as in the collection letters described earlier,
there often is a difference in the tone of the first letter
for employment and in the fourth or fifth. The letters
below humorously illustrate the very serious problem
of adjusting the tone of the application for employment to suit the situation.

Vice-President of Development
Glucksville Dynamics
Glucksville, California

Dear Sirs:

I am writing in regard to employment with your firm. I
have a BS from USC and PhD in physics from the California
Institute of Technology.

In my previous position I was in charge of research and
development for the Harrington Chemical Company. We did
work in thermonuclear energy, laser beam refraction,
hydrogen molecule development, and heavy-water computer
data.

Several of our research discoveries have been adapted for
commercial use, and one particular breakthrough in linear
hydraulics is now being used by every oil company in the
country.

Because of a cutback in defense orders, the Harrington
Company decided to shut down its research and development
department. It is for this reason I am available for immediate
employment.

Hoping to hear from you in the near future, I remain

                    Sincerely yours,
                    EDWARD KASE

Dear Mr. Kase:

We regret to inform you that we have no positions
available for someone of your excellent qualifications. The
truth of the matter is that we find you are "overqualified"
for any position we might offer you in our organization.
Thank you for thinking of us, and if anything comes up in
the future, we will be getting in touch with you.

                    Yours truly,
                    MERRIMAN HASELBALD
                    Administrative Vice-President

Personnel Director
Jessel International Systems
Crewcut, Mich.

Dear Sir:

I am applying for a position with your company in any responsible capacity. I have had a college education and have fiddled around in research and development. Occasionally we have come up with some moneymaking ideas. I would be willing to start off at a minimal salary to prove my value to your firm.

Sincerely yours,

EDWARD KASE

Dear Mr. Kase:

Thank you for your letter of the 15th. Unfortunately we have no positions at the moment for someone with a college education. Frankly it is the feeling of everyone here that you are "overqualified," and your experience indicates you would be much happier with a company that could make full use of your talents.

It was kind of you to think of us.

HARDY LANDSDOWNE
Personnel Department

To Whom It May Concern
Geis & Waterman Inc.
Ziegfried, ILL

Dere Ser,

I'd like a job with your outfit. I can do anything you want me to. You name it Kase will do it. I ain't got no education and no experience, but I'm strong and I got moxy an I get along great with peeple. I'm ready to start any time because I need the bread. Let me know when you want me.

Cheers

EDWARD KASE

Dear Mr. Kase:

You are just the person we have been looking for. We need a truck driver, and your qualifications are perfect for us. You can begin working in our Westminister plant on Monday. Welcome aboard.

CARSON PETERS
Personnel
(Courtesy G. P. Putnam's Sons for Art Buchwald [3])

FOLLOW-UP LETTER
Employment

A follow-up letter can determine whether or not you get the job. After you mail your letter of application for employment, sometimes several weeks go by without any reply from the company. A follow-up letter can remind them that you are alive, well, and still eager to be considered for employment. It can also be very helpful after you have had an interview. You can simply thank the employer for the interview. This type of letter shows that you can write effectively—a plus quality regardless of the type of job for which you are applying.

There are several reasons you can use to correspond further with the company:

1. Stress your growing interest in the firm.
2. Add to or change some of the information that you included in your letter or interview.
3. Ask some question about the company.

Other Types

Follow-up letters can be used effectively in situations other than employment. You may write them at the end of the year to former customers, or you may use them as letters of appreciation to the customers listed in your active files. When you are waiting for a client to make up his mind or take action, a tactful follow-up letter may spur him to make a decison.

The tone of the follow-up letter, as that of all technical writing, must be confident, obliging, and sincere. Stress the *you* attitude, the benefits for your reader rather than for you. As you revise it, eliminate some of the *I*'s and any statements that will be difficult to substantiate.

The first three follow-up letters below are for employment; the fourth is an end-of-the-year letter to a former customer. All begin on a pleasant note, explain an interest, and tactfully request action.

(1)

Dear Mr. Johnson:

Pleasant beginning and reminder Thank you for considering my resumé and letter of application for the position of Special Agent, mailed September 2, 19—.

Growing interest My interest in the FBI continues to grow. Since I have been stationed with the U.S. Army at Fort Riley, Kansas, I have become quite familiar with the Kansas City area. My wife is a native of Joplin, Missouri, and shares my desire to make the Midwest our permanent home.

Request for action I am eager to work for your organization and look forward to hearing from you at your convenience.

Yours truly,

(2)

Dear Mr. Johnson:

Courteous reminder Since I mailed my resumé and letter of application for the position of Special Agent with the FBI September 2, I have taken further steps to

Purpose prepare myself for the job.

Explanation I have enrolled in two courses required for the Master's degree in Administration of Justice at Wichita State University: a three-hour seminar in the criminal intelligence and a three-hour course in the court system.

Request for action I am much interested in the FBI and will appreciate any information about my employment opportunities.

Sincerely yours,

(3)

Dear Mr. Block:

Courteous reminder On October 3, 19—, I completed and mailed the job application form sent to me by the John Deere Corporation. I was very eager to return
"You" attitude this job application and, in my enthusiasm, overlooked one point that may be of interest to you.

Additional information During the summer of 19— I worked at the John Deere dealership in Anthony, Texas; I assembled your 6600 and 7700 series combine, the model 47 mower, various models of cultivators, and the LM and DRB model drills.

"You" attitude Mechanical knowledge of these much-used pieces of farm equipment will contribute to my ability to excel with your company.

Appreciation I am happy that John Deere has considered my potential and allowed me to fill out an applica-
Request for action tion form. I am free to come to Dallas for an interview at any time convenient for you.

Very truly yours,

(4)

Dear Mr. and Mrs. Smith:

Purpose It is never pleasant to lose a member and customer, and we are sorry that you have found it necessary to close your account. It was our pleasure to serve you and we assure you that your account was very much appreciated.

Explanation It is a serious matter with us when we lose a customer. If there has been a misunderstanding
Expression of goodwill of any kind, please let us know. We are very anxious to do all we can to insure complete satisfaction.

"You" attitude We are glad to have had an opportunity to serve you and we sincerely hope circumstances will change later on so that once again you will wish to have a savings account with us. Remember, if you are saving, you are getting ahead. And *where* you save *does* make a difference (especially to us).

Very sincerely,

SUMMARY

There are accepted rules for writing the following basic types of letters: complaint, granting and refusing of credit, collection, inquiry, answer to complaint and inquiry, invitation, instruction, form letter, application for employment, and follow-up. If you will follow the general principles that are set forth in this chapter for writing these letters, you will be able to handle business correspondence quickly and easily.

The tone for all these types of letters involves the *you* attitude. Always imply that you are more interested in the welfare of the reader than in your own. Always appear to be contributing to the future well-being of your reader. Even the carefully prepared form letter can be written so that it has this personal tone and specifically applies to each reader. The purpose of business letters is to affect in some way the attitude or conduct of the reader, and this purpose can best be accomplished through diplomacy and courtesy.

Although the parts of business letters are arranged in various patterns depending on the type and purpose, there are some basic organizational rules to follow. Begin and end on a pleasant note. Give good news immediately; delay bad news until you have had a chance to explain your position. Often you can temper a refusal by offering some other information or service or by making some promise for the future.

The appearance of a business letter is important because it represents you and your company. Maintain 1- to 1½-inch margins on the sides and 1½- to 2½-inch margins at the top and bottom. Use short paragraphs and mechanical devices such as headings, numbers, and underlining so the letter will look easy to read. If there are erasures, strikeovers, and misspelled words, retype. Eliminate some of the *I*'s as you revise the body of the letter and again as you type.

All business letters are not as clear-cut as the specimen letters used in this chapter. Some do not fit any special type; others seem to be a combination of several types. For example, an invitation may also include persuasion and instructions.

A business letter is a personal communication. Each letter should represent you at your best and should be adapted to fit a specific situation. Thus the sample letters in this chapter are useful as examples, but do not copy them or borrow phrases and sentences from them. Do, however, imitate their tone, organization, and appearance.

WRITING ASSIGNMENTS

Write the letter called for in the situations described below. Invent any names, addresses, and details that are necessary.

1. You have purchased an article of clothing from a mail-order company. After you wore the clothing once, the faulty construction was obvious. Write a letter of complaint.

2. The representative of an out-of-town firm has called on you and has been extremely rude. Complain to the head of the firm.

3. Your next-door neighbors are mistreating their pet. You have complained to them, but they have not remedied the situation. Write the local humane society.

4. The book you ordered from a certain publisher is unsatisfactory in some way. You want it replaced. Write a letter of complaint.

5. A person representing an ecology group has accused the chemical company for which you work of pollution of a nearby river. In a rude letter, reason after reason has been given why you are guilty and you have been challenged to a public

discussion of the problem to be broadcast over a local television station. You are in the public relations department. Write a letter accepting or rejecting the challenge.

6. Ask several questions of a local company. You need this information for the formal report you are writing this semester in technical writing.

7. You are a consumer who desires specific information about a new product you have heard about. Write a letter of inquiry.

8. You have received a request from a business executive who has had a number of problems with a product from your company. A refund of $1000 for the faulty product is requested. You have the authority to grant all, part of, or none of the amount.

9. You have received a letter from a dissatisfied customer complaining that your product is faulty. You believe the product is not being operated correctly. Tactfully give instructions telling how to use the product.

10. Invite a celebrity to speak to a campus group about a specific topic.

11. Write a form letter to credit card customers announcing a forthcoming increase in interest rates charged on their accounts.

12. Write a resumé sheet (data sheet) and the covering letter setting forth your qualifications for a position you might plausibly apply for. Assume you definitely know an opening exists and the reader knows nothing about you until reading your letter. In stating your qualifications, limit yourself to the facts, but assume you will be graduating at the end of this semester. Include any experience you would be likely to gain before graduation. Use the resumé sheet of the placement bureau of your school or pattern yours after the one used in this chapter.

13. Write a traditional letter of application setting forth your own qualifications for a position you might plausibly apply for. You do not know whether an opening exists. In stating your qualifications, limit yourself to the facts, but assume you will be graduating at the end of this semester. Include any experience you would be likely to gain before graduation. Do not include any personal information.

14. Assume you have written an unsolicited letter of application for employment to a certain company. You have not received a reply. Write a follow-up letter.

15. Assume it is the end of the fiscal year and your company wants you to write a follow-up letter to customers who have done business with you during the last year.

16. Urge a campus group to donate time to a community project.

17. Employees of the water department destroyed the roots of a valuable tree on your property when they repaired a water main that crossed your front lawn. You want the city to pay for replacing the tree.

18. You own a camera equipment store. You do not solicit credit accounts, but when your steady customers ask to charge merchandise, you usually agree. But some customers do not pay promptly and usually shop elsewhere while their accounts remain delinquent. Write a letter in which you attempt to collect while retaining their goodwill.

19. Assume you are a credit manager for a department store in a large city. At least 20 of your accounts are delinquent and you have sent them the usual form reminders. Some represent good risks and some poor risks. Write a personal letter suitable for the good risks and one suitable for poor risks.

20. As credit manager for a furniture store, you have many accounts that are good risks but slow to pay. Prepare a series of three collection letters to be sent at intervals to those whose accounts continue to be delinquent.

21. A person who has been a good cash customer for five years has recently applied for a charge account. Your investigation shows this person will not be a good credit risk because of a precarious financial situation. Refuse the application and yet try to retain the person as a cash customer.

22. You are a wholesaler of women's coats. A local clothing store manager has applied for a credit account and has been approved. As you grant the request, tell about the rules, services available, and other factors.

23. One of your good credit customers for the past 20 years has, in the last six months, run up a past-due balance of $529.50. Write an appropriate collection letter.

REFERENCES

1. The Ford Motor Co. Dearborn, MI 48120.
2. Whirlpool Corporation. Benton Harbor, MI 49022.
3. Art Buchwald. *I Never Danced at the White House.* New York: G. P. Putnam's Sons, 1973.

CHAPTER 11

Catalogs, Advertising Copy, Direct Mail Letters, and Product News Releases

THE job of preparing industrial catalogs and other advertising and promotional pieces should fall to the employee who has the most extensive communication skills. This is a highly specialized form of technical writing, and to be successful at it, you must heed many of the same basic guidelines used in other types of technical writing. You will continue to consider the audience; appeal to their needs and desires; and strive for clarity, economy, and accuracy. Classifying the audience can help you distinguish between catalogs and advertising. In general, buyers use catalogs and sellers use advertising.

CATALOGS

Catalogs are the strongest links between the company and the consumer, who is often a well-trained technician. Catalogs serve two purposes: to inform potential users about what products are available and to motivate sales.

Definition

The catalog can be a one-page sheet or a thousand-page volume. It is usually a special booklet that gives brief, accurate listings of a company's merchandise; prices are sometimes included. When the listings contain detailed descriptions and explanations, the catalog becomes a form of technical writing. The catalog tells the buyer what is for sale and, since it is frequently consulted before a sales representative calls, the catalog must give enough information so a decision can be made about the merits of the product.

Purpose

Why is this catalog being prepared? Will it be a mail-order catalog, a single-product catalog, a distributor's catalog, a condensed catalog, or a prefiled catalog? What kind of audience are you trying to reach? Are you writing for laypersons, technicians, or highly trained professionals? Do they need prices, design information, dimensions, or weight? Or do they want all this information? Are they interested in color, materials, speed, range, or fuel consumption? After you have satisfactorily answered these questions, you will be ready to plan an effective catalog that will sell your product.

Remember that a catalog is not designed for entertainment; there should be no jarring colors, junky layouts, involved foldouts, or irresponsible claims. Technically knowledgeable readers prefer a brief description of the product, detailed dimensions, a statement of the product's capabilities and limitations, its proper applications, and prices when available. Give relevant facts instead of a blatant sales pitch, but do not hesitate to stress your product's good qualities.

Illustrations

Dimensional drawings, diagrams, and other pertinent illustrations are vital parts of a useful catalog, so it is wise to choose the visual parts of your layout first. Then as you write the copy, you can refer to each illustration. Detail drawings should be large enough so the buyer can read the dimensions and figure out how much space is needed and how to handle unit placement. Photographs are especially valuable for showing design features, various models available, and installation procedures.

Economizing on illustrations will not help sell the product; the more attractive the appearance of the catalog, the more likely that sales will result.

Steps in Writing Catalogs

1. *Collect* the data and illustrations. You will want to keep in touch with the departments of your firm that supply the latest information. Strive to make the catalog as timely and accurate as possible. Satisfied customers are often glad to provide (or let you take) photos of your product in use. These are particularly effective sales tools, along with testimonials from pleased users.

2. *Organize* the data. Correlate the text with the visual elements you select. Take the information the buyer will need and arrange it in logical order. There are no hard, fast rules for presenting material, but if the catalog describes more than one product, you will want to include a title page, table of contents, design and specification data, special features, ratings, prices, ordering procedures, and the names of sales representatives.

3. *Write* the rough draft. Be concise, but give enough information so the reader can take action. Use adjectives carefully because they can detract from professional-sounding copy. Break up the text with illustrations, tables, and lists of product applications so the catalog will be easier to read. Clearly state but do not dwell on any limitations of the product, so the buyer will be accurately informed.

4. *Check* the facts. Then double-check the facts, especially when you are promoting highly technical merchandise. Always have the approval of your supervisors and concerned departments before you proceed further. If you work for a large corporation, you must often send the text and visuals to the engineering, sales, and public relations departments and get written clearance from each.

5. *Polish* the rough draft. Follow the same procedures used in other types of technical writing. Continue to strive for clarity, economy, and correctness. Be professional, but remember the goal of the catalog is to promote your product.

6. *Send* the catalog to production. Large corporations have their own printing plants, and production is handled in-house. If your firm is smaller, you may work with an advertising or public relations agency. Select a catalog format most suitable for your technical audience, and then insist on the best printer, paper, and binding for the job.

7. *Proofread* the catalog carefully. When you receive galleys or roughs of the catalog prior to printing, check them carefully for errors. Incorporate any changes or new information you have compiled since the catalog went into production. The catalog represents your company and your efforts are important to make sure the catalog is not outdated by the time it is printed.

Specimen Catalog

The following pages illustrate a single-product catalog advertising DeWalt Radial Arm Saws.

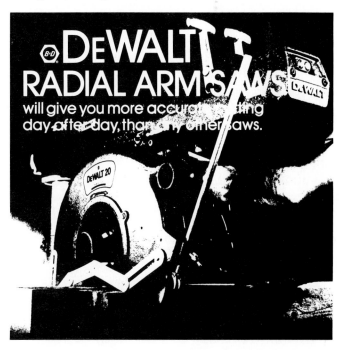

(Courtesy Black & Decker Manufacturing Company [1])

You benefit four important ways from DeWalt's 50 years of heavy-duty saw experience.

1. DeWalt Radial Arm Saws stand up to the toughest work. DeWalt reliability has been proved by tens of millions of production hours. One reason: all DeWalt-built motors are designed specifically for use on Radial Arm Saws.

2. You get the convenience of up-front low-voltage (115V) controls that put the operator completely in charge, plus lower blade guards (OSHA approved). Many models give you automatic electric brakes and overload and low-voltage protection.

3. You get repeatable accuracy. The cutting angle stays the same as you set it. Precision Miter Scale allows 360° miter capacity. Positive bevel stops automatically position at 0°, 45° and 90°. Precision Bevel Scale assures repeatable accuracy at any angle. Rip Scale maintains accuracy on ripping cuts. Lifetime adjustment and accuracy are insured by ball bearings in the interior roller head riding in precision machined tracks. Eight ball bearings on all 14″, 16″ and 20″ models. Four on 10″ and 12″ models.

4. You get a wide variety of cuts: cross cut, rip, miter, bevel and compound. With repeatable accuracy . . . cut after cut, shift after shift, day after day.

DeWalt.

18 MODELS TO CHOOSE FROM.

TWO 20" GIANTS

Model 3533, 44" arm. Model 3558, 52" arm.
Largest ripping capacity—to 48¾"
Largest miter capacity—to 23" (at 45° R)
Greatest depth of cut—6¼" with lower blade guard
All with standard equipment, which includes:
- Exclusive automatic electric brake. Stops saw in seconds.
- Electrical controls are of the magnetic type with low voltage at the operator's switch. "No-voltage" protection is provided. 3-phase models feature 3-leg overload protection.
- Exclusive column lock, plus lower blade guard.

Model	HP	Voltage	Phase	Cycle
3553	7½	230/460	3	50/60
3558	7½	230/460	3	50/60

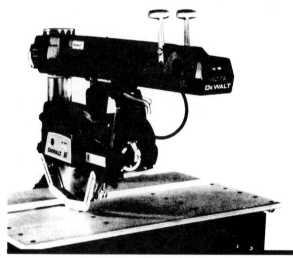

SIX SUPER DUTY 16"s

Models 3551, 3556, 3561, 3566, 3571, 3576

2 Arm sizes. All models with automatic electromechanical brakes. Electrical controls are of the magnetic type with low voltage at the operator's switch. "No-voltage" protection is provided. 3-phase models feature 3-leg overload protection. *Versatile*—they do the work of a shopful of special-purpose saws and shapers.

Model	Arm Size	HP	Voltage	Phase	Cycle
3551	44"	5	230	1	60
3556	52"	5	230	1	60
3561	44"	5	230/460	3	50/60
3566	52"	5	230/460	3	50/60
3571	44"	7½	230/460	3	50/60
3576	52"	7½	230/460	3	50/60

TWO HEAVY DUTY 16"s

Models 3573 and 3574

Big production capability at the lowest price on the market. Cuts 5⁷⁄₁₆" deep without lower blade guard, or 4⅝" with lower blade guard (OSHA required). Pushbutton switch. Electrical controls are of the magnetic type with low voltage at the operator's switch. "No-voltage" protection is provided. 3-phase models feature 3-leg overload protection.

Model	HP	Voltage	Phase	Cycle
3573	5	230/460	3	60
3574	3	230	1	60

DeWALT TRADE CATALOG

DeWALT RADIAL ARM SAWS ARE FAMOUS FOR REPEATABLE ACCURACY. These features are standard on all 10" and 12" models: 10" blade cuts 3" deep (12" blade cuts 4" deep on 12" models). Up-front push button switch with key lock prevents unauthorized use. Precise blade elevation control and depth adjustment to ¹⁄₆₄". Sawing operations include accurate crosscutting, mitering, ripping, bevel crosscutting, bevel mitering and bevel ripping. Bevel pins give quick, true settings at 0°, 45° and 90° positions. No "play" after years of use. The roller head has four shielded, adjustable, permanently lubricated ball bearings which ride on tracks machined into the solid one-piece arm casting. Yoke swivels 360° and automatically locates at 0°, 90°, 180° and 270°. The precise miter locator locks at 0° and 45°. The scale is marked in 1° increments.

DeWALT MOTORS. DeWalt does not use general-purpose, commercially available motors. Instead, we design, engineer and build each direct drive, fan-cooled induction motor for a specific use as an integral part of each saw. We make our own ball bearing-lubricated and sealed for life—motors to handle the precise requirements of radial saw applications. Low maintenance Powershop motors eliminate gears, brushes, grease and oil. An integral thermostat protects against overload and burnout. Saws come complete with combination blade, lower blade guard, anti-kickback attachment, sawdust elbow and control function chart.

DeWALT ADJUSTMENTS. DeWalt saws are fully adjustable. This maintains their accuracy for life. All wear caused by use can be adjusted out at each metal-to-metal point. DeWalt accuracy gives you precision cuts at any angle. Miter, bevel, rip, compound. You get repetitive precision cut after cut, year after year.

VERSATILITY. With accessories, a DeWalt radial arm saw can do almost anything in woodworking. Each of these 10" and 12" saws will sand, joint, shape, surface and sabersaw. Accessories allow you to apply the rigidity and precision of your saw to all types of woodworking operations. GET DeWALT.

MODEL
7740/3421
$334.95

[183]

MODEL 7745/3445
$349.95

INCLUDES MODEL 7740/3421 DeWALT 740 10" POWERSHOP WITH T/R1201 LEG STAND, T/R 1445 RADIAL ARM SAW BOOK AND T/R 1444 SAWDUST CATCHER.
$400.80 IF PURCHASED SEPARATELY.

YOU SAVE $50.85

SPECIFICATIONS

Motor	120V., 1 ph.
Motor Rating Develops	2 HP
Full Load Speed—60 cy. AC	3450
Standard Guard (includes lower blade guard)	10"
Standard Blade	10"
Arbor Size	⅝" x 1½" long
Maximum Depth of Cut	3"
Maximum Depth of Cut at 45° Bevel	2⅛"
Cross Cut Capacity—1" stock	13"
Spindle Dado Cap.—Width	¹³⁄₁₆"
Ripping Capacity—Width	24¹¹⁄₁₆"
Miter Locating Latch	0° and 45° R or L
Scales	Miter, Rip, Bevel
Bevel Locating Pin	0°, 45°, 90°
Column Diameter	2¾"
Steel Table Size	18" x 21½"
Work Table Overall Size	26⅜" x 36"
Height Work Table on Cabinets	37"
Height Work Table on Legs	35"
Net Weight	127 lbs.
Gross Shipping Weight	140 lbs.

DeWalt 740 10" Powershop. Its consistent precision and modest price make it the most popular saw for the home owner. Versatile! It crosscuts, rips, miters, bevel miters, bevel crosscuts and bevel rips. With accessories, it does almost any job in woodworking. Sand, shape, dado . . . it has dozens of uses.

In addition to all the standard features, this saw has . . .
- 10" blade that cuts 3" deep
- Blade guard
- 120 volt operation
- Open motor construction develops 2 HP at the blade.

Get famous DeWalt quality at the lowest cost!

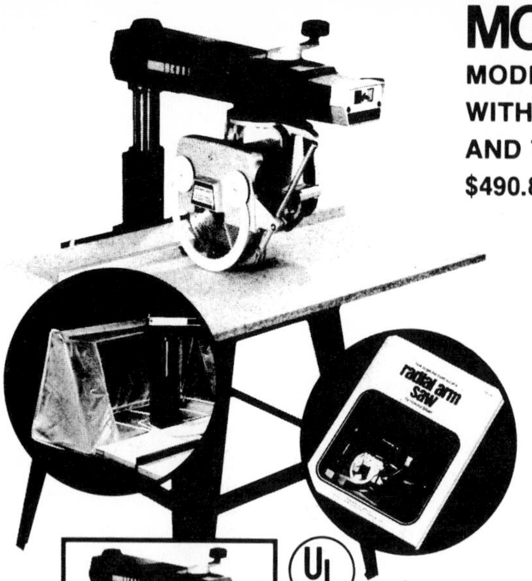

MODEL 7775/3475 $439.95 INCLUDES

MODEL 7770/3427 DEWALT 770 10" DELUXE POWERSHOP
WITH T/R 1201 LEG STAND, T/R 1445 RADIAL ARM SAW BOOK,
AND T/R 1444 SAWDUST CATCHER.

$490.80 IF PURCHASED SEPARATELY. YOU SAVE $50.85

MODEL 7770/3427 $424.95

SPECIFICATIONS

Motor	120/208-240V, 1 ph.
Motor Rating Develops	2¼ HP
Full Load Speed—60 cy. AC	3450
Standard Guard (includes lower blade guard)	10"
Standard Blade	10"
Arbor Size	⅝" x 1½" long
Maximum Depth of Cut	3"
Maximum Depth of Cut at 45° Bevel	2⅛"
Cross Cut Capacity—1" stock	14½"
Spindle Dado Cap.—Width	13/16"
Ripping Capacity—Width	24 11/16"
Miter Locating Latch	0° and 45° R or L
Scales	Miter, Rip, Bevel
Bevel Locating Pin	0°, 45°, 90°
Column Diameter	2¾"
Steel Table Size	18" x 21½"
Work Table Overall Size	26⅜" x 36"
Height Work Table, on Cabinets	37"
Height Work Table on Legs	35"
Net Weight	136 lbs.
Gross Shipping Weight	153 lbs.

The DeWalt 770 10" Deluxe Powershop is DeWalt's finest 10" model. It develops more power—2¼ HP. The motor is totally enclosed. Dirt, moisture and dust never touch the winding. This gives longer life, troublefree service. Automatic brake built into the motor, stops the blade in seconds after the switch is turned off. Dual voltage motor is factory connected for 120 volt use and can easily be reconnected for 240 volt use. Two piece backboard gives more rip fence positions. The well is precut for drum sanding operations. Here's our better 10" Powershop at a popular price!

MODEL 7790/3431 DEWALT 790 12" CONTRACTORS' POWERSHOP

INCLUDING LEG STAND $639.95

SPECIFICATIONS

Motor	120/208-240V., 1 ph.
Motor Rating Develops	3½ HP
Continuous Duty	1½ HP
Full Load Speed—60 cy. AC	3450
Standard Guard (includes lower blade guard)	12"
Standard Blade	12"
Arbor Size	⅝" x 1½" long
Maximum Depth of Cut	4"
Maximum Depth of Cut at 45° Bevel	2¾"
Cross Cut Capacity—1" stock	16"
Spindle Dado Cap.—Width	13/16"
Ripping Capacity—Width	27"
Miter Locating Latch	0° and 45°, R or L
Scales	Miter, Rip, Bevel
Bevel Locating Pin	0°, 45°, 90°
Column Diameter	2¾"
Steel Table Size	26" x 32"
Work Table Overall Size	29⅜" x 38½"
Height Work Table on Legs	33"
Net Weight	208 lbs.
Gross Shipping Weight	242 lbs.

DeWalt 790 12" Contractors' Powershop. Engineered for the professional contractor or serious hobbyist who demands more power and precision with frequent use. Motor designed for continuous duty applications: ripping, gang cutting, wide miters and other frequent applications. Blade cuts full 4" deep. Totally enclosed motor. Automatic brake. Control function chart gives easy set-ups. Saw is assembled, aligned, kerfed and use-tested at the factory. Net weight is 60% greater than other Powershops. Develops 3½ HP. Class 130 insulation. Cadmium plated column. Individual "Wedge-Lok" miter and clamp handles for accurate, positive positioning for miters. The top of the twelves!

MODEL 7717/3417 DEWALT 10" POWER MITER BOX $239.95

Power and accuracy for faster, better finish and trim in home building, cabinet making, picture framing, boat building, mobile home production. Cuts wood, plastics, compositions, thin-wall lightweight aluminum extrusions. It's the finest, most accurate miter!

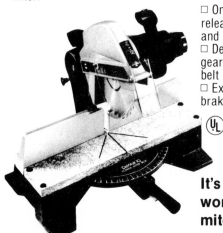

☐ One-handed trigger release miter pivot handle and lock
☐ Dependable 1½ HP gear-driven motor. No belt to break.
☐ Exclusive automatic brake.

It's the world's finest miter!

DEWALT 6", 7" & 8" BENCH GRINDERS

Six smooth running, dependable heavy-duty grinders . . . designed for many applications in toolrooms, welding, woodworking and machine shops, schools, factories, homes, farms, garages, and maintenance shops.

MODEL 3455

MODEL 3451 6" WITH EYE SHIELDS $149

MODEL 3452 6" WITH ILLUMINATED EYE SHIELDS $169

MODEL 3453 7" WITH EYE SHIELDS $189

MODEL 3454 7" WITH ILLUMINATED EYE SHIELDS $209

MODEL 3455 8" WITH EYE SHIELDS (1 PHASE) $389

MODEL 3456 8" WITH EYE SHIELDS (3 PHASE) $399

WITH ACCESSORIES, POWERSHOPS DO MORE THAN SAW WOOD

POWERSHOPS DADO

Cut uniform slots, grooves, half laps, drawer corners, rabbet cuts with these great DADO SETS

Quickset Advantages at Lowest Cost—
35004 6" Quick-Set II™ Adjustable Dado. Single unit construction; carbon steel cutter. Infinitely adjustable ¼"—¹³/₁₆" **$28.95**

Our Best Quickset—
T/R2860 6" Quick-Set™ Dado, easily adjustable in width from ¼" to ¹³/₁₆" without removing the head from the saw arbor. Cuts smooth, clean grooves without vibration, wobble, chatter, burning or chewing **$52.95**

These Dado Sets with Spacers and Chippers Assure Finest Quality Cut and Precision over Longest Life—

T/R6024 6" Dado Head Set. Flat Ground (2 Blades, 4 Chippers ⅛", 1 Chipper ¹/₁₆") ⅝" bore **$37.95**

T/R6001 6" Dado Head Set. Hollow Ground (2 Blades, 4 Chippers ⅛", 1 Chipper ¹/₁₆") ⅝" bore **$48.95**

T/R6025 8" Dado Head Set. Flat Ground (2 Blades, 4 Chippers ⅛", 1 Chipper ¹/₁₆") ⅝" bore **$53.95**

POWERSHOPS PLANE AND SAND

Rotary planers surface and size boards. Sanders finish surfaces with either straight or curved edges.

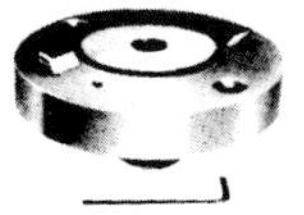

T/R6380 Rotary Planer (includes knives and wrench) Surface planes. Excellent for thickness sizing, panel raising **$36.95**

T/R6383 Knife Set.
2 knives for T/R6380 .... **$15.95**

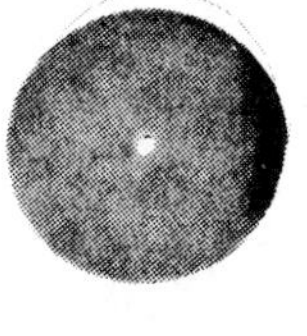

Disc Sander, ⅝" L.H. thread.
T/R7470 8" dia. Sander Disc Set (includes bevel edge disc, one 8" dia. pressure-sensitive sandpaper disc No. 60 grit) Fast material removal. Surface, end grain and bevel sanding **$17.95**

T/R467 6 assorted 8" pressure-sensitive sandpaper discs (1 No. 50, 2 No. 60, 3 No. 80 grits) **$10.95**

Drum Sanders, no adaptor necessary.
T/R7468 2½" dia., 3" long Drum Sander, ⅝" L.H. thread. Fits arbor shaft of all 9", 10" and 12" models for straight and curved edges up to 2" thick **$15.95**

T/R7473 1" Drum Sander, 3" long, ⅝" L.H. thread. Fits arbor shaft of all 9", 10" and 12" models for small radius curves and delicate sanding **$13.95**

POWERSHOPS SABER SAW

T/R1254 Saber Saw. Does curve work the fast easy way in wood, plastic, metal. Complete with 3 blades **$38.95**

T/R8028 Saber Saw Blades Consists of one each: Fine, Medium, Coarse **$2.95**

POWERSHOPS ROUT

35500 Router Attachment. Holds router motor for overarm routing applications. Ideal for variety work. **$32.95**

POWERSHOPS DRILL

T/R1208 ⅜" Drill chuck w/key fits right hand arbor on models R-1250, R-1350, 7740/3421, 7770/3426, 7780 for horizontal drill. A must for dowel jointing **$11.95**

POWERSHOPS SHAPE AND JOINT

Make finished edges for glue jointing long boards. Edge & surface shape with many different knife sets for decorative mouldings and cabinet making, panel raising and other special woodworking effects.

T/R3472 Jointer Cutter Head, solid 4-wing cutter includes special ⅝" L.H. thread arbor nut. 2" dia. x 2" long **$38.95**

T/R9220 Shaper-Jointer Fence. Converts saw for precise shaping and jointing operations. Feed fence has micrometer adjustments from 0 to ½" **$69.95**

Deluxe Shaper & Knives Yield Finest Quality Work

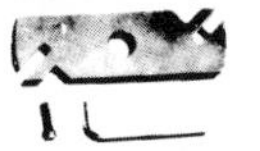

T/R6480 2-Knife Shaper Head: 5" long, 1½" wide, ⅝" arbor hole **$23.95**

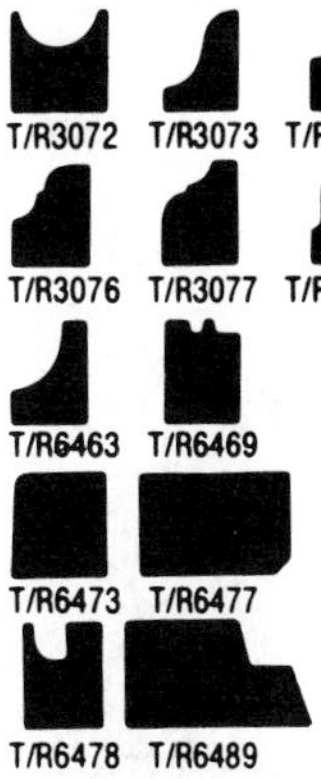

Sets of 2 Knives—Self Aligning. ¼"-⅜" thick, 1"-1½" long. High speed steel with one hole and held by ¼" socket screw.

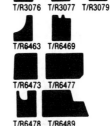

T/R3072	T/R3073	T/R3075
T/R3076	T/R3077	T/R3079
T/R6463	T/R6469	
T/R6473	T/R6477	
T/R6478	T/R6489	

T/R3072 Nosing Cutter, ¹⁵/₁₆" Nose Knives .. **$22.95**
T/R3073 Ogee Moulding, ⁷/₁₆" Bead and Cove Knives **$16.95**
T/R3075 ⅝" Quarter Round Knives **$16.95**
T/R3076 ⁵/₁₆" Bead and Cove Knives .. **$13.95**
T/R3077 ⁵/₁₆" Cove and Bead Knives .. **$16.95**
T/R3079 Fluting Cutter ⁷/₁₆" Knives **$14.95**
T/R6463 ¾" Quarter Round Knives ... **$16.95**
T/R6469 Glue Joint Knives **$16.95**
T/R6473 Panel Raising Knives **$31.95**
T/R6477 2" Jointing Surfacing and Panel Knives **$13.95**
T/R6478 Cabinet Door Lip Knives, ⅜" radius, 7° rake **$23.95**
T/R6489 Cabinet Door Lip Knives, Straight, 7° rake **$16.95**

Economical Starter Set and Knives

T/R6501 3-Knife Shaper Head Set: 1 T/R6500 Head; 1 T/R6505 Glue Joint Knives; 1 T/R 6512 Universal Bead Knives; 1 T/R6515 Cabinet Door Lip Knives; 1 T/R6517 ⁵/₁₆" Bead and Cove Knives. Purchased separately, $53.75, Kit **$38.95**

T/R6500 3-Knife Shaper Head for Bench and Radial Saws, ⅝" arbor hole **$17.95**

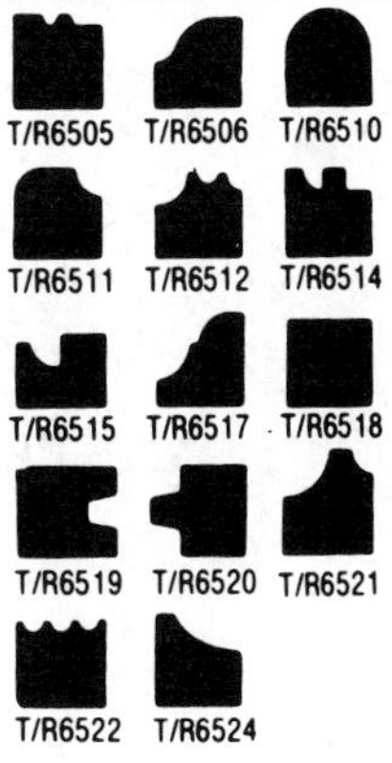

			SETS OF 3 KNIVES:
T/R6505	T/R6506	T/R6510	
T/R6511	T/R6512	T/R6514	
T/R6515	T/R6517	T/R6518	
T/R6519	T/R6520	T/R6521	
T/R6522	T/R6524		

T/R6505 Glue Joint Knives **$8.95**
T/R6506 Ogee Casing Knives **$8.95**
T/R6510 1" Round Flute Knives **$8.95**
T/R6511 Drop Leaf Flute Knives **$8.95**
T/R6512 Universal Bead Knives **$8.95**
T/R6514 Panel Cupboard Door Knives .. **$8.95**
T/R6515 Cabinet Door Lip Knives **$8.95**
T/R6517 ⁵/₁₆" Bead and Cove Knives ... **$8.95**
T/R6518 1" Straight Knives **$8.95**
T/R6519 Tongue Knives **$8.95**
T/R6520 Groove Knives **$8.95**
T/R6521 ¼" and ½" Quarter Round Knives **$8.95**
T/R6522 Triple ¼" Bead Knives **$8.95**
T/R6524 Base Mold Knives **$8.95**

To Edge-Shape Use This Guard
T/R119826 Tool Guard. Replaces standard blade guard for all shaping, dadoing, disc sanding and planing operations. Will accommodate tools up to 8" diameter **$25.95**

... and this kit can get you started at less cost than if purchased separately.

T/R1428 Shaper Accessory Group. Includes: T/R119826 Tool Guard. T/R 6500 Shaper Head, T/R6505 Glue Joint Knives, T/R6512 Universal Bead Knives, T/R6515 Cabinet Door Lip Knives, T/R6517 ⁵/₁₆" Bead and Cove Knives. Purchased separately, $79.70 Kit ... SPECIAL **$56.95**

ACCESSORIES (CONT'D.)

— POWERSHOPS SAW All blades listed have ⅝" arbor hole.

Catalog Number	Size	Type	No. of Teeth	Quality	Price
35025	8"	Combination, Chisel Tooth	22	Standard	$ 5.95
T/R2919	8"	Plywood, Veneer	176	Standard	10.95
T/R997	9"	Combination, Chisel Tooth	28	Premium	13.95
T/R1011	9"	Planer, Hollow Ground	65	Premium	17.95
T/R1013	10"	Planer, Hollow Ground	75	Premium	18.95
T/R1014	10"	Plywood, Veneer	200	Premium	19.95
T/R1036	10"	Non-Ferrous Metal Cutting	80	Premium	84.95
T/R1041	10"	Combination, Chisel Tooth	30	Premium	10.95
T/R1426	10"	Rip	36	Standard	10.95
T/R2010	10"	Combination, Novelty Tooth	60	Standard	10.95
T/R2114	10"	Combination, Chisel Tooth	30	Premium	17.95
30010	10"	Combination, Chisel Tooth	28	Standard	8.95
T/R1034	12"	Combination, Chisel Tooth	44	Premoum	17.95
T/R2112	12"	Combination, Chisel Tooth	38	Standard	18.95
T/R2115	12"	Combination, Chisel Tooth	38	Premium	24.95
T/R2311	12"	Rip	32	Standard	18.95
35150	12"	Combination, Chisel Tooth	32	Standard	18.95

CARBIDE SAW BLADES

35502	8"	Combination Planer	25		$ 74.95
35504	8"	Veneer	40		81.95
T-1032	8"	Combination	44		179.00
T/R2508	9"	Combination	8		36.95
T/R989	10"	Combination	8		33.95
35521	10"	Combination	24		69.95
35522	10"	Combination Planer	35		94.95
35523	10"	Rip	12		41.95
35524	10"	Veneer	50		97.95
35525	10"	Plastic Veneer	80		144.95
T/R2510	12"	Combination	12		49.95

CAT. NO. 77-990
DeWALT POWERSHOP ACCESSORY CENTER

Contains one (1) each of the following:

Item	Total Retail
T/R1205	$ 6.95
T/R1208	11.95
T/R1254	38.95
T/R1445	6.95
T/R2860	52.95
T/R3076	13.95
T/R6001	48.95
T/R6024	37.95
T/R6380	36.95
T/R6477	13.95
T/R6478	23.95
T/R6480	23.95
T/R6501	38.95
T/R6506	8.95
T/R6515	8.95
T/R6517	8.95
T/R7468	15.95
T/R7470	17.95
T/R119826	25.95
Rack	FREE
T/R1445	
8 Free Goods	55.60
TOTAL	$498.65

— EVEN MORE POWERSHOP VERSATILITY WITH THESE ACCESSORIES

T/R9362 Deluxe Utility Cabinet. Convenient and neat storage for blade and accessories. Door has tray for wrenches. For 7700, 7740/3421, 7770/3427, 7780 ... **$79.95**

T/R9361 Utility Drawer for utility cabinets. Complete with mounting hardware **$28.95**

T/R1201 Leg Stand for models 7740/3421, 7770/3427, 7780 ... **$37.95**

T/R1518 Leg Stand for 7790/3431, 3436 ... **$40.25**

T/R9363 Caster Set (4) For Cabinets. Includes toe-locking casters **$13.95**

35021 Deluxe Machine Stand. Use with DeWalt #7700, 8" Saw and B & D Bench Grinders and 7717 Miter Box. A stable work shop bench for many uses. Work surface 23" x 18¾" x 30½" high. Rubber foot grommets. ... **$42.95**

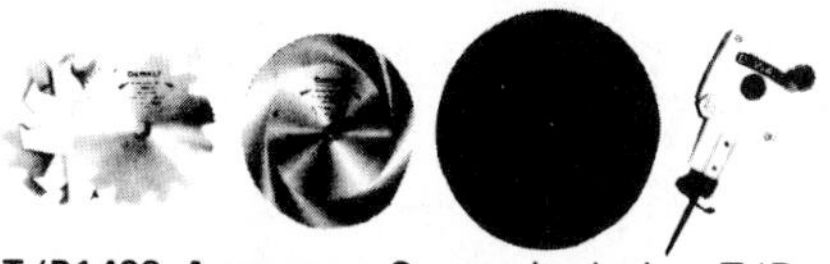

T/R1429 Accessory Group. Includes T/R-6024 6" Dado Head Set, T/R7470 Disc Sander, T/R2919 8" Taper Ground Plywood Blade, T/R1254 Sabre Saw Attachment. Purchased separately, $105.80 Kit **$87.95**

35016 Deluxe Goggles. Gives complete eye protection. Comfortable elastic band holds goggles in place. Air vents allow you to work safer and in comfort. Meets OSHA requirements **$5.95**

35015 Operator's Glasses. Lightweight, one-piece, impact resistant, clear plastic glasses with side shields. Can be worn directly over eyes or over prescription glasses. Comfortable **$2.95**

Spacing Collars:
T/R2432 ¹/₁₆" thick, ⅝" arbor hole **$3.95**
T/R2433 ⅛" thick ⅝" arbor hole . **$4.95**
T/R2434 ¼" thick, ⅝" arbor hole . **$6.95**

35010 Roller Head Stop. Mounts on arm of 10" and 12" machines to limit travel of roller head to any desired cutting width **$6.95**

T/R1205 Adjustable Cutoff Gauge Use with any radial arm saw. Clamps to fence for repeated accurate length cutting. Fine adjusting screw provides precise setting for exact length **$6.95**

Automatic Return Device. Fastens to rear of machine arm. Returns saw carriage to rear position: **T/R1438** for 1250, 1350, T1810, 3420, 7700, 7740/3421, 7770/3427, 7780 .... **$19.95**
T/R1506 for 925, 1030, 1200, 1400, T1531, T1533, 3430, 3435, 3436, 7790/3431, 7791/3432 .... **$17.95**

T/R1445 "How To Get The Most Out Of A Radial Arm Saw" Book. A complete guide to radial arm saw techniques. 64 pages. Fully illustrated. Designed to lie flat when open for easy reference ... **$6.95**

T/R1516 Splitter and Anti-Kickback Device for 10" Saw Guard-splitter, separates wood when ripping—prevents saw bind. For 1400, T1810, T1812, 3420, 3425, 7740/3421, 7770/3427 ..... **$29.95**

T/R1818 Splitter and Anti-Kickback Device for 12" for 7790/3431, 7780 ..... **$28.95**

Lower Blade Guards Free floating device rides over stock being cut.

T/R1508 12" Ring-type lower blade guard fits R1512, 3430, 7790/3431 ..... **$29.95**

34001 Complete guard assembly for current 12" saws and 1500 series... **$39.95**

35017 10" New style lower blade guard, fits all 10" DeWalt models **$21.95**

T/R1444 Saw Dust Catcher. Sturdy wire frame with translucent vinyl cover. Collects dust in crosscut, miter and bevel positions. Fits R1250, R1350, R1450, 7740/3421, 7770/3426 machines and fits other models if modified **$20.95**

WARRANTY Black & Decker warrants this product for one year from date of purchase. We will repair without charge, any defects due to faulty material or workmanship. Please return the complete unit, transportation prepaid, to any Black & Decker Service Center or Authorized DeWalt Service Station listed in your owner's manual. This warranty does not apply to accessories or damage caused where repairs have been made or attempted by others.

DeWalt ®
Stationary Power Tools/A Division of The Black and Decker Manufacturing Co., Lancaster, Pa. 17604

DeWalt®

The greatest choice of saw capacities, arm lengths and power ratings in the industry.

FOUR 14" MODELS

Models 3511, 3516, 3521, 3526

2 Arm sizes. All models cut 4⁷⁄₁₆″ deep, the maximum for any 14″— or 4⅛″ with lower blade guard (OSHA required).

The 40″ Arm Models give the greatest capacity of any 14″ saw: Cross cuts 1″ material up to 24″. Rips to 37⅞″ wide.

Electrical controls are of the magnetic type with low voltage at the operator's switch. "No-voltage" protection is provided. 3-leg overload protection on 3-phase models.

Model	Arm Size	HP	Voltage	Phase	Cycle
3511	32″	3	230	1	60
3516	40″	3	230	1	60
3521	32″	5	230/460	3	60
3526	40″	5	230/460	3	60

TWO 12" MODELS

Models 3431 and 3436

Repeatable accuracy and speed make it a favorite of contractors, builders, industrial maintenance departments. Cuts a full 4″ deep with lower blade guard. Automatic built-in motor brake. Totally enclosed motor.

Model 3436 features electrical controls of the magnetic type with low voltage at the operators switch plus "no voltage" and 3-leg overload protection.

Model	Continuous Duty HP	Total Developed HP	Voltage	Phase	Cycle
3431	1½	3½	120/208-240	1	60
3436	2	5	208-240/480	3	60

TWO 10" MODELS

Models 3421 and 3427

Cuts 3″ deep. Built-in motor brake, manual on 3421, automatic on 3427. Front push-button switch with fingertip 115V control. Safety-key lock. Direct drive fan cooled motor. Model 3427 has heavy duty totally enclosed motor.

Model	Developed HP	Voltage	Phase	Cycle
3421	2	120V	1	60
3427	2¼	120/208-240V	1	60

DeWALT 10" POWER MITER BOX
16 Features prove it's the world's finest miter.

Power and accuracy for faster, better finish and trim in home building, cabinet making, picture framing, boat building, mobile home production. Cuts wood, plastics, compositions, thin-wall lightweight aluminum extrusions. It's the finest, most accurate miter!

■ One-handed trigger release miter pivot handle and lock for fast, smooth, accurate, positive angle selections. ■ Dependable 1½ HP gear-driven Black & Decker/DeWalt motor. No belt to break—downtime eliminated! ■ Exclusive automatic brake stops blade in seconds. Just release trigger. Cuts production time. ■ Miters up to 47°, R and L. No slop! Miters out-of-square corners. Plus 12 more high performance features.

DeWALT 3-WAY PANEL SAW
Cross cut ■ Right hand rip ■ Left hand rip

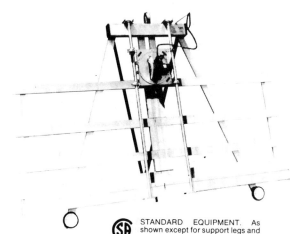

STANDARD EQUIPMENT. As shown except for support legs and wheels, optional at extra cost.

Fastest, cleanest, most accurate cutting...at low cost per cut for plywood, fibreboard, hardboard, thin aluminum sheets, tileboard, Plexiglas®, plastic laminates, doors, corkboard, metallic chipboard, corrugated paper, asbestos board, compositions.

Here are just a few of the features of this DeWalt Panel Saw: ■ NEW! Extruded Aluminum Structural members for extra strength, rigidity and maintained accuracy. ■ NEW! Heavy-duty counterbalance spring designed for the life of the saw. ■ NEW! Rips two ways, to right or left for flexibility, convenience; adapts to flow of operation. ■ EXCLUSIVE! Nonmarring face boards will not scratch material to be cut.

Model	B&D Motor	Standard Voltage	Shipping Weight	Cutting Capacities Panel Width	Material Thickness
3481	2 HP	115V* 25 to 60 cycles single phase AC or DC	157 lbs.	48" (+ 2 inches)	2"
3486	2 HP		167 lbs.	60" (+ 2 inches)	2"

*220 volt motor is available. Contact factory for price and availability. Motors carry full Black & Decker Warranty.

DeWALT 6",7" & 8" BENCH GRINDERS

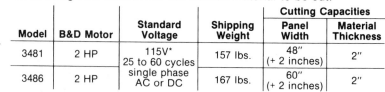

MODEL 3455

NO. 3451 6"
WITH EYE SHIELDS
NO. 3452 6"
WITH ILLUMINATED
EYE SHIELDS

NO. 3453 7"
WITH EYE SHIELDS
NO. 3454 7"
WITH ILLUMINATED
EYE SHIELDS

NO. 3455 8"
WITH EYE SHIELDS
(1 PHASE)
NO. 3456 8"
WITH EYE SHIELDS
(3 PHASE)

Smooth running, dependable grinders...designed for many applications in toolrooms, welding, woodworking and machine shops, schools, factories, homes, farms, garages, and maintenance shops. Six DeWalt models to choose from for tough, heavy-duty use.

All models are Underwriters' Laboratories-listed, comply with OSHA standards, rated for continuous heavy-duty use, have heavy-duty ball-bearings with eye shields. For greater visibility in all grinding operations, 6" Model No. 3452 and 7" Model No. 3454 come equipped with 2 15-watt illuminated eye shields.

	No. 3451	No. 3452	No. 3453	No. 3454	No. 3455	No. 3456
Wheel Size	6" dia. ⅝" face ½" hole	6" dia. ¾" face ½" hole	7" dia. ¾" face ½" hole	7" dia. ¾" face ½" hole	8" dia. ⅞" face ⅝" hole	8" dia. ⅞" face ⅝" hole
Motor Rating	⅓ HP	⅓ HP	⅓ HP	⅓ HP	¾ HP	¾ HP
Phase	1	1	1	1	1	3

STATIONARY POWER TOOLS
A Division of The Black & Decker Manufacturing Co.
Lancaster, Penna. 17604

ADVERTISING

Technical writers rarely produce entire ads without help, but you should know enough basic advertising to communicate with media representatives. You may be called upon to rewrite or edit ads prepared by an ad agency. Or you may have to come up with creative ways to distinguish your firm's copy from your competitors'. The newspaper, radio, or television sales representative may be generating copy for twelve different auto parts supply houses and not be able to spend the time required to make your ads distinctive. You may need to feed ideas to this copywriter.

Industrial advertising is done for many reasons. Ads aim to find new markets for established products, to introduce new products, to give information about product uses, or to publicize the name of the firm (known as institutional advertising). In print and radio advertising, the text (copy) is all-important, while the visuals communicate the message in television ads. The layout (arrangement on the page) in newspapers and periodicals also contributes to the readership of the ad.

General Rules for Preparing Advertising

1. Know your viewers, listeners, or readers. These considerations will help you determine where and when your ad will run. Will it run on television or radio during the pro football game or during the afternoon talk shows? Will the ad appear in popular, semitechnical, or technical periodicals? Television and radio stations, newspapers, and other publications can give you a detailed breakdown of their audiences' needs, interests, and preferences.
2. Have something specific to say to your audience. Emphasize time, money, or labor saved by your product, or focus on its superior quality, reliability, or performance.
3. Keep the message simple and direct. Use understandable language. Stress only one theme or product.
4. Be professional. State your claims and then document each claim with testimonials, statistics, demonstrations, or other appropriate support.

The Five I's

As you write an ad, try to accomplish these five things:

1. *Interest* the audience. Get their attention by showing or saying something pleasant or helpful that relates them to the product.
2. *Indicate* the product. Smoothly move from the initial point of interest to the product.
3. *Inform* the viewer or reader about the product. Let the camera show and demonstrate, or let the visuals and copy describe the product.
4. *Inspire* the viewer, reader, or listener to use the product and enjoy the promised benefits.
5. *Invite* the audience to take action—by placing an order or going to a certain place to buy the product.

Basic Layout

There is an endless variety of layouts for ads. But most of these stem from six basic formats:

1. *The Mondrian* layout (named for a design originated by an artist of the early part of the century) is based on good proportion achieved by using a fitted set of vertical and horizontal rectangles, all in different sizes. These lines and the resulting rectangles of type or art tend to break the ad into sections that may be scattered optically but that are balanced informally.
2. *The picture window* layout involves a generous display of picture and tight editing of copy so it will fit the small space remaining, the space often below the picture. The copy is usually lined up with some axis within the picture.
3. *The frame* layout uses a border to frame the headline and copy placed in the center of the ad. This frame prevents the ad from being associated with another on the same page, but it does decrease the optical size of the ad.
4. *The circus* layout is loud because it is filled with reverse blocks, large type, sunbursts, tilts, and other attention-getters. It gives the impression of disarray, but all the elements must be organized into a unified pattern. This format gets variety through size, shape, and tone changes within the ad, but is difficult to do well. Grocery store ads often use this format.
5. *The multipanel* layout is the comic strip technique with photographs replacing the drawings and with conversation set in type beneath the pictures instead of in the balloons within the drawing.
6. *The silhouette* layout has its elements arranged to form an overall silhouette. The side view is used with the white space pushed to the outside to form an irregular frame. Some element of the ad should touch the very edge so the white frame will not become an even halo that could lessen, optically, the ad's size.

Examples of these layouts may be found in *Advertising Management Handbook* (1977) by Richard Stansfield, Dartnell Corporation of Chicago, Illinois, publishers.

Principles of Design

After the basic layout has been selected, all the elements within the ad must be examined. Five principles of design should be applied to each element and to the arrangement of elements as a whole:

1. Balance
2. Proportion
3. Sequence (directional pattern)

4. Unity
5. Emphasis (one element dominating the others)

As many of these principles—and as much of each principle—must be worked into each ad as possible. When you have arranged the elements into a good layout, see if you can remove one of them without hurting the ad's balance, its proportion, and its unity. If you can, the basic structure is questionable.

Copyfitting

Copyfitting includes tracing letters from a type-specimen book or lettering them freehand in their approximate sizes. Then the copy must be fitted in the allotted space for the ad. If the copy is too long (1) the layout can be adjusted to fit it, (2) a smaller typeface can be used, (3) extra space between lines of type, the leading, can be removed, or (4) the copy can be shortened. If the copy is too short (1) the layout can be adjusted, (2) a larger typeface can be used, (3) more leading can be used, or (4) a few words can be added to the text.

Body Type. In most cases, when trying to decide how much space typed copy will take in an ad, you may count the characters in a line and multiply that average by the number of lines. Decide the width of the copy block and select the typeface and size. Consult a copyfitting chart to find out how many characters you can get in the line width you have chosen. Divide the total number of characters in the manuscript by the number of characters you get in a line of type. Now you have the number of lines of type you can expect. Multiply the number of lines by the point size of the type. (Be sure to allow for any leading.) Convert the points into picas.

Square Inch. An easier but less accurate way to fit copy is through the square-inch method. Draw several one-inch squares over random parts of copy already set in the type style and size you want and count the number of words in each. Take an average. Then count the words in the type manuscript and divide by the average number. This will give you the number of square inches of typed matter you can expect.

Column Inch. A variation of the square-inch method is the column-inch method. You must find copy set exactly as you want your copy set; simply measure a block an inch deep and then count the words. Do it in a few more places and then take the average. Divide the average into the number of words in the typed manuscript and you will have the number of column inches the ad will take in type.

Headline. The headline can be considered as part of the copy. It must catch the attention of the reader; in fact, about 75% of the readers usually notice only the headline. It should always include *a, an,* and *the* since the rhythm is more important in advertising than the amount of space used. It need not contain a subject and predicate, but merely be a tag or a label. The headline should convey the essence of the message of the whole ad; it can report the facts, offer advice, make a promise, give an order, stir up curiosity, or single out a certain segment of the audience.

There are basically six different arrangements of advertising headlines: (1) the straight across line, (2) flush left lines, (3) centered lines, (4) flush right lines, (5) ragged left and right lines, and (6) ragged left and right lines with an axis involving part of either the right or the left edge of the headline. See Figure 11.1.

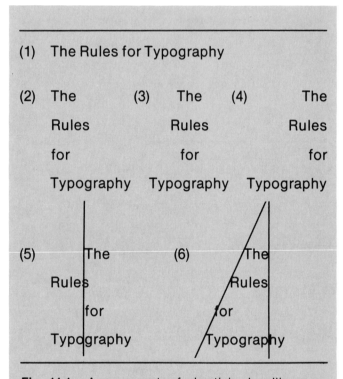

Fig. 11.1. Arrangements of advertising headlines.

Color

Color lures the reader into the ad and thus sells more of the product or service. Psychologists believe that extroverts are more responsive to color, and anyone who responds to color is more easily influenced by shade than by shape. The additional cost of using color in long-run ads is minimal.

There is no such thing as an ugly color, just unattractive combinations and uses of color. Bright colors radiate and expand the size of the object. Cool colors are calming greens and blues; warm colors are stimulating reds and yellows. Warm colors seem to advance from the page, and cool colors recede. In the famous "Uncle Sam Needs You" pose, the hand appears in warm tones while the area around it is painted in cool tones.

For more information on basic advertising principles, consult one of the many excellent texts in the field. A recommended source is *Advertising Management Handbook.*

Television Advertising

Television advertising is intended to sell the product or the firm. But sometimes the best-remembered commercials are not the most effective sales motivators. "I can't believe I ate the whole thing" became a popular catch phrase across the country, but there was no increase in the sales of Alka-Seltzer so the company changed ad agencies. Yet Charmin has built a very successful campaign around the tag-line "Squeezably soft."

In spite of the popularity of television slogans and phrases, the visual impact is often most important. You should plan the visuals first and then write the audio (copy). Variety is a must, so try to incorporate videotape, slides, and film in the video and several types of voices in the audio.

A recent trend in television commercials has been to show competing brands and prove that yours is best. Just remember to impress the viewer with your product and not that of the competition. And whatever the current trend, creativity is always desirable. The do's and don'ts listed here will increase your creativity and contribute to the overall effectiveness of the commercial.

FOR EFFECTIVE COMMERCIALS—LIVE AND TAPE

DO'S

In copy, speak the viewer's own language.

Concentrate on the picture side first and add the audio copy later.

Use interesting staging and appropriate props and keep the pictures moving or changing with motivation.

Run through the pictures without the sound. Make the visual side tell a complete story. Strive for unusual and memorable graphics at all times.

Try to involve viewers emotionally.

Use optical and electronic effects where possible in the tape commercial. Make it creatively interesting and technically right for production.

Stress close-ups to make your message personal, vivid, and more effective.

Use situations, questions, dramatic statements by people, cartoons, etc.

Keep the progression of ideas, pictures, and sales points moving to your objective.

Strive for extremely clear visuals.

Create mood and effect lighting to enhance the commercial.

Let the camera show and demonstrate products.

Prove selling features as you would in person.

Feature *one major* theme or item in a commercial.

DON'TS

Don't talk too much and especially don't talk *advertisingese.*

Don't develop the words first . . . this is radio and print technique.

Don't rely on the announcer's sheer personal magnetism to hold the audience even for one 60-second commercial.

Don't rely on the combination of radio-style copy and whatever pictorial sequences are at hand and easiest to use. Don't write too much copy.

Don't create unrealistic situations and hope to convince.

Don't write a *live commercial* and simply record it on tape.

Don't wait more than a few establishing seconds before coming in close.

Don't use printed headlines to arrest attention.

Don't use an unrelated opening or *stopper* merely to get attention.

Avoid cluttered backgrounds in pictures.

Don't rely on flat lighting.

Don't merely mention their benefits.

Don't just point to the product and *talk* selling features.

Don't use television to list items as you use newspapers.

———————————

The following specimen television commercials illustrate various degrees of creativity and incorporate the 5 I's into the video and audio.

	VIDEO	(1) *1 minute* AUDIO

(Peppy music up and under)

Interest George Washington   "I cannot tell a lie." Gordon's in Pittsburgh asked me
and indicate   to say a few words about their big Presidents' Sale-A-

Inform pantsuits   Bration going on. They have ladies' pantsuits for just

slacks $9.00, slacks for $5.00, and children's clothes too.

girls' pants   Girls' slacks are just $3.00 and toddlers' pants are

$2.47. Styles have changed since my day but Gordon

prices are pretty low compared to other places. Honest

Abe likes Gordon's prices too.

Abe Lincoln   "I'll agree, George. Did you see those men's

coveralls   coveralls for just $19.00 when they were $25.97 or

jeans   jeans at $8.00—shirts, jackets, everything I need. Wish

jackets   we had Gordon's a long time ago. I've got my eye on

rugs   those room-size rugs for $18.00. Sure beats the cold

wood floors we had in the cabin. Hey look! There's ole

Thomas Jefferson   Tom Jefferson. Wonder what he's lookin' for. . . ."

Inspire Other shoppers   Well, it's a real Presidents' Sale all right. It's hard to

decide with so many great things to choose from. So

everyone come on out to Gordon's today. The sale

ends tomorrow and they have everything in one store

Invite Store sign   at 3001 N. Broadway. Gordon's, Pittsburg.

---

(2) *30 seconds*

Interest Cowboys rounding up cattle (Sound effects of the cattle roundup.)

Saddle up and head for the big "Roundup Sale" on

Indicate   Quasar Color televisions at BARRESSI BROTHERS

in Arla.

Inform	Roomful of televisions	The whole herd are heading for the savings they can get on their old televisions during the sale.
	Close-up of Quasar	Real double-barreled savings . . . you get the quality of Quasar Color TV . . . at reduced prices.
Inspire	Service personnel	And you get the same fine service dependability you've counted on from BARRESSI BROTHERS.
	Person lassoing the TV	Com'mon pardner! Lasso your old TV and trade it in
Invite	Sign with name and address	for a new model at BARRESSI BROTHERS APPLIANCES in Arla.

---

(3) *20 seconds*

Interest and indicate	trees and rock	New shipments of trees, shrubs, and decorative rock are now on hand at COPE NURSERY in Springfield . . . ready
	*Shrubs and trees	*for immediate planting. Come to 4th and Highland for best selection at lowest prices. Low overhead allows COPE NURSERY
Inform and inspire		
	*Shrubs and trees	*to provide you with QUALITY NURSERY STOCK at BIG SAVINGS . . . from small shrubs to
Invite	*Picture and name	*beautiful trees. COPE NURSERY, 4th and Highland, in Springfield, growers of beautiful trees and evergreens.

---

(4)   *1 minute*

Interest Announcer keyed over picture of interior sound department	If you want a component quality music system but don't want to fool around with all those little boxes, here's how to get what you want in one easy step. Come into MARDICK'S in Fort Henry and
Indicate *Zoom in to close-up of component system.	*listen to the new Sony Integrated Component Music Systems. Sony has taken the finest components—tun-
Inform *Pan of the items	*ers, amplifiers, pre-amps, turntables, and cassette and 8-track cartridge player recorders—and integrated them into compact music systems that will please both your *ears* and your pocketbook. And these components include
*Fast pan of items as names are mentioned	*some of the most highly regarded names in the world of sound . . . names like Dual, Pickering, BSR, and, of course, SONY. Every system features a 3-speed auto-manual professional quality turntable with a cueing lever for manual placement of the tone arm. There are
Inspire *Announcer keyed into showroom again	*systems for the most demanding audiophile. And if you're on a budget there are systems with a quality of sound you couldn't duplicate on your own for the same price. Come listen
Invite *Mardick sign and exterior	*to them at MARDICK'S of Fort Henry, on city route 69 across from the Post Office.

Radio Advertising

The variety and creativity so necessary in television commercials are also vital to the success of a radio advertisement. The radio ad must also interest the listeners, indicate the product, inform about the product, inspire the listeners to buy, and invite them to make their purchases at a specific place. When you are informing the listeners about your product, you should repeat the key point in several different ways so it will be remembered.

The following specimen radio commercials were prepared by Ford Motor Company for their local dealers. These tapes can be ordered by local dealers for a nominal fee and provide an inexpensive, professional means of airing a sales message. Personalized radio scripts are also offered free of charge to retailers by some large companies. If you must write your own radio ads or edit those written by local sales representatives, these ads can serve as models of good selling pitches.

TAPED RADIO COMMERCIALS

Here are the messages your taped radio commercials will be carrying. They begin with Ford's bouncy ". . . looking for excitement . . ." musical chorus introduction, swing into a 30-second announcer product message, then back to the vocal chorus, followed by space for your own 10-second tag line (see suggested copy). They provide you with an inexpensive and professional way to put your message on the air. Order your tape today.

LIMITED EDITION FULL LINE 50-SECOND

VOCAL: If you're looking for excitement, come look at Ford. If you're looking for good value . . .

ANNCR: Hold it, hold it, change that song because your Ford Dealer has news. Real news about his Limited Edition Sale based on manufacturer's price reductions to dealers on special value models. Sportier looking Mustang II's that include added features in the base sticker price. A specially equipped, specially priced Limited Edition of the elegant mid-size Elite. A strikingly beautiful specially priced Torino that you've never been able to buy before. And the Ford Truck Explorer Specials with special prices and options. Limited Editions . . . limited quantities . . . special value . . . at your local Ford Dealer's Limited Edition Sale. So change that song.

VOCAL: So come and buy now, buy now, buy now the value's hot. What a sale it is your Ford Dealer's got. What a sale it is he's got.

Suggested 10-Sec. Tag—Local Live Announcer: Buy now at (Hometown Ford) for extra value on Limited Edition Ford Mustang II's, Torinos, Elites, and Explorer Special Trucks.

LIMITED EDITION MUSTANG II 50-SECOND

VOCAL: If you're looking for excitement, come look at Ford. If you're looking for good value . . .

ANNCR: Hold it, hold it, change that song. Because your Ford Dealer has news. Real news about his Limited Edition Mustang II's. Now during his Limited Edition Sale you get a $137 worth of added manufacturer's suggested retail value on these Mustang II's. Including selected 2-tone paint and trim with matching sporty interior and styled steel wheels. All at the standard Mustang II base sticker price. The Limited Edition Mustang II's Hardtops or 2 + 2's. Beautiful values you can buy right now while supply lasts at your local Ford Dealer Limited Edition Sale. So change that song.

VOCAL: So come and buy now, buy now, buy now the value's hot. What a sale it is your Ford Dealer's got. What a sale it is he's got.

Suggested 10-Sec. Tag—Local Live Announcer: Hurry on into (Hometown Ford) while we still have a fine selection of Limited Edition Sale cars with real values.

PERSONALIZED RADIO SCRIPTS

MUSTANG II:
30-SECOND

ANNCR: Now you can give the Mustang II an even sportier look and added value . . . just by saying, "Limited Edition Sale" to (Hometown Ford). That's right. Now, you can get a Limited Edition Mustang II with selected two-tone paint and trim and matching sporty interior and styled steel wheels . . . all at the standard Mustang II base sticker price. Available in 2-Door Hardtop or 3-Door 2 + 2 models. Limited quantities. Come in and save at (Hometown Ford).

TORINO:
60-SECOND

ANNCR: If you're looking for excitement and value . . . look to (Hometown Ford). Now, during our Limited Edition Sale, you can get a specially priced, strikingly beautiful Limited Edition Torino that you've never been able to buy before. This Torino has half-vinyl roof, opera windows, special interior, dual racing mirrors, sport wheel covers, and your choice of selected colors . . . even Silver Metallic . . . all for 159 dollars less than the total retail value of items added to the base Torino. (This is based on traditional suggested retail pricing.) Of course, you also get the popular value features already standard on Torino like: automatic transmission, power brakes and steering. Come to (Hometown Ford) and see this beautiful Torino value that you can buy *now* during our Limited Edition Sale. Act now . . . time's limited.

TORINO:
30-SECOND

ANNCR: If you're looking for excitement and value . . . look to (Hometown Ford). Now, during our Limited Edition Sale, you can get a specially priced, strikingly beautiful Limited Edition Torino with half-vinyl roof, opera windows, special interior, racing mirrors, and in a choice of colors . . . even Silver Metallic . . . for 159 dollars less than the total retail value of items added to the base Torino. (This is based on traditional suggested retail pricing.) Quantities are limited. Buy now for extra value at (Hometown Ford) during our Limited Edition Sale.

(Courtesy Ford Motor Company [2])

Advertising in Newspapers and Semitechnical Periodicals

An effective newspaper ad or ad for a semitechnical periodical includes (1) the attention-getting headline, (2) the personal approach of *you* and *your,* (3) the data on capacities, ratings, and delivery, (4) the expression of willingness to help the reader, and (5) the coupon for encouraging inquiries.

The headlines below are forceful enough to attract the attention of the nonprofessional, and all feature some benefit to the reader.

"Now! Run Your Car without Spark Plugs"
"What This Country Needs Is a Good Abrasive Planer for under $12,000"
"Forget about Fuel Shortages"
"Waste Is Fuel without a Gatz/Rennicke Metered Feeding Device"

"If You Don't Believe You Can Improve Quality and Reduce Costs, Ask AP about Yorkite"

Data should be explained and reinforced by illustrations having some connection with the heading. Tell your story with pictures so the reader with little specialized information can understand. Photographs are best for installation views and cutaway drawings for the actual workings of the product. Charts and graphs are suitable for newspaper and periodical ads because the reader has time to study them.

The following specimen ads should be examined for general effectiveness. Check them for the attention-getting headline, the supporting illustrations, the play on words, the personal approach, and willingness to help the customer.

Headline

ENGINEERING, INC.
3011 POWER DRIVE (18TH & MERRIAM LANE)
KANSAS CITY, KANS. 66106   (913) 831-3733

NEW, LARGER CAPACITY
AKIN PORTABLE HYDRAULIC
Filter & Pumping Units

Photograph

Model EA 8166-1800/1500 gal. cap. per hr.

Data

CLEAN HYDRAULIC OILS! CLEAN CUTTING FLUIDS! CLEAN SOLVENTS! By recirculating while in the machine. . . OR WHILE TRANSFERRING FROM Barrel to Machine, Machine to Barrels, Barrels to Barrels. Clear plastic tubing. Filter gauge indicates when dirty. Filter as fine as you want. 10 micron standard. SAVE MAN HOURS, VALUABLE OILS, SOLVENTS SOLUTIONS.

"You" attitude

Make Akin headquarters for Air & Hydraulic Equipment.

(Courtesy Engineering, Inc. [3])

AUTOMATIC WELD-LOC POLY STRAPPER

Headline

Photograph

The Automatic Weld-Loc Poly Strapper is manually operated with push-button or foot switch, or can be made fully automatic. Compact and portable. Unique strapping material used is available in 3/8" or 1/2" AMS widths. Extra strength through embossed design. Heat sealed joint is strong, up to 90% of band strength. Won't pop in cold weather. Call Alexanders today for more information and a free demonstration.

Data

"You" attitude

ALEXANDERS MATERIAL HANDLING
800 HICKORY   816-474-6290   KANSAS CITY, MISSOURI

(Courtesy Alexanders Material Handling [4])

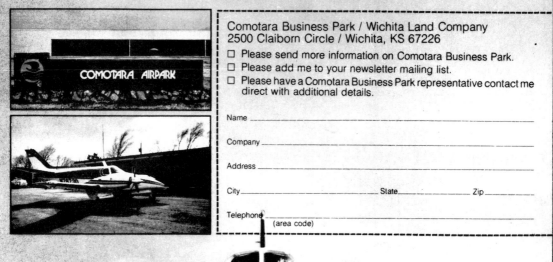

(Courtesy Comotara Business Park [5])

The following two-page *Farmland News* ad was designed as a four-color presentation.

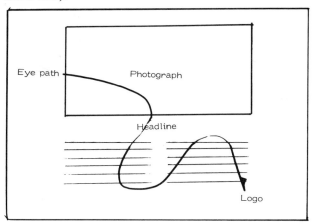

(Courtesy Farmland Industries, Inc. [6])

Advertising in Technical Periodicals

Advertisements in technical periodicals are intended for the highly skilled professional audience. The interest of the reader is assumed, so attention-getting headlines are less important. There are few plays on words and a more formal approach is used. However, illustrations are still necessary to attract the reader and to explain the product, and the tone is still one of willingness to help the customer.

Because the advertisements in technical journals are intended to inform the specialized reader and because the products and services advertised are often complex, such ads can consist of several pages. Cutaway and exploded drawings as well as photographs are important to the message; prices are not quoted when the product or service must be tailored to each individual client. In such cases, the potential customer is invited to write for more information.

Eye path is important. Tests show the eyes are attracted to the upper half of the page—and to the left side before the right side. Therefore the illustration is usually placed at the top of the one-page ad and used as a lead-in to the title which, in turn, directs the eyes to the text and finally to the logo (identification of the advertiser).

Headlines and subheads are easier to read in caps and lower-case letters rather than in all caps, and the text is easier to read when arranged in copy blocks of no more than 40 characters. Indented paragraphs and *widows* (lines of only a few words) contribute to easy reading and give an impression of space.

Five or six elements make the most striking ad: perhaps a photograph, headline, two copy blocks, and the logo. Color should be used where there is some justification for it: it can tie one element to another, define the eye path, highlight key words, attract attention, indicate action, separate the product from the background, show the color of the product if color is important (the orange of a hunting jacket, for instance), or identify the company (yellow for Kodak).

The following specimen ad provides data on a complex product and is suitable for publication in technical journals. This two-page advertisement uses the full-page photograph on the left to *lead* the reader into the ad. The eye path moves from the heading to the copy blocks—which are linked by the cutaway drawing—to the logo. Notice the lower-case headline, indented paragraphs, and *widows* that give a feeling of space.

Direct Mail Sales Letters

A special kind of promotional piece that you may be called upon to write or edit for your company is the direct mail sales letter. This letter, along with accompanying flyers, brochures, and order forms, allows you to make a detailed written presentation about your company's products or services. It is usually sent via third class bulk mail to sales prospects on a direct mail list you purchase from a professional direct mail broker or to those on your own in-house mailing list compiled from past sales and inquiry records. Sending a direct mail sales letter to a special list of sales prospects allows you to provide more information than in a catalog listing and at a lower cost per prospect than most mass media advertising. Firms that use direct mail often do extensive testing to see what type of package works best.

The basic direct mail letter attempts to persuade the reader to take some action: either purchasing a product or service or contacting a sales representative.

Form. The length of a direct mail letter is important. You should say enough to present your product or case effectively, but not so much that the reader will resist reading the entire letter. The first paragraph (or lead) is

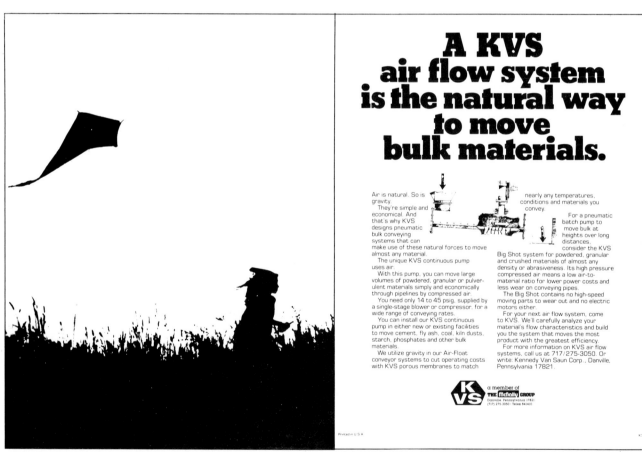

(Courtesy McNally Pittsburg Manufacturing Corporation [7])

vital. It should be intriguing enough to capture and sustain the reader's interest, yet brief enough so the reader will be encouraged to continue reading.

Placement of the facts also affects the success of a direct mail letter. An effective sales letter delays mentioning expense or responsibility until the reader's interest is thoroughly engaged.

Parts. There are four parts to the standard direct mail letter:

1. Attracting attention and getting the reader's interest
2. Arousing some desire in the reader
3. Persuading the reader that if a certain action is taken, a desire will be satisfied
4. Encouraging that action

To get the necessary attention, suggest that the reader's needs or desires are involved. Then clearly connect the reader's wants with the action you are proposing. Explain the assets of using your product, joining your organization, or participating in your activity. Stress the many benefits to the reader, using the personalized *you* and *your* approach. As you convince the reader of the value of a specific action, tactfully explain the steps that will lead to the intended results. Describe exactly what the reader must do and give a valid reason why action must be taken by a definite date. ("We must have your order before the special prepublication price ends April 15.")

Here is an example of a direct mail sales letter in which the reader's attention is secured, a certain desire is aroused, the benefits of satisfying that desire are stressed, and then action is requested.

Dear Mr. Hoffman:

Attention-getter Quite frankly, the American Express Card is not for everyone. And not everyone who applies for Cardmembership is approved.

Arousing of desire However, because we believe you will benefit from Cardmembership, I've enclosed a special invitation for you to apply for the most honored and prestigious financial instrument available to people who travel, vacation, and entertain.

Benefits that will satisfy the desire For example, you get the unique benefits of a worldwide network of offices of the American Express Company, its subsidiaries, and representatives. You can turn to these offices for a wide range of services that make traveling more enjoyable and worry-free.

You will have emergency cash available when you need it. For instance, the Card guarantees your personal check for up to $50 at participating hotels and motels across the United States where you're a registered guest. You can also cash a check for $50 in cash and up to $450 in Travelers Cheques at most travel offices of American Express Company, its subsidiaries, and representatives worldwide. And now Cardmembership includes $25,000 Travel Accident Insurance, too.

With the Card, you have unequaled mobility. It's welcomed by all the world's major airlines and car rental agencies. It pays for tires and auto servicing. You can use the Card to dine out or to outfit yourself with a set of new golf clubs. You can buy gifts, send flowers, cable money abroad, host a dinner, select a new wardrobe . . . all without cash in your pocket.

Many more additional benefits are fully described in the special Membership Brochure you receive when the Card is issued. Yet they are all yours to enjoy for the modest fee of only $20 a year.

Request for action Why not apply for Cardmembership today? All you have to do is fill out and mail the enclosed application by October 15, which marks the end of our "open membership" period. When your application is approved, we'll send along the Card, without delay.

Cordially,

(Courtesy American Express Company [8])

Product News Releases

Product news releases are a way of generating publicity and are considered free advertising. Some small firms depend on publication of releases as their only form of promotion until they can afford an advertising budget. Such releases are published in the new equipment or new products departments of industrial and business periodicals. The important thing to keep in mind when writing these releases is that they should be "news" and not overt promotion. Copy should be restrained and limited to the facts about the product. Well-prepared releases should be short, no more than one double-spaced page; have a good drawing or photograph of the product, in use if possible; and state the product capacity, size, use, and materials included in its construction.

A photograph enclosed with a product news release may cause the editor of a trade publication to give you double the space the text would take. Although you cannot pressure the editor into using your release, a genuinely newsworthy release should receive editorial consideration.

Honesty is especially important in all product releases. You should stress why this product will be helpful to readers. And you should prepare releases only for new products; a different color of paint or a variation in size does not make a product new. The following typical product news releases observe three basic guidelines: they avoid implied criticism of competitors' products, limit the release to the new product, and omit details of personnel who worked on its design and development.

Apex finder

Description

The Apex-Finder is a battery-operated, low-voltage, high-frequency oscillating apparatus designed to locate the apex of a root canal. The instrument has a large microammeter that compares the impedance of the patient's periodontal membrane at the neck of the tooth to the impedance of the same periodontal membrane at the apex of the canal. When the probe is touching the periodontal membrane at the neck of the tooth, the dial should be adjusted to give a reading of 40. The probe can then be inserted in the canal, and the apparatus will give readings of 20,30, or more. A reading of 40 should indicate that the apex has been reached. The

Uses

Apex Finder can reduce the number of radiographs needed.
Ellman Dental Mfg. Co., Inc.
1135 Railroad Ave
Hewlett, NY 11557

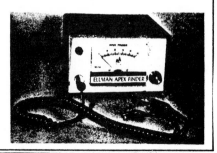

Photo

Casting system

Description

The CA Chrono-Matic casting system functions on the basis of vacuum and pressure. The alloy is melted in a thermostatically controlled electric furnace with temperature settings up to 2,500 F. Open flames and bottled gas are not required. According to the manufacturer, the CA Chrono-Matic is simple and economical to operate and uses a minimum of precious alloy because vents and reservoirs are not necessary. The system, which requires less than 1 sq ft of space, runs on 115-v, 15-amp electric outlet and house air (60 to 120 psi), eliminating the need for flammable bottled gas. The unit needs no special mounting. There are no rotating or rapidly

Uses

moving components. The system features a stainless steel casting chamber.
Whaledent, International
236 Fifth Ave
New York, 10001

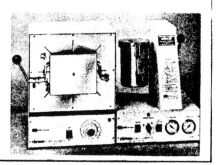

Photo

(Courtesy American Dental Association [9])

SUMMARY

Catalogs and television, radio, and newspaper advertising copy are parts of technical writing when technical descriptions and explanations are involved. As in other types of technical descriptions and explanations, the audience is of prime importance. Catalogs are buyer oriented; advertising copy is seller oriented.

The catalog gives brief, logical listings of a company's products. Each listing describes the product, explains its applications, any of its limitations, and the price. There should also be many informative and easy-to-read illustrations. The steps in writing a catalog include collecting the data and illustrations, outlining the data, writing the rough draft, checking the facts, polishing the rough draft, and arranging for printing.

There is a wide range of industrial advertising copy, but each ad should include the 5 I's: interesting the

viewers, listeners, or readers; indicating the product; informing the viewers, listeners, or readers; inspiring them to buy; and inviting them to buy at a specific place. The *informing* section should be simple and support your claims.

When planning a television commercial, consider the video first and then the audio. Arrange the visuals so they tell the whole story about one major theme or item. Stress close-ups to make your message personal and vivid and to involve the viewer emotionally. Let the camera demonstrate the product, and keep the pictures and sales points moving toward your objective.

Variety in repetition is the key to effective radio advertising. Sometimes the manufacturer will supply tapes and scripts for live spots for a small fee. These tapes and scripts can serve as models for ads written locally. The manufacturer will not only supply advertising but frequently will also offer the retailer co-op funds to help pay for advertising promoting the product.

The headline, the *you* approach, data and illustrations, and obvious willingness to help the reader are all found in good newspaper and periodical ads.

The direct mail sales letter is a detailed, written presentation of the product or service sent to a special list of sales prospects. The attention-getting lead paragraph, statement of facts, and call for reader action are important elements in a successful letter.

Product news releases that are short, include an illustration, and describe a new product can be called free advertising when they appear in the new products column of trade magazines.

Catalogs, advertising copy, direct mail sales letters, and product news releases should have the clarity, economy, and accuracy of all technical writing. Although you may not be asked to do all the writing for a catalog or other advertising, you should be familiar with the basic principles so you can communicate with media sales representatives and agencies.

WRITING ASSIGNMENTS

1. Write a one-minute television commercial (about 160-word text) advertising a business that you might be operating after graduating. Plan the slides, film, and background music you will use. Then write the audio.
2. Plan and write a twenty-second television spot advertising an after-Thanksgiving sale at a local department store.
3. Write a thirty-second television spot for the local Honda dealer stressing the Christmas gift theme.
4. Write a one-minute television commercial for a bookstore stressing the graduation theme. Plan the background music and the use of slides in the video.
5. The representative of a bakery tells you that he does not want the announcer holding up a loaf of bread and *talking* about it in his new one-minute television commercial. He wants ingenuity and creativity. It is Easter time. Write the commercial.
6. You work for a large organization and have been assigned the job of planning the attention-getting opening of three radio commercials (one minute each). Each commercial will run once a day for a

week; then another commercial will run for a week, etc. The *attention-getter* for each of the three commercials should be coordinated in some way.
7. Plan the layout and text for a Fourth of July Sale for an auto parts store or for a grocery store. This will be a half page newspaper spread.
8. Prepare two periodical ads, each advertising a car. One ad should be suitable for a popular magazine and the other suitable for a technical publication.
9. Prepare a new product release for some piece of equipment needed in your major area.
10. Assume that you own a business after graduation. You are preparing a catalog. Plan the layout and text for one page on which you advertise three items.
11. Observe three ads presented during this last week. Analyze the use of the five I's in these ads (either stated or implied) and rate them 1, 2, and 3 for their general effectiveness. Justify your rating system.
12. Persuade a recent graduate of your school to purchase a one-year membership in the alumni association for $10.
13. Write a direct mail letter to a list of 20,000 animal hospital supervisors explaining your company's new animal restraint harness. Offer readers the option of placing a direct order or having a sales representative call.

REFERENCES

1. DeWalt Trade Catalog. Lancaster, PA: The Black and Decker Manufacturing Co., n.d.
2. *Taped Radio Commercials: Personalized Radio Scripts.* Dearborn, MI: The Ford Motor Co., 1976.
3. Engineering, Inc. 18th & Merriam Lane, Kansas City, KS 66106.
4. Alexanders Material Handling Co., Inc. 800 Hickory, Kansas City, MO 64101.
5. Comotara Business Park. 2500 Claiborn Circle, Wichita, KS 67226.
6. Farmland Industries, Inc. P.O. Box 7305, Kansas City, MO 64116.
7. The McNally Pittsburg Manufacturing Corp. Pittsburg, KS 66762.
8. American Express Co. Card Division. 770 Broadway, New York, NY 10003.
9. "New Products Information," *Journal of the American Dental Association,* Feb. 1976, pp. 448, 450.

CHAPTER 12

Technical Writing as a Career

THE purpose of this textbook has been to prepare you to handle successfully the writing chores with which you will be confronted before graduation and later during the first years of your supervisory-management level careers. Throughout, the emphasis has been on training you to write effectively in your chosen area of work even though your principal interest is not writing. Writing is simply a valuable skill for you to acquire because it can call attention to your technical skills and help you advance in your field.

However, those of you who write well should also consider technical writing as a career. The professional technical writer has been in great demand for the last three decades. Every year the necessity of communicating technical information in the clearest, simplest way possible has become more urgent.

DUTIES

The professional technical writer prepares written work under the name of the company or acts as a silent partner in collaboration with the technical employees who must write. If you want to see your name in print, you should not enter this field because the technical writer must always remain anonymous.

Beginning technical writers are often responsible for handling correspondence, a formidable task when some companies take pride in answering every letter personally and not depending on form letters. The same standards of clarity, economy, restraint, and courtesy must be maintained for every letter regardless of the tone and content of the letters received. Your letters represent the company.

You will prepare progress reports to be submitted to

federal offices if you are working for a corporation with government contracts. It will be your job to communicate to the government exactly what your company is doing. Any government-regulated industry must hand in dozens of federal reports each year.

When a technical worker in your firm is asked to read a paper at a meeting, convention, or institute, you will play a vital role in the project. After the employee writes the rough draft of the paper, you will edit it for style, format, and content. In some organizations the technical worker merely describes the type of paper needed and then you write the rough draft as well.

You will have a wide range of daily duties. You may write articles, ads, and even biographical sketches for the plant newspaper whether it is *Farmland News, Plane Talk* (Boeing), *Penney News, Ford World,* or *Marketing World* (Hallmark). Many publications are consumer oriented and are more informative sales support than technical instructions. You may prepare instruction manuals, explain processes, analyze performance, and write feasibility or lab reports, depending on the product or service offered by your company. There is always the continuous process of creating maintenance manuals and inspection forms for new products while revising existing ones. Language skills are necessary for technical writing in large corporations because many current manuals must be translated into Spanish, French, German, Japanese, and other languages.

You will provide information to the news media by preparing releases that will be published in the name of the company or in the name of an administrative official and by giving editorial assistance to magazines that feature articles about your company. Such articles are then submitted to you for clearance and final approval of the data and illustrations. You must be willing to consult experts as you write: the technical personnel for factual input, the artists for visuals, public relations experts for clearances, and representatives of the legal department for analysis of the validity of supporting data.

At Ford Motor Company, for example, the duties of technical writers range from automotive research and design to describing the various technical aspects of the production automobile and its components. The media request information on innovations; and releases, booklets, and speeches must be prepared.[1]

The Commercial Publications Department at Beech Aircraft Corporation is divided into four specific areas: (1) Operation Data, (2) Maintenance Overhaul and Wiring Data, (3) Special Projects, and (4) Parts Catalog Data. These areas are so highly specialized that if a writer were to move from one area to another, it would mean some retraining.[2] The writer usually does most of the actual research himself from engineering documents or laboratory data and is responsible for its accuracy and timeliness. At Beech the writer oversees complete production of his materials to final camera-ready copy. The writer orders composition and art as required by the job and handles the proofreading, layout, and paste-up of the final copy.[3]

Technical writers at Farmland Industries, Inc., list speech writing, technical writing, human relations work, and preparation of legislative testimony and background material as their primary duties.[4] The agricultural technical writer may translate highly technical information on crops, machinery, and cattle into simple, readable articles for farm workers.[5]

The technical writers at Boeing report the following duties:

The primary duty of an engineering writer is to develop complete technical manuals to support systems, subsystems, and components. The manuals contain system-component descriptions, operating procedures, maintenance procedures, repair procedures, troubleshooting procedures (including fault isolation procedures), and component breakdowns. These procedures are developed by analyzing engineering drawings (blueprints), researching design documents, and application of personal engineering and scientific knowledge. During technical manual development, procedures are validated by the engineering writer and verified by actual performance with the customer to ensure technical accuracy and adequacy.[6]

The wide range of duties assigned technical writers makes it difficult to decide on their primary job functions. In the 1974 survey of members of the Society for Technical Communication, almost half the respondents saw their primary function as one of management. See Figure 12.1. One implication of these figures is that many technical writers function as management only part of the time and have many other responsibilities. The size of the technical writing department determines the types of duties assigned each writer; sometimes the management title is more in name than in fact.

Regardless of job classification, though, the types of media on which the respondents of the Society for Technical Communication survey work have remained the same over the years: manuals are still the primary assignments of a large portion of the respondents.

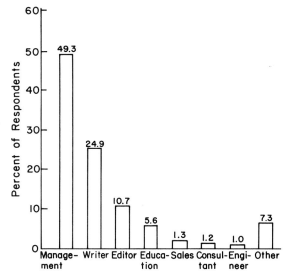

Fig. 12.1. Major job function.[7]

Significant gains occurred in the areas of presentation, technical books, and specifications. Smaller gains were found for proposals, procedures, catalogs, and house organs. Activity in the teaching area dropped the most from that of past years. See Table 12.1.

TABLE 12.1. Major work area[8]

Medium	1974 No.	1974 %	1970 No.	1970 %	Change in %
Manuals	588	20.8	473	35.8	−15.0
Reports	410	14.5	263	19.9	−5.4
Proposals	232	8.2	76	5.7	+2.5
Presentations	229	8.1	27	2.0	+6.1
Technical books	194	6.9	27	2.0	+4.9
Articles/journals	163	5.8	76	5.7	+0.1
Procedures	159	5.6	42	3.2	+2.4
Specifications	157	5.6	28	2.1	+3.5
Catalogs and parts lists	130	4.6	31	2.3	+2.3
House organs	92	3.3	8	0.6	+2.7
Advertising	85	3.0	20	1.5	+1.5
Information retrieval	83	2.9	27	2.0	+0.9
Textbooks	50	1.8	24	1.8	0.0
Technical film	45	1.6	9	0.7	+0.9
Sales/PR materials	26	0.9	36	2.7	−1.8
Teaching	18	0.6	68	5.2	−4.6
Training program	17	0.6			+0.6
Data processing	13	0.5	42	3.2	−2.7
Other	133	4.7	48	3.6	+1.1
	2,824	100	1,325	100	

TRAINING

Several years ago the large corporation looked for someone who had technical training and wrote well to develop as a technical writer. Now most corporations seem to be searching for graduates in English, journalism, advertising, or marketing who have some interest in technical work—on the theory that any new employee will have to be trained in a particular technical area anyway. As long as the applicant can describe a stapler or other office tool clearly and economically and can use headings and figures and tables effectively, that person is trainable.

However, Boeing technical writers report that technical training or experience is indeed necessary for an understanding of the product or technology involved. The technical writer does not have to know the same things the engineer had to know to design the product or the shop people had to know to manufacture it, but an understanding of the technical jargon associated with the technology is necessary for the writer to translate that jargon into understandable English.[9]

Notice in Table 12.2 that, at least among members of the Society for Technical Communication, technical writers with English and journalism degrees have increased from the 1970 survey to the 1974 survey. The 1970 and 1974 surveys also revealed that a large percentage of technical writers had bachelor's degrees. Technical writers often reveal work experiences on newspapers and trade publications. The agricultural technical writer must have practical work experience in the field; the mechanical engineer can write more successfully right out of college with little practical work in the mechanical engineering field.[11] Women have, in the past, been restricted from the technical writing fields due to their lack of training and experience in mechanical and other technical fields, but now they are preparing themselves.[12] Women are now listing a bachelor's degree, a year or two of technical experience, and on-the-job training.

In 1974 over one-third of the employers of technical

writers were in manufacturing; over 75% of the employers were in manufacturing, government, or educational institutions. Almost one-third of these employers hired 1,000–4,999 persons. See Tables 12.3 and 12.4.

TABLE 12.3. Employers of technical communicators[13]

Business	1974 No.	1974 %	1970 %
Manufacturing	445	34.9	
Government	193	15.1	17
Research and development	120	9.4	24
Printing/publishing services	117	9.2	7
Educational institutions	110	8.6	5
Data processing	62	4.9	
Consulting	59	4.6	
Mining/construction	16	1.2	
Bank, finance, insurance	15	1.2	
Medical	13	1.0	
Public relations/sales	12	0.9	
Public utilities	11	0.9	
Retired	8	0.6	
Professional societies	6	0.5	
Engineering	5	0.4	
Free lance	4	0.3	2
Trade magazines	3	0.3	
Engineering services	2	0.2	
Other	74	5.8	
Total	1,275	100	

TABLE 12.4. Total employees in respondents' plants[14]

Plant Size	No.	%
1–49	150	12.3
50–199	134	11.0
200–499	182	15.0
500–999	147	12.1
1,000–4,999	365	30.0
5,000 and over	238	19.6
Total	1,216	100

Some writers move up from within the company, products of in-house training programs calculated to help them handle their wide range of writing duties—for instance, training in blueprint reading and shop practices. Industrial seminars in technical writing are periodically offered free of charge to company personnel. In this program workers in technical areas may transfer to the technical writing department if they wish.

WORKING CONDITIONS, PAY, AND OPPORTUNITIES
Working Conditions

The technical writing department seems to be the focal point of the company with ringing telephones and clattering typewriters and office machines. The noise level is high because the usual working area is one large room either with no partitions or half partitions that do nothing to decrease the high noise level. In the technical

TABLE 12.2. Degrees of respondents[10]

Discipline	1974 No.	1974 %	1970 No.	1970 %	Change in %
Engineering	312	26.3	275	19.9	+6.4
English	289	24.3	173	12.5	+11.8
Science	133	11.2	58	4.2	+7.0
Journalism	115	9.7	127	9.2	+0.5
Business	95	8.0	59	4.3	+3.7
Fine and applied arts	53	4.5	4	0.3	+4.2
Education	35	3.0	64	4.6	−1.6
Technical communication	34	2.9	21	1.5	+1.4
History	15	1.3	19	1.4	−0.1
Mathematics	11	0.9	37	2.7	−1.8
Language	8	0.7	10	0.7	0.0
Electronics	7	0.6	2	0.2	+0.4
Photography/visual comm.	5	0.4			+0.4
Psychology	5	0.4	13	0.9	−0.5
Law	4	0.3	6	0.4	−0.1
Library science	3	0.2	9	0.6	−0.4
Home economics	3	0.2	2	0.2	0.0
Political science	3	0.2	9	0.6	−0.4
Social science	3	0.2	6	0.4	−0.2
Sociology	3	0.2	8	0.6	−0.4
Printing	2	0.2			+0.2
Data processing	2	0.2			+0.2
Nursing	2	0.2	1	0.1	+0.1
Medicine	0	0.0	1	0.1	−0.1
Other	46	3.9	479	34.6	−30.7
Total	1,188	100	1,383	100	

writing department of one large corporation the most productive employee is totally deaf. Whether the office is part of a large room accommodating many writers or a small cubbyhole, it is usually cluttered with texts and visuals. The technical writing department should be close to the art department or any photography, printing, or television facilities that the company has. It should be near typing groups; blueprints should be immediately available. The ideal situation is to make the technical writing department easily accessible to the technical employees in the plant. However, sometimes the technical writing department is located with the administrative offices, often miles away from the plant itself; researching a manual or a report can involve a lot of commuting.

Most technical writers "are allowed considerable freedom of movement in and out of work areas and wide latitude as to 'how' to accomplish their work. Sometimes there is a great deal of pressure and overtime pay when a deadline has to be met."[15] Essentially, though, technical writing is still a desk job because the actual production work comes from researching and writing at a desk.[16]

Pay

Technical writers work the same 40-hour, 5-day-a-week shift as other employees, but the pay is generally higher. In most corporations technical writers begin at a few dollars more an hour than other technical workers and are also protected by unions. Even so, there is a wide variation in the pay to match the diversity of duties. It would seem that experienced technical writers earn the top salaries in their organizations possibly because they have a valuable overview of the whole operation that a specialist in one area can never have. One writer interviewed stated that she had been paid less than the minimum wage working for a small distributor and later fifteen times as much as a free-lance business writer.[17] In general, manufacturers tend to pay according to their size and offer numerous employee benefits not available to free-lance or independent writers: savings and investment opportunity, retirement security, life and disability and health insurance, military leave, paid holidays and vacation, and relocation expenses.[18]

A large percentage of the respondents to the previously mentioned survey, who saw their tasks mostly as management, revealed annual salaries in the $15,000 to $19,999 bracket. But 2% earned in the $30,000 to $39,999 bracket and 0.6% made $40,000 and up. The average salary for members was $16,800 in 1974 and 71% made between $10,000 and $20,000. Percentages of members in the lower pay brackets have decreased, generally showing that the technical writing field has attracted more experienced people into the ranks. The upper pay ranges show long-time technical writers advancing to the top levels of their companies. See Figure 12.2.

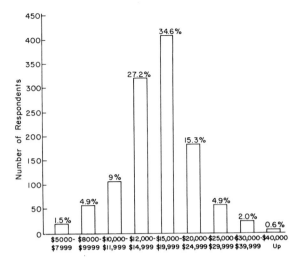

Fig. 12.2. Salary respondents.[19]

Opportunities and Advantages

Some college graduates have selected the company they want to work for and, when there have been no openings in their professional area, they have taken a temporary job in the technical writing department. Often they enjoy the activity and variety of their writing jobs so much that they stay on even when positions in their technical areas become available.

Variety of on-the-job work is the big advantage of technical writing. Correspondence, sales promotions, instruction manuals, feasibility or lab reports, news releases, and speech writing all add to the challenge and excitement of the job. Such diversity of responsibilities contributes to the freedom of movement and relaxed atmosphere on the job.

Advancement often comes rapidly to the technical writer. Communications skills bring about promotions within the department and within other departments of the plant, and contact with other job opportunities outside the plant through outside vendors.[20] The technical writer can move "from writer to group leader or crew chief, then to editor or administrator and, depending upon the structure of the company, to publisher or director of publications."[21]

Women have been especially sought after as technical writers since 1970. They are praised for their flexibility and attention to detail. According to the U.S. Department of Labor, technical writing ranks third in careers offering the most opportunity to women—outranked only by medicine and law. Women hold key public relations management positions in industry; some have moved from journalism careers into the very top levels of organizational management. Some have used technical writing as a stepping-stone to other careers within the publishing industry.

Because the technical writer is constantly exposed to new ideas, there is the opportunity to learn and to develop skills applicable to other fields as well as to technical writing.[22] "Opportunities in the field . . . are as numerous and varied as the kinds of technical information required by our modern society. The background in research and training in relaying information required by a technical writer are valuable in middle management. The ability to communicate effectively and knowledgeably opens many opportunities for career advancement both within the individual company and in a broader range of areas."[23]

Self-improvement is another advantage. As a technical writer you have the opportunity to expand your knowledge of the various aspects of the industry. "Since technical writing involves a working knowledge of several disciplines, such as engineering, typesetting, graphic arts, and printing, the writer can gain an overall view of the commercial publication industry."[24]

SUMMARY

Most technical writers list as the advantages of their jobs (1) their contacts with the technical employees, (2) the opportunity to learn the fundamentals of the business, (3) their being at the center of all activity, (4) desirable hours, and (5) financial rewards. They use their technical writing jobs to develop careers in public relations, advertising, and management.

Technical writing is a skill much admired in private business, industry, and governmental agencies. It can help you advance in your technical or professional area and can also offer you a career option in a new, challenging field.

NOTES

1. Derwood A. Haines, Technical and Product Information, Ford Motor Co., Dearborn, MI, in response to a letter dated October 25, 1976, asking for comments on his duties, training, working conditions, pay, advantages, and opportunities.
2. J. C. Hiebert, Administrator, Commercial Publications, Beech Aircraft Corp., Wichita, KS, in response to a letter dated October 25, 1976, asking for comments on his duties, training, working conditions, pay, advantages, and opportunities.
3. Maureen Werdann, Commercial Publications, Beech Aircraft Corp., Wichita, KS, in response to a letter dated October 25, 1976, asking for comments on her duties, training, working conditions, pay, advantages, and opportunities.
4. Bill Matteson, Executive Director, Communication Services, Farmland Industries, Inc., Kansas City, MO, in response to a letter dated October 25, 1976, asking for comments on his duties, training, working conditions, pay, advantages, and opportunities.
5. George Earle, Field Editor of *Farmland News,* Farmland Industries, Inc., Kansas City, MO, in response to a letter dated October 25, 1976, asking for comments on his duties, training, working conditions, pay, advantages, and opportunities.
6. C. A. Miller, Product Support Manager, Boeing, Wichita Division, Wichita, KS, in response to a letter dated October 25, 1976, asking for comments on the duties, training, working conditions, pay, advantages, and career opportunities for technical writers at Boeing.
7. Austin C. Farrell, "1974 Membership Profile of the Society for Technical Communication," *Technical Communication,* Second Quarter, 1975, p. 2.
8. Farrell, p. 5.
9. Miller.
10. Farrell, p. 6.
11. Earle.
12. Werdann.
13. Farrell, p. 5.
14. Farrell, p. 5.
15. T. Alan Gonia, Commercial Publications, Beech Aircraft Corp., Wichita, KS, in response to a letter dated October 25, 1976, asking for comments on his duties, training, working conditions, pay, advantages, and opportunities.
16. Miller.
17. Werdann.
18. Haines.
19. Farrell, p. 4.
20. Charles E. Gray, Jr., Commercial Publications, Beech Aircraft Corp., Wichita, KS, in response to a letter dated October 25, 1976, asking for comments on his duties, training, working conditions, pay, advantages, and opportunities.
21. Gonia.
22. Miller.
23. Werdann.
24. Gonia.

Index